"This bountiful volume of independent and cross-pollinating essays offers a tour d'horizon of the state of Christian-Jewish dialogue and touches upon nearly all of the heady critical issues of interfaith conversation. Scholars, theologians, clergy, interfaith dialogue participants, and all who marvel at the transformation of the Christian-Jewish relationship will gain new insights from each of the contributors."

> — **Rabbi Noam E. Marans**
> *Interreligious and Intergroup Relations,*
> *American Jewish Committee*

"Always profound and often provocative, these essays testify to the potential for Jews and Christians to think creatively together."

> — **Rabbi David Sandmel**
> *Catholic Theological Union, Chicago*

COVENANT AND HOPE

Christian and Jewish Reflections

ESSAYS IN CONSTRUCTIVE THEOLOGY FROM
THE INSTITUTE FOR THEOLOGICAL INQUIRY

Edited by

Robert W. Jenson *&* Eugene B. Korn

WILLIAM B. EERDMANS PUBLISHING COMPANY
GRAND RAPIDS, MICHIGAN / CAMBRIDGE, U.K.

Published 2012 by
Wm. B. Eerdmans Publishing Co.
2140 Oak Industrial Drive N.E., Grand Rapids, Michigan 49505 /
P.O. Box 163, Cambridge CB3 9PU U.K.

Printed in the United States of America

18 17 16 15 14 13 12   7 6 5 4 3 2 1

Library of Congress Cataloging-in-Publication Data

Covenant and hope: Christian and Jewish reflections: essays in constructive theology from
    the Institute for Theological Inquiry / edited by Robert W. Jenson & Eugene B. Korn.
        p.   cm.
    ISBN 978-0-8028-6704-9 (pbk.: alk. paper)
    1. Judaism — Relations — Christianity.   2. Christianity and other religions — Judaism.
    3. Covenants — Religious aspects — Judaism.   4. Covenants — Religious aspects —
    Christianity.   5. Hope — Religious aspects — Judaism.   6. Hope — Religious aspects —
    Christianity.   I. Jenson, Robert W.   II. Korn, Eugene B., 1947-   III. Institute for
    Theological Inquiry.

    BM535.C728   2012
    261.2'6 — dc23

                                                                    2011049622

www.eerdmans.com

Contents

Contents

Introduction

Eugene B. Korn

This volume celebrates the original research developed by the fellows of the Institute for Theological Inquiry's theology project conducted between 2008 and 2010. Over those years, ITI fellows met in America and Israel to conceptualize, draft, and finely hone the ideas presented in this book. The scholars also benefited from the insights of the faculties of the Yale Divinity School and the Yale Judaic Studies Program as well as the research fellows of the Van Leer Jerusalem Institute, whose institutions graciously co-sponsored conferences in New Haven and Jerusalem centered on the research.

As an ongoing enterprise, ITI is the theological division of the Center for Jewish-Christian Understanding and Cooperation in Efrat and Jerusalem, Israel, founded in 2008. Both ITI and CJCUC are profoundly grateful to Roger Hertog, of New York, NY, whose vision and generosity have been critical to the launch and continuing success of both institutions. Without his support, this volume would not have been possible.

ITI's American partner is the Witherspoon Institute of Princeton, New Jersey. Robert Jenson and I serve as ITI's co-directors. The Institute invites world-class thinkers to break new theological ground in projects focusing on subjects critical to Judaism, Christianity, and world culture. Through its research, ITI aims to develop fresh constructive foundations for Jewish-Christian understanding and for spiritual and moral values that bear on contemporary religious, cultural, and political life. With the successful completion of the 2008-2010 project, ITI has planned future research projects centering around the topics of Judaism and Christianity: Single or Dual Covenants; Religion, Violence, and War; The Significance of the Jewish Return to Zion; Jewish and Christian Biblical Interpretation; Love and Death; Democracy and Religious Authority; Modern Messianism; Family,

Children, and Fidelity; Election and the People of Israel; and Judaism and the Ministry of Jesus. It is ITI's hope that the fruits of its research will be adapted and utilized as pedagogical tools in educational settings.

New constructive thinking on these topics is needed now that Christian-Jewish relations have passed from the era of polemics to one with the possibility of sympathetic understanding and partnership — on theological, moral, and political levels. There are many reasons for this fundamental transformation that began in the second half of the twentieth century, and perhaps the primary one is the Holocaust. The near success of Hitler's Final Solution threw both Judaism and the Jewish people into an existential crisis and precipitated a deep spiritual crisis for Christian theology. The Nazi plan to exterminate the Jewish people found an all-too-ready acceptance in the heart of Christendom, and for the most part those who implemented the grisly plan were believing Christians. As the initial trauma of the Holocaust began to recede, both Christian and Jewish scholars found that the Christian *Adversus Judaeos* tradition had played a substantive role in Europe's easy acceptance of the idea that Jews were subhumans deserving of extermination. Something in Christendom had gone horribly wrong, and after deep introspection many Christian theologians began to understand that Christian theology had to repair itself and the church had to reconcile with the Jewish people.

The Jewish people's return to their historic homeland and the reality of the State of Israel also changed Jewish thinking profoundly. After the Holocaust and Israel's struggle for survival, Jews in the second half of the twentieth century recognized perhaps as never before the perils of living without friends in a world that had lost the presence of the sacred and the reality of transcendent moral authority. Thus both thinking Christians and Jews came to understand that the old thinking about, and alienation from, each other had proved disastrous for the past, and that they could no longer be operative if Jews and Christians are to fashion a better future for themselves and humanity.

The papers in this volume center around two interrelated topics: Covenant, Mission, and Relation to the Other, and Hope and Responsibility for the Human Future. Both Jewish and Christian religious life is grounded in God's covenant with Abraham and his descendants as it unfolds throughout human history. For Jews, this has meant primarily the revelation of Torah at Sinai and its interpretation by Jewish thinkers, as well as Jewish historical experience as God's chosen people. For Christians, it has meant the fullness of the Jewish covenant through Jesus and its universal redemption for gentiles. The covenant thus mediates the texture of daily religious life for both Christians and Jews, as well as forming the foundations for their theological, moral, and eschatological aspirations. Fulfilling God's covenant, as Christians and Jews respectively understand it, constitutes the "mission" of both Christian and Jewish life.

The directors of ITI selected a group of Jewish and Christian scholars headed by Robert Jenson and asked them to analyze their faith tradition's concept of covenant, how it determines their religious commitments, behavior, and theology, and how their covenantal theology shapes their relations with people outside their religious community in general. The Christian scholars were asked to examine the implications of their covenantal theology for relations with Jews and Judaism, while Jews were asked to probe the covenantal implications for Jewish relations with Christians and Christianity.

I headed a second group of scholars, asking them to reflect on the possibility of hope and responsibility for the future. Conviction in the promise of the messianic era appears to commit Jews and Christians to the belief in the redemption of humanity and its moral progress over history. Normatively, the prophetic vision of a future messianic redemption obligates Jews and Christians to take responsibility for the human future. Yet an honest recognition of the tragic history of the twentieth century that includes mass murders, genocide, and nuclear warfare, when combined with the trajectory of events in the young twenty-first century (e.g., extreme wealth conjoined with extreme poverty, ascending extremism and violence, scarcity of life-sustaining resources, and unprecedented proliferation of war and lethal weaponry), discourages a rational belief in human progress. The scholars of ITI were asked to present their understanding of the grounds of religious hope and how belief in the future can be nourished, and to outline the nature of the philosophic and practical responsibility that could ensure the improvement of future human life and culture.

In "What Kind of God Can Make a Covenant?" Robert Jenson examines the difference between, to use the medieval poet Yehuda Halevi's phrase, "the God of the Bible and the God of the philosophers." He laments the long history of Christian theological discussion about whether God is "impassible," insisting that this is a Greek philosophic conception of God that is ultimately incongruent with the God who strikes reciprocal covenants with his creatures and who relates to them with love and compassion, as delineated by Jewish and Christian Scriptures.

In his "Covenant, Mission, and Relating to the Other," Gerald McDermott argues that according to Scripture, covenant is a differentiated plan of blessing in which God relates in different ways to gentiles and Jews, blessing the world universally through the particular Israel. The apostle Paul held to the Jewish covenant, and was neither anti-Torah nor a supersessionist Christian. Moreover, God's covenant with Israel is not understood properly unless its promise of land is taken seriously. The notion of mission as bearing witness is fundamental to covenant, which was God's choice of Israel to be a light to the nations (mission).

In "Covenant and Mission," David Novak reflects on three questions: What should be the Jewish reaction to the missionary attempts of various Christian to proselytize Jews? Does Jewish exclusion of gentiles from the covenantal community imply that gentiles *cannot* become members of the community (and hence converting gentiles should be prohibited) or may gentiles become members of the community, so that proselytization of gentiles should be permitted? *Ought* gentiles to become members of the community by conversion, so that proselytization of them should be mandated? Novak finds no objection — moral or otherwise — to conversion attempts in a democratic pluralistic society as long as those attempts are honest and noncoercive.

Richard Sklba examines the covenantal theology of Josef Ratzinger, now Pope Benedict XVI, in "Covenant Renewed: Josef Ratzinger, Theologian and Pastor," with a particular eye to what Ratzinger's conception of the covenant implies for Jews and Judaism. Over the millennia this issue has long bedeviled relations between Jews and Christians, which were so often hostile due to the traditional Christian assumption that after Jesus, the biblical covenant with the Jewish people was transferred to the church and was no longer operative in the Jewish people. Is there a way to square the circle and assert the universality of the Christian covenant and still make room for a living Judaism?

In "Three Forms of Otherness: Covenant, Mission, and Relation to the Other in Rabbinic Perspective," Naftali Rothenberg sees the Jewish covenant as a boundary-setting concept that precludes positive theological relations with gentiles in general and Christians in particular. He prefers to ground Jewish-gentile relations in the foundational principles of Jewish ethics that treat all human beings as creatures made in the image of God and therefore worthy of love and respect. From such a perspective, it seems that there is nothing distinctive about Jewish-Christian relations or theology. Jewish relations with Christians are governed by the same principles as those with Muslims, Hindus, or even secularists.

Shlomo Riskin, in "Covenant and Conversion: The United Mission to

Redeem the World," examines how Jewish rabbinic tradition regards God's covenants with Abraham and later with the Jewish people at Sinai. He posits a third covenant, the one that God seals with the Jewish people on the plains of Moab before entering the Promised Land (Deuteronomy 27 and 28). Riskin insists that this third covenant has universal implications because, at a minimum, it obligates Jews to teach universal ethical values to all humanity. He also considers whether the Sinai covenant mandates the mission that Jews try to convert gentiles to the Mosaic covenant and commandments revealed at Sinai — what we now know as Judaism. He sees Christianity partially fulfilling the universal covenantal mandate and argues for future cooperation between Christians and Jews.

Michael Wyschogrod probes the political implications of covenantal society. In "Judaism, the Political, and the Monarchy," he recommends that Israel establish a regent as a reminder of biblical monarchy. The regent would function only symbolically to stress that the new Jewish national political order in Israel has retained its Jewish and biblical connection. Wyschogrod contends that this would strengthen the faith of biblically oriented Jews and Christians and revive the biblical purpose of the Jewish people in the world and history.

In "The People Israel, Christianity, and the Covenantal Responsibility to History," I argue that the *telos* of God's biblical covenant with the Jewish people is that the Jewish people become a nation of priests throughout history, bringing the knowledge of God and divine moral authority to the nations of the world. Lacking Mosaic commandments, Abraham was a theological Noahide who shared the biblical mission later articulated to the Jewish people at Sinai. Although Jews cannot accept Christianity (and Christians) as part of, or heirs to, the Sinai covenant, they can rightly understand Christianity as part of Abraham's biblical covenant and mission. I contend further that if we combine a number of modern rabbinic theological views sympathetic to Christianity with the contemporary Christian rejection of hard supersessionism, we create a logical opening for removing the impediments to a Jewish appreciation of Christianity. Because of these modern theological turns, Jews and Christians should cooperate with each other, bearing common witness to the spiritual center of human experience, the intrinsic sanctity of human life, and the necessity of moral values for human flourishing in the twenty-first century.

Russell Reno, in "The Antinomian Threat to Human Flourishing," critiques modern culture, assessing it as fundamentally antinomian. The underlying metaphysical dream of our culture is to be an Empire of Desire, in which norms are justified solely by serving the goal of maximizing individual desires. This is exemplified best by Norman O. Brown, who rejected all norms of rational autonomy or authenticity, be they derived from Moses, Kant, or Wordsworth, and even Freud's self-limiting imperatives of the Ego, in order to advocate living in "the timeless immediacy of desire." Our age has become anticultural in Brown's antinomian sense; hence moral ideals can only propagate themselves ineffectually. Reno believes that postmodern culture has morphed into a socially sanctified and rhetorically disguised expression of the material desires of the powerful. Despite their long argument over the validity of law, the Empire of Desire should unify Jews and Christians today. Christians and Jews must assert a pronomian picture of life and culture, a metaphysical dream at odds with postmodern antinomian fantasies. Both need to heed Moses' plea in Deuteronomy to "choose life," which requires the full commitment to obedience and moral norms. As articulated both by Pope John Paul II and Rabbi Joseph Soloveitchik, Christians and Jews must revitalize the concept of law as a foundational category for realizing human flourishing.

Miroslav Volf reflects on hope, love, and accounts of reality in "God, Hope, and Human Flourishing." He traces the narrowing of the idea of human flourishing, from its initial center around a transcendent, loving, cosmic God, to a humanistic or national imperative that entailed loving others, to personal satisfaction devoid of all reference to something higher for humans to love. In the end, only moral solipsism remains — ultimate concern for the self and its satisfaction. Love as the ability to transcend oneself has been lost. So too with hope, initially diminished from the vastness of God to the national ideal of a redeemer nation, and ultimately "to the vanishing point of the self alone." Real hope has disappeared since it depends on the pursuit of an end greater than desire. Yet the concern for human flourishing — how to be successful *at being human* — is central to Christianity, Judaism, and Islam; essential to all these conceptions is each human being fitting into the larger cosmos and drama of human history. Malfunctions of faith, flourishing, and hope are rooted in a failure to love the God of love or a failure to love the neighbor. Today's challenge to Christians — and all religious persons — is to love God and neighbor rightly. This means explicating God's relation to human flourishing in light of concrete issues we face today (poverty, environmental degradation, war, sexuality) and more so, transforming our belief that God is fundamental to human flourishing into an active conviction that shapes the way we think, preach, write, behave, and live.

Douglas Knight, in "Hope and Responsibility: The Assembly with the Promise of God," finds hope through the covenanted community of Israel. Because Israel covenanted with the God of all humanity, the covenant is simultaneously particular through Israel and also universal. Knight claims that God's love for Israel heralds good news for all humankind, since Israel witnesses the truth of humanity with God. He understands the church as the second assembly called into being around Israel's first assembly and thus he rejects supersessionism. Christianity is dependent on the witness of Israel, deferring to it rather than displacing it. When Christians speak or act against Israel, it is the pagan within speaking. God's covenant is a metaphysics of promise. We flourish only as we know we are loved, which enables us to serve our neighbor. And because no generation is sufficient to itself and needs affirmation from another, we are required to pass on life and culture by which those after us can affirm life as good. Knight believes that Christianity is assessed by the extent that it ameliorates contemporary material culture. Once again it is only the assembly of Israel and the baptized gentiles added to her who can give this warning against cultural, political, and demographic crises — really the crisis of humanity in paralysis before the summons of God. Imbued with covenantal confidence, the assembly of God testifies that God invites us to find the divine image in each another, giving us hope for the future.

In "Messianic Hope," Alan Mittleman explores the Jewish tradition of realist messianism as a locus of perennial Jewish hope. The realist tradition envisions that the Messianic Age will not differ from the present age in fantastic ways. The laws of nature will not change, but people in the Messianic Age will live peacefully. Goods will be sufficient for everyone's consumption and poverty will be eliminated. This tradition has roots in the Bible and Talmud, but its most famous proponent was the medievalist, Maimonides. Mittleman focuses on three modern philosophers in this tradition, Hermann Cohen, Steven Schwarzschild, and Lenn Goodman, and considers the difficulties of domesticating an eschatological concept into a realistic portrayal of economic and political possibilities by explicating and critiquing these three thinkers.

In "Moral Agency, Sin, and Grace: Prospects for Christian Hope and Responsibility," Darlene Fozard Weaver offers six theses about the character of Christian hope and responsibility, with occasional reference to Jewish conceptions of moral responsibility. The theses outline a theological and ethical argument about the scope of moral agency given the pervasive influence of structural violence and the power of grace. Noting that structural violence is a social construction, Weaver argues that social sin disorients the human will and blocks human transcendence. Yet in the end, it is a product of human freedom and therefore malleable. God empowers our moral self-transcendence, and it is God's grace that reconciles us to the good of our being and incorporates us into a new economy of relations with others and the world. For Jews and Christians both, hope is principled because it rests on faith in God, nourished by the faith that God acted in history. Christian hope is grounded in Jesus Christ and that the Holy Spirit continues to act in our lives and the world, sanctifying us. Christian hope thus reckons with the bondage of freedom and disorientation of desire. In contrast to the modern understanding of responsibility, Christian responsibility is not about fixing completely a world that is broken, but rather about learning to share it in ways that permit God to heal it and us. In the end, hope bears fruit in just love for ourselves and our fellow creatures.

In "Zionism as Jewish Hope and Responsibility," Deborah Weissman considers Zionism as a translation of the Jewish hope for redemption into human agency, for in Zionism the Jewish people assumed responsibility for their own destiny. Although most traditionalists initially opposed the Zionist movement because they believed one must wait passively for the Messiah, Weissman makes the case that human agency has always been part of the classical Jewish tradition. She views the classical themes of creation, revelation, and redemption as calling for a partnership between the divine and the human, and asks what religious meaning Zionism and the State of Israel can have for Jews. Established only three years after the end of the Holocaust, the State of Israel's continued existence amidst a host of challenges and accomplishments can give us a sense of wonder and help us cope with despair — all without equating those accomplishments with the fulfillment of biblical or messianic prophecies.

When we conceived of this project, Robert Jenson and I hoped that the scholars of both groups would create a community of dialogue. This hope was realized as the fellowship gradually assumed synergy. The scholars often found common points of inquiry and analysis, and a significant topical overlap emerged from their reflections, even within those of different groups. For instance, Naftali Rothenberg, Richard Sklba, Shlomo Riskin, and I addressed and debated the implications (or lack thereof) of using covenant as a basis for relationship with the Other. Riskin, David Novak, and Gerald McDermott all addressed the implications that covenant and mission have for converting others. Douglas Knight, Miroslav Volf, Russell Reno, and Michael Wyschogrod reflected on the implications of faith for the political, moral, and social orders, as well as for human flourishing in light of contemporary cultural trends and values. Darlene Fozard Weaver and Alan Mittleman both reflected on the nature of religious ethics, while Alan and Michael Wyschogrod also touched on the idea of a messianic polity and its problems. Darlene Fozard Weaver and Deborah Weissman sought a basis for religious hope amidst the turbulence and moral confusion of modern culture and history.

The ITI scholars came from the varying disciplines of theology, ethics, philosophy, rabbinics, and political thought. When read as a collective, their research can be divided into secondary categories, such as "Conversion and Mission" (Gerald McDermott, Riskin, Novak, Sklba), "Covenant and Hope" (Mittleman, Jenson, Knight), "Covenantal Ethics and the Other" (Rothenberg, Korn, Sklba, Riskin), "God and Human Flourishing" (Volf, Reno, Mittleman), and "Covenantal Ethics and Politics" (Weaver, Wyschogrod, Weissman).

Robert Jenson and I share the hope that the continuing work of ITI and CJCUC will make vital contributions not only to the theology of contemporary Christians and Jews, but also to the living reality of Christians and Jews, their ever-growing appreciation for each other, and indeed to the entire human family and the values and world culture in which that family toils and thrives. Together, we may consider anew this God's ancient yet still-inspiring call to Abraham and his descendants at the moment both our spiritual communities were born: "Be a blessing. . . . Through you may all the nations of the earth be blessed" (Gen. 12:2-3).

Covenant, Mission, and Relation to the Other

What Kind of God Can Make a Covenant?

Robert W. Jenson

I

The title of my essay presupposes that there are putative gods of more than one kind. To be sure, this supposition is disputed by some theorists, who hold that although different religions may appear to identify God or the gods differently, this appearance is superficial. Instead of arguing directly with this ideology let me simply ask: What leads us to attach the label "god" to a reality or aspect of reality in the first place? Let me propose: a particular community will use the word "god" or some equivalent to invoke whatever it is that this community relies on to survive moving from its past to its future — or perhaps we should say, from its future to its past. And there are many different and often irreconcilable ways in which communities specify that "whatever."

The one ineluctable metaphysical experience is the passage of time. As Augustine in his *Confessions*[1] pondered that experience, he identified the threat posed by time's passing: every moment of our lives seems to go immediately from the future into the past, from what we are not yet into what we no longer are. If this seeming is veridical, temporal creatures are finally nothing, and creation fails. Augustine was always haunted by the emptiness where the light of being runs out; with these reflections he found the location of that emptiness. As Greek myth dramatized it, *Chronos* eats his children.

Only if the moment between future and past is not in fact a merely "passing" moment, only if it dwells in some reality that transcends the

1. Augustine, *Confessions* xi.

3

abrupt difference between the future as it comes on and the past as it departs, can we live stories that are coherent through time, that is, can we *live* at all. Willy-nilly, we all bank our lives on some eternity or other — including those who think they do not and perhaps loudly proclaim it.

Let me insert a disclaiming excursus, lest it be supposed that I fully endorse Augustine's analysis. His reflections on time have been a foundational blessing for Western thought, but it seems to me that he slips at two related points. First, he finds a more-than-passing present in a *distentio animae*, an "expansion of the soul" by anticipation and memory, which brings future and past together as an experienced present; then he describes eternity by analogy to this feature of human nature. In Augustine's anxiety to avoid anthropomorphism when speaking of God, here as sometimes elsewhere he somersaults into it, for the biblical God has indeed a *spiritus* but surely no *anima*, not even analogously. Second, the human nature Augustine invokes is that of an individual, whereas it is first in communities that time is experienced and eternities are then invoked. It is as you, a person who differs from me, confront me, that I face the possibility of being other than I am, that is, that an actual future comes on for me. It is you and I together who experience time — or perhaps you and I with him/her. But that is a matter for another time.

Returning to the line of my argument, in analyzing the meaning of "god/s" we must indeed speak of "some eternity or other." For even a brief acquaintance with religious history will discover that "eternal" is a *portmanteau* word, accommodating very different supposed bridges over the nothingness that threatens as the future becomes past. Indeed, there are as many kinds of supposed eternity as there are different communities to rely on them. There is, for example, the eternity of Plato's still geometrical point at the center of time's turning wheel; or there is, for a quite different example, the eternity of ancestors, the eternity of the dead who in their own way live but no longer change.

A god or pantheon is then the embodiment of some eternity. That is, a god or pantheon is an eternity insofar as it is *available* to a community, insofar as its community can pray or sacrifice to it, obey it, or perhaps merely contemplate or long for it. We might plunder Hegel and say that a god is the representation, the *Vorstellung*, of an eternity, if it is understood that, à la right-wing Hegelians, the representation is the actuality of the concept.

II

So there are supposed gods of various kinds and the way to my question is therefore free. I ask, "What kind of God could make a covenant?" What sort of eternity would such a God embody?

Let me suggest that making a covenant would take a very particular, indeed a quite odd kind of God — or at least odd by the standards of the main Western intellectual tradition. The high deity of the pagan Greek religious thinkers, who still rule our tradition, would not and indeed could not do anything so compromising as making a covenant with an other than itself — and "it" is the right pronoun. At a minimum, to make a covenant the covenant-maker must address the other, and to do that he must, again at a minimum, be interested in the other's existence. But whether we think of Plato and his followers, of Aristotle and his, or directly of Parmenides' great vision in which the God of the Greeks was primally revealed,[2] their God is God — "truly," "really" God — precisely by the total absence of such concern.

Aristotle's God is a sheer consciousness of itself as consciousness, which moves the worlds by lesser beings' longing for such autonomy. The article with the first "consciousness" above is needed, for this God is included in the cosmos, and so is indeed "a" being with the other beings.[3] Plato's God is even more self-contained; and in his case we may dispense with the article. Plato's vision of deity was first brought to fully coherent statement by his late disciple Plotinus, as "the One," which is so sheerly oneness that even saying "The One is," since this is a synthetic statement, diverts our intention ontologically down from the One.[4] Within the inexorable logic of the Greek dream of deity, "God is not . . . ," with the ellipsis and with a stipulation against filling it, must be the final word — if indeed any word at all is possible, if an apophaticism to the limiting case is not the inevitable path.

It would be blasphemy to depict this deity negotiating with Abraham or dining with Israel's elders on the mountain of his self-revelation. And as for Moses seeing the God of Sinai from behind, a greater offense to the Greek dream of deity can hardly be imagined. This is not to say that religion in the train of the pagan Greeks cannot be grand and ennobling, just that it cannot be a communication between God and others, and therefore cannot involve a covenant. Its highest expression had to be the unique

2. Martin Heidegger, *Einführung in die Metaphysik.*
3. It is the prime example of Heidegger's warned-against *Ontotheologie.*
4. Plotinus, *Enneads* i.6; ii.9; iii.8; v.5.

drama we call tragedy, in which gods and humans alike are instruments/ sports of impersonal and unseeing Necessity — "Let us call no one happy, until he has died without disaster."

So what would a God be like who was *not* like the Unmoved or the One? Apart perhaps from inklings in so-called "primitive" religions, it is the Jewish and Christian Scriptures in which we hear of such a God. Thus my investigation must be a blend of exegesis and conceptual analysis.

We may start with the observation that a God who could make a covenant would be a God who *creates,* that is, who willingly instigates an actual other than himself. For if God is to make a covenant, there must be an other with whom to make it. And the being of this other cannot be independent of God, nor yet can God's relation to that other be such as to mitigate or threaten either its reality or its otherness.

Humanity's religions do not posit such a relation between the gods and their others. They may conceive what is other than the divine as a realm of darkness[5] or illusion.[6] Or they may posit the raw material of the cosmos as co-eternal with God[7] or indeed identify the cosmos itself with God.[8] Or, most often, they will in one way or another conceive what is other than the divine as emanating from it, in a fashion ambiguously envisioned as birth[9] and as logical consequence;[10] most actual construals appear somewhere on a spectrum between these poles. With either an opposed or co-eternal or precariously other as other than the god, there would be no space for a covenant.

So strict is the correlation of covenant and creation, that in Scripture the Lord's creating is modeled on his covenant-making, and vice versa. As God made covenant with Israel by speaking, by saying, "I will be your God and you will be my people," so God creates by speaking: "Let there be . . ." The God who can make a covenant must like the God who creates be a verbally able God: he must have a Word.[11]

5. As did the Gnostics of late Mediterranean antiquity.
6. As does Buddhism.
7. Plato once summarized standard ancient mythology: "When ["the Demiurge"] took over the visible stuff, and found that it was not stable but was in unharmonious and disorderly motion, he brought it to order from disorder. . . ." Plato, *Timaeus* 30A.
8. E.g., and gloriously, Spinoza.
9. Most mythology, in one way or another, tells or presupposes the story of Mother Earth and Father Sky.
10. E.g., Middle- and Neoplatonism.
11. John 1:1-3 is plainly a gloss on Genesis 1.

And as the people God established by speaking were just so to be good *for* something, were to know and follow his will and bring blessing to the nations, so in Genesis 1 it belongs to the act of creating that God affirms the purposefulness of the creature: ". . . and God saw that it was good," where the Hebrew *tov* surely means "good for. . . ." God's certification of the creature's purposefulness is not an addendum to the act of creating; it is the form of the act — to break into medieval categories. Thus the God who *can* make a covenant must be in himself a God who does and so can prescribe moral purposes: he has, or is, a moral will.

Moreover, both Judaism and the church have claimed to know what it is that the creation is good for. For Judaism, 2 Esdras is often cited — at least by Christians — because of its bluntness: "It was for us that you created the world."[12] And early Christian thought could simply appropriate the teaching, sometimes, to be sure, with a supersessionist twist. The second-century visionary Hermas is as blunt as 2 Esdras: "The world was made for the church's sake."[13] Not only is creating modeled on covenant-making, covenant-making is the purpose of creating. As Karl Barth put it, with unprecedented clarity, creation is the "outer basis" of the covenant and the covenant is the "inner basis" of creation.[14] The goal of all things is a holy community.

Moreover, the God who can make a covenant is not a Creator in the style of the Enlightenment, who instigates an other than himself and then maintains that otherness by himself remaining exterior to his other. At inconsistent best, such a God could act within the creation only by "intervening" from time to time; but making a covenant is not an intervention from outside history: it is an act within it. A good deal of intellectual energy was recently devoted by some Catholic and Reformed philosophers of traditional theological persuasion to the question: How can an eternal God act within time? The effort was mostly wasted, because it was assumed that "eternal" meant "timeless," and when the question is set that way no answer is possible. It is all but obvious: a sheerly timeless God simply could not *act within* time. He could — again at incoherent best — only interfere with it from a distance.

Making covenant is initially a unilateral act by one party, but it inaugurates a future shared by both parties: "I will be your God and you will be

12. 2 Esdras 6:55. Though see Eugene Korn's paper for another possibility.
13. Hermas, *Vision* ii.4.1.
14. Karl Barth, *Kirchliche Dogmatik* (Zürich, 1932-) III/1, 103-377.

my people." The covenant-maker thus acquires a joint history with his other. Yet the covenant-making God remains nonetheless Creator of this other, and his joint history with it remains an act of grace. Thus a God who can make a covenant is a God who is, and so can be, as one and the same unique God, both the author of the history he makes with creatures and one or more of the *dramatis personae* of that history.

Israel's Scriptures are rife with figures that are actors in the history determined by the Creator yet who turn out to be the same Creator God. Perhaps the most striking is "the Angel of the Lord" who appears so regularly in the Pentateuchal narrative and the Deuteronomic history. In each instance of his appearing he is initially identified as a messenger *from* the Lord, a reality distinguished from the Lord by the construct/genitive construction that makes his name. Yet as each such narrative continues, the Angel turns out to speak and act not *for* the Lord, but *as* the Lord, and indeed is rightly worshiped as the Lord.[15] We find the same pattern in narratives about "the Glory of the Lord"[16] or "the Word of the Lord."[17]

One body of such narrative was perhaps most central to Israel's theological experience, and provides a name for the general phenomenon. In the stories of Israel's wilderness journey, the Angel of the Lord duly appears in the cloud and the pillar of fire.[18] But the Tent was different: it was to be the place where the Lord *dwells* (the Hebrew verb form in Exodus is "*shakhan*") among his people.[19] For this Presence, the rabbis took a word from this same root. In both the Tent and later the Temple, the central holy place became the place of the *Shekhinah,* in the Temple the Lord's usually but not always invisible presence above the cherubim-throne. Was God beyond his creation or was he in the created Tent and then in the created Temple? To be faithful to the texts we must say he was both: he is the one God as God ruling over his people's history from beyond it, and he is the same God as one who in that history is himself among its carrying *dramatis personae.*

The God who can make a covenant is a God who indeed *can* do all of the above. That is to say, his own life somehow has an antecedently covenantal structure, as indeed does all personal life, made in the divine

---

15. E.g., Genesis 21:17-19; 22:11-12; Exodus 3:2-4; spectacularly, Judges 13:2-22.

16. E.g., 1 Kings 8:10-13.

17. Above all, as the Word comes to a prophet: "The Word of the Lord came to . . . ," which turns out not to mean simply that the Lord comes and speaks to the prophet, remarkable as that too would be.

18. Exodus 23:20-23.

19. Exodus 25:8.

image. Now, of course, a God who has a life, or more precisely *is* a life, and whose being has personal structure, is no proper God at all by the standards of that part of our metaphysical tradition most indebted to the Greek theologians. We observed that at the start. He is not "simple" in the usual — and in my judgment disastrous — Christian-theological sense: his relation to creation in its temporality cannot be modeled by the relation of a point to a line or of a center to a circle.

Otherwise stated, a God who can make a covenant is indeed eternal, but not by sheerly lacking time, as was the God of the ancient Greeks or the God of some other sophisticated religions. A God who can be so involved with his creatures' history as is the God of Scripture cannot in himself be merely timeless. Saying this need not infringe God's "eternity," for as we have seen, the real question is always "*How* does a particular alleged divinity transcend time?"

What then is the Lord's particular "eternity"? A passage in Isaiah has always seemed to me something like a definition by parallel construction. At Isaiah 55:3 the Lord promises "a *berit olam*," an eternal covenant, which is then seen to be "Davidic mercies faithfully kept." The eternity of the biblical God is his faithfulness. He is faithful in his history with us, here to his promises to or about David; and that he *can be* triumphantly faithful is the how of his eternity. Or we can appropriate another of Karl Barth's maxims, which has been an axiom for me since I encountered it fifty years ago: it is not that there is not in eternity beginning, present, and goal; it is that in the eternity of the biblical God these are in no tension.[20] Precisely God's goals are his eternal plenitude.

Christian theology has always had to struggle to maintain a biblical apprehension of God's eternity. It has again and again been seduced by the serenity and conceptual manageability of the Greek vision. This does not mean that Christian theology's engagement with that vision has been a mistake or unproductive, merely that it has its perils. When Christian theology has spoken of God's eternity, it has too often assumed that the only conceivable eternity is that of Plato's or Aristotle's deity. Indeed, much of the history of Christian theology is the history of a repeated rearguard action in defense of this assumption, against the impact of the way Scripture actually talks about God.

To pick a major arena in which this rearguard defense has played out, the "christological" controversies that plagued the church through the

20. Barth, *Kirchliche Dogmatik* II/1, 690.

whole patristic period, i.e., for 600 years, were all at bottom occasioned by insistence on the supposed "impassibility" of God, his alleged complete lack of affect, his immunity to temporal events. This root of the successive christological quandaries was perhaps most blatantly displayed in the so-called "theopaschite" controversies, which dragged on for decades until the issue was more or less settled by the Fifth Ecumenical Council in 553.[21] It came to center around the originally liturgical acclamation, *hena tes hagias triados peponthenai sarki,* "One of the holy Trinity suffered, in the flesh," a slogan beloved by the politically powerful Eastern monastic communities and by most of the faithful East or West.

If indeed Jesus is God the Son, and if indeed he was killed, the proposition of course follows. Yet even when it was recognized as orthodox by the council of 553, this was done only indirectly, by condemnation of its contradictory, and under strong pressure from the theologian-emperor Justinian — he who finally put Athens' philosophical schools out of their misery and built the church of Holy Wisdom in what is now called Istanbul.

Neither is this dispute a matter of ancient history only, nor indeed was it in practice squelched by the council's decision. It will doubtless seem preposterous to many that so ancient and *outré* a controversy should still agitate anyone, but in fact God's impassibility/passibility is a current hot issue in American Catholic and some "mainline" Protestant theology. Entire books and conferences have recently been devoted to the errors of those who have their doubts about describing the God who appears in Scripture as "impassible."[22]

Those with such doubts can recruit some prestigious if sporadic support from theological history. Thus Origen of Alexandria, the third-century founder of both Christian systematic theology and methodologically self-conscious Christian biblical exegesis, wrote a remarkable commentary on the book of Ezekiel — much of which has been lost. In chapter 16, Ezekiel develops an allegory, or sort-of allegory, of the covenant, under the figure of Jerusalem as a foundling and later faithless bride.[23] The Lord, on his way to an unspecified destination, happens upon

21. For the text of the council's decrees, see Norman P. Tanner, ed., *Decrees of the Ecumenical Councils* (Washington, DC: Georgetown University Press, 1990), I:107-22.

22. E.g., and with some essays in response, James F. Keating and Thomas Joseph White, eds., *Divine Impassibility and the Mystery of Human Suffering* (Grand Rapids: Eerdmans, 2009).

23. On both the Ezekiel passage and Origen's reading, see Robert W. Jenson, *Ezekiel,* Brazos Theological Commentary on the Bible (Grand Rapids: Brazos Press, 2009), ad loc.

the infant Jerusalem, exposed by her Canaanite parents to the elements and scavengers, the ancient pagan world's favored way of dealing with unwanted or disappointing pregnancies. The Lord saves her life and, returning to find her sexually mature, takes her to wife. Origen notes thus that what pagan humanity did not show the child, *pity*, is exactly what the Lord manifests. And Origen catches the profound implication for the Scripture's vision of God, as against that of his own milieu and education, for pity is an *affect*, a *passio*. Specifically, Origen defines it as the affective dispositional possibility of love, the *caritatis passio*. It was a great dogma of Origen's intellectual heritage — he had the same Alexandrian teacher as Plotinus — that since to be timelessly perfect deity must be immune to temporal events, it must be utterly without affect, that is, "impassible," *impassibilis*. Contemplating Ezekiel 16, Origen is nevertheless compelled to say, *ipse pater non est impassibilis*, "Not even the Father is impassible."

If the God who can make a covenant is not "impassible," is he then "passible"? Here it seems to me that we cannot bind our discourse to a two-valued logic — a point about which the self-described "kabbalist" Peter Ochs is tirelessly urgent.[24] Perhaps, *in divinis*, 'P or -P' does not equal 'T', as the truth-tables of propositional logic stipulate; perhaps that this God is not impassible does not imply that he is passible. Perhaps Origen's double negative is precisely the needed rule: "God is *not im*passible" — as I will take up below, adducing Maimonides, Jewish theology has gone through the same discussion. The God who can make covenant is not "impassible" in any plausible sense of the word, but is nevertheless not subject to change inflicted by others. He is not a sort of hyper-stoic, but neither is he at any temporal agent's mercy. He is, however, at the mercy of himself — which is the great difference between him and the impassible deity of the religions.

In general, it seems to me that much Christian theological discourse, deploying all those abstract divine attributes that begin with "omni . . ." or a privative, hides a rather subtle *petitio principii*. It is presumed that if God can ever be said to be, e.g., "impassible," this predicate must apply in every context. That is, in the present case, that he must be impassibly impassible. I suggest that Christians should get over this — and that perhaps also some Jewish thinkers have a problem here.

The Christian gospel is primally neither religious wisdom nor moral insight. It is first and foremost a narrative, and therefore Christians have at

24. E.g., Peter Ochs, *Peirce, Pragmatism and the Logic of Scripture* (Cambridge: Cambridge University Press, 1998).

their classical best read Scripture first of all as a single encompassing narrative. In any good narrative, the "attributes" of the *dramatis personae,* and indeed of the story itself, are not abstractly fixed, but rather ride the story's waves. Is the Lord "passible" in his pity for foundling Jerusalem? Yes, since he in fact shows this affect. Is the Lord, precisely by that affect, impassibly committed to Jerusalem? Yes.

To this outsider, it seems that Jewish theology has sometimes had the same problems with Scripture's way of speaking about God. At least the great Maimonides did — a judgment about which I am comforted in that I share it with Michael Wyschogrod, another scholar in our research project. In the *Guide of the Perplexed* Maimonides makes mastery of Aristotelian thought the necessary preparation for "divine science," a preparation without which any further venturing could only lead to disaster;[25] the inevitable result is that he must explain away much of the Scripture's actual language about God. Indeed, the "perplexed" person for whom the *Guide* is intended is precisely the man perfected in Aristotle and consequently offended by Scripture's language.

Centrally in Maimonides' explanatory project, he insists that God has no dispositional properties.[26] Therefore when he is said to do things that resemble human actions that proceed from moral dispositions, this must not be thought to reveal anything truly present in God. If God is said to love or hate, this is said only to awaken our love or hatred. And so on. However you may massage the concepts — including the concept of covenant itself, as Maimonides does — such doctrine does not fit a God who has a history with creatures.

Finally in this paper on this line, a God who could and would make a covenant must be a God who can meaningfully be petitioned. Since a covenant-maker and those with whom he makes covenant have a common history, those with whom covenant is made must have their own voice within the relation, unless they are simply to be protected slaves. And since in this case the covenant-maker is the Creator, that voice will be the voice of petitionary prayer. If the covenant is to be real, we must be able to address God and tell him how we think events should go in our history together, in trust that somehow he will take our opinion seriously. And that reliance must be able to appeal to something real in God.

---

25. E.g., Maimonides, *Guide of the Perplexed* I:34. In reading such passages, we should remember that most of what we would call philosophy is included in Aristotle's "physics."
26. Maimonides, *Guide* I:54.

But every pastor is familiar with the question: "If God is omniscient and omnipotent (as we have been taught), then he already knows what we need or want and has already decided what he will do. So why tell him?" The frequent and evasive response of Christian pastors is that prayer cannot of course influence *God's* mind, but that it can open *our* minds to his will. Now to be sure, prayer does this last also, but to say that this is its only ·or chief agency is to deny its actual content, which is asking for something from one in position to grant it. It is patent that the evasive response is dictated by Aristotle and Plato rather than by Scripture, for Scripture can entirely without embarrassment have the cries of the people in Egypt remind God of his covenant with their fathers, or describe a negotiation in which Abraham talks God down from his initial demand on Sodom. I have sometimes said (only half in jest) that of course God knows everything, but that this does not settle how he finds it out.

I have the impression that Jews are not as reluctant as Christians to emulate Scripture in their prayers, indeed on occasion to emulate Abraham's negotiations. But if they followed the strain of thought represented by Maimonides they would be. For in the *Guide* he is explicit that petitionary prayer is not to inform God of what he of course already knows, but to assure ourselves and others that he knows it.[27]

And indeed, if we suppose that our petitions come to God from an instance merely exterior to him, the case for petitionary prayer is hopeless. But we need not suppose that. If we take seriously that God is not only the Creator of his history with us, but at the very same time God is with us as a *persona* in that history, we may suppose that in prayer we join with God in petition to God. Providence need not be construed as a determining exterior to us; it would be more faithful to Scripture to think of prayer as our *involvement* in Providence.

A first necessary step on this line is the notion that God himself prays, and necessarily to himself. Here a passage from the rabbinic tradition goes very far: "What does the Holy One, blessed be He, pray? Mar Zutra said in the name of Rav: 'May it be My will that My mercy suppress My anger, and that My mercy prevail over My other attributes so that I may deal with My children out of mercy and act above and beyond the strict requirement of the law.'"[28] And the next step is recognition that, because the biblical God,

27. Maimonides, *Guide* III:24.
28. Babylonian Talmud, *Berakhot* 7a. I owe this reference to Eugene Korn.

as his *Shekhinah,* is among us as fellow agent in our history, we may join our prayer with God's prayer to himself.

III

It will be apparent that I have been sneaking up on the Christian assertion of God's triunity. And indeed, Christians must say that the God who could make a covenant is the triune God, which does not mean that to rely on this God one must acknowledge his triunity.

It is often supposed that the doctrine of Trinity is the breaking point between Judaism and Christianity. To the contrary, let me assert a proposition that many in our group will doubtless — I hope only at first — find preposterous: "There is one God in three identities" is actually a repetition of the *Shema,* in the situation where it is believed that the God of Israel has raised his servant Jesus from the dead.

I will try to unpack that proposition in a moment. In this paragraph I note that if it holds, then belief in Jesus' resurrection is the true division between Judaism and Christianity, and not the consequent apprehension of God's triunity. Obviously, Judaism and Christianity are divided by what Christianity says about Jesus under the rubric of incarnation and by the doctrine of Trinity — though perhaps less decisively than is usually thought. But these divisions are *consequences* of division over a matter of fact: Did the Lord raise Jesus or did he not?

In the book of Acts, Luke presents Peter preaching the first and paradigmatic Christian sermon, preached to a wholly Jewish gathering.[29] Apart from the Scripture-proofs, Peter's sermon is very simple: in ignorance you gave Jesus up, but God has raised him. According to Luke many believed this, and were forthwith baptized — without, one must suppose, much other alteration in their theology, certainly without instruction in trinitarian dialectics. Luke does not dwell on those who did not believe, but extrapolating from known later results, they may have been most of those present. Those who did believe the resurrection were separated from those who did not only by this belief and by the communal meal that celebrated it; for the rest, they worshiped in the Temple with the other Jews,[30] only taking such occasion as they found for preaching on the lines of Peter's sermon.

29. Acts 2:14-36.
30. Acts 2:46-47.

To return to the promised unpacking: To do it completely, I would have to discuss something I have elided, the "third identity" of the Trinity, the Scripture's pervasively present "Spirit of/from the Lord." I will not now make up that deficiency, only ask readers to remember the general biblical role of the Spirit, who enlivens Israel in its darkest moments and, as the creed of Nicea-Constantinople has it — "spoke by the prophets." That noted, we are in position to proceed.

The doctrine of Trinity is at its root the insistence that the history God has with his people, plotted by the relations of its *dramatis personae,* is not only our life but his. In his history with us, precisely as Israel's Scripture plots it, God is the Author of the story, a personal Do-er and Sufferer within the story, and the Breath of Life that enlivens and binds the two — in Christian jargon, he is Father, Son/Logos, and Spirit. The doctrine of Trinity, right to the farthest reaches of its dialectical development, is merely the conceptualized insistence that God is not Father, Son/Logos, and Spirit only for us, but for himself. In theology, formulations that push language to the brink of its powers are nevertheless sometimes illuminating. Let me propose this one: God is *the life lived between* the divine Presence in sacred history and the Author of the history, in their mutual bonding Spirit; and there is only one such life.

It does not seem to me that there is anything in the previous paragraph that absolutely must divide the spirits between Christians and Jews in this colloquium. Obviously, it looks at Scripture from an angle that Judaism does not occupy, and uses concepts that Judaism will hardly adopt for herself. But it seems to me that if the two communions make an effort to think within each other's language, they may decide that we have not yet reached a point of mutual dissent.

That point, of course, is reached when Christians identify Jesus of Nazareth as the Son/Logos. Here we must first ask what is involved in that, and then why Christians would do it.

According to the Prologue of John's Gospel, the Logos/Son "became flesh and dwelt among us."[31] That is, the content — the Son — or plot — the Logos — of the Lord's history with Israel came, at the beginning of the End of Days, to dwell in Israel as the teaching and suffering and action of one Israelite. What the Lord and Israel are together as a joint reality, appeared as one concrete person, and so as one personal and simultaneous participant in God's life and in the life of his people. At a session of this col-

---

31. John 1:14.

loquium, I was asked whether I would be willing to say that God is incarnate in the people of Israel. I answer that he is, if we read the whole history of Israel as the coming of the Son/Logos, as the church does — or did before she lost her exegetical nerve.

But why ever would one make so extravagant a claim as that of the previous paragraph about this one man, Jesus of Nazareth? What can possibly justify it?

The claim was and is called forth and founded by his resurrection. For by raising him from the dead in anticipation of the general resurrection, the Lord fulfilled on this one Israelite the great and encompassing promise to all Israel, that she will live with death behind her and even bring gentiles into this new life. Thus Jesus is Israel in and for Israel. The resurrection of all God's folk is discovered to be participation in this one's resurrection; we are ". . . united with him in a resurrection like his" (Rom. 6:5). All the host of the apocalyptic visions are to be raised *in* and even *as* this one: as Paul once put it, "as his one body."

I certainly do not hope with such explanations to make the Trinity doctrine convincing in this gathering, only to make it less puzzling. What kind of God can make a covenant? Christianity must answer, a triune God; Judaism does not. But perhaps Judaism and Christianity can together affirm some of what Christians mean with that answer; if that is so, it will be a chief fruit of this paper. Moreover, where in the foregoing we must part may vary from theologian to theologian, in both communities.

IV

I cannot entirely avoid the question of the relation of the church, which claims a covenantal relation with the God of Israel, to the covenant/s established with the Jewish people by Abraham's call and at Sinai — much as one might wish to elide so historically delicate a matter. Is the covenant with the God of Israel claimed by the church the same covenant made with Abraham or at Sinai? Judaism mostly says No. The church has not quite known what to say; though it is clear that assignment to the covenant with Noah will *not* answer her claim. We may ask: Do the above reflections on the character of a covenant-making God contribute any clarity here?

Let me approach this question by positing the situation supposed, if sometimes only subliminally, by the sort of theology I have been lamenting: there is God, who is eternal by being timeless; and nevertheless there is a temporal community in constituting covenant with him. This community has a history, and therefore so does its constituting covenant: on different occasions, it is made with different features. Are these covenant-makings sheer repetitions of the first making? Or are the covenants made on some occasions new, perhaps in the sense of Jeremiah 31? And what sense of newness is that, exactly?

The question will, on the supposition, be undecidable. For there will be one answer if we consider the matter with respect to God and the opposite answer if we consider the matter with respect to the community. While the community will experience novelty, for the covenant-making God the times of the several covenant-makings will all be the same eternal instant and there will be no extension to accommodate variation.

Next, let us suppose that foreigners appear, who with what seems to them sufficient reason claim to have been brought into covenant with the community's God. Should they or should they not suppose that their alleged ingathering is into the same covenant as that of the prior community?

This question also will, on the supposition, be undecidable, for much the same reasons as those just adduced. The prior community will probably altogether reject the claim, and will in any case surely hold that their covenant and the covenant of the newcomers are separate and different. The newcomers will have to take this judgment seriously. But on the other hand, if they consider the matter with respect to the supposedly timeless God, they will have to claim that their covenant and the prior covenant are but one for him and so in reality.

What, however, if the community's history, including its history of covenanting, is also and indeed primally God's own history? What if God is not eternal by being merely timeless? Two things would follow.

First, the *aporia* just canvassed disappear. However Judaism is led to construe its history of covenanting, its historicality is no longer contradicted by God's lack thereof. And however Judaism or the church may each construe their entangled history of covenanting, the church will not need to suppose an either/or between simply belonging to Israel's covenant and simply being a new phenomenon.

Second, we are freed to take the history of the Lord's covenant-making with his people seriously as narrative, embodying logic appropriate to narrative rather than logic appropriate to deductions. We can believe that also God's own living of that history does not posit some other abstract logic.

It has long seemed to me that Aristotle got the logic of true narrative exactly right.[32] To be sure, he did not believe it applied to anything but fiction, since his cosmos had no narrative; but that is another matter. An event in a true — that is, dramatically coherent — narrative, he said, is unpredictable before the fact but after the fact can be seen as just what had to happen.

If the covenant-making God and the people of his covenant are joined in a history whose possibilities are not characterized by the either/or of propositional logic but by dramatic coherence, then new covenant-makings can be in some aspects repetition of the existing covenant and in other aspects truly new, without violating either God's eternity or the community's temporality. Then the relation between God and his people rides with the waves of its own narrative.[33]

And then at least this Christian will want to claim that the church's covenant with Israel's God is at once the same as Judaism's continuing covenant and different. If so, Paul's metaphor of grafting wild-olive sprigs into a cultivated olive tree is just right, precisely in its horticultural ambiguity.

32. Aristotle, *Poetics* 1452a.3.
33. Further on this, see Robert W. Jenson, *"Ipse pater non est impassibilis,"* in Keating and White, eds., *Divine Impassibility,* pp. 117-26.

Covenant, Mission, and Relating to the Other

Gerald McDermott

This paper explores the relation between covenant and mission for Jews and Christians as they seek to understand each other and work together. The first section argues that covenant is the main story of the Hebrew and Christian Scriptures. It is a differentiated plan of blessing in which God relates in different ways to gentiles and Jews, blessing the world (the universal) through Israel (the particular). Jesus was an observant Jew who taught this covenant, and saw himself as teaching and fulfilling the inner meaning of Torah. Paul held to the same covenant, and was neither anti-Torah nor supersessionist Christian.

The second section maintains that God's covenant with Israel is not understood properly unless its promise of land is taken seriously.

The last part of the paper claims that mission is fundamental to covenant, which was God's choice of Israel to be a light to the nations (mission). I argue that mission means bearing witness, and in fact that this truth-bearing (not coercive proselytism) is inevitable in all true dialogue. I close with some brief suggestions of what Christians can learn from Jewish witness-bearing, and what Jews might learn from Christians testifying to what they see.

I am grateful to Brian Kvasnica, Scott Horrell, Paul Hinlicky, Alan Pieratt, Mark Nanos, Harold Netland, Terry Muck, Dan Juster, David Pileggi, and Avihu Zakai for helpful comments on earlier drafts of this essay.

Gerald McDermott

One Covenant for Jesus and Paul

Covenant is *the* story of the Scriptures, both First and Second.[1] One-sided and asymmetrical, unlike the bilateral agreements of the ancient Near East, it might therefore be better described as a "testament" — to reflect its unconditional character. The God of the Hebrew Bible fixes on an elderly, childless couple in what is now Iraq and declares to them that they will bring blessing to all the nations of the world. Jesus and his followers claim to be children of that couple and recipients of the blessing. Despite repeated failures by God's people in both sets of Scripture, God insists the promise remains. His faithfulness is one-sided. Yet at the same time, he treats his people as partners in the history of redemption.

This overarching single covenant of unconditional promise subsumes several other covenants (those made to Noah, Jacob-Israel, Moses, and David), some of which were conditional. Paul distinguishes between "covenants of promise" and covenants with commandments, but suggests the unconditional covenant made with Abraham and his offspring is the master covenant incorporating all the others (Eph. 2:12-15; Gal. 3:15-18). I shall argue below that for Paul and other NT authors, the Abrahamic covenant was primary, but obedience to the Mosaic covenant of law was still required for Jewish — not gentile — disciples of Jesus. They believed Torah was "for Jews but provides a standard for" gentiles.[2]

Jesus' "new" covenant was similar: his use of Jeremiah's *berit ḥadashah* (31:31) might be translated "renewed" covenant, since there is no Hebrew word to distinguish "brand new" from "renewed." According to Matthew and Mark, Jesus said simply, "This is the blood of *the* covenant," suggesting

---

1. Not all Christians, especially those outside the Reformed tradition, would put the matter so pointedly. But most orthodox Christian theologians, even those who find covenantal theology problematic, might agree that the biblical canon, notwithstanding the non-narrative character of parts such as its wisdom literature, is to be read, and has been so read in the Great Tradition, as "a coherent story." Richard Bauckham, "Reading Scripture as a Coherent Story," in *The Art of Reading Scripture,* ed. Ellen F. Davis and Richard B. Hays (Grand Rapids: Eerdmans, 2003), pp. 38-53.

2. Michael Wyschogrod takes a similar approach to the Abrahamic and Mosaic covenants: "God could have begun his relationship with Abraham by bestowing the law on him. But he did not do this. . . . [The law] is not the deepest layer of God's relationship with the Jewish people." Wyschogrod, *Abraham's Promise: Judaism and Jewish-Christian Relations,* ed. R. Kendall Soulen (Grand Rapids: Eerdmans, 2004), p. 234. The quote is from Pamela Eisenbaum, *Paul Was Not a Christian: The Original Message of a Misunderstood Apostle* (New York: HarperOne, 2009), p. 219.

20

there is only one fundamental (Abrahamic) covenant (Matt. 26:28; Mark 14:24). Luke suggests the same when he has Zechariah bless the Lord God of Israel for the one "holy covenant, the oath he swore to our ancestor Abraham" (Luke 1:72-73). Jesus said he did not come "to abolish the law or the prophets" but to "fulfill" them, and that "not one letter, not one stroke of a letter,[3] will pass from the law until all is accomplished" (Matt. 5:17-18) — suggesting that he also believed in the continuing validity of Mosaic law. More on this below.

If Jesus and Paul both regarded the covenant with Abraham and his seed as primary, they understood this to mean that God has an eternal and inviolable relationship to the Jewish people. For the last fifty years Christian theologians have begun to see with new force Paul's declaration that Jews who did not accept Jesus as messiah were specially loved by God: "As far as the gospel is concerned, they are enemies on your [gentile Christians'] account; but as far as election is concerned, they are *loved* on account of the patriarchs, for God's gifts and his call are irrevocable" (Rom. 11:28; added emphasis).

Supersessionist Christians assumed for most of the last two millennia that once the Abrahamic mission (to be a blessing to the world) was shared with the gentiles through the gospel, God transferred the covenant from Israel to the church. God had universalized the particular. Now God's fullest love could be manifested in only one way: Jews were to become Christians and leave their Jewishness behind, since the covenant with Israel no longer existed.

But this was a misunderstanding of the biblical covenant. From the first promises to Abraham that his seed would bless the nations — to the prophets' visions of the gentiles coming to Israel to know the true God, there was always a *differentiated* plan of blessing: God would bless the Jews directly and the world indirectly (but *through* the Jews!). The covenant was expanded to include gentiles, but without obliterating its original promise to Israel.[4] For the early church, this differentiation extended not only to

---

3. Irving Greenberg helpfully suggests that this is a "probable reference to the Rabbinical Oral Law tradition, which derived laws from the strokes/jots/tittles that are part of the calligraphy of the Torah's letters." Irving Greenberg, *For the Sake of Heaven and Earth: The New Encounter between Judaism and Christianity* (Philadelphia: Jewish Publication Society, 2004), p. 228.

4. Recent scholars have pointed to Second Temple Judaism's "universal" concern. Terence L. Donaldson has traced Jewish patterns of universalism to 135 CE, concluding that while scholars typically speak of Christian particularism and Christian universalism, "the

the relation between the *ekklesia* and Temple community, but also among different races within the *ekklesia*: Jews who worshiped Jesus were to retain their Jewishness and commitment to Torah, while gentile converts were held only to a variation on what the rabbis would later call the Noahide commandments (Acts 15:28-29). Just as equality of blessing among men and women did not lead to androgeny in biblical and rabbinic Judaism or the early church, so too the first-century church did not require gentiles to become Jews, or Jews to become gentiles.[5] Pamela Eisenbaum, in her new *Paul Was Not a Christian,* suggests that the apostles' sense of differentiation was similar to that of first-century rabbis: "Both groups [Jews and gentiles, according to the rabbis] are supposed to be in concord with the will of God, both are called to obedience, and in their different roles, both are being faithful to the Torah. There are different components that encompass redemption and different stages in realizing it, and those different stages may affect people differently or require them to play different roles, but that does not mean there are two different systems of redemption."[6] Of course Jewish disciples of Yeshua differed with other Jews on Jesus' role in that redemption, but both groups agreed that redemption came through one fundamental covenant.

Perhaps the chief reason for Christians' misunderstanding of the covenant has been their oft-recurring Marcionism, which fundamentally mis-

---

Judaism within which Christianity came to birth was just as universalistic in its own way as was its upstart offspring"; Donaldson, *Judaism and Gentiles: Jewish Patterns of Universalism (to 135 CE)* (Waco, TX: Baylor University Press, 2007), p. 513. Donaldson points to Jewish belief that gentiles who variously adopted Jewish ways were acceptable to God, the practice of gentile conversion, Jewish understanding of Torah as a particular formulation of universal natural law, and the belief by some Jews that some gentiles would worship Israel's God in the eschatological future. Magnus Zetterholm writes of a "universalistic tendency within first-century Judaism that presented the Torah as a superior way of achieving the Greco-Roman ideal of 'self-mastery' *(enkrateia).*" He cites Philo's claim that "each seventh day . . . in every city [there are] thousands of schools [synagogues] of good sense, temperance, courage, justice and other virtues." These were open to gentiles because, as Philo put it, Jews were placed in the civilized world because "they have a mission to be to the whole world as the priest is to the whole Jewish people." Zetterholm, "Paul and the Missing Messiah," in *The Messiah in Early Judaism and Christianity,* ed. Zetterholm (Minneapolis: Fortress Press, 2007), pp. 42, 43.

5. "The church's mistake has been to consider the law as abstractly addressing some generic human rather than as addressing Jews and, in a different way, gentiles." Jon C. Olson, "Which Differences Are Blessed? From Peter's Vision to Paul's Letters," *Journal of Ecumenical Studies* 37, nos. 3-4 (Summer-Fall 2000): 458.

6. Eisenbaum, *Paul Was Not a Christian,* p. 252.

reads Jesus' attitude toward the Mosaic law. But in recent years scholars such as Mark Nanos, Mark Kinzer, and Markus Bockmuehl — building on the earlier work of W. D. Davies, Krister Stendahl, and E. P. Sanders — have argued that Jesus saw himself as an observant Jew claiming to teach the inner meaning of the Law but in no way abrogating it.

Let me illustrate with some of the familiar flashpoints. This "new perspective on Jesus" points to a Jesus who endorsed sacrifices and voluntary offerings to the Temple. He commended the poor widow's offering (Mark 12:41-44), assumed his disciples would bring their gifts for sacrifice at the altar of burnt offering in the inner court (Matt. 5:23), told the healed leper to be purified by offering a gift for sacrifice (Matt. 8:4; Mark 1:44; Luke 5:14), retold the Isaiah 5 parable of the vineyard so that it became directed against its tenants (the priests) rather than the vineyard itself (the Temple) (Luke 19), and showed jealousy over the administration of the Temple, calling it "my house" (Luke 19:45-46; Matt. 21:23-27).[7] Luke says that Jesus' parents went up to Jerusalem every year for Passover, no doubt making their own family sacrifice of the Pesach lamb (Luke 2:41-42), and shows Jesus' cousin's parents praying outside the Temple during the time for incense offering (Luke 1:10).[8]

Sometimes it is asserted that Jesus' emphasis on the "weightier things of the Torah" (Matt. 23:23) meant indifference to the rest of Torah. But this appeal to higher principles within the Torah was not uncommon in the rabbinic tradition. First-century Rabbi Yohanan b. Zakkai, for example, used Hosea 6:6, just as Jesus did, to argue that deeds of kindness are more important than Temple observance.[9]

Jesus continued to appeal to biblical purity laws, such as when he

---

7. See Randall Buth and Brian Kvasnica, "Temple Authorities and Tithe-Evasion: The Linguistic Background and Impact of the Parable of the Vineyard Tenants and the Son," in *Jesus' Last Week: Jerusalem Studies on the Synoptic Gospels*, vol. 1, ed. R. S. Notley, B. Becker, and M. Turnage (Leiden: Brill, 2006), pp. 53-80, 259-317.

8. Contra David E. Holwerda, who claims Jesus never offered sacrifice or engaged in any cultic practices of the temple; Holwerda, *Jesus and Israel: One Covenant or Two?* (Grand Rapids: Eerdmans, 1995), p. 68. See Susan Haber, "Going Up to Jerusalem: Purity, Pilgrimage and the Historical Jesus," in *They Shall Purify Themselves: Essays on Purity in Early Judaism*, ed. Adele Reinhartz (Atlanta: SBL, 2008), pp. 181-206.

9. Bockmuehl refers to the rabbinic *kelal gadol ba-Torah* ("great principle of the Torah"), e.g., Rabbi Akiva in y. Ned. 9.4, 41c36-7; *Sifra* Qedoshim 4 on Lev. 19:18, §200.3.7; Bockmuehl, *Jewish Law in Gentile Churches: Halakhah and the Beginning of Christian Public Ethics* (Grand Rapids: Baker Academic, 2000), p. 6, 8n. See also Shmuel Safrai, "The Jewish Cultural Nature of Galilee in the First Century," *Immanuel* 24, no. 25 (1990): 147-86.

warned of walking over unmarked graves (Luke 11:44) and giving dogs what is holy (Matt. 7:6), not to mention his bidding unclean spirits to enter pigs that would rush off a cliff into the sea (Mark 5:1-13). As we have already seen, he approved of the need for priestly purification after leprosy. He regarded camels and gnats as unclean (Matt. 23:24), and was "not entirely at ease with gentiles and Samaritans (Matt. 10:5; 18:17; Mark 7:26-27), even if these boundaries [were] on occasion signally transcended."[10] Therefore he did not abolish the distinction between clean and unclean or the purity laws generally. He denounced what he saw as a discrepancy between the words and actions of Pharisees, but not their attention to ritual observance per se. In an oft-missed aside, Jesus commands his disciples to "practice and observe whatever [the Pharisees] tell you" (Matt. 23:3a).

Jesus affirmed the sanctity of the Sabbath by arguing about its purpose (Mark 3:4) and telling his disciples to pray that the days of tribulation would not cause them to flee on the Sabbath (Matt. 24:20). He seems to have approved of tithing (Matt. 23:23b) and wore tassels on his garments. The same Greek root — κράσπεδ — is used for the "fringe" of Jesus' garment which was touched by the woman who had hemorrhaged for twelve years and the sick in Gennesaret, the fringes which the Pharisees wore long, and the tassels God commanded his people to wear in the Septuagint (Matt. 9:20; 14:36; 23:5; Num. 15:37-39).

Perhaps the most allegedly "law-free" statement of Jesus is the response he gave to a disciple whose father had died: "Follow me, and leave the dead to bury their own dead" (Matt. 8:22). Bockmuehl has argued at length that this cannot be used to illustrate a casual attitude to the Law. While the Torah commands children to bury their parents, it excepts High Priests and Nazirites (Lev. 21:11-12 and Num. 6:6). Jesus' vow not to "drink again of the fruit of the vine until that day when I drink it new in the kingdom of God" has parallels with Nazirite vows in the Mishnah, and Nazirite vows were "extremely popular in first-century Palestine" where "obligation to purity before God was [regarded as] greater even than . . . duty to parents."[11] The implication is that this statement about the burial of one's father cannot be the linchpin for a position that Jesus felt free to dispense with Mosaic law. There is no clear sign that Jesus failed to uphold the moral or ceremonial law — a distinction that is foreign to Judaism in early Second Temple Judaism.

10. Bockmuehl, *Jewish Law in Gentile Churches*, p. 10.
11. Bockmuehl, *Jewish Law in Gentile Churches*, p. 45.

This attitude to the Law seems to have continued in the first generation of the church. As Michael Wyschogrod, Mark Nanos, and Mark Kinzer have contended, both sides in the dispute at the Jerusalem conference (Acts of the Apostles 15) accepted as a given the obligation of Jewish Yeshua-disciples to live as Jews, observing the Law.[12] They differed only on whether gentiles had to do the same.

> It is clear that both parties agreed that circumcision and Torah obedience remained obligatory for Jewish Jesus believers since, if that were not the case, one could hardly debate whether circumcision and Torah obedience were obligatory for gentiles. Such a debate could only arise if both parties agreed on the lasting significance of the Mosaic Law for Jews. Where they differed was its applicability to gentiles. But both sides agreed that Jewish believers in Jesus remained obligated to circumcision and the Mosaic law.[13]

Peter's dispute with Paul at Antioch was not about whether he could eat *like* a gentile, but whether he could eat *with* gentiles. The resolution of the dispute — that he could eat kosher food with gentile Yeshua-disciples — was in fact not unlike the practice of other observant Jews who felt free to eat with gentiles "given the right conditions."[14]

It is widely agreed that Paul argued for this practice of Jewish Christians eating with gentile Christians. But it is fiercely contested whether his attitude toward Torah was similar to Jesus' approach as described above.[15] I think the evidence shows it was — despite what *seem* to be internal con-

---

12. Wyschogrod, *Abraham's Promise*, pp. 163, 192, 194, 197, 232-33; Mark Nanos, *The Mystery of Romans: The Jewish Context of Paul's Letter* (Philadelphia: Fortress Press, 1996), ch. 4; Mark S. Kinzer, *Post-Missionary Messianic Judaism: Redefining Christian Engagement with the Jewish People* (Grand Rapids: Brazos, 2005), pp. 65-68.

13. Wyschogrod, *Abraham's Promise*, p. 209.

14. See Nanos, "What Was at Stake in Peter's 'Eating with Gentiles'?" in *The Galatians Debate: Contemporary Issues in Rhetorical and Historical Interpretation,* ed. Nanos (Peabody, MA: Hendrickson, 2002), p. 296; and Chris A. Miller, "Did Peter's Vision in Acts 10 Pertain to Men or the Menu?" *Bibliotheca Sacra* 159 (July-September 2002): 302-17.

15. Jon Levenson, for example, has recently argued that, for Paul, Torah is the problem and not a solution. While he is right to say that Paul's approach to Torah is different from that of rabbinic Judaism and so at one level suggests a different God and different Torah, I think Paul was more positive toward Torah and its role for Jewish Christians than Levenson seems to think. Levenson, "Did God Forgive Adam? An Exercise in Comparative Midrash," in *Jews and Christians: People of God,* ed. Carl E. Braaten and Robert W. Jenson (Grand Rapids: Eerdmans, 2003), pp. 148-70.

traditions. There is tension, for example, between Paul's treatment of law in Galatians, where he is "almost stridently negative" and in Romans, where law is "good in and of itself but does not provide a sufficient solution to the problems occasioned by the fall." Yet when the two letters are read together, Romans seems to "subsume the more pointedly negative construal of Galatians into a larger synthetic whole."[16]

Let me try to flesh this out a bit. Paul said that "every man who lets himself be circumcised is obligated to obey the entire law" (Gal. 5:3). Granted, he also said he was "not under the law" (1 Cor. 9:20), but Bockmuehl and Kinzer suggest that by this Paul meant he was not like Jews who lived in strict separation from those "outside Torah (τοῖς ἀνόμοις)." He was for bringing together "within" the Torah (ἔννομου) Jews and gentiles now that the messianic era had begun. So Paul was "within" Torah (ἔννομος) but not "under Torah" (ὑπὸ νόμον): "While Paul himself does not affirm the narrowly ethnic type of halakhah, he can happily adapt to it and operate within it, if thereby he can win some of his stricter compatriots."[17] Thus Paul exercised halakhic flexibility but not complete freedom. We have no grounds for "thinking that he ever actually violated basic Jewish practice (i.e., by eating nonkosher food or by profaning the Sabbath or holidays)."[18]

One problematic Pauline text has been Galatians 3:10-14, where he said Christ "redeemed us from the curse of the law by becoming a curse for us" (v. 13). Since this is the same Paul who said "the law is holy, and the commandment is holy and righteous and good" (Rom. 7:12) and that faith in Christ does not "overthrow the law" but in fact "we uphold the law" (Rom. 3:31), it seems odd to follow the suggestion of many that for Paul the law itself is the curse. Wyschogrod's interpretation of the Galatians 3 text makes much better sense of these Pauline texts. He says that in the rabbinical framework God is both law and mercy, but there is no way of knowing which aspect of God's character will predominate — the curse that is attached to disobedience to Torah or the mercy that tempers God's justice. "Jewish existence is thus a very insecure one." But for Paul, Jesus on the cross was the "lightning rod which drew all punishment to itself, thereby

16. Gary Anderson, review of Brevard Childs's The Church's Guide for Reading Paul, in First Things 194 (June/July 2009): 46.

17. Bockmuehl, Jewish Law in Gentile Churches, p. 171.

18. Kinzer, Post-Missionary Messianic Judaism, p. 88. See David J. Rudolph, A Jew to the Jews: Jewish Contours of Pauline Flexibility in 1 Cor 9:19-23 (Tübingen: Mohr-Siebeck, 2010).

protecting all others." So the curse of the law is the punishment that comes from disobeying the law, which itself is holy and good.[19]

John G. Gager contends that Galatians has been misunderstood because its audience has been misunderstood. In reality, he says, Paul addresses only gentiles in this letter, and his purpose is to explain the relation of law to gentiles — which for Paul means none at all. "The Gentiles [in Galatia were] . . . being pressured by other apostles, within the Jesus-movement, to take on circumcision and a selective observance of the law." So Paul explains that "the law was never the intended path for Gentiles." Gager reasons that Galatians is addressed only to gentiles because "the descriptions of the circumstances of the Galatians before Christ can *only* apply to gentiles: 'we were slaves to the elemental spirits of the universe' (v. 3); 'you did not know God' (v. 8); and 'you were in bondage to beings that by nature are no gods' (v. 8)" [emphasis added]. Even the phrase "those who were under the law" refers to gentiles because it "is not a characteristic phrase in Jewish texts for describing the relationship of the law and Jews." Thus the Paul of Galatians can be reconciled to the Paul of Romans. Galatians tells gentiles the law is not for them, while Romans insists the law is "holy and just and good" (7:12). The two are compatible because Torah is for Jews not gentiles.[20]

Wyschogrod's and Gager's interpretations are supported by an abundance of other signs of Paul's respect for the Law: he circumcised Timothy, made and kept a Nazirite vow, and participated in another Nazirite vow (Acts 16:1-3; 18:18; 21:21-24). In the latter vow Paul proved to "James and all the elders" of the Jerusalem church, who seemed pleased that "thousands among the Jews [who] have believed" were "zealous for the law," that he himself was "liv[ing] in observance of the law" (Acts 21:18, 20, 24). Luke goes out of his way in this story to show that Paul was *not* "teach[ing] all the Jews among the Gentiles to forsake Moses, telling them not to circumcise their children or walk according to our customs" (21:21). In Romans Paul claimed that God's purpose in sending Jesus was that his disciples would fulfill "the righteous requirement of the Law" (Rom. 8:4).

In one respect, Paul was even more Jewish, if you will, than Jesus: he took a more positive approach to Pharisees than we see in the gospels. He

19. Wyschogrod, *Abraham's Promise*, pp. 196-97. See also Hillary LeCornu and Joseph Schulam, *A Commentary on the Jewish Roots of Galatians* (Jerusalem: Academon, 2005).

20. John G. Gager, *Reinventing Paul* (New York: Oxford University Press, 2000), pp. 86, 89, 91.

proudly presented himself as a Pharisee (Acts 23:6), and Luke reports that Pharisees came to his defense (Acts 23:9). In Acts 21 through 26, Paul "affirms his identity as a Torah-observant Jew, indeed, a Pharisee, and one not guilty of breaching the Torah or desecrating the Temple."[21] Raymond Brown speculated that if Paul had had a son, he would have circumcised him. Wyschogrod wonders, "Could it be that Paul was, after all, an Orthodox Jew?"[22]

For Nanos, Paul "affirmed Torah unambiguously." His differences with his fellow Jews were not over Torah observance, but the identity of Jesus: "The differences in Paul's time [between the Judaism of Paul and that of other Jews] did not turn around the traditional derogatory views of Torah, or reactions to those views. . . . They turned instead around the meaning of Christ for the people of Israel . . . and the rest of the nations."[23] Perhaps then the real question for Jews and Christians is not whether Jesus or Paul accepted the continuing validity of the law — for there is mounting evidence that they did — but whether Jesus was, as Irving Greenberg has put it, "a would-be redeemer for the nations."[24] It might seem impossible for Israel to see Jesus as Son of God, but it may be possible for Jews "to see Jesus as the Servant of God who carries the light of his God to the nations."[25] In other words, perhaps they could agree that it is Jesus [and his disciple Paul] who "invite gentiles to worship the God of Israel."[26]

21. Mark Nanos, "The Myth of the 'Law-Free' Paul Standing Between Christians and Jews," online paper at Nanos's website, http://www.marknanos.com/Myth-Lawfree-12-3-08.pdf, 6. See also Nanos, "Paul and the Jewish Tradition: The Ideology of the Shema," in *Celebrating Paul: Festschrift in Honor of J. A. Fitzmyer and J. Murphy-O'Connor*, ed. Peter Spitaler (Washington, DC: Catholic Biblical Association of America, 2011); Nanos, "Rethinking the "Paul *and* Judaism" Paradigm: Why Not 'Paul's *Judaism*'?" online article at http://www.marknanos.com/Paul%27sJudaism-5-28-08.pdf.

22. Wyschogrod, *Abraham's Promise*, pp. 232, 234.

23. Nanos, "Myth," pp. 2, 6. See also Daniel R. Langton, "The Myth of the 'Traditional View of Paul' and the Role of the Apostle in Modern Jewish-Christian Polemics," *Journal for the Study of the New Testament* 28, no. 1 (2005): 69-104.

24. Greenberg, *For the Sake of Heaven and Earth*, p. 229.

25. Joseph Ratzinger, *Many Religions — One Covenant: Israel, the Church, and the World*, trans. Graham Harrison (San Francisco: Ignatius, 1999), p. 104. See also Paul Hinlicky, "Lutheran Contribution to the Theology of Judaism," *Journal of Ecumenical Studies* 31, nos. 1-2 (Winter-Spring 1994): 123-52.

26. David P. Goldman, "Jewish Survival in a Gentile World," *First Things* 194 (June/July 2009): 23.

Covenant and Land

If the covenant is *the* story of both Scriptures, and at its heart is unconditional promise to Israel, land is integral to that promise. The word "land" is
the fourth most frequent noun or substantive in Hebrew Scriptures, repeated 2504 times. In fact, it is more dominant statistically than the idea of
covenant.[27] Next to God himself, "the longing for land dominates all others [in the Old Testament]." Land is presented by Torah as a place of spiritual testing; its pollution by sin and Israel's consequent exiles are portrayed
as analogous to humanity's fall from grace in Eden and consequent expul-
sion. Adam, formed from land, failed to protect it and therefore allowed
the serpent (evil) access to it. Land also represents the human condition:
"Good in principle, land is cursed as a result of humanity's sin, and people
are alienated from it as well as being joined to it."[28]

Yet most Protestant and Catholic affirmations of the Jewish covenant
ignore this central component. A recent letter writer to the *Christian Century* complained that the editor's approach to the land of Israel "is roughly
equivalent to a Jew asking a Protestant teenager: 'Hey, what's up with the
resurrection thing?' A Judaism without the [covenantal] component of the
land of Israel is a faith shorn of most of its power." This is in part because,
as the National Council of Synagogues has proposed, "God wants the nations to see the redemption of Israel and be impressed. . . . They will therefore learn, if they had not learned before, that the Lord, God of Israel, re-
stores His people to His land."[29]

After the Holocaust, a rereading of Scripture and particularly of Paul
led to a new vision for Israel's future (and hence the land) among some
theologians and New Testament scholars such as Karl and Marcus Barth,
C. E. B. Cranfield, Peter Stuhlmacher, and numerous evangelical scholars.
Cranfield, for example, concluded that an impartial reading of Paul's epistle to the Romans demanded a revision of supersessionism: "These three

---

27. Elmer A. Martens, *God's Design: A Focus on Old Testament Theology* (Grand Rapids:
Baker, 1981), pp. 97-98.

28. *Dictionary of Biblical Imagery*, ed. Leland Ryken, James C. Wilhoit, Tremper Long-
man III (Downers Grove, IL: InterVarsity Press, 1998), pp. 487-88. Walter Brueggemann
adds that the single central symbol for the promise of the gospel is land; *The Land: Place as
Gift, Promise, and Challenge in Biblical Faith* (Philadelphia: Fortress Press, 1977), p. 179.

29. Jeffrey K. Salkin, *Christian Century* 119, no. 22 (23 Oct.–5 Nov. 2002): 52; "Reflections
on Covenant and Mission," issued by the National Council of Synagogues and Delegates of
the Bishops' Committee on Ecumenical and Interreligious Affairs (12 August 2002), p. 8.

chapters [9–11] emphatically forbid us to speak of the church as having once and for all taken the place of the Jewish people."[30] Like Cranfield, scholars began to notice that Paul seemed to believe that Jewish rejection of Jesus as Messiah did not abrogate God's covenant with them, for in Romans 11 he says explicitly that "God has not rejected his people whom he foreknew" (v. 2; NRSV). As W. D. Davies noted in his landmark work on the biblical concept of land, "Paul never calls the Church the New Israel or the Jewish people the Old Israel."[31] Craig Blaising submits that Paul's forecast of Israel's future in Romans 11 is based on Isaiah 59:20-21, where the prophet forecasts the return of divine favor on Zion and follows this promise with another: "Then all your people will be righteous; they will possess the land forever" (Isa. 60:21).[32]

Thomas McComiskey adds that this last promise of land is not dropped by Paul, even if many Jews in Paul's day were rejecting Jesus. McComiskey thinks Paul has in mind the Abrahamic promises in Galatians 3:15-29, all of which (Gen. 12:7; 13:15; 15:18; 17:8) refer to the land. Since Christ is the offspring to whom Paul refers ("Now the promises were made to Abraham and to his offspring . . . that is, to one person, who is Christ" 3:16), McComiskey reasons that it cannot be only justification that the offspring inherits. In other words, the promise may function differently under the "new" covenant, but it has not lost its territorial connotations. In this case, the land has become a world (under the dominion of Christ) but *typified* by Israel's inheritance of Palestine.[33]

If Paul research has shown new hope for the future of Israel and its land, so too has research into the historical Jesus, with E. P. Sanders, N. T. Wright, John P. Meier, and Ben F. Meyer among the most important scholars showing that Jesus was far more interested in Israel than scholars had previously imagined.[34] Scot McKnight has pushed this further by ar-

30. C. E. B. Cranfield, *A Critical and Exegetical Commentary on the Epistle to the Romans* (Edinburgh: T. & T. Clark, 1979), vol. 2, p. 448.

31. W. D. Davies, *The Gospel and the Land: Early Christianity and Jewish Territorial Doctrine* (Berkeley: University of California Press, 1974), p. 182.

32. Craig A. Blaising, "The Future of Israel as a Theological Question," paper presented to the annual meeting of the Evangelical Theological Society, 19 November 2000, Nashville, TN.

33. Thomas Edward McComiskey, *The Covenants of Promise: A Theology of Old Testament Covenants* (Grand Rapids: Baker, 1985), pp. 55, 204-5.

34. E. P. Sanders, *Jesus and Judaism* (Philadelphia: Fortress Press, 1985); N. T. Wright, *Jesus and the Victory of God* (Minneapolis: Fortress Press, 1996); John P. Meier, *A Marginal*

guing that Jesus intended to renew Israel's national covenant, not found a new religion. He wanted to restore the twelve tribes, which would bring the kingdom of God in and through Israel. By his death, Jesus believed the whole Jewish nation was being nailed to the cross, and God was restoring the nation and renewing its people. Hence salvation was first and foremost for Israel; if the nations wanted salvation they would need to assimilate themselves to saved Israel. By his claim to dispense forgiveness of sins and create a new community of restored Israel that would inherit the kingdom of God, his disciples saw Jesus as the savior of Israel, as God coming to them through Jesus, leading the nation out of exile to regain control of the land.[35] Robert Wilken has observed that "hope of restoration and the establishment of a kingdom in Jerusalem were not, it seems, foreign to early Christian tradition." The angel tells Mary that "the Lord God will give to [Jesus] the throne of his father David, and he will reign over the house of Jacob forever" (Luke 1:32-33). Jesus himself seemed to anticipate the day when Jerusalem would welcome him: "Jerusalem, Jerusalem, I tell you, you will not see me again until you say, 'Blessed is he who comes in the name of the Lord'" (Matt. 23:39). He told his disciples they would "judge the twelve tribes of Israel" (Matt. 19:28). And, as Wilken points out, the word translated "earth" *(gen)* in Jesus' beatitude ("Blessed are the meek, for they shall inherit the earth" Matt. 5:5) is the word usually translated as "land" in the phrase "possess the land" elsewhere in the Septuagint.[36]

Most Christians have assumed that the promise of land to Israel has changed with Christ to the promise of inheritance in his kingdom to all peoples of the world. They have drawn this conclusion for two reasons, principally: first, the prophets' promise of a universal messianic kingdom, not limited to the land of Israel, and second, the New Testament's relative silence on land.

The prophets' promise of a universal kingdom seems to supersede all particular promises to Israel. But this is true only if a universal promise must abrogate an earlier particular promise. The biblical prophets as-

---

Jew: Rethinking the Historical Jesus, Anchor Bible Reference Library, 3 vols. (New York: Doubleday, 1991); Ben F. Meyer, *The Aims of Jesus* (London: SCM, 1979).

35. Scot McKnight, *A New Vision for Israel: The Teachings of Jesus in National Context* (Grand Rapids: Eerdmans, 1999).

36. Robert Wilken, *The Land Called Holy: Palestine in Christian History and Thought* (New Haven: Yale University Press, 1994), pp. 49, 52, 48.

sumed the fulfillment of both kinds of promises. While they expanded the promised inheritance of God's people beyond the definable boundaries of Canaan to include the world, they nevertheless retained their expectation that Israel would return to the land of Palestine. According to Hebrew Scriptures scholar McComiskey, "We cannot conclude that the prophets considered that promise to have been abrogated."[37] In other words, with the prophets we find new promises made for the messiah and his world-wide reign, but these new promises do not overrule the earlier promises of a particular land for a particular people. "Expansion [of the promise] is not synonymous with abrogation."[38] As Eliezer Berkovits has put it, "The universal expectation is inseparable from Israel's homecoming. The very passage that directs man's hopes to the time when 'nation shall not lift up sword against nation, neither shall they learn war any more' also envisages that 'out of Zion shall go forth Torah, and the word of the Eternal from Jerusalem' [Isa. 2:3-4]."[39]

The relative silence about land in the New Testament does not mean that the New Testament authors believed that the Abrahamic promises concerning land had been abrogated. Josephus was also silent about land. But Josephus deleted the theology of covenanted land because of its revolutionary implications for the messianism of the Zealots, whom he feared and despised. Political circumstances and Josephus' purposes thus determined his presentation about the promise of the land; any claim that he did not share the Jewish view concerning the land as promised or covenanted land because of his omissions would be precarious.

The same is true of any argument from silence concerning the New Testament authors themselves.[40] Paul, for example, "does not mention the land in Romans 9 . . . [because he lived] before the devastation of the Second Temple in A.D. 70[, and] the right of the Jews to their land was an inarguable commonplace in his own day."[41] Paul and his fellow Jews were already in the land — if not controlling it — and there was little or no debate about Jews' right to the land. Thus the relative silence.

McComiskey argues further that while Jesus does not speak directly in

---

37. McComiskey, *The Covenants of Promise*, p. 51.

38. McComiskey, *The Covenants of Promise*, p. 205.

39. Eliezer Berkovits, *Essential Essays on Judaism*, ed. David Hazony (Jerusalem: Shalem Center, 2002), pp. 178-79.

40. McComiskey, *The Covenants of Promise*, p. 207n. McComiskey cites B. H. Amaru, "Land Theology in Josephus," *Jewish Quarterly Review* 71 (1981): 201-29.

41. Gary Anderson, reply to letters, *First Things* 155 (August/September 2005): 7.

the gospels about God's promise of land to Israel,[42] neither did the Mishnaic tractate, "The Sayings of the Fathers." Yet the "Fathers" were known for their belief in the promise.[43] Similarly, the Mosaic law never included the earlier promise of gentile inclusion, yet the earlier promise was never abrogated.[44] McComiskey links the two promises, both referring to land, typologically: they are two aspects of the promise of land in the prophets — restoration to the land of Palestine, and the rule of the world by the Messiah. The first is the earnest of the second.[45]

Covenant and Mission

Whether land belongs to the *esse* or the *bene esse* of Israel's covenant, mission is fundamental. It is the Bible's answer to the question, What will God do about evil in the world? That answer starts with an elderly, childless couple in the land of Babel, who become the launching pad for God's mission *(missio dei)* to save the world.

The pivotal text is Genesis 12:1-3, where God calls Abraham to go to "a land that I will show you." From there God promises to make of him "a great nation," and "in [him] all the families of the earth [would] be blessed" (v. 3). This promise is repeated five times in Genesis (12:3; 18:18; 22:18; 26:4-5; 28:14).

Throughout the Hebrew Bible, there is oscillation between the particular and the universal, but a certain pattern recurs — God is on mission to redeem the world (the universal) through Israel (the particular). It is not a matter of *either* the particular *or* the universal, but the universal *through* the particular. For example, God calls Abraham and his seed because he wants to show Pharaoh his power in order "to make my name resound through *all the earth*" (Exod. 9:16). The Lord says he will establish Israel as a holy people because then "*all the peoples on earth* shall see that you are called by the name of the Lord" (Deut. 28:10). Joshua tells Israel that God dried up the waters of the Jordan "so that *all the peoples of the earth* may know that the hand of the Lord is mighty" (Josh. 4:24). David tells Goliath

42. But his telling the disciples they would judge the twelve tribes of Israel (Matt. 19:28) might have been an indirect suggestion of this.

43. McComiskey cites S. Talmon and D. Flusser, "The Gospel and the Land: Early Christianity and Jewish Territorial Doctrine," *Christian News from Israel* 25 (1975): 132-39.

44. McComiskey, *The Covenants of Promise*, p. 208.

45. McComiskey, *The Covenants of Promise*, p. 208.

that he would strike him dead "so that *all the earth* may know that there is a God in Israel" (1 Sam. 17:46). Solomon prays the Lord to hear foreigners' prayers "so that *all the peoples of the earth* may know your name and fear you, as do your people Israel" (1 Kings 8:43). The psalmists pray that "*all the ends of the earth* shall remember and turn to the Lord (22:27), "that your way may be known upon earth, your saving power *among all nations*" (67:2), and that "*all nations* be blessed in [Israel's king]" (72:17).[46] Isaiah predicts a day when Israel's enemies, Egypt and Assyria (representing all the nations), will share the blessings of Israel (19:24-25). Jeremiah predicts a day when "the nations" shall hear of all the good God does for Jerusalem, and then "fear and tremble" (33:9).[47]

Notice the pattern. The purpose of the covenant with Abraham and his progeny is to bless them so they in turn would bring blessing to the world. God does great acts for Israel in order to educate the nations. Israel comes to know God so that in turn the nations might come to know Israel's God. Hence the covenant of election is not simply soteriological (to bless and save Israel) but also missional (to bring blessing to the nations).[48]

Mission as Bearing Witness

Mission means, among other things, bearing witness. It must bear witness because it has been given truth and blessing, the knowledge of which is a blessing to others. The patriarchs did not hesitate to give witness to the God who had blessed them.

> Theirs is not a mute faith. The patriarchs verbalize to others the reality of Yahweh that they have experienced in their lives: they tell of his provision of wealth ([Gen.] 30:30; 31:5-13; 33:10-11; cf. 24:35), his protection and guidance (31:42; 50:20; cf. 24:40-49, 56); his giving of children (33:5); . . . and their commitment to his moral standards (39:9).[49]

46. For more of this theme in the psalms, see Psalms 86:9 and 145:12.

47. All emphasis is added.

48. Christopher J. H. Wright, *The Mission of God: Unlocking the Bible's Grand Narrative* (Downers Grove, IL: IVP Academic, 2006).

49. M. Daniel Carroll R., "Blessing the Nations: Toward a Biblical Theology of Mission from Genesis," *Bulletin for Biblical Research* 10 (2000): 29; cited in Wright, *The Mission of God*, p. 210.

After millennia of coercive and murderous "witness" by Christians, Jews are understandably wary of any talk about bearing witness. It can seem to be an excuse to eliminate either Jews or Judaism. But they might reflect on the notion that bearing witness is inevitable in all meaningful dialogue. For all real communication is concerned with conveying truth — even if the "truth" is that all truth is relative! And when it comes to religion, a simple profession of faith, even if one has no intent to convert the hearer, seeks to persuade the hearer that this faith is coherent. Often (but not always) implied is that for the speaker — the profess-or — this faith has more coherence than any of its rivals. The religious Jew is presumably convinced that his faith makes more sense of the world than Christian faith, since, among other reasons, Jesus seems not to have redeemed the world and so is not the messiah. The Christian might concede the unredeemed state of the world, but still think her faith is more coherent because of other things about Jesus that seem messianic. The point at the moment is not which one is right, but that all profession of faith bears within it the sense that it is a coherent construal of reality — even if the profess-or cannot always explain logically the inner *sense* of coherence. She bears witness to the rationality of the faith she senses simply by professing. She bears witness to what she thinks to be *true,* because of what she has seen and lived. This is different from proselytizing, which too often is coercive and demeaning. True witness is testimony, without demanding that the other accept the truth of the testimony in order to retain dignity as a human being or believer in God. Because this conference is about Jews and Christians, it is important for me to note that an important orthodox Christian scholar has recently concluded that when Jews resisted Christian proselytism that demanded they give up Torah observance, they were showing fidelity to the true God.[50]

Some participants in interreligious[51] dialogue think the dialogue

---

50. Kinzer suggests that Jewish rejection of Christian testimony has been fidelity to God when Christian testimony distorted the God of Israel. Kinzer, *Post-Missionary Messianic Judaism,* p. 224; Kinzer, "Post-Missionary Messianic Judaism, Three Years Later: Reflections on a Conversation Just Begun" (The 2008 Lindsey Lectures, delivered on 1 July 2008, at Narkis Street Congregation, Jerusalem, available at www.narkis.org), pp. 9-10.

51. I am reluctant to use this word for Jewish-Christian dialogue because I believe the New Testament covenant is a renewal and fulfillment of the one Abrahamic covenant. Hence, at one level, Judaism and Christianity are not two religions that are entirely distinct. But at another level, because the rabbinic tradition and the New Testament interpret Tanakh in very different ways, they are two religions that see God differently.

should not be about truth-bearing because such talk is hegemonic and intolerant, implying that one religion is superior to another. But it is hard for anyone who takes any position on religion to avoid concluding that her settled conviction is not better than its alternatives. Why would she take that position otherwise? Think of the religious pluralist who thinks all the religions are equally truthful paths to the Divine. It would be difficult for him not to conclude that religious exclusivists (those who think their religion has the most truth) have in fact *less* truth — since after all, they wrongly think their religion is the best. But now the religious pluralist, who said no one religion is better, has concluded that his *own* religious view is better than that of the exclusivist. So he is now doing, perhaps unwittingly, the very thing he thinks is hegemonic and intolerant.[52]

Thus interreligious dialogue that claims it avoids truth-bearing cannot avoid truth-bearing. If this is true, then engaging in Jewish-Christian dialogue[53] with the sole purpose of making one another better in our respective faiths is not enough. It fails to take the religious other seriously as a professor of truth-claims, and thus misses the highest goal of Jewish-Christian dialogue — "common search for truth in light of the Word of God."[54]

Because both of our communities have been given truth, and because none of us sees clearly all the truth we have been given, we need to bear witness to one another. We can learn from one another as our different versions of the one covenant are "corrected and refreshed" by dialogue about covenant. Perhaps this is part of a "general divine strategy of redemption."[55]

We Christians need Jews to bear witness to us. They need to bear witness, especially to evangelicals and Lutherans who sometimes flirt with cheap grace and antinomianism, that law is a gift from God and in fact a manifestation of love. They need to remind us that God's wrath is against that which destroys his covenant relationship with his people and therefore is love — as they have learned from Israel's biblical history.

Jews need to bear witness to Christians of the danger of dualisms that speak of spirits only, for which the Jewish emphasis on carnal matters, on

52. I think this is what Greenberg means by going "beyond tolerance" and pluralism to "partnership." Greenberg, *For the Sake of Heaven and Earth*, p. 211. He too seems to believe in our need to learn from one another while retaining our theological distinctions.

53. This term should be understood to include dialogue between messianic Jews and Jews who do not see Yeshua as messiah.

54. R. Kendall Soulen, in Wyschogrod, *Abraham's Promise*, p. 14.

55. Greenberg, *For the Sake of Heaven and Earth*, pp. 44, 38.

law and land, is a wonderful corrective. God's election, Jews need to remind us, is not only spiritual but also carnal. He lives in his people just as he lived in his temple.[56] As Wyschogrod and Greenberg point out, it is this carnality of God's work, if you will, that makes plausible the idea of Jesus' incarnation — if not finally credible to most Jews' sensibilities.[57]

Jews need to warn us of the danger of submitting to philosophy and abstractions (alleged eternal verities of reason or some global sensibility) rather than God's Word. As Wyschogrod has put it, "The God of Israel is the lord of all frameworks and subject to none."[58] Of course, Karl Barth also taught this. But he got it from the greatest Christian theologians, who got it from the New Testament, whose Jewish authors got it from the Hebrew Bible.

To a church that has often been triumphalist, Jews need to bear witness again to the fact that God's relationship to Israel and the gentiles has been by God's initiative. We need to be reminded that if we think we are in the Promised Land, it is "not because of your righteousness or the uprightness of your heart" but simply "because the Lord loves you" (Deut. 9:5; 7:8). And in a church that is too frequently Marcionite, we need the people of Israel to testify to us that their biblical story is "a flesh-and-blood map to the salvation of every Christian."[59] To Christian reductionists they need to testify that the ceremonial parts of Torah are intrinsic to the Hebrew Bible and therefore fundamentally meaningful, not to be separated artificially from moral injunctions.

All of this truth-bearing by Jews to Christians will help Christians keep from "regressing to the paganism from which we emerged."[60] For without the Hebrew Bible, "the figure of the Christ is reduced to a mythical or purely pagan figure of divinity over which western reason proclaims its triumph."[61]

Some Jewish truth-bearing will challenge orthodox Christians. Wyschogrod says Jews have a "responsibility" to teach gentiles of the danger of idolatry, and that Christian doctrines of incarnation and Trinity risk

56. Wyschogrod, *Abraham's Promise*, p. 102.
57. Wyschogrod, *Abraham's Promise*, p. 178; Greenberg, *For the Sake of Heaven and Earth*, p. 156.
58. Wyschogrod, *Abraham's Promise*, p. 42.
59. Goldman, "Jewish Survival," p. 23.
60. Richard John Neuhaus, "Salvation Is from the Jews," in Braaten and Jenson, eds., *Jews and Christians: People of God*, p. 71.
61. Cardinal Jean-Marie Lustiger, *The Promise* (Grand Rapids: Eerdmans, 2007), p. 73.

idolatry. Therefore "it is my duty as a Jew to persuade my Christian friends to abandon these teachings."[62] I dare say that this is the kind of theological resolve that will move dialogue from mutual affirmation of least-common denominators to stimulating exchange that might enable all involved to see more "truth in the light of the Word of God." It is risky and frightening — for "there is always the chance that some Jews will finally accept the Christian revelation as original just as some Christians will finally accept the Jewish revelation as original."[63] But there would be something artificial and contrived if either Jew or Christian decided they should not bear witness to the truths they have seen and lived, and not engage one another at points of deepest difference, especially when they profess to seek truth in the light of the Word of God.

This is not the place for a full-orbed presentation of Christian witness-bearing. But just as I have sketched briefly some lines of Jewish thought that should inspire Christians, let me suggest some lines of exploration that Jews might consider.

1. That the idea of incarnation is not foreign to Judaism, but in fact integral to the idea, as Wyschogrod has written, of "the indwelling of God in Israel." Christians see "the intensification of that indwelling in one Jew."[64]
2. That differentiation within God's unity is an idea with Jewish provenance. Daniel Boyarin has written recently of the "widely held [belief] by Jews in the pre-Christian era" of "a second divine entity, God's Word (Logos) or God's Wisdom, who mediates between the fully transcendent Godhead and the material world."[65]
3. That resurrection from the dead "was a weight-bearing beam in the edifice of rabbinic Judaism" (Jon Levenson).[66]
4. That, as Boyarin puts it, "the borders between Christianity and Judaism are as constructed and imposed, as artificial and political as any of the borders on earth."[67] This might be hyperbole, but if (as I have ar-

62. Wyschogrod, *Abraham's Promise*, p. 158.

63. David Novak, "From Supersessionism to Parallelism in Jewish-Christian Dialogue," in Braaten and Jenson, eds., *Jews and Christians: People of God*, pp. 112-13.

64. Wyschogrod, *Abraham's Promise*, p. 178.

65. Daniel Boyarin, *Border Lines: The Partition of Judaeo-Christianity* (Philadelphia: University of Pennsylvania Press, 2004), pp. 30-31, 112-37.

66. Jon D. Levenson, *Resurrection and the Restoration of Israel: The Ultimate Victory of the God of Life* (New Haven: Yale University Press, 2006), p. x.

67. Boyarin, *Border Lines*, p. 1.

gued above) Jesus and Paul were neither anti-Torah nor anti-Jewish, the most fundamental distinctions between these two communities are not Torah/law, resurrection, incarnation or God's unity, but Jesus' role within the covenant and its mission.

5. That the notion of who is a Jew might need to be reevaluated. My Jewish friends may think it is inappropriate for me, a Yeshua-follower, to suggest this. But I speak on behalf of fellow Yeshua-followers with Jewish blood and Torah-devotion who also seek to be accepted as Jews — messianic followers of Yeshua. It strikes this outsider to the Jewish community odd or inconsistent to accept "BuJus" (some of whom integrate Judaism and Buddhism and others who have renounced Jewish religion for Buddhism) as Jews,[68] and atheists (who have renounced the Jewish G-d for what most sociologists of religion would call a religion) as Jews, but not messianic Yeshua-followers (who say they embrace the G-d of Israel, have Jewish mothers, teach their children Jewish identity, and passionately support Israel/serve in the IDF, and many of whom keep Torah). Even in the famous 1958 Brother Daniel decision by the Israeli Supreme Court to deny registration on his identity card as a Jew to a Polish man who was raised as a Zionist Jew and became a Catholic priest,[69] "it was accepted on all sides that for *other* purposes of Israeli law [besides those entailed by the Law of Return], Rufeisen [the petitioner] was indeed to be regarded as a Jew." One of the judges on the Court wrote that "Jewish law itself regards a person born to a Jewish mother as remaining a Jew, notwithstanding a conversion to another religion." Another cited "the Jewish religious ruling which holds that 'a Jew who sins nevertheless remains a Jew' [*Sanhed*

68. The claim by the former to worship the G-d of Israel while seeing the Buddha or buddhas as expressions of that G-d seems comparable to the claims that "messianic Jews" make — that they worship the God of Israel and deny nothing of what Tanakh asserts. In fact, the messianic claim to the religion of Israel appears to be far stronger than that of Buddhist-Jews, for the Buddha was for all practical purposes an atheist while Jesus worshiped Israel's G-d. Some messianics, like Kinzer, see the rabbinic tradition as inspired by God.

69. Oswald Rufeisen was reared as a Jew in Poland by two Jewish parents, was active in the Zionist Youth Movement, trained to immigrate to Israel, was imprisoned as a Jew by the Gestapo twice and escaped both times, infiltrated the German police and saved 150 Jews by informing them of German plans against them, and converted to a Catholic monastic order which had a chapter in Israel so that he could accomplish his goal of *aliyah*. Bernard S. Jackson, "Brother Daniel: The Construction of Jewish Identity in the Israel Supreme Court," *International Journal for the Semiotics of Law* 6, no. 17 (1993): 115-19.

rin 44a], and 'even though he changes his religion does not cease to be part of the Jewish people.'" The most religiously committed of the judges concluded that "if the *religious* categories of Jewish law [rather than secular] applied, the petitioner would indeed be regarded as a Jew."[70]

Our Common Mission

This troubled world needs the "partnership"[71] of Jews and Christians to bear common witness to what they share in the Abrahamic covenant. We have a common mission. To a world of postmoderns who despair of any ultimate truth or meaning, we need to bear witness to final truths we have seen and a love that is more than human construction. In a Western culture that has lost confidence in its legitimacy while under siege from a radical Islam that denies religious freedom, we need to testify together of religious freedom as the first principle of justice. As we strengthen our own respective convictions and perhaps learn from dialogue about our shared covenant, we will be better prepared to respond to forces that would want to diminish or destroy both of our communities.

70. Jackson, "Brother Daniel," pp. 120, 128, 146.
71. Greenberg, *For the Sake of Heaven and Earth*, p. 201.

Covenant and Mission

David Novak

The Question of Covenant and Mission

Formulated as a question, the term "covenant and mission" seems to ask: Is a community elected by God for an ongoing relationship with God required by that relationship to seek to bring outsiders into their community? The relationship itself, in scriptural language, is called a *berit* or "covenant." Formulated as an imperative, "covenant and mission" seems to say that the elected community is obliged to go out and actively recruit others for membership in *their* community, a community designated by scriptural revelation to be the *unique* people of the unique God.[1]

As an imperative, *mission* is like *covenant*. It basically follows from divine election. Those who advocate mission seem to be saying that divine election is meant for all human beings, some of whom have already accepted it and are thus members of the covenanted community. Their task is now to get as many outsiders as possible to accept divine election and thus become members of the covenanted community that has already accepted it.

But Jews and Christians are the only people in the world who regard themselves as elected by God to be members of the community God has covenanted with in history. That is why the relation of covenant and mission could only be of concern to Jews and Christians. By contrast, Muslims, who do not have a notion of divine election of a community, do not have a notion of covenant. Though Muslims do have a notion of mission, that means they are obliged to get outsiders to choose to serve God (which is what *Islam* means) as proclaimed by Muhammad. However, that is quite

1. See David Novak, "Why Are the Jews Chosen?" *First Things* 202 (2010): 35-37.

41

different from being obliged to persuade outsiders that they too are elected by God and are thereby obliged to confirm that election by becoming one with the covenanted community. In Islam, the faithful choose to become a community; in Judaism and Christianity, God chooses the community whose members are to respond to their election faithfully.

At the *prima facie* level, the very term "covenant and mission" seems to have a decidedly Christian connotation. It is well known that most Christian churches advocate some sort of mission to non-Christians. And it is just as well known that no Jewish group advocates any such mission to non-Jews. So, whereas proselytization seems to be endemic to Christianity, it seems to be foreign to Judaism. In other words, are covenant and mission correlative for Christianity, but antithetical for Judaism?

In dealing with this and related questions in this paper, I can only attempt to speak as a Jew who accepts the covenant between God and Israel as the central reality of my life, and who therefore regards the commandments of the Torah — the Torah being the constitution of the covenant — as obligatory for me and all my fellow Jews. Whether we Jews who willingly (and happily) confirm our covenantal status and its attendant rights and duties favor a Jewish mission to the gentiles or not, mission is an issue we have to take seriously: by accepting or rejecting it as our task in this world. But we cannot be indifferent to it, regarding it as irrelevant to our covenantal identity.

For Jews who do not confirm God's specific election of Israel, mission cannot be an issue. After all, "mission" comes from the Latin *missio:* "being sent"; but "being sent" by whom? A mission without a sender is like an ambassador without credentials because he or she represents no sovereign state. That is why secularized Jews who object to Jews being proselytized can only do so on nontheological or anti-theological political grounds (it is "undemocratic" to "push religion" in public) or "cultural" grounds ("we don't want to be told to adopt another communal identity"). Having no basis for understanding how mission could be of concern for them, secularized Jews cannot understand how mission is of concern to any non-Jew. Yet a religious commitment coupled with theological awareness gives Jews a much better way to answer the claims made upon them by missionaries representing other religions than do the rather weak political and cultural arguments of the secularists just noted.

In the dialogical milieu of a conference such as this, whose participants are Christian and Jewish theologians, the arguments should be theological, and they should only be political when politics and theology overlap (as they inevitably do for covenantal faiths). So, in dealing with covenant and mission in our respective traditions and what that means for the other, Jewish participants need to ask the following questions: (1) Since Christian proselytization of Jews has been an ever-present fact, what has been and what should be Jewish reaction to the missionary attempts of various Christians to proselytize Jews? (2) Does Jewish exclusion of gentiles from the covenanted community in this world mean gentiles *cannot* become members of the community; hence proselytization of gentiles should be prohibited? (3) *May* gentiles become members of the community by conversion *(gerut),* so that proselytization of them should be permitted? (4) *Ought* gentiles become members of the community by conversion, so that proselytization of them should be mandated?

The answer to (1) is easiest: Jews have resisted, do resist, and should resist the efforts of any other religious community to proselytize them. However, the question we shall deal with shortly is whether or not Jews should advocate the civil prohibition of proselytizing in a democratic polity where freedom of religion obtains for everybody. A positive answer to (2) implies that the Jews are a "race," since the only way to become a Jew is to be born a Jew. (And that, by the way, does not necessarily mean gentiles are to be regarded by Jews as inferior to Jews, just permanently different.) A positive answer to (3) implies that there is no obligation for any gentile to convert to Judaism, thereby becoming a member of the Jewish people. (But, as many "secular" Jews have discovered, often to their chagrin, even in the "secular" State of Israel, their gentile spouses and their gentile children can only become members of the Jewish people by conversion to the Jewish religion.) As such, a gentile may decide not to become a Jew with impunity, which surely implies there is no obligation on the part of the Jewish community to proselytize gentiles (yet this doesn't imply any prohibition). But a positive answer to (4) certainly implies that Jews *ought* to proselytize gentiles. After all, if gentiles are obliged to become Jews, aren't Jews obliged to inform them of their duty, even persuade them of it, in the same way Jews are obliged to inform each other of their duty, even persuade each other to do it?

Jewish Reaction to Christian Proselytization

Let us now deal with the first question raised at the beginning of this paper: Since Christian proselytization of Jews has been an ever-present fact, what has been and what should be Jewish reaction to Christian attempts to proselytize Jews? This question shall be addressed in the light of what seem to be some renewed Christian efforts to proselytize Jews. I do not regard these efforts as illegitimate from either a Christian perspective or from a democratic perspective. That is, there are no doubt valid Christian reasons for Christians to actively proselytize non-Christians in good faith (even though there are Christian churches that do not actively proselytize). There is nothing un-Christian about that. Moreover, if one's commitment to a democratic society is part of one's general moral commitment, then proselytizing anybody is only immoral if coercive or deceptive. And if Judaism and Christianity rightfully claim to be more than moralities but never less than them, then neither Christianity nor Judaism should permit their adherents to coerce anyone to convert, or coerce anyone to be kept within their religious community against his or her will, or deceive anybody about anything, and surely not about one's religious agenda. Coercion, whether violent or threatening violence, and even psychological deception, are both immoral. If coercion is like rape, deception is like seduction. In both cases the victim is violated. Nevertheless, I fail to see why any attempt, short of coercion or deception, to win over converts to one's religious conviction is immoral in a democratic society (which most Jews and Christians regard as the most morally attractive sort of political arrangement available today). Indeed, religious proselytizing is no more immoral than attempting to win over people to one's political conviction, short of coercion or deception. And, just as political convictions are the business of political groups (usually called "parties"), so are religious convictions the business of religious groups (usually called "communities" or "communions" or "confessions"). Both political parties and religious communities, *mutatis mutandis,* are certainly legitimate associations in any truly democratic society.

Jewish reaction to Christian proselytization of Jews, therefore, should not be made on general moral grounds, but only on specifically Jewish theological grounds. Only Jews, however, are obliged by Jewish theology. ("Theology" here means God's word as revelation — *dvar ha-Shem* — as transmitted to, by, and through the covenanted community; it is not human philosophical speculation about God, what we now call "God-talk.") Hence a Jewish theological reaction to Christian proselytizing is not a general moral argument made to Christians as human beings, especially to Christians as citizens of a democracy. And it is not a theological argument made against Christianity. In fact, this theological reaction only contains a political argument made to Christians when it reminds them of how a specific mission *to* Jews makes dialogue with Jews impossible (which is not the case when Christians simply proclaim the gospel to the whole world in general). But it is for Christians, not Jews, to decide whether the abandonment of a specific mission *to* Jews for the sake of dialogue with Jews can be a genuinely Christian public policy or not. In other words, Christians like Jews have to ponder whether or not Christian-Jewish dialogue is theologically justified.[2] In fact, the Roman Catholic Church, which since the Second Vatican Council in the 1960s has abandoned any specific mission to the Jews, is still struggling with this issue, as we shall presently see.[3]

Short of anti-Semitic proposals for the persecution or even the murder of Jews, nothing is more offensive to Jews than concerted programs by adherents of some other religion that target Jews to convert. Most Jews have always understood that to follow such calls for conversion is to commit religious and cultural suicide. Even when such programs simultaneously denounce the injustice of anti-Semitism, and even when they express "genuine friendship and love for the Jewish people," by their very call for the conversion of the Jewish people to a religion other than Judaism, they can at best only denigrate Judaism as a religion insufficient for the salvation (that is, the ultimate reconciliation of all humans with God) of the Jews who live it. At worst, such programs can further denigrate Judaism as a false religion altogether. All of this is hardly new. In fact, there is hardly a Jew in the world who has not been the target of some overt attempt to cause him or her to convert to another religion, especially another monotheistic religion of revelation: Christianity or Islam.

There has been very little attempt of late on the part of Muslims to convert Jews to Islam. Many Muslims today regard Jews as much more of a political threat than a theological opportunity. (And, it needs hardly be mentioned that today, as distinct from the not-so-distant past, hardly any Jews are now living in Muslim societies anyway.) However, two very recent events have made Jews wonder whether Christians, and even Christians who claim to be our friends otherwise (such as being supportive of the State of Israel), are now embarking on a renewed effort to convert us through ministries specifically directed to the Jewish people. Nevertheless,

2. See David Novak, *Jewish-Christian Dialogue: A Jewish Justification* (New York: Oxford University Press, 1989).

3. See Bruce Marshall, "Elder Brothers: John Paul II's Teaching on the Jewish People as a Question to the Church," in *John Paul II and the Jewish People*, ed. D. G. Dalin and M. Levering (Lanham, MD: Rowman & Littlefield, 2008), pp. 113-29.

before criticizing Christian proselytizing efforts that target us Jews, the announcement of such proposals should first cause us to more adequately bring the message of the sufficiency of the Torah, the supreme gift of the One who chooses us, to those Jews most likely to be targeted by Christian missionaries and most likely to accept their message. These vulnerable Jews first need to be convinced that the Jewish community wants to more fully include them in our communal-religious life by responding to their genuine religious concerns with empathy; and second, they need to be convinced that conversion to Christianity (or to any other religion) in effect removes them from the life of the Jewish people and thus from any actual Jewish identity for themselves in this world or the world-to-come.[4]

Of course, we have a much bigger problem with those Jews who are simply dropping out of normative Judaism through assimilation and intermarriage, let alone those who overtly leave Judaism for various forms of atheistic secularism. Yet, even though these "dropouts" should be of bigger concern to us (if for no other reason than there are a lot more of them) than Jews being targeted by Christian missionaries, there is still a greater likelihood of our bringing them back into Judaism than bringing back those who have actually converted to another religion. The former are still only heretics; the latter, however, are apostates. That is why they are an object of perennial Jewish concern. (I strongly suspect that the church has a similar problem with those baptized Christians who have dropped out of Christianity more than it has with those who were never Christians in the first place.) We want them back with us in the normative Jewish community, even those who were never here with us in our community in any real way.

Two events that have caused this Jewish concern are the recent act of Pope Benedict XVI to reintroduce into the Latin Good Friday liturgy the hope that Jews will "accept Jesus as their Savior," and the recent statement of some (but not all) prominent Evangelicals about Christian missions to the Jews. Even though it is easy to lump these two statements together and complain about both of them in tandem, they are quite different in essence, and thus they need to be addressed differently by perceptive Jews.

At face value, the statement of the Pope is the less problematic of the two. After all, it only expresses an eschatological hope, not an actual proselytizing strategy here and now. In fact, Walter Cardinal Kasper, who was

---

4. See David Novak, *The Election of Israel: The Idea of the Chosen People* (Cambridge: Cambridge University Press, 1995), pp. 189-99.

the Vatican's chief authority on Catholic-Jewish relations, has emphasized that this does not mean the Catholic Church is planning to reestablish the special missions to the Jews that it terminated after Vatican II. Nevertheless, as the late Rabbi Michael Signer (one of the four authors of the year 2000 Jewish statement on Christianity, *Dabru Emet*) pointed out: "Why was it necessary to compose a new prayer?" After all, the earlier efforts of Pope John XXIII and Pope John Paul II had been to remove from the Catholic liturgy *all* references to Jews, simply hoping for the salvation of all humankind. Even though the negative references to Jews have not been reintroduced (like calling Jews "perfidious"), nonetheless by singling Jews out, this new prayer (albeit reiterating old Christian doctrine) seems to be saying that the Catholic Church is more concerned with the salvation of the Jews than with the salvation of any other non-Christians, which still could very well suggest that present-day Catholics get busy again with that concern as an act of *imitatio Dei*, becoming God's advance men to the Jews as it were. That is because liturgy is theology expressed in the second person as in "Thou O Lord" (thus *lex orandi est lex credendi*); theology is liturgy expressed in the third person as in "God is unique" (thus *lex credendi est lex orandi*); and praxis is theology expressed in the first person as in "we are commanded to do this act" (thus *lex credendi est lex faciendi*). In other words, in liturgy we ask God to do for us; in theology we declare what God does for us; and in praxis we do for God. These three elements of the religious life are certainly inseparable, whether in Judaism or in Christianity. Any distinction between them is formal, not substantial. (*Lex credendi* that doesn't at least imply *lex faciendi* seems to be rather empty, like faith without works.)

It is important that the Catholic Church (either the Pope himself or Cardinal Kasper) answer the questions raised by Jewish leaders, most thoughtfully and sympathetically the question raised by Rabbi Signer (who until his untimely death this past year, taught at the University of Notre Dame), and which Cardinal Kasper could hardly dismiss as an "emotional" reaction. It came from a major player in the dialogue, a scholar and theologian respected by both Jews and Catholics. I might also add: Why is this prayer about the hoped-for salvation of the Jews only inserted in the Latin version of the Good Friday Liturgy, which is said by only a small minority of Catholics, rather than in the vernacular versions of that liturgy, which are said by the vast majority of Catholics? Is the magisterium different for "Latin" Catholics than it is for "vernacular" Catholics? Nevertheless, so long as the Catholic Church keeps its proselytizing efforts separate from its involvement in Jewish-Christian dialogue, and as long as it does not reintroduce proselytizing programs specifically directed at Jews, I see no problem as yet for the dialogue with this recent act of the current Pope.

As for proselytizing in general, the fact that the Catholic Church eagerly accepts converts whatever their origins should be no more offensive to Jews than the fact that Jews accept converts to Judaism whatever their origins (religious or ethnic) should be offensive to Catholics, even though Catholics who convert to Judaism are apostates in the eyes of the Church, much as Jews who convert to Catholicism are apostates according to Jewish theology. Neither Jews nor Catholics (nor any Christians) can expect the other community to regard either apostasy or conversion with indifference. Moreover, one community's apostate is the other community's "righteous convert" and vice versa. One cannot honestly criticize the practices and policies of another community when there are similar practices and policies in one's own community.

The declaration, "The Gospel and the Jewish People — An Evangelical Statement," is another story, since it does advocate explicit proselytizing of Jews *as Jews*. Obviously, unlike the Catholic Church, these people have not separated their dialogical agenda (if they ever had one) from their proselytizing agenda, especially their regularly announced programs to convert Jews. But, how many of the Evangelicals who signed or would sign "The Gospel and the Jewish People" have ever been part of the dialogue? Indeed, how could they become part of the dialogue in good faith? (That ought to calm the fears of those Jews who think that Christians who are part of the dialogue are using it as a ruse for a covert proselytizing agenda.) That is why their statement has had little or no effect on the dialogue itself. After all, there seem to be three prerequisites for membership in what might be loosely called "dialogical space." They are: one, firm commitment to one's Judaism or one's Christianity; two, not using dialogical occasions to proselytize a "captive audience"; three, absence of any syncretistic vision that leads to a "Jewish Christianity" or a "Christian Judaism."[5] Clearly, these Evangelicals do not fulfill the first prerequisite, and probably not the third either. Although in a free democratic society they have every right to engage in whatever kind of proselytizing they want, they must recognize the right of any potential convert (Jewish or gentile) to strenuously avoid

5. See David Novak, "What to Seek and What to Avoid in Jewish-Christian Dialogue," *Talking with Christians: Musings of a Jewish Theologian* (Grand Rapids: Eerdmans, 2005), pp. 1-7.

them. Just as we must respect their democratic right, so must they respect our democratic right. (We Jews still have vivid memories of being forced to listen to conversionist tirades directed at us by Christian evangelists in the Middle Ages, something that democratic secular societies have happily saved us from.)

There is a giant misconception in the view of these Evangelicals of who Jewish Christians (that is, Jewish converts to Christianity) really are. And, I might add, they have been helped in that misconception by Jews who have misunderstood the ethnic component of Jewish identity. Therefore, this response to their statement is my way of clarifying the issue at hand both for them and for the Jews who have lent their confusion to the notion that in any real sense one can be a Jew and a Christian in tandem.

In the Evangelical statement, it is stated that "we reject the notion that it is deceptive for followers of Jesus Christ who were born Jewish to continue to identify as Jews." And they cite Romans 11:1, namely Paul's assertion: "Has God cast away his people? God forbid! For I am also of the seed of Abraham, of the tribe of Benjamin." However, the citation of Paul is misleading for two reasons. One, Paul was writing at a time when many still regarded the Christian community as an essentially Jewish sect, and when Paul himself was still trying to convince Jews that faith in Jesus Christ was a fulfillment of the Torah. But today, nobody could make a cogent case that Christianity is a form of Judaism rather than being a gentile religion. Two, even if some Christians maintain Paul's view of "Jewish" Christianity or "Christian" Judaism, no Jew committed to the normative Jewish Tradition (our magisterium) could agree with this Evangelical definition of Jewish identity. Do we Jews tell Christians they must accept as authentic the Christian identity of those who have adopted a non-Christian religion, or accept as authentic Christianity the beliefs and practices of those who are clearly heretics by traditional Christian criteria?

This confusion is one, however, that has been fed by some Jews over the years. Many times Christians have heard from "secular" Jews (and their sympathizers) that being a Jew is not a religious identity but an ethnic one. After all, they cite the fact that according to Jewish law anyone born of a Jewish mother is a Jew, even if that person never affirmed any Jewish religious dogmas or engaged in any Jewish religious practices.[6] Unlike religious faith that can be accepted or rejected, ethnic identity is a matter of natural or historical necessity. It cannot be denied; and those who do deny

---

6. See Novak, *The Election of Israel*, pp. 189-93 re Babylonian Talmud, *Sanhedrin* 44a.

it are like blacks attempting to "pass" as whites, that is, until they are eventually "outed." From this, some Christians can make the following inference: Since Christianity is a universal religion as distinct from particular ethnic identities, one can be a Christian without giving up one's ethnic identity (even though, in the not-so-distant past, most Jewish converts to Christianity were most eager to do just that). If so, why then cannot one be a Jew, even a proud Jew, as a matter of ethnic origin, yet be even more so a Christian as one's universal or cosmic identity? To this inference, the proponents of secular Jewish identity have no good answer other than the suspicion that any Jew converting to Christianity (or any other non-Jewish religion) must really be a "self-hating" Jew, all protests (and even evidence) to the contrary.

So, what is the error in this assumption of some Jewish secularists and the inference drawn from it by some faithful Christians? The error here is the spurious use of the categories of "universal" and "particular," and the equally spurious distinction between "religion" and "ethnicity" in Judaism (and, I think, in Christianity as well). In truth, Judaism is both universal and particular. It is universal in the sense that *anyone* can become a Jew through proper conversion. Thus calling Jews a "race" is false and offensive because, if Jews are a race, then Judaism is racism. The Jews are a particular people, open to the whole universe of humankind — and open to the eschatological hope that all humankind will in the end become Israel. Yet almost all Jews over the centuries have not drawn from this hope any proselytizing imperative. As for religion and ethnicity in Judaism, there is no real divide between the two since the Jewish people is a community elected by the Creator of heaven and earth. Even though one has no choice about being born into such a community, one does have the choice of whether one is going to confirm the covenant by living according to the body of revealed norms *(the Torah)* that enables members of the community to put their covenantal identity into tangible, audible, and visible practice.[7]

I daresay a Christian who was baptized in infancy by a church that regards baptism as indelible is as much a Christian by birth as I am a Jew by birth — *Christianos non nascitur sed fiat* notwithstanding. Yet, even though one's "Jewishness" by birth is indelible and inalienable (as even infant baptism is indelible and unalienable for most Christians), the religiously determined privileges of Jewish identity are not indelible and not

---

7. See David Novak, *In Defense of Religious Liberty* (Wilmington, DE: ISI Books, 2009), pp. 73-80.

unalienable. For example, a Jew who is a public Sabbath violator loses the privilege of being a witness in a Jewish religious proceeding. Recently, more traditional Jews have refused rabbinical ordination to those who openly and willingly engage in homoerotic relationships. Now the most serious sin a Jew can commit in terms of his or her relationship with the God who chooses Israel is to officially join another religion. Such a Jew is called a *meshummad* (literally, "one who has been destroyed"); in other words, what Christians call an apostate (literally, "one who stands apart"). Accordingly, that person is denied such Jewish religious privileges as being counted in the quorum for public worship or being buried in a Jewish cemetery. And, though arguable on legal grounds, some Jews have even publicly mourned members of their own families who have converted to another religion as they would mourn a family member who had died, or in this case had committed suicide.

In the view of many Jewish theologians, especially of the mediaeval period when Jewish apostasy was rampant, Jewish converts to Christianity are to be treated as one would treat any other gentile. And that treatment need not be hostile, though it usually is. (Most family members resent relatives who have left the family for another family.) Yet there are three ways in which these Jewish converts to Christianity (or any other religion) are still treated as Jews. One, if their marriages to other Jews were initiated under proper Jewish auspices (that is, they had a "kosher" Jewish wedding), then that marriage can only be terminated under proper Jewish auspices in the event of divorce. Two, their children (if the mother is Jewish), even if born after the conversion of the parents, are considered Jews. Thus their male children are to be circumcised (and the Jewish community is required to accommodate their circumcision). And three, this also means that should these Jewish converts to Christianity (or any other religion) decide to return to Judaism and renounce their conversion to another religion as a mistake, they are to be taken back into the Jewish fold without any formal conversion procedures (though it has been strongly recommended over the years that the returned apostate undergo certain purification rites as a penitent or *ba'al teshuvah*).

Evangelicals who target Jews for conversion need to know that even though there are Jewish converts to Christianity who consider themselves still to be Jews, there is no basis in Judaism for that opinion. They might still be Jews *de jure*, but for the most part they are not Jews *de facto*. (And it is in the *real, de facto* world that Judaism as a way of life is practiced, whereas it can only be thought in the more abstract, *de jure* world.) So, for example, very few traditional Jewish congregations would accept a Jewish convert to Christianity (that is, a Jew voluntarily baptized) as a member, for whatever reason he or she did convert. This indicates that there are two kinds of Christians with whom Jews can have a dialogical relationship: gentile Christians who do not attempt to proselytize us, and Jewish Christians who do not claim to still be Jews — let alone "fulfilled Jews" — and who do not attempt to influence other Jews to follow suit. But we can have no dialogical relationship with any Christian, whether of Jewish or gentile origin, who attempts to proselytize us, whether overtly or covertly.

As for those Jewish converts to Christianity who call themselves "Messianic Jews," and who do not seem to be proselytizing other Jews to follow suit, I do think dialogue is possible, because we Jews are not being asked by them to convert to Christianity, but only not to read them out of the Jewish people. While I think they are very much in error, they are at least making a nonthreatening claim that can be discussed and explored further within the Jewish community. Nevertheless, even this last group of Jewish Christians should not be regarded as any kind of "bridge" between the Jewish community and the church, because of both Jewish and Christian doubts about whether anyone or any group can be equally Jewish and equally Christian.

Jewish Proselytization of Gentiles

Let us now deal with questions two, three, and four, which were raised at the beginning of this paper: (2) Does Jewish exclusion of gentiles from the covenanted community mean that gentiles *cannot* become members of the community, so that proselytizing them should be prohibited? (3) May gentiles become members of the community by *conversion (gerut)*, so that proselytizing of them should be permitted? (4) *Ought* gentiles become members of the community by conversion, so that proselytizing of them is mandated?

As for question (2), even though the institution of conversion to Judaism does not necessarily entail active proselytizing of possible converts, proselytizing itself necessarily presupposes the institution of conversion. One cannot honestly solicit new residents of a cooperative building that never accepts any new residents.

Ever since the rabbis established the procedures for conversion to Judaism *(gerut)* in the second century CE, no one within the normative Jewish community (i.e., those who accept the authority of Halakhah completely) could categorically exclude gentiles who want to become part of the Jewish people as the covenanted community. Moreover, the rabbis obviously considered conversion to be not only a Jewish necessity but, also, a Jewish desideratum. That is evidenced by the fact that the rabbis could have easily eliminated conversion *de facto* halakhically. They could have eliminated it after the destruction of the Second Temple in 70 CE inasmuch as ancient tradition stipulated that in order for the process of conversion to Judaism itself *(giyyur)* to be complete, the full convert *(ger tsedeq)* had to bring a sacrifice to the Temple.[8] Nevertheless, the rabbis ruled that this was not an impediment *(iqquv)* to conversion when circumstances beyond the control of the community (i.e., the Roman destruction of the Temple and the subsequent inability of the Jews to rebuild it) prevented anyone from bringing a sacrifice, since any sacrifice could only be offered in an extant Temple. Furthermore, ancient tradition stipulated that those supervising a conversion had to have the type of rabbinical ordination *(semikhah)* that would qualify them to be members *(haverim)* of the Sanhedrin. With the demise of the Sanhedrin within about one hundred years after the destruction of the Temple, this too could have been made a necessary condition of conversion. Nevertheless, later authorities ruled that all that was needed in the post-Temple was three adult Jewish males to supervise the conversion proceedings.[9] This whole approach to the institution of conversion was especially emphasized by those Jewish theologians who gave greater priority to voluntary conviction than to involuntary birth.

However, truth be told, there have always been rabbis (and their lay followers) who have been uncomfortable with the institution of conversion. Of course, they couldn't come out and say they are opposed to conversion in principle inasmuch as it is a permanent, biblically grounded, and halakhically structured Jewish institution. As such, no one within normative Judaism could argue for its repeal, for its excision from Judaism *de jure.* Furthermore, once the option of eliminating conversion *de facto* due to the two legal reasons cited above has itself been eliminated, the only way to avoid conversion has been to make the preconditions for converting such that the vast majority of would-be converts will simply give up their quest in frustration.

8. Babylonian Talmud, *Keritot* 9a.
9. See Maimonides, *Mishneh Torah,* Isurei Biah 13.16; Novak, *The Election of Israel,* pp. 177-88.

Many of those who would make conversion virtually impossible have been influenced in one way or another by kabbalistic theology, in which Jews are considered to be a different species from other human beings. In kabbalistic theology, the difference between Jews and gentiles is ontological. In fact, some of these kabbalistic or neo-kabbalistic theologies actually suggest, in a way that can only be considered racist, that the difference between Jews and gentiles is biological. As such, they have no theological basis for affirming the institution of conversion; they can only not deny it in principle. Conversely, non-kabbalistic theologies regard the difference between Jews and gentiles as legal, hence the legal power of conversion annuls the legal difference between a Jew and a gentile when a gentile is accepted as a full convert to Judaism in a legally valid way.[10]

To be sure, no one involved in Jewish theology can ignore Kabbalah, since from the fourteenth to the eighteenth century it was the predominant way Jews did theology. One cannot repeat the myopia of the nineteenth- and early twentieth-century rationalists who simply ignored Kabbalah because they were embarrassed by its metaphysics, which seemed to border on the occult. Nevertheless, for those of us who do not regard Kabbalah as authoritative revelation, or even as good theological speculation most of the time (thus we only employ it quite sparingly), and who reject it when it seems to go against general tendencies of Rabbinic Judaism, to reaffirm the necessity and desirability of conversion is one way we can reaffirm Rabbinic Judaism. Moreover, this has great political significance insofar as it enables us to reject the racist implications of kabbalistic theology. Rejection of any racism, even our own, should be Jewish policy after the Holocaust, when Jews were the chief victims of a virulent form of racism that made us a species wholly apart from those taken to be real humankind. (In all fairness to the premodern kabbalists, though, their theology did not lead them to the violent xenophobia that has been the practical conclusion drawn by most adherents of modern, ideological racism.) So, even though there are those within the normative Jewish community who, if they are honest, would admit they would like to eliminate conversion altogether, there is enough in both the rabbinic tradition and in recent Jewish experience to counter their attempt to make converts to Judaism a null class *de facto*.

10. See Menachem Kellner, *Maimonides on Judaism and the Jewish People* (Albany: State University of New York Press, 1991), pp. 81-95; also, *Maimonides' Confrontation with Mysticism* (Oxford: Littman Library of Jewish Civilization, 2006), pp. 216-64.

As for question (3), it is clear that the best case can be made for the permissibility of accepting converts, perhaps even the desirability *(mitsvah)* of doing so. But even the most enthusiastic proponents of welcoming converts could not argue that there is any true obligation *(hovah)* to do so actively, to the point of engaging in what could easily be called proselytizing or mission. That leads one to answer question (4) with a No. In fact, the only Jews who used the term "mission" were some nineteenth- and early twentieth-century Reform Jews who spoke of "the mission of Israel."[11] However, their "mission" was not an attempt to get gentiles to convert to Judaism and thus adopt all the particularly Jewish practices mandated for Jews alone by the Torah and Tradition. Instead, the mission of these Jews to the gentiles was basically Jewish advocacy of the universal "enlightened values," which it was claimed Jewish "genius" had first discovered and best preserved. Therefore, in this liberal vision Jews are in the vanguard of universal progress. Today, we still see secularized remnants of this "mission" in attempts to proclaim a "secular Judaism" as a paradigm for those attempting to overcome the seemingly narrow restraints of their own traditions. Therefore, traditional Jews who have attempted to bring the wisdom of the Jewish tradition into current discussions of universal moral questions have carefully avoided seeing themselves as missionaries to the gentiles.

This leaves us with a fifth and last question: (5) If conversion cannot be eliminated from the contemporary Jewish religious agenda, is Jewish proselytizing of gentiles something to be encouraged (but not strictly mandated) or discouraged (but not strictly prohibited)? And I ask this question as someone who as a rabbi has officiated at the conversion of many persons who have greatly enriched the Jewish community — spiritually, intellectually, and politically. Nevertheless, Jewish proselytizing of gentiles, as distinct from welcoming conversion to Judaism, should be discouraged for two reasons.

First, most Jews have bad (even painful) memories of having been proselytized by gentiles, especially Christians. If, as Hillel the Elder taught as the most basic Jewish norm: "What is hateful to you, do not do to anyone else,"[12] advocating a Jewish mission to the gentiles would get, especially from traditional Jews, either a laugh or a shudder.

11. See David Novak, *Jewish Social Ethics* (New York: Oxford University Press, 1992), pp. 228-32.
12. Babylonian Talmud, *Shabbat* 31a.

Second, proselytizing inevitably involves some sort of triumphalism. Maximally, proselytization tells its gentile objects that their own religion is absolutely evil. Minimally, it tells them it is inadequate by comparison with the religions of those proselytizing. Yet that is decidedly unbiblical, for it can be shown that the prophets of Israel never condemned the idolatry of the gentiles per se. Those not born into the covenanted community cannot be held responsible for not worshiping the covenanting God. Thus the prophets only condemned gentile idolatry when Jews were attracted to it to the point of practicing it. Thus the few gentiles in the Bible who became attracted to the religion of Israel, like Jethro or Naaman or Ruth, came to worship the God of Israel and became members of the people of Israel, like Ruth, on their own initiative. This comes out when one correctly interprets one of the most misinterpreted verses in the Bible. Many have spoken of Israel being "a light *to* the nations." But the verse actually reads: "I have made you a covenanted people, to be a light *of* nations [*l'or goyyim*]" (Isa. 42:6; see 49:6). In other words, the gentiles are to be impressed with what God has done to his people, not that his people are to go out and bring enlightenment to or even for the gentiles. So, for example, in rabbinic interpretation, Jethro — who could be considered the first convert — became one with the people of Israel when he heard that God had revealed the foundation of the Torah, the Decalogue, to the whole people at Mt. Sinai. Even in the end of days, when gentiles en masse will say: "Let us go up to the mountain of the Lord, to the house of the God of Jacob, that he might instruct us in his ways, that we might walk in his paths" (Isa. 2:3), the initiative will be, as the kabbalists would say, an "awakening from below" (*it'aruta de-le-tatta*).[13]

Finally, the discouraging of proselytization should not lead one to think that conversion itself is futile because one religion is as good as the other, so everyone should simply stay put in the religion of their own culture. Or, since one religion is as false as the other, then everyone should be encouraged to drop the religion of their own culture rather than going from one falsehood to another. Such relativism, whether tolerant or intolerant, makes one's Judaism (or one's Christianity) something of less than ultimate significance, something that could hardly require one to die as a martyr if that is the only alternative to apostasy, which is something Judaism requires of all Jews and Christianity requires of all Christians, and

13. See Gershom Scholem, *Major Trends in Jewish Mysticism* (New York: Schocken Books, 1946), p. 233.

which faithful Jews and faithful Christians should never forget. That is why we Jews have to argue against the mistaken conviction of those of our brethren who have become apostates or who are tempted to do so. And that is why we have to applaud the true conviction of those gentiles who want to experience the closest connection possible with God in this world in the company of the covenanted community to whom God has come closest. Welcoming converts enables us to proclaim the righteousness of God. Proselytizing could too easily lead us to the false proclamation of our own righteousness.

Covenant Renewed:
Josef Ratzinger, Theologian and Pastor

Richard J. Sklba

A major figure in the recent development and restatement of Catholic Christian teaching regarding the ongoing vitality of Judaism in our contemporary world has been Josef Ratzinger, theologian, curial official, and now Pope Benedict XVI. Against the historical backdrop of negative Christian beliefs regarding the role of Judaism in the salvation of the world, his teaching on the singularity of God's covenant with both Jews and Christians, as rooted in the teachings of the Second Vatican Council and expressed in the *Catechism of the Catholic Church,* is crucial to an appreciation for the way in which our mutual partnership may deepen. This essay also offers some suggestions for further reconciliation and renewal.

Josef Ratzinger has been a major figure in the theological implementation of the teachings of the Second Vatican Council. With a magisterial career spanning over forty years, he has become an increasingly significant interpreter of the Catholic Christian tradition and an official spokesperson for the belief of the Catholic Church. For that reason, it seems useful to examine briefly but carefully his teachings, especially as related to the question of God's covenant with Abraham and subsequent generations of the Chosen People. As a Christian, Ratzinger sees himself among the recipients of the blessings attached to that covenant. The perennial question, sharpened by the teachings of the Epistle to the Hebrews in the canon of Christian Scriptures, has revolved around the question of whether there are "one or two covenants." At stake are three issues: first, the degree of individual distinctiveness of the two faith traditions; second, their interrelated nature; and finally, the manner in which Catholics, especially after the dramatic reversal found in the affirmations of Vatican II's *Nostra aetate* and subsequent official teachings, view their relationship with the Israel of God.

The question is a vast one, and therefore I shall attempt a sharper focus for my essay. The intent of this study is to offer a very brief review of the focal teachings of the New Testament regarding the proposed topic, then that of early Christian theologians. This will provide a backdrop for examining the writings of Josef Ratzinger and the major magisterial documents of the Catholic Church that have been produced with his participation and developed under his guidance. I will offer some final personal conclusions as a possible modest contribution to the assigned topic for our conversation, namely, "Covenant, Mission, and the Other."

The Early Ages of Catholic Christian Teaching

There were many traditions that the early Jewish followers of Jesus of Nazareth borrowed from the Tanakh to describe their understanding of his person and mission. Those motifs represented clues of sorts that then defined those early disciples of the rabbi from Nazareth and their presumed task in history. Among the ideas taken from the Scriptures of Israel, one might list such diverse themes as the figure of Adam from Genesis 1–3, the Suffering Servant from Isaiah 53, prescriptions for the annual Passover celebration of the paschal lamb (Exodus 12), and the apocalyptic figure of the meek lamb (Rev. 5:6-14, possibly influenced by such intertestamental literature as the animal allegories in Ethiopic 1 Enoch 85-90) who rises victorious over all the terrifying beasts of the earth.

Certainly the notion of kingship in Judah and Israel also offered a major contribution to the theological repertoire of early Christianity, especially through the ritual of anointing for royal leadership and sacred mission. The early Christians likewise studied the promises and dreams of all the ancient prophets of Israel, and found themselves somehow prefigured in them. "Covenant," *berit*, was invoked to describe the divine initiative, the communal character of this religious experience, and the successive forms into which that relationship was cast at various periods in history.

The Scriptures of Israel spoke in a voice of their own, without Christian interpretation and indeed prior to the development of Christianity. Christians must respect that legitimate voice, even if they subsequently hear a unique message for themselves in the same texts. Those ancient documents that witnessed to the faith of Israel were then read through Christian belief in the Resurrected Jesus, victorious over sin and death. Through that latter lens those same texts revealed to early Christian teachers and preachers a deeper meaning, a *sensus plenior* as it were. Acknowledging both aspects of historical development in this history of interpretation is important for our conversation.

The Divine Gift of Covenant in the Two Testaments

As noted above, a major theme in the Scriptures of Israel was that of covenant.[1] Against the background of God's gifts of covenant with Noah and Abraham, the book of Exodus describes the historical Sinai covenant of God with Moses and those whom he had led out of the house of slavery in Egypt. Through the ritual of sacrificial blood sprinkled on the altar at Sinai and then upon the people, Israel became chosen, and, at least in my analysis, adopted members of God's own family.[2] Thus the First Testament[3] gives clear witness to the divine election and its implications for the history of Israel.

A key element in the background of any consideration of the interrelationship of the Jewish and Christian experiences of covenant must be the oracle of Jeremiah, whose promise of a new covenant engraved on human flesh, not stone (Jer. 31:31ff.), initially served as a beacon of hope for those who had been exiled from the northern kingdom by the Assyrian conquest in the late eighth century BCE and the subsequent Babylonian conquest of the southern kingdom in 597 and 587 BCE. The politically and theologically devastating destruction of the Temple must have seemed to extinguish all hope of divine protection and appeared to destroy any trace of an enduring divine promise. The tragic and virtually inconceivable loss of kingship, Temple, and land signaled a finality beyond belief.

The interrelationship of the two realities of covenant as described by

---

1. Scholars debate the question of its centrality. A minority seek the taproot for Israelite faith elsewhere, as for example in Divine Presence — cf. Samuel Terrien, *The Illusive Presence* (New York: Harper & Row, 1978); or Witness — cf. Walter Brueggemann, *Theology of the Old Testament: Testimony, Dispute, Advocacy* (Minneapolis: Augsburg Fortress, 1997).

2. Exodus 24:3-8. For an effort to apply historical-critical methodology to the account of the Sinaitic covenant, see Richard Sklba, "The Redeemer of Israel," *Catholic Biblical Quarterly* 39 (1972): 1-19.

3. This term of reference, namely First Testament or First Covenant, is the one preferred by myself, even as I recognize the recent debates, inspired no doubt by a combination of respectful sensitivity and theological accuracy, surrounding the most appropriate and useful title for that ancient collection of inspired texts.

Jeremiah, whether of renewal and development within a single enduring divine election with Israel or of eventual replacement by some future people, has been a focal point of discussion of covenant between Christians and Jews over the centuries. The New Testament attributes to Jesus himself an allusion to the promise of Jeremiah in the very words of Eucharistic institution, as cited in the Gospels.[4] This serves to underscore the manner in which Jews and Christians viewed the promise of Jeremiah and their own interrelationship. The Jeremian promise remains central and crucial to our study; our purpose is not so much to determine which interpretation is correct, but rather to understand the variations within each religious tradition. One cannot explore the teachings of Josef Ratzinger without an understanding of this prophetic oracle of Jeremiah and the ways in which the notion of covenant was woven into the inspired writings of early Christianity.

Paul's Teaching to the Romans

In the New Testament there are two primary theological *loci* that deal with the theme of covenant and the use of that construct to describe the interrelationship between Israel and the followers of Jesus of Nazareth. One such *locus* is in the letter of Paul to the Romans, especially chapters 9-11, where the apostle Paul treats the relationship of the Jews and gentiles who follow Jesus the Christ to those Jews who do not. The other major *locus* is in the Epistle to the Hebrews.

In his letter to the Romans Paul, himself of Jewish heritage within the Pharisaic tradition, stresses the continuity of the relationship. Paul acknowledges that he and his Jewish colleagues together with their ancestors have been chosen by God, and therefore to all of them "belong the sonship, the glory, the covenants, the giving of the law, the worship and the promises; to them belong the patriarchs, and of their race according to the flesh is the Christ" (9:4-5).[5] Paul knows that Israel has never been definitively

---

4. "This cup which is poured out for you is the new covenant in my blood" (Luke 22:20; 1 Cor. 11:25). Mark's text, namely "This is my blood of the covenant which is poured out for many" (Mark 14:24; similarly Matt. 26:28, adding "for the forgiveness of sins," which could be an oblique allusion to Jer. 31:34), is more clearly related to the Fourth Servant Song of Isaiah 53.

5. Problematic at times has been the tendency of some vernacular translations of the New Testament to insert a past tense of the verb into this citation, namely ". . . to them *belonged* . . ." even though the text itself is without verbal specification and the context of Paul's

Richard J. Sklba

rejected (11:1) throughout their long history of sin, forgiveness, and redemption, and so he views the Christian people as but a wild gentile olive branch grafted into the true people of divine election (11:24).

Paul alludes to the Jeremian promise of the new covenant (Jer. 31:31ff.), and insists that "the gifts and call of God are irrevocable" (Rom. 11:29).[6] This statement was reclaimed anew by Christians in the post-Shoah era, and it was used to affirm a conviction of the theological validity and vitality of the ongoing existence of Israel. The irrevocable nature of that call was an often-repeated theme in the statements of the late John Paul II.

This stands in sharp contrast to earlier centuries of Christian teaching, which seemed to have forgotten the authentic apostolic teaching. Many ancient patristic writers spoke rather of the rejection of Israel by God, and they quoted prophetic oracles to prove the point, sometimes presuming in those texts a definitive character of final judgment that the verses themselves did not intend. The apostle Paul himself, however, recognized the enduring character of Israel's relationship to the God of their ancestors, and he understood the gentiles as saved only to the extent that they could be incorporated into that original covenantal bond of Israel and their Lord.

Paul remained a faithful Jew throughout his life. Moreover, his address to the Christians in Rome praised the inhabitants of the city whom he hoped to visit on his way to the new territories of Spain. For many reasons, therefore, the author of the letter to the Romans would uphold the faith of his prospective Jewish hosts, and he would affirm profound commonalities with their ancestral religious convictions.

The Epistle to the Hebrews

The other key New Testament source for Catholic Christian reflection on the covenant is the Epistle to the Hebrews. Long debated in terms of its ca-

---

statement is precisely the opposite. More recently approved translations are more accurate and use the present tense in the verse.

6. Recently, Catholic scholars and Roman authorities have attempted to refine the precise translation of that word, preferring to stress the fact that the word literally means "not rued, not regretted, not wished differently or otherwise." Unfortunately, the very fact of the quest for precision in this matter has raised a fear among Jewish neighbors that the teaching itself was being backpedaled or rejected, thus signaling that a return to the hostility of earlier ages might again be possible. This was never the implication in that intra-Catholic discussion.

nonical authority,[7] and perennially (erroneously) attributed to Paul, this epistle has been viewed as a prime source for radical supersessionism. That opinion stems from the work's repeated contrast between the worship by priests of Aaronide genealogy offered in the Temple at Jerusalem, on the one hand, and the eternal worship offered by Jesus, the risen victorious high priest at the heavenly throne of God, on the other. The consistent teaching of Hebrews is the superiority of the heavenly worship offered by a sinless Jesus once and for all, as contrasted with the daily repetition of sacrifices by human priests confronted by their own sinfulness. Invoking Platonic categories, the Epistle to the Hebrews states that the earthly tabernacle is only the "copy and shadow" of its heavenly counterpart (Heb. 8:5).

In particular this contrast is presented in the central section of the text (Heb. 8:1–9:28), which compares the true and everlasting heavenly tabernacle with the earthly structure in Jerusalem. The Epistle's author insists that the limitation of the first covenant consists in its inability to give people the capacity to keep its laws (8:7-12); and that the newness of Jeremiah's promised covenant is found in a new interior capacity given by God to human beings as faithful partners in that covenant. The author of the Epistle to the Hebrews was convinced that the former covenant had already either disappeared, or perhaps developed into its newer form.

It is interesting that the theologians at the Second Vatican Council chose to highlight the writings of Paul to the Romans rather than that of Hebrews in their effort to readdress the relationship of the Church to Israel. In my judgment this choice in fact left the debate within Christianity unfinished, and demanded an eventual reconsideration by subsequent Catholic theologians in order to achieve a more comprehensive and balanced doctrine. If there is to be a universally accepted priority of one Christian tradition over the other, some clear theological rationale must be provided. Thus far, such has not been developed.

It may well be that a potential approach to the resolution of this difference can be found in the Platonic categories themselves as expressed in the Epistle to the Hebrews, namely the categories of philosophical thought that insist on the contrast of contemporaneous earthly and material shad-

---

7. Many early writers hesitated to include the work within the approved canon of inspired writings, as demonstrated by the fact that the work was not included among the list of canonical writings provided by the Muratorian Canon (ca. 200 CE). Under the influence of the practice of the church in Alexandria, however, the work's Pauline character and canonical status was finally accepted in the West by the end of the fourth century and the beginning of the fifth.

ows, on the one hand, and their heavenly substance, on the other, rather than on the contrast interpreted as a temporal prior and post. The latter historical contrast has often been seen as laying the foundation for radical supersessionism, but this may not be necessary if the categories are seen as Platonic in essence. I offer this suggestion as grist for the Christian debate still to be resolved. Contrasting texts within the New Testament itself must be given the opportunity to speak with one another in their quest for mutual nuance and ultimate truth. This type of inner dialogue seems demanded by the very fact that diverse books have been bound together into a single codex since the fourth century at the latest.

It remains imperative, therefore, for Christian theology to find a way to affirm its renewed conviction about the enduring importance of Judaism in the modern world, while still holding fast to its central belief in the universality of salvation achieved in Christ for all ages and all people. Precisely how to interrelate and balance those two key areas of Christian belief, while retaining both, is the focal challenge for contemporary Catholic members in the Jewish-Christian dialogue.

The introduction of the topic of "mission" in the title of our project acknowledges that interrelationship. If each group, namely Jewish and Christian, lives in a covenantal relationship with God, what is the consequent mission to each other flowing from that common bond?[8] One can only hope that Jewish colleagues can be patient while Christians work out their synthesis of these convictions.

To understand the manner in which mission flows from covenant, we need to return to the early decades of Christian experience, and to the way in which the gifts of the Holy Spirit were understood as a means for the deepening and development of Judaism into what became Christianity. The Holy Spirit is both the bond of unity and the source of creative energy for the ongoing work of Christian believers.

The Final Age of Fulfillment

The gift of the Spirit had often been associated with the charism of prophecy, beginning perhaps with the bands of charismatic prophets who gath-

8. A very useful summary of current considerations on this topic can be found in *Two Faiths, One Covenant? Jewish and Christian Identity in the Presence of the Other,* ed. Eugene Korn and John Pawlikowski (London: Sheed & Ward, 2005).

ered around ancient figures such as Samuel (1 Sam. 10:5) and Elijah (2 Kings 2:7). That same spirit, *ruach,* was associated with the mysterious Servant as described by Second Isaiah (Isa. 42:2; 61:1). Both priestly and royal election were ritualized by an anointing with fragrant oil symbolizing the outpouring of divine power that was absorbed into the very physical being of the new leader. The action signified transformation and new authority given to the persona of both priest and king. In Christian experience, these traditions became so focused on the person of Jesus as to become a personal name as well as a title: "Jesus the Christ."

Of particular interest to some of the early Christian communities was the promise of the Spirit in the writings of the prophet Joel (3:1-3). Inspired by God, that prophet envisioned a time when the Spirit of God would fall upon all people, young and old alike. The entire social fabric of Israel would become prophetic in character.

That prophecy of Joel subsequently shaped some of the passages in the Gospel of Luke and its counterpart document about the early history of the Christian movement, the Acts of the Apostles. In the account of the baptism of Jesus by John the Baptizer, for example, the Spirit is given to Jesus (Luke 3:22) as a prophetic inauguration of his public ministry of heralding a year of jubilation (Luke 3:22; 4:1-18 citing Isa. 61:1). The same Spirit is given to the entire early Christian community on Pentecost with the sense of extending God's Spirit to the nations (Acts 2:17f.).

Further Patristic Reflections

It would seem that only in the later writings of Justin, a Christian philosopher from Nablus in the second century CE and an early martyr (ca. 180 CE), do we find a new and somewhat ominous twist to the earlier teaching of the New Testament. For Justin, the Spirit given to Jesus and then to the Christian community represented the Spirit originally given to Israel and its leaders but transferred to Jesus and his disciples.[9] This would seem to be one of the earliest roots of radical supersessionism, which then became entangled in the life and teaching of the Christian Church for almost two millennia.

This was, however, by no means the universal teaching of early Chris-

9. Susan Wendell, "Justin and the Descent of the Spirit," in *Justin and His Worlds,* ed. Sara Parvis and Paul Foster (Minneapolis: Fortress Press, 2007), pp. 95-103.

tianity. By contrast for example, Origen, the brilliant teacher from Alexandria and Caesarea († ca. 253), insisted on the perennial vitality of the Sinaitic covenant:

> As for me, I do not apply the name "Old Testament" to the Law when I consider it spiritually. The Law only becomes an "Old Testament" for those unwilling to understand it according to the spirit. For them it has necessarily become "old" and has aged because it cannot preserve its strength. But for us who understand and expound it in spirit and according to the sense of the Gospel, it is always new. The two Testaments are one new Testament for us, not according to date but in the newness of their meaning.[10]

Subsequent teachings of the early Christian writers, however, tended to follow the path of Justin. The homilies of religious leaders like John Chrysostom, Patriarch of Constantinople (†398 CE), were stern in their condemnation and uncompromising in their dismissal of Judaism. Mary Boys describes and documents the gradual parting of Christianity from the Judaism of its time, highlighting the stages of differentiation as occasioned by (1) the destruction of the Temple in Jerusalem, (2) the controversy over the necessity of observing circumcision and the dietary laws for gentiles at Antioch, and (3) the developing Christology that saw their acknowledgment of Jesus (problematic for the radical monotheism of Judaism) as mysteriously yet fully participating in divinity.[11]

It has been proposed that one of the motives for the sometimes-bitter patristic denunciation of Judaism can be found in the recurring attraction that the synagogue held for Christians into the fourth and fifth centuries CE! Precisely because the seekers and God-fearers of that age continued to

---

10. *Ninth Homily on Numbers.* The text was cited with approval by Pope Benedict XVI at his weekly Wednesday audience on 25 April 2007. The extensive influence of Origen upon the theology and catechesis of the early Church can be understood by the fact that Jerome himself once cited the titles of all of Origen's 320 books and 310 homilies (*Epistle* 33)!

11. "The Partings: Christianity's Prolonged and Polemical Break with Judaism," in *Has God Only One Blessing? Judaism as a Source of Christian Self-Understanding* (New York: Paulist Press, 2000), pp. 149-59. Boys also noted that Chrysostom used the stinging traditional rhetorical form of invective *(psogos)* to hold up Jewish practice to ridicule (p. 55). Yet a different scholarly study comes from Larry W. Hurtado, *How on Earth Did Jesus Become a God? Historical Questions about Earliest Devotion to Jesus* (Grand Rapids: Eerdmans, 2005), who insists that devotion to Jesus occurred within twenty years of his death and was not viewed by early Jewish followers as incompatible with their traditional monotheism!

frequent Sabbath services, the Christian leadership of the time felt compelled to repeat and perhaps even intensify their critique.

Another major figure in Christianity's patristic tradition is the witness of Augustine of Hippo (†410 CE), bishop of a North African church located in what is now Tunisia. Often cited because of the volume of his writings, the theological sharpness of his teachings, and the eloquence of his preaching, Augustine stands out as a prominent voice whose thought must be reviewed if any fuller sense can be made of the long twenty centuries of tradition behind the writings of Josef Ratzinger/Benedict XVI.[12]

Whether Augustine's teaching regarding God's protection of Judaism as a valuable enduring witness was a blessing, or whether it only emphasized the radical otherness of Judaism and provided a clearer target for the age's teaching of contempt will undoubtedly be an object of debate for centuries to come.[13]

The Teachings of the Second Vatican Council Regarding Covenant

The earth-shaking experience of the Catholic Church's Second Vatican Council (1962-1965), whether revolutionary or evolutionary depending upon one's perspective,[14] did not arrive out of thin air. The Council's teachings and prescriptions in many areas of church life were the accumulative result of over a century of historical, biblical, and liturgical research. Scholars from the various Jewish communities and Christian churches gradually worked together with increasing frequency. Looking over each other's shoulders and through each other's glasses, they sometimes saw the biblical texts anew. The horror of the Shoah had a curious and completely unexpected side effect, namely a renewed mutual respect for the faithful practice of each other's respective religious traditions. Ever-deepening sorrow for the tragedy of the Shoah led to a review of Christian teaching re-

---

12. This is of particular importance since much of Ratzinger's theological work has been viewed as permeated with Augustinian theology, thought, and sentiments. His doctoral dissertation (1950) was titled "The People and the House of God in Augustine's Doctrine of the Church"; cf. Joseph Ratzinger, *Milestones: Memoirs 1927-1977* (San Francisco: Ignatius Press, 1998), p. 97.

13. These questions are neatly summarized in the review of Paula Frederickson's book by Jerome Chanes, "A Church Father with a Stroke of Mercy," *Forward* (23 January 2009): 17.

14. John W. O'Malley, *Did Vatican Two Change Anything?* (New York: Continuum, 2007).

garding the Jewish people and their faith. This is an ongoing challenge for Catholics and other Christians, and one that still demands constant vigilance from preachers, teachers, and writers of devotional literature.

The debates among the bishops who gathered in Rome for the four sessions of that Council were gradually garnered into some sixteen documents of varying magisterial authority.[15] Given the Council's conviction that the Church's teaching, preaching, and praying should be articulated in biblical language, it is not surprising that there were several references among those documents of the Second Vatican Council to the notion of covenant as a means of describing God's relationship to humanity and our consequent human relationship with each other.[16]

In *Lumen gentium,* the *Dogmatic Constitution on the Church,* for example, the bishops of the Council taught that God "chose the race of Israel as a people unto Himself. With it he set up a covenant. . . . All these things, however, were done by way of preparation and as a figure of that new and perfect covenant which was to be ratified in Christ" (§9).[17]

In *Nostra aetate,* the *Declaration on the Relationship of the Church to Non-Christian Religions,* a later document of the Council, the bishops concluded their years of deliberation by recalling "the spiritual bond linking the people of the New Covenant with Abraham's stock." The paragraph goes on to insist that "the Church, therefore, cannot forget that she received the revelation of the Old Testament through the people with whom God in His inexpressible mercy deigned to establish the Ancient Covenant" (§4).[18] This reference to the "new" covenant reflected the Jeremian oracle and underscored the common Christian conviction regarding the new teachings of Jesus, faithful Jew and herald of God's kingdom.

Finally in *Dei verbum,* the *Dogmatic Constitution on Divine Revelation,* the same Council fathers taught that God "chose for Himself a people to whom He might entrust His Promises. First He entered into a covenant

15. A major account and assessment in four volumes can be found in the work of Giuseppe Alberigo, English edition by Joseph Komonchak, *The History of Vatican II,* 4 vols. (New York: Orbis, 1996).

16. Following the reference of the full covenant with Noah and all the creatures of the earth (Gen. 8:22), this has even been recently extended to include the pressing ethics of ecology in a world under the destructive human touch!

17. 21 November 1964 (Third Session). The motif of continuity and development will be constant and consistent in all the contemporary teachings of the Church when referring to the people of Israel.

18. 28 October 1965 (Fourth Session).

with Abraham (cf. Gen. 15:18) and, through Moses, with the people of Israel (cf. Exod. 28:4). To this people which He had acquired for Himself, He so manifested Himself, through words and deeds, as the one true living God that Israel came to know by experience . . ." (§14).

"The principal purpose," that same document teaches, "to which the plan of the Old Covenant was directed was to prepare for the coming both of Christ, the universal Redeemer, and of the messianic kingdom" (§15). Thus, quoting Augustine, the document went on to repeat a frequent summary: "God, the inspirer and author of both testaments, wisely arranged that the New Testament be hidden in the Old and the Old be made manifested in the New" (§16).[19]

The conviction of Catholic Christianity as expressed in the documents of the Second Vatican Council, therefore, is that its faith is rooted in the witness of the Tanakh and in the lives of the people who have venerated God's word over the centuries, and that consequently Christianity itself is a legitimate and providential development from that ancient biblical witness. Through the lens of the death and resurrection of Jesus of Nazareth, Christians see a pattern that foreshadows and prepares for Christianity. Jewish religious leaders and teachers do not.[20]

The Writings of Josef Ratzinger

Over the decades Cardinal Ratzinger had distinguished himself by his voluminous writings on almost all aspects of theological understanding, especially revelation, ecclesiology, and Christology. His doctoral dissertation focused on the writings of Augustine of Hippo.

A summary of his views on the relationship between Israel and the Christian people can be found in a small volume of four essays initially published in German, then in English under the title of *Many Religions — One Covenant: Israel, the Church and the World*. In the opening sections of the work Ratzinger insists that the Church and Israel belong together because of their faith in the One God and their commitment to his will. In the wake of the blood and tears of centuries stained by so much mistrust

---

19. 18 November 1965.

20. Nevertheless, Jewish scholars such as Jon D. Levenson have written extensively on the pattern of death and resurrection already present in the Scriptures of Israel; cf. *The Death and Resurrection of the Beloved Son* (New Haven: Yale University Press, 1993).

and hostility between the two, he states that reconciliation is an object of Christian faith.[21]

The focal point of his thought for our discussion seems to be found in the second chapter, "The New Covenant: On the Theology of the Covenant in the New Testament."[22]

In that second essay, to establish the theological sources for his teaching, Ratzinger explores the writings of Paul. Following Paul's teachings, Ratzinger acknowledges a multiplicity of divine covenants with Noah, Abraham, Jacob-Israel, Moses, and David, but insists that God's covenant with Abraham is "real, fundamental and abiding."[23] Perhaps, by way of summary, it may be useful to cite two entire paragraphs from this essay:

> By contrast [with the Mosaic covenant on Sinai], the covenant with the Patriarchs is regarded as eternally in force. Whereas the covenant imposing obligations is patterned on the vassal contract, the covenant of promise has the royal grant as its model. To that extent Paul, with his distinction between the covenant with Abraham and the covenant with Moses, has rightly interpreted the biblical text. This distinction, however, also supersedes the strict opposites of the Old and the New Covenant and implies that all history is a unity in tension: the one Covenant is realized in the plurality of covenants.
>
> If this is so, there can be no question of setting the Old and the New Covenants against each other as two different religions; there is only one will of God for men, only one historical activity of God with and for men, though this activity employs interventions that are diverse and even in part contradictory — yet in truth they belong together.[24]

In this same essay Ratzinger goes on to study the primary New Testament texts that provide focus and teaching regarding this "new covenant," namely the institution narratives of the Eucharist. For Christians that new covenant is, in Ratzinger's view, continually presented as new in the regular celebration of the Eucharist, thus once again remaining "ever new and is always one and the same Covenant."[25]

---

21. *Die Vielfalt der Religionen und der eine Bund* (Hagen: Verlag Urfeld GmbH, 1998). The English is a translation by Graham Harrison (San Francisco: Ignatius Press, 1999), p. 25.

22. Originally produced as a lecture by the Parisian Academy of Moral and Political Sciences and published in *Internationale Katholische Zeitschrift Communio* 24 (1995): 193-208.

23. *Many Religions — One Covenant*, p. 55.

24. *Many Religions — One Covenant*, pp. 56f.

25. *Many Religions — One Covenant*, p. 65.

Although Christian tradition has generally thought in terms of two covenants, conceived as antithetical alternatives, often described as first particular and then universal, such a contrast is superficial at best. Ratzinger insists that the new covenant is found in the prophetic promise of renewed friendship that places God as the single Source who does everything. Thus, from the Catholic Christian perspective there is but one God, one covenant of family kinship and friendship, and a single religious tradition.[26]

The Catechism of the Catholic Church

Josef Ratzinger served as Prefect for the Congregation for the Doctrine of the Faith for over two decades. His earlier academic and pastoral experiences served as invaluable background for the task of guiding the preparation and publication of the *Catechism of the Catholic Church*.

In 1985 at a special Synod of Bishops to reflect on the initial twenty years of postconciliar implementation, Cardinal Bernard Law of Boston among others had called for a new Catechism that could summarize the teachings of the Council.[27] The proposal was widely endorsed because such a compendium was envisioned as a much-needed resource for bishops, pastors, and catechists. Because the project was officially referred to the Congregation for the Doctrine of the Faith by John Paul II, it came under the careful guidance of Cardinal Ratzinger.[28]

A review of the topical index for the English translation[29] reveals no

26. There may be an analogical reference here to the bitter debate within the Council over the sources of revelation. One group of theologians insisted on the double source, namely, Scripture and Tradition, while the other eventually dominant theory spoke of a single source, the Revealing God alone.

27. The text of Cardinal Law's intervention was published as a sidebar comment to the final message of that Extraordinary Synod in *Origins* 15, no. 27 (19 December 1985): 443.

28. Among the members of the chief drafting committee for that project during the years of its preparation was then-Archbishop William Levada of Portland, Oregon, who was later appointed by Benedict XVI in 2005 to be his successor as Prefect of that same Congregation for the Doctrine of the Faith.

29. The English translation, titled *Catechism of the Catholic Church*, was published by the United States Catholic Conference in 1994, using Scripture quotations from the *Revised Standard Version of the Bible* with copyrights of 1946, 1952, and 1971, as well as the *New Revised Standard Version of the Bible* (1989). This was based upon the *editio typica, Catechismus Catholicae Ecclesiae* as published by the Libreria Editrice Vaticana in 1997.

entry under "covenant" or "testament." The entries under "Abraham" are restricted to the following: "call of Abraham," "faith of Abraham," "hope of Abraham," "in the Muslim religion," "prayer of Abraham," and "promise to Abraham," which includes "fulfillment of the promises."

Although the word "covenant" is not used in the *Catechism's* main treatment of God's choice of Abraham,[30] the summary appended to that section introduces the concept and clearly states: "God chose Abraham and made a covenant with him and his descendants. By the covenant God formed his people and revealed his law to them through Moses."[31] Later in the text under the heading of *"The Church — Prepared for in the Old Covenant,"* there is no reference to Abraham and the covenant, but only to the prophets who accuse Israel of breaking the covenant and announce a new and eternal covenant.[32] Such references could contribute to the false conclusion that the prophetic judgments and condemnations were definitive. In fact, virtually every prophetic book in the inspired canon ends with a promise of renewed hope.

In another section dealing with prayer in the Old Testament, the text states that "Abraham believed in God and walked in his presence and in covenant with him."[33]

For the most part, the *Catechism* treats of Abraham in references to the promises he received and his faithful response to those promises. Those promises, as the Church from its apostolic writings and earliest convictions insisted, included Christ and the people of the New Covenant who were also called holy and beloved by God. The divine gift of covenant through Moses was a specific form of the Abrahamic relationship given as special and permanent blessing to the Jewish people.

Speeches and Addresses

Over the past years since his election on 16 April 2004, Benedict XVI has viewed the visits to synagogues as significant events in his various pastoral journeys throughout the world. These have sometimes in fact become op-

---

30. *Catechism*, §59-61. The structure of the reference book includes an initial description of each topic, followed by a brief summary of the main points made in the prior explanation.

31. *Catechism*, §72.

32. *Catechism*, §762.

33. *Catechism*, §2571, citing Genesis 15:6; 17:1f.

portunities for clarifying his comments and intention, especially when skewed by other controversies of the moment. Of particular significance for our assessment of Benedict's teaching are his convictions regarding Jewish and Christian relationship in covenant, and their shared faith which is often described as in some fashion identical. It may well be that Jewish partners in the renewed dialogue of our age do not share that view, and even vigorously deny that conclusion.

On 19 August 2005, Benedict visited the *Roonstrasse* Synagogue of Cologne, which had been destroyed during the *Kristallnacht* of 1938 and rebuilt in 1959. This historic visit marked only the second time a modern Pope has visited a Jewish place of worship.[34] Although once again the word "covenant" was not used explicitly, the Pope referred to the fourth chapter of *Nostra aetate,* and he noted "the immensely rich spiritual heritage that Jews and Christians share. Both Jews and Christians recognize in Abraham their father in faith (cf. Gal. 3:7; Rom. 4:11ff.) and they look to the teachings of Moses and the prophets."[35] In this fashion Benedict reiterated the teachings of the Second Vatican Council forty years earlier, and he brought that solemn conviction into the twenty-first century CE.

On 17 April 2008, in the context of his first pastoral visit to the United States, Benedict XVI offered special Passover greetings in a private meeting with Jewish leaders at the John Paul II Cultural Center in Washington, DC. He referred to the reality of a shared covenant twice during that address:

> At this time of your most solemn celebration, I feel particularly close, precisely because of what *Nostra aetate* calls Christians to remember always: that the church "received the revelation of the Old Testament through the people with whom God in his inexpressible mercy concluded the ancient covenant" (§4).[36]

He used the word "ancient" in the sense of venerable, not outmoded. Later in the same address Benedict returned to the theme of covenant and placed it within the larger framework of eschatology in order to include the existence of Christianity:

34. The first such visit was that of Pope John Paul II to the Great Synagogue of Rome on April 13, 1986; cf. *Origins* 15, no. 45 (24 April 1986): 729ff.

35. *Origins* 35, no. 12 (1 September 2005): 207.

36. *Origins* 37, no. 46 (1 May 2008): 746. The day of the meeting as a matter of fact coincided with the eighty-first birthday of Benedict XVI.

At the Passover seder you recall the holy patriarchs Abraham, Isaac and Jacob and the holy women of Israel, Sarah, Rebecca, Rachael and Leah, the beginning of the long line of sons and daughters of the covenant. With the passing of time the covenant assumes an ever more universal value as the promise made to Abraham takes form: "I will bless you and make your name great, so that you will be a blessing. . . . All the communities of the earth shall find blessing in you (Genesis 12:2-3)."

Indeed according to the prophet Isaiah, the hope of redemption extends to the whole of humanity: "Many peoples will come and say: 'Come, let us go up to the mountain of the Lord, to the house of the God of Jacob; that he may teach us his ways and that we may walk in his paths'" (Isaiah 2:3). Within the eschatological horizon it offered a real prospect of universal brotherhood on the path of justice and peace, preparing the way of the Lord (cf. Isaiah 62:10).

Christians and Jews share this hope; we are in fact, as the prophets say, "prisoners of hope" (Zechariah 9:12). This bond permits us Christians to celebrate alongside you, though in our own way, the Passover of Christ's death and resurrection, which we see as inseparable from your own, for Jesus himself said, "Salvation is from the Jews" (John 4:22).[37]

This manner of expression highlights the Christian conviction that there is a single covenant, which has been blessed by an eschatological development that is not as yet experienced by Judaism. The degree and the manner in which eschatology is claimed by each of the two peoples who claim membership in the covenant with Abraham remains a fundamental difference in our two religious self-consciousnesses.

Another important statement occurred on 28 January 2009. Shortly after the debacle of misunderstanding and hurt occasioned by the lifting of the penalty of excommunication against four bishops illicitly ordained in 1988 by the schismatic archbishop Lefebvre, and the subsequent revelation that one had denied the existence of the Holocaust, Benedict felt an obligation to offer an additional word of reconciliation and apology to the Jewish people. At his first opportunity, namely, the next customary Wednesday audience, his comments included the following statement:

In these days when we remember the Shoah, images come to mind from my repeated visits to Auschwitz, one of the concentration camps in which the heinous slaughter of millions of Jews occurred, innocent vic-

---

37. *Origins* 37, no. 46 (1 May 2008): 746.

tims of a blind racial and religious hatred. As I affectionately renew the expression of my full and unquestionable solidarity with our fellow receivers of the first covenant, I hope that the memory of the Shoah will lead humanity to reflect upon the unfathomable power of evil when it conquers the heart of man.[38]

Conclusions

A fundamental conclusion to this study would seem to be that Josef Ratzinger both as theologian and as Pope holds to a single covenant of God with Abraham and through Abraham with the entire people of Israel. Both Jews and Christians each subsequently found a place in that single covenantal relationship with God, through the promises to Abraham. A son would be given beyond normal natural limits, and Abraham's faith would be credited as righteousness. Christians brought the lens of their belief in the resurrection of Jesus to that covenant, and they see clear lines of development between its initial formulation and later developments, all of which are held by Christians to be organic and logical.

Ratzinger would find it impossible to propose a theory of two covenants because they might then easily be conceived as parallel and essentially unrelated except in terms of their common historical origins or final destiny.

The truth of the centrality of Christ's redemptive mission as held by Christians for two millennia becomes a controlling criterion for judging other theological questions. Without a doubt Jesus remained a faithful Jew throughout his entire life, certainly as portrayed by the four canonical Gospels of Christian tradition. Jesus prayed regularly in the synagogues of his day. Like the great Rabbi Akiva he invoked the essential centrality of the dual command to love God (Deut. 6:4ff.) and neighbor (Lev. 19:18) as the key to the Torah. He demanded obedience to the Decalogue as a fundamental obligation for anyone claiming to be his disciple (Matt. 19:17ff.). He celebrated the Passover with his disciples. His teachings and even his debates were all within the great Pharisaic traditions of his age.

Matthew's Gospel, written for a community comprised both of Torah-observant Jewish "Christians" and of gentile converts, insisted that Jesus

38. *Origins* 38, no. 36 (19 February 2009): 571.

came to fulfill the Torah, not abolish it.[39] Thus, as repeatedly articulated in Matthew's Gospel, there remained a firm continuity between the ancient faith of Israel and the faith of the Jesus movement of the first century CE. Moreover, there existed a radical similarity, if not identity of faith, between that early Jesus movement and contemporary Jews outside the movement. For this reason, Catholic Christians see themselves as sharing a single faith in the One God of Abraham and in submission to his divine Will. There may be some Jewish colleagues who would reject the notion of a single Judeo-Christian tradition, and insist on plurality, but Christians see the issue in the singular.

The truth of the universal salvific mission of Jesus the Christ remains a bedrock of Christian conviction. In recent years, however, Christian contact with the other major religions of the world, and a genuine Christian respect for the deep spirituality and powerful witness of the lives of those adhering to them, has forced Christians to confront their own sense of theological superiority and to recontextualize that conviction within the sense of their mission. A greater humility, however, and the recognition of the activity of the Holy Spirit in all the major religions of the world, does not and cannot negate the fundamental Christian belief regarding the universal redemptive nature of the life and death of Jesus of Nazareth.

Another seriously debated question, therefore, is the scope of the Christian mission as such, or to state it more precisely, the relationship between the two "Israelite" families. Does the fact that the great commission of Jesus, which commands making disciples of all the "nations" of the world (Matt. 28:16ff.), focuses precisely on the gentile nations rather than the Jewish people, limit the mission of Christianity, and preclude any mission to Jewish people? How does the fact that elsewhere Jesus sent his disciples to the "lost sheep of Israel" (10:16ff.) and claimed to have been sent himself to that same group (15:24), and not to the groups embodied in and represented by the Syro-Phoenician woman, fit into the subsequent mission of his disciples today? Thus there must be some ongoing relationship to Judaism itself on the part of the disciples of Jesus, but it may now be a fraternal call to ongoing mutual fidelity to the covenant they both share. Is the Christian "mission to the Jewish other" a summons to delve more deeply into the Abrahamic covenant in order to see what might be discovered? Can there be a commitment to one's own witness that does not seek

---

39. Matthew 5:17; cf. Anthony J. Saldarini, *Matthew's Christian-Jewish Community* (Chicago: University of Chicago Press, 1994).

to make converts of the other? These are serious questions that are not easily answered, but refuse to go quietly away! Conversely, can it be a mission of Judaism to insist on the core Judaism of Christianity?

If the salvific mission of Jesus the Christ is in fact universal, how do Christians see themselves related to the Judaism of today? This is a key question, especially in view of the many centuries of painful and tear-stained relationships that included forced conversions when Church and state were allied, and in view of the countless violent pogroms against those who resisted and refused to be assimilated into Christianity, ancient or medieval. There is a longstanding Christian tradition about the eschatological conversion of Jews to the reforming message of Jesus at the end of time. How can this be held in fidelity to one's deepest convictions without at the same time reverting to the mentality that produced the dreadful forced conversions of an earlier age? What utter humility must mark the true Jewish or Christian member of the Abrahamic covenant before the total mystery of God's will for the world?

Thus the inner logic and conceptual dynamic must flow from an understanding of the Christian view of the universal mission of Jesus to the unity of the faith as shared by Christians and Jews, at least as we understand it, and finally to the mission of Christianity. If we in fact share one faith in the same God, is it not logical that we share one covenant? Each tradition may develop a distinctive sense of its primordial covenant with God in Abraham; thus both Jews and Christians have developed and evolved from the faith of Israel. One and the same God may be shared by both traditions, though experienced differently. That difference, however, must include an eternal mutual relationship.

Thus we return to the question raised from the beginning of this paper and from the beginning of the Jewish/Christian dialectic of the first centuries of our Common Era.[40] Some contemporary Christian theologians would attempt to resolve the tension between Judaism and Christianity by asserting two covenants, running in parallel fashion through the ages, each perhaps with its own blessing.[41] The benefit of that position would be its affirmation of the ongoing validity of Judaism in the modern world and the deep respect of such a theory for their witness to God's faithful promises embodied in the Jewish people of our time.

40. The very fact that we persist in naming our Era "Common" might suggest a bond deeper than mere historical coexistence!

41. Cf. the historical and theological study of Mary Boys, *Has God Only One Blessing?*

For many Catholic Christians the downside of the theory of two covenants would be the difficulty of seeing any relationship between a universal salvific notion of the mission of Jesus of Nazareth and the reality of contemporary Judaism. Although Jesus may have been historically and genealogically of Jewish origin, in such a theory he has no ongoing salvific relationship with Judaism. He served as the focal point of the historical bifurcation of the religious traditions in the early period of the Common Era, but the separation of both Christianity and Judaism from the ancient people of Israel would have severed any further relationship between Jesus and his people.

Central to that moment of historical and theological bifurcation remains the reality of God's covenant with Israel at Sinai. To what degree are the ethical prescriptions embodied in the "Ten Commandments" which bind all Christians to be distinguished from those commands which address issues such as diet and circumcision? Can the latter, which are viewed by Christians as part of the treasure of Judaism, be respected even though an early apostolic decision (Acts 15) decreed them as nonbinding for gentile Christians, who now constitute the vast majority of the disciples of Jesus? The relationship of the Mosaic to the Abrahamic covenant still presses for further mutual understanding by Christians and Jews alike.

Benedict XVI, however, insists that there can be only one covenant between God and humanity, given through Abraham and the entire people of Israel, from which Jesus the Christ was born as the final expression of the love of God for Israel. For Christianity, the fundamental enduring reality remains the historical and theological sequence of the one from and after the other. This is not simple replacement. Christian conviction regarding development, that the second is hidden in the first and the first revealed in the second, does not invalidate the first by any means. To the degree that Christianity sees itself as a logical unfolding of the Abrahamic faith, it offers the witness of its existence and its conviction as part of the divine design of God for the salvation of the world. Thus the Christian witness to the other, inherent in its understanding of covenant, is one of finding in the Abrahamic covenant ever-fresh and fruitful meaning for the redemption of humanity.

Many Jewish colleagues conclude that one cannot be truly Christian and affirm the historical and theological development of Christianity from its Judaic roots without being at least "developmental supersessionists." To claim otherwise, they note, would be to deny one's being! I respond by questioning whether every development essentially negates its predecessor. These are the deeper questions of our new age, and I pray that a renewed friendship may find new answers that bring us ever more profound reconciliation and peace.[42]

If Judaism remains an ongoing witness to God's fidelity, can Christianity be a similar ongoing witness to the presence of the last age already experienced? Because Christianity believes itself to be a fulfillment and "new" in that sense (to evoke the Jeremian oracle once more), it must be open to welcoming individual Jewish members of the Abrahamic covenant, and it must consider itself a valid development and completion. Formal mission to the Jewish nation as such, however, cannot be held by Christians if such a conviction would presume the historical termination of Judaism.

A recent encounter on 23 September 2009 between Cardinal Angelo Bagnasco, president of the Italian Episcopal Conference, and the Italian Jewish leaders Rabbi Giuseppe Laras, president of the Italian Rabbinic Assembly, and Rabbi Riccardo Di Segni, Chief Rabbi of Rome, included the Cardinal's clear articulation of this "mission": "The Italian Episcopal Conference reaffirms that it is not the intention of the Catholic Church to actively work for the conversion of Jews."[43]

During the Lenten season of the Great Jubilee of 2000, the late Pope John Paul II joined with the then-Cardinal Ratzinger for a series of profound apologies in the context of a penitential service held in Saint Peter's Basilica in Rome. Those apologies were an effort on the part of the Catholic Church to purify human memories and to ask pardon for the sins of the Church involved in those memories. Among the statements was an apology for imposing our truth upon others, and indeed by means that were often violent and disrespectful of human dignity and the personal conscience of others. That sentiment of humble apology and the quest for the truth of God must mark our steps forward as we are embraced by God's "Covenant, Mission, and the Other"!

---

42. Ephesians 2:14.

43. Cited in *30 Giorni/30 Days* 27, no. 9 (2009): 44. The same issue reported a meeting between Benedict XVI and Rabbi Di Segni on 14 October 2009, to prepare for a then-future visit of Benedict XVI to the Great Synagogue in Rome (17 January 2010). His address on that occasion was published in *Origins* 39, no. 33 (28 January 2010): 538-40.

Three Forms of Otherness: Covenant, Mission, and Relation to the Other in Rabbinic Perspective

Naftali Rothenberg

Introduction

The interfaith Jewish-Christian discourse is frequently a dialogue of the oblivious: oblivious to differences of belief and oblivious to halakhic (Jewish legal) positions intended to keep Jews apart from Christians. This not because a harmonious or sterile dialogue is wanted, given that participants are not oblivious to the long history of hatred and persecution.

It is interesting to compare the two main themes of this discourse. During decades of participation in interfaith dialogue I have almost never seen that differences of belief were at the core of the discussion. I have never heard a Jewish participant mention the halakhic definition of Christianity as idolatry, or other laws intended to keep the Jews from having contact with Christians (or with non-Jews in general). Rather, in most cases the discussion has focused on parallel images or on emphasizing what the two cultures have in common. Anti-Semitism and persecution are an integral part of the dialogue, and Jews and Christians have not ignored it. These two features — the obliviousness to differences of belief and halakhic principles that aim at isolation, and the recognition of the Jews' status as victims — contribute to the shallowness of the interfaith discourse.

From a Jewish perspective the great loss is that the discourse has had no internal influence and has made no contribution to the way in which Jews perceive their self-identity and consequently to their attitude toward the Christian Other. That is, the widespread Jewish perception is that Christianity is an enemy that seeks to destroy us physically or spiritually, with violence or with soft words. This Jewish stance makes only a negative contribution to Jewish identity.

There is a difference between avoiding a theological discussion and ignoring the halakhic principles intended to keep Jews away from Christians. Most rabbinic leaders in the Jewish world have nothing to do with theology and consequently cannot be part of a theological discourse, whether internal to the Jewish world, between Jews and Christians, or between Jews and others. For these rabbis, Judaism is a religion not of theology but of practices — practices that aim at forging a way of life. Some see the theological lacuna as a defect, but I do not share this view. A Jewish-Christian dialogue focused exclusively on theology would always be limited, on the Jewish side, to a very small group.

What is more, theological principles and creeds do not have the status of dogma in Judaism. Jewish-Christian theological discourse is liable to take place on a plane that is too narrow and marginal for many Jews. This is why their avoidance of such discourse is not particularly significant.

In this article I would like to take up the challenge of the attitude toward the Other in the face of the halakhic strictures against relations with non-Jews. I would like to show that the rejection of "the others" does not totally rule out some kinds of relations and may even set a foundation for their positive existence. I hope that at the end of the process it will be possible, from a Jewish rabbinic perspective as well, to place Jews and Others on the same plane.

This paper was written as part of a group's work. The outline of our research project steers us to a discussion of the attitude toward the Other based on two prior concepts: *Covenant* and *Mission*. I will begin by clarifying their significance and role in Jewish culture.

Covenant

The word *berit* = covenant appears in the Hebrew Bible hundreds of times in different connotations and forms. There are three categories of covenants:

a. Covenants between God and humanity *or* between God and the people of Israel.
b. Covenants between human beings for a positive aim.
c. Covenants with idols and pagans.

The message of covenants of the third category is negative, standing in opposition to the first.

The *Torah* as a whole (*Sefer Habrit* = Book of the Covenant) carries the message of the covenant between God and the people of Israel. However, it is customary to specify two founding appearances: the Abraham covenant and the Sinai covenant. These are exclusively between God and the people of Israel. Their practical implementation is the observance of God's commandments.

But there is another covenant in the *Torah,* prior to these two — the first time when the word *berit* appears: the covenant between God and the children of Noah — with the entire post-Flood humanity:

> And God spoke unto Noah, and to his sons with him, saying: "As for Me, behold, I establish My covenant with you, and with your seed after you. . . ." And God said: "This is the token of the covenant which I make between Me and you and every living creature that is with you, for perpetual generations: And the bow shall be in the cloud; and I will look upon it, that I may remember the everlasting covenant between God and every living creature of all flesh that is upon the earth." (Gen. 9:8-9, 12, 16)

This is of course an inclusive covenant. It contains promises of God on the one hand and commandments (Gen. 8:15-22; 9:1-7) on the other. As we'll see in the last part of this paper, this covenant plays an important role in classifying the relations between Jews and gentiles.

To no less extent we can see the creation of Adam in the image of God as a covenant between the Creator and the created, i.e., the entire humanity. This was breached when Adam sinned in paradise but still will contribute to establishing a model of common denominator between Jews and gentiles.

The Abrahamic covenant appears in Jewish tradition and internal Jewish discourse as a particularistic and private process; in the words of the *Midrash:*

> *And told Abram the Hebrew* (Gen. 14:13). Rav Judah said: "Hebrew [Hebrew *ivri*] [signifies that] the whole world was on one side [Hebrew *ever*] and he was on the other side."[1]

The fact that the world described here, from which Abraham separated himself and from which he wished to isolate his descendants, is that of pagan idolatry did not keep this *Midrash* from being invoked also after the

1. *Genesis Rabbah* 42:8.

spread of monotheistic faiths; it has served as a key element in Jewish education to enforce segregation from them. In Jewish tradition, the covenant with Abraham is a covenant of separation, which begins with his obedience to the divine injunction to "Go forth from your native land and from your father's house to the land that I will show you" (Gen. 12:1) and concludes with the covenant of circumcision (Gen. 17:1-14, 24-27).

The word *berit*, "covenant," occurs nine times in this passage. Four of them refer to the practical side of the covenant: "This shall be the covenant between Me and you and your offspring to follow, which you shall keep: every male among you shall be circumcised" (Gen. 17:10). We are not dealing with a monotheistic creed that invites all believers to take shelter under it, nor with a theological principle to bond them together, but with a practical act, removing a bit of flesh, a physical modification of the body, which establishes total separation between Abraham and his household on the one hand and all the nations of the world on the other.

In Jewish culture, however, the covenant par excellence is the covenant at Sinai. The covenant at Sinai is first and foremost an exclusive covenant between God and the people of Israel. At the same time that it is a covenant that excludes all those who are not of the people of Israel,[2] it is also one that includes all of the coming generations of the Jewish people, including all future converts.[3] According to the Midrashic tradition, all future generations of Israel, including proselytes, have their root in the souls of the Israelites who witnessed the revelation at Sinai.

Over the generations, one of the best-known and most frequently quoted *Midrashim* is the one that recounts how God offered the Torah to every single nation, who refused to accept it; but when He offered it to Israel the answer was, "We will do and [then] we will hear" (Exod. 24:7). Thus this is a covenant of doing, a covenant of commandments or precepts. The covenant is directly linked to the *mission* assigned to the people of Israel, who are the "community of those commanded," and to every individual member thereof.

Every individual who is affiliated with the people of Israel and who is obligated by the 613 precepts is a "member of the covenant" *(Ben Berit)*, while every individual who does not belong to the people of Israel and on whom the Torah and precepts are not incumbent is defined by negation as "not a member of the covenant" *(She-eino Ben Berit)*. So "covenant" cannot

2. *Sifre Deuteronomy* 343; *Exodus Rabbah* 5 (and parallels).
3. BT *Shau'ot* 39a.

be the starting point for making the Other present by a positive definition of partnership or participation: neither the covenant with Abraham, which culminates in the rite of circumcision, nor the covenant at Sinai, which distinguishes those who were present at the giving of the Torah — the people of Israel and all those who joined them over the generations — from those who were not present, meaning all others. The covenant, as an obligation to the precepts, and the mission, which is fulfilling the precepts, are in practice identical.

Mission

The mission is to serve the Lord in every human action in this world. This is not necessarily by means of prayer but in every action of the body — eating and drinking, marital relations, at work and at play.

The mission defines otherness: there are those who are with you — "your fellow in the Torah and precepts" — and there are those who do not belong to this fellowship. Practical life, as framed by this mission, raises barriers and defines the others: Jews' attitude toward sex is not like the gentiles'; Jews do not intermarry; a Jewish menu is different and Jews do not eat at gentiles' tables; Jews refrain from labor for sixty days out of the year, in a complete and meticulous fashion that has nothing in common with gentiles' vacations, which in any case do not coincide with Jewish holidays.

Were all of these not enough to create a distance and separate the Jew from the non-Jewish Other, the Sages enacted additional rules and regulations whose sole intent is to keep Jews away from non-Jews — for example, not only a ban on eating meat at their tables, or cooked dishes to which some forbidden ingredient might have been added, but also a prohibition on drinking their wine, and (for some authorities) on eating their bread or drinking the milk of their cows.

We have seen that in the Jewish tradition the concept of covenant generally implies isolation, exclusion, and separation between those who are members of the covenant and those who are not. This means that covenant cannot be the starting point for a discussion of the attitude toward the Other or a foundation for a common denominator between Jews and other monotheistic communities.

We have seen, too, that the mission — observing the precepts — distances Jews from those who do not share the Torah and precepts with them and erects a wall, seemingly impassable, between Jews and non-Jews (and, in modern times, between observant and nonobservant Jews as well). This background offers a far from comfortable point of departure for a discussion of the attitude toward the Other in general and the attitude toward the Christian Other in particular.

Otherness and the Attitude toward the Other

This section will present the main exercise of this article: a presentation of possible inclusive models of the Other within the exclusive Jewish self-identity views. But first I want to mention two approaches to Otherness.

Exclusion and Inattention. Certain others, those who are not part of our[4] affinity group, are perceived — if they are perceived at all — as part of the undifferentiated backdrop of our lives. Aside from the fact of their exclusion from our affinity group, they have no substantial presence. In their insubstantiality they might as well not be there, so that the attitude toward them is more than just obliviousness to their existence.

Negative presence. Then there are the Others who are our enemies, in the past or in the present, actively or passively. As such, not only do they have real existence in their own place, but they are also present, in their negative essence, in shaping the identity of our own group.[5]

One might have expected that it would be more difficult to modify the attitude toward the Other who is negatively present. As I shall try to show, however, the possibility of ameliorating the attitude toward the Other with whom we have some form of relationship, even if it is negative, has stronger anchors than does the possibility of giving a presence to the Others who are excluded so far that we are oblivious of them.

The various forms of exclusion I have mentioned thus far, both those that derive from the concept of the covenant and those that stem from the definition of the mission, constitute a barrier to a respectful relationship with the Other. It may be possible to construct a meaningful bond between Jews and others precisely by recognizing the difference and uniqueness of

---

4. The word "our" used here and subsequently reflects a common position in Jewish communities but does not represent the author's personal identification.

5. In this context I will mention Carl Schmitt's cogent argument that any national identity (as well as a separate group identity) depends on the existence of an enemy. Leo Strauss was ineffective in his attempts to parry Schmitt's assertions, and Jean-Paul Sartre registered only limited success. See Carl Schmitt, *The Concept of the Political,* trans. G. Schwab, with notes by Leo Strauss (Chicago: University of Chicago Press, 1996).

these concepts (covenant and mission) in Jewish civilization, and treating them as part of a complex structure that employs them as building blocks rather than as obstacles. There are several forms or models for this in the classic Jewish texts, and here I will suggest and review three of them.

Model 1: The Presence of Every Individual in the Image of God

The first model is based on the ideas of Rabbi Akiva,[6] who follows a process that begins by reinforcing our limited obligations toward ourselves, toward our family, and toward other Jews, and ultimately attains a sense of obligation and responsibility toward the Other, without waiving our responsibility toward those with "prior claims."

> Love thy fellow as thyself (*Leviticus* 19:18) — Rabbi Akiva says: This is a great principle in the Torah. Ben Azai says: "This is the book of the generations of *Adam*" (*Genesis* 5:1) is a greater principle than that. (*Sifra, Kedoshim* 2)

Rabbi Akiva and Ben Azai were attempting to determine the categorical imperative from which all morality can be inferred. Ben Azai's claim rests upon the creation of man in God's image: "This is the book of the generations of *Adam*. In the day that God created man, in the likeness of God made He him" *(Gen. 5:1)*. According to this principle, all human beings were created equal, and humanity — of which each and every individual human being is a part — embodies the image of God. Each part of humanity therefore has its own worth, just as every limb in the body has a place and value of its own. Ben Azai further developed this idea in the following *mishnah*:

> Do not despise any man and do not dismiss any thing. For there is no man without a time and no thing without a place. (Mishnah *Avot* 4, 3)

---

6. Rabbi Akiva ben Yosef (50-135?) was one of the leading sages of the Mishnaic period, if not the greatest among them. His legendary figure, leadership, and Halakhic method and thought occupy a central place in the Talmudic literature, edited over a period of centuries. See N. Rothenberg, *The Wisdom of Love: Man, Woman, and God in Jewish Canonical Literature* (Boston: Academic Studies Press, 2009), pp. 94-103 (ch. 6, "Love Thy Fellow as the Basis of Human Socialization"). See also N. Rothenberg, "Akiva Ben Yosef," and "Love Your Neighbor in Judaism," in *Encyclopedia of Love in World Religions*, ed. Y. Kornberg (Santa Barbara/Denver/Oxford: Greenberg ABC-CLIO Publishers, 2008).

Ben Azai thus resolves the great dilemma of the principle of equality: the fact that in reality men are not equal in any sense — not in ability, not in behavior, and not in the contribution or disturbance they offer society and their surroundings. Nor are the limbs of the body equal, but since none can be eliminated without "diminishing [God's] image," the principle of equality is upheld inasmuch as each has its proper place. They are equal in their right to exist, and every person is responsible for the existence of her/his fellow. The idea that man was created in God's image is, in Ben Azai's opinion, a greater moral/social principle than the commandment to love one's fellow.[7] According to Ben Azai, the categorical imperative is a rational law from which responsibility for one's fellow man derives. It is thus written in the Talmud (*Berakhot* 6b): "The entire world was created only for the sake of fellowship" — i.e., it is a categorical imperative from which all moral behavior stems. In relation to our main topic: the creation of human beings in the image of God is the first covenant with Him, and it is totally inclusive.

Rabbi Akiva's criticism of Ben Azai's approach derives first and foremost from the fear that it is not practicable and therefore unsuited as a practical basis for morality. The debate regarding the "great[est] principle in the Torah" is not an abstract philosophical discussion, but a practical discourse on human nature, and it is in this context that Rabbi Akiva claims that rational knowledge is not enough to create a sense of mutual responsibility and commitment to one another. Moreover, he is skeptical regarding the rationality of this sublime principle, since absolute equality goes against reason. One always takes precedence over one's fellow man, and one's responsibility to oneself comes before one's responsibility toward others.

The following debate in the *Midrash* demonstrates the profound difference between the two approaches on a practical moral level:

> "That thy brother may live with thee" (Leviticus, 25,36) — Ben Peturei taught: Two are walking in the desert, and only one has a jug of water. If he drinks it, he will reach an inhabited place, and if they both drink, they will both die. Ben Peturei taught: They should both drink and die, as it is written "that *thy* brother may live *with* thee." Rabbi Akiva said to

7. The version in Midrash, *Bereshit Rabbah* 24, presents Rabbi Akiva's opinion as "a greater principle than that": "Ben Azai says: 'This is the book of the generations of *Adam*' (*Genesis* 5:1) is a great principle in the Torah. Rabbi Akiva says: 'Love thy fellow as thyself' (*Leviticus* 19:18) is a greater principle than that."

him: "that thy brother may live *with thee*" — your life takes precedence over that of your fellow. (*Sifra, Behar* 5)

Ben Azai's principle of equality between all who are created in God's image is represented in this debate by Ben Peturei,[8] who rules that both men have equal right to live and therefore equal right to the water, regardless of the fact that the water is presently in the possession of one of them. The principle of equality is the categorical imperative from which the laws of morality derive. Ben Peturei therefore rejects the principle of ownership and dismisses the fact that the water belongs to only one of the two. Rabbi Akiva does not believe that the principle of equality is practicable, and therefore qualifies the responsibility one has for one's fellow, making it conditional upon first fulfilling one's responsibility toward oneself: "your life takes precedence over that of your fellow" — in the sense that your duty toward another begins from the point at which you have favored and ensured your own life.

From this we can understand the deep meaning of the principle "love thy fellow *as thyself*" according to Rabbi Akiva. One cannot love one's fellow man unless one first loves oneself. According to Ben Azai, the principle of equality that stems from man's creation in God's image precludes the individual's independent existence, projecting it to the totality of the divine image. From this derive the rational moral principles, including one's responsibility for each and every human being by virtue of her/his humanity. Rabbi Akiva restricts this principle in two stages: first, love thy fellow as thyself — love of yourself takes precedence over love of another, and is a precondition for its existence; second, love thy fellow — specifically your fellow and not just anyone. Boundless, unreserved love is limited to one's immediate surroundings — family, friends, fellow townspeople, members of one's people — and is not shown toward all human beings per se. Limiting one's love of man to a smaller circle of people is a practical necessity.

Rabbi Akiva's criticism of Ben Azai's categorical principle is, once again, that it is impracticable. In his opinion, moral behavior cannot proceed solely from a rational tenet, even when that is accepted as a sublime principle founded upon a clear intellectual premise. One cannot exercise responsibility toward another if one is not first at peace with oneself. Just as love of one's fellow depends upon love of oneself, so moral responsibility

---

8. Panaetius, the Stoic, discussed a similar moral dilemma, presented in Cicero, *De Officiis* III.23.

toward humanity as a whole — with an emotional as well as a rational basis — depends first upon love for one's own people. Rabbi Akiva believes that universal moral values can be developed and practiced, but only by a gradual process, layer upon layer. One must begin from the most basic principle, as expressed by Hillel the Elder: "What is hateful to you do not unto your fellow."[9] Before you can perceive something as being hateful to you, which you can then be required not to do unto another, you must first have a basic sense of self-worth. Here too, the basis is not purely rational, but rests upon feelings — toward oneself and consequently toward one's fellow. Henceforth: "the rest is commentary — go and learn," i.e., the principle of mutual responsibility can be expanded and applied to a broad range of areas, such as saving the life or property of another, charity, kindness, etc. A system of moral practice thus arises, on a social and national, as well as a personal level. At this point, it is possible to demand that one exercise responsibility toward all of humankind — every human being created in the image of God — as Rabbi Akiva himself explains:

> He [Rabbi Akiva] would say: Beloved is man for he was created in the image of God; he was accorded great love, being created in God's image, as it is written: "for in the image of God made He man" (*Genesis* 9:6). Beloved are Israel for they were called children of God; they were accorded great love, being called God's children, as it is written (*Deuteronomy* 14:1): "Ye are the children of the Lord your God. . . ." (Mishnah, *Avot* 3, 14)

The phrase "beloved are Israel who were called children of God" qualifies the *mishnah*'s previous assertion — "beloved is man who was created in the image of God" — making it clear that the first statement should be construed as referring to every human being, whether of Israel or the nations.

In this *mishnah* in *Avot*, Rabbi Akiva establishes the principle that all men were created in God's image, whence arises the mutual responsibility expressed in the words "beloved" and "great love." When we wrong one another, we do so less from hatred than from self-absorption and ignorance of the other's existence. Responsibility for one's fellow man does not derive solely from the principle of equality mandated by creation in God's image, but from being encouraged to develop a positive attitude toward him/her.

9. BT *Shabbat* 31a, and *Targum Yehonatan* on the verse "love thy fellow as thyself." The verse itself does not refer only to refraining from doing harm to others, but to doing good as well. See commentary of R. Shmuel Eliezer Halevi Eidels (Maharsha) on BT *Shabbat* 31a.

It is not merely a matter of rational solidarity, but of real empathy toward all human beings, be they of Israel or of the nations. One can only develop a sense of responsibility toward one's fellow man based on awareness of the other's existence, if one has already developed love toward those in one's immediate circle: friends and compatriots. Such love can only be felt by one who has attained basic recognition of his/her own worth.[10] The process that leads up to the principle of equality based on the premise that all men were created in God's image is thus a gradual one: first "love thy fellow as thyself," and only then "beloved is man for he was created in the image of God."

Rabbi Akiva offers a basic and comprehensive model for constructing a process to make the Other present in the Jews' own world without surrendering the elements of individual and group identity that exclude the Other. I believe that his is a worthy alternative to Carl Schmitt's approach,[11] one that demonstrates that there can be a group identity that does not depend on the existence of an enemy. Rabbi Akiva's model emphasizes the presence of every individual in the image of God seen in human creation itself, an inclusive covenant for all human beings.

Model 2: Relation to Ultimate "Other" by Definition of a Common Basis

Rabbi Akiva's model does not provide a specific answer when the other, or the other's views, run counter to or threaten the group's own hallowed principles. Is it possible to relate to the other in that case? To accept him on the basis of a partial common denominator? If so, how?

To deal with this challenge let me introduce a second model, developed by Rabbi Meir, one of the most important sages of the Mishnah, in his relations with one of his teachers — Elisha ben Avuyah, whom the Talmudic literature usually designates by a cognomen that is precisely our topic — *Akher (Aḥer)* or "Other."

Elisha ben Avuyah was one of the leading scholars of his generation and one of the four sages who "entered the orchard" — that is, who devoted themselves to the study of esoteric lore. But it was precisely his engagement with this that led him to apostasy.

10. See Erich Fromm, *The Art of Loving* (New York: Harper Perennial, 2000), pp. 23-30.
11. See footnote 5.

The Rabbis taught: Four entered the (esoteric) Orchard, and they were: Ben Azai, Ben Zoma, *Aher** ("Other") and Rabbi Akiva. . . . Ben Azai glimpsed and died. . . . Ben Zoma glimpsed and was harmed. . . . *Aher** slashed among the plants, Rabbi Akiva emerged safely. (B.T. *Hagigah* 14b)[12]

As noted, *Akher* denotes Elisha ben Avuyah, but the Talmudic literature systematically refrains from mentioning him by name and almost always refers to him as "Other."

According to the Talmudic interpretation, Elisha ben Avuyah's study of esoteric wisdom caused him to abandon his faith in the One God, in the strict sense, and to believe in a dualist system. In the wake of this apostasy he realized that he was condemned to forfeit his share in the world to come; even were he to repent fully it would be of no avail and his soul was doomed to perish utterly. Consequently he decided to forsake observance of the precepts as well and to transgress all of the commandments in the Torah. Elisha's behavior caused a great shock among the people and even more so among his fellow scholars, who had learned together with him, and often from him, in the House of Study, where he was one of the main pillars. Their response was categorical: he immediately ceased to be accounted a great and revered scholar; he was stripped even of his name and relegated to the category of Other. They kept their distance from him, did not speak to him, and in practice decreed his total ostracism.

The result of this reaction should have been that his name and story would be forgotten and blotted out from Jewish history. But this did not happen. The sages' reaction and its expected outcome were frustrated by Rabbi Meir. He, who was one of the leading scholars of his generation[13] and a disciple of Elisha's, did not sever his relations and continued to study Torah with him.[14]

We read that one Sabbath Rabbi Meir was sitting in the synagogue in Tiberias, expounding the Torah. Elisha ben Avuyah rode by outside on his horse. Some of the students came and told Rabbi Meir, "Your teacher is outside." R. Meir cut off his sermon at once and went out to him. Elisha ben Avuyah asked him what they had been learning that day in the House

12. See parallel: *Tosefta Hagigah*, ch. B3.

13. "Rabbi Aha bar Hanina said: It is revealed and known before Him Who spoke and the world came into existence, that in the generation of R. Meir there was none equal to him" (BT *Eruvin* 13b). Rabbi Meir was one of the redactors of the Mishnah.

14. See BT *Hagigah* 15a-b; JT *Hagigah* 2:1 (77b).

of Study and what he had been teaching. The two began moving along the road, discussing Torah together — Elisha on horseback, profaning the Sabbath in public, and Rabbi Meir on foot:

> Our Rabbis taught: Once *Akher* was riding a horse on the Sabbath, and R. Meir was walking behind him to learn Torah from him. Said [*Aher*] to him: Meir, turn back, for I have measured by the paces of my horse that this is the limit of the Sabbath boundary. He replied: You, too, turn back! [*Aher*] answered: Have I not already told you that I have heard from behind the Veil: "Return, O backsliding children" (Jer. 3:22) — except *Aher*. (B.T. *Hagigah* 15a)

Akher and Rabbi Meir are divided by high walls of Otherness: Rabbi Meir's observance of the precepts distinguishes them unambiguously. One of them is on foot; one of them is astride a horse on the Sabbath. Rabbi Meir's belief is the antithesis of *Akher's* apostasy. We would expect that there neither should be nor could be any bond or relationship between them. Nevertheless, it seems that for Rabbi Meir there is no wall whatsoever. Not only does he continue to learn Torah from his teacher; he even does so while the latter is desecrating the Sabbath. Nor can we miss *Akher's* respect and concern for his disciple-colleague. It is one thing for Rabbi Meir to be learning Torah with him in this situation; but to cause him to violate a Sabbath prohibition on his account by walking beyond the distance permitted on the Sabbath — this Elisha will not do. He interrupts his discourse to warn Rabbi Meir to turn back toward the town, because even as they have been walking/traveling and talking together and he has been desecrating the holy day, he has been counting his horse's paces so that he would know when they reached the Sabbath boundary.

Rabbi Meir's approach to building a bridge between himself and *Akher* is a model for counteracting the reality of Otherness produced by a painful situation burdened by unpleasant emotions. Despite his status, Rabbi Meir's conduct is fiercely criticized in rabbinical texts, especially the Babylonian Talmud,[15] and he evidently paid a personal price for it. But his defenders viewed his behavior in a different light: "Rabbi Meir found a pomegranate, ate the fruit and threw away the peel."[16] Here Otherness is perceived as a peel or rind that can be discarded or ignored; but the fruit

---

15. N' Be'eri, *Went Forth into Evil Courses, Elisha Ben Abuya — Aher* (Hebrew) (Tel Aviv, 2007), pp. 105-70, 173-84.

16. BT *Hagigah* 15b.

itself, the shared basis of the intellectual discourse or the study of Torah, is far more important. A significant and real common basis can be built for both. Whereas Rabbi Akiva's model, which we examined first, offers an option for respectful relations with the Other who remains in his or her Otherness, Rabbi Meir's model permits significant relations with the Other, canceling out the Otherness by turning it into a mere peel or rind.

Rabbi Meir survived the criticism (but paid a certain price, as noted). His model came to occupy an increasingly important place in the canonical literature over the generations and became a familiar narrative of Jewish culture. I can imagine that Rabbi Meir's model might serve as a solid basis for a significant and profound relationship with Others for a limited Jewish group (whose members are at a high moral and spiritual level). What is important for our present discussion, however, is that it supports a significant relationship and profound bond with Others who do not share Jewish beliefs and are not partners in observance of the precepts.

Model 3: A Shared Covenant and Mission: Partnership in Practice of Jews and Gentiles

Both forms — Rabbi Akiva's, which leaves Otherness untouched but finds a way to relate to it positively, and Rabbi Meir's, which neutralizes and almost ignores Otherness — pose an elitist, complex, and hard-to-achieve challenge to a positive and meaningful relationship with the Other. The powerful reality created by observance of the precepts — by the mission — constitutes a fortified wall and impassable barrier between the observant Jew and all others. This means that we must find a new model, one that is linked to the observance of the precepts and ethical practices that can serve as a bridge between the observant Jew and the non-Jewish other. This third model is based, somewhat surprisingly, on a partnership of practice, on collaboration in the mission.

It turns out that it is precisely the mission — the service of the Lord by observing the precepts — that can establish lines that unite Jews and non-Jews; it is just in that place of greatest separation and distance that the exclusion is not hermetic. The Jewish people are a collective that is obligated to the precepts of the Torah, the 613 commandments.[17] But all human beings

17. This precise number of 613 precepts seems to be of late origin. It first appears in a homily of R. Simla'i, who lived in Eretz Israel in the third century (B *Makkot* 24a). The total

are obligated to comply with the seven so-called Noahide commandments;[18] if they do so, they are partners in the mission and merit the designation of "righteous of the nations" even if they do not participate in the covenant:

> The difference between the righteous of Israel and the righteous of the nations: The righteous of Israel are not designated "righteous" until they have observed the entire Torah, but the righteous of the nations, when they have fulfilled the seven commandments incumbent on the descendants of Noah, both the commandments and all their details, are designated "righteous." To what does this refer? When they perform them and say, "it is by virtue of the fact that our ancestor Noah, who had them from On High, commanded us, that we do them; if they did so, they will inherit the World to Come like Israel, and this even though they do not observe the Sabbaths and festivals, because they were not commanded to do so. But if they observed the seven precepts and said, "we heard them from such-and-such a person," or they did it of their own accord, or because it is rational to do so, or if they mixed them up with idolatry — then, even if they observed the entire Torah, they receive their reward exclusively in this world. (*Mishnat Rabbi Eliezer* 6, p. 121)

This is the beginning of a possible partnership between Jews and non-Jews. As noted, it is essentially a shared covenant and mission. The covenant is the first one to appear in the Scriptures. It is an inclusive covenant between God and all humanity. Human beings' part in this covenant, their mission, is the observance of seven commandments God gave to the children of Noah.[19]

I imagine this must sound rather strange. It is easier to understand

---

is not based on a meticulous count of all the commandments in the Torah, but on a hermeneutic idea that the precepts correspond to each of the 248 organs and 365 limbs of the human body. In the Middle Ages halakhists set themselves the task of enumerating precisely 613 precepts; their attempts produced countless disputes that have never been resolved. Rabbi Simeon ben Zemah Duran (1361-1444), for example, proposed restoring the number of 613 to its original aggadic context and suspending all attempts to develop halakhah on its back. All authorities agree that no Jew can fulfill all 613 precepts. In the introduction to his work, the thirteenth-century author of *Sefer ha-Hinnukh* counts only 270 precepts that are binding in the post-Temple era. See also Yakov Levinger, "The Sixty Essential Precepts, according to Maimonides," in Moshe Idel, Zev Harvey, and Eliezer Schweid, eds., *Shlomo Pines Jubilee Volume* (Jerusalem, 1988), vol. 1, pp. 399-421 [Hebrew].

18. *Tosefta, Avodah Zarah* 8:4.

19. Genesis 9:1-7 and related rabbinic interpretation.

some version of a partnership that is theological, ethical (on the level of principles), or ideological, rather than a practical collaboration in the service of God. I do not rule out joint ventures like those. But sharing divine commandments, even if only some of them, and the consequent possibility of accepting the Other as one of the righteous of the nations strikes me as more meaningful — not because the Others may prefer it, but because it is an important start to introduce the acceptance of the Other into the Jewish worldview, to make this acceptable to Jews who could not arrive at authentic acceptance of the Other in any other way, and to deepen their own self-understanding through this acceptance.

If we look closely at the passage cited above, we may detect a deeper aspect that is latent in this collaboration. In theological discourse the path leads from the covenant to the mission. The covenant exemplifies the vision and sets the itinerary; the mission defines that actual implementation, the content of life according to the covenant. But this model, which makes the Other present as a partner in the accomplishment of the precepts, a partner in the mission, inverts the order. It is the practice that counts, first of all: if the Others observe the seven Noahide precepts they are the Jews' collaborators in the mission. The next question is *why* they observe these precepts. What ethical principle or vision guides them? If it is an innate ethical principle or a vision derived from a particularistic or even pagan culture — their action is positive and a human partnership certainly exists. But the non-Jewish Others may observe the seven Noahide precepts because they believe that God enjoined Noah and his descendants to do so; that is, they observe them because they see themselves as commanded to do so. It follows that their collaboration with the Jews is not merely a practical or ethical partnership of observing precepts. It is not just a partnership in a mission, but also a partnership in the covenant, in belief in the divine source of the injunction to observe these commandments. What emerges from the shared mission is a shared covenant of Jews and non-Jews. "If they did so, they will inherit the World to Come like Israel." This is as well the order in Genesis: first God commands the Noahide precepts (Gen. 9:1-7) and later He declares the covenant (Gen. 9:8-17).

Summary and Conclusions

Both Abraham's covenant with God and the covenant at Sinai between the Israelites and God exclude all others. The implementation of those covenants, the mission of observing the precepts, reinforces this exclusion and gives it concrete form in daily life. There are three common ways to proceed: (1) Affirming total segregation of the Other as the enemy, as nonexistent, or irrelevant. (2) Attempting to reinterpret the notion of covenant. To neutralize its isolationist sense, and at the same time to ignore the mission — the obligation to comply with hundreds of precepts whose practical import is to isolate the Jew from the non-Jew or to interpret the mission as *tikkun olam* — reforming the world — and in this way to export it from the obligatory particularistic and communal milieu into the airy spaces of universalism. (3) Trying to deal with the isolationist significance of the covenant and mission as they really are, and inquiring whether the self-segregation and exclusion are hermetic or whether the rabbis have produced positive and constructive models that can be applied to the Other.

The first path is common in large Jewish groups. This fact intensifies the challenge I have taken upon myself in this article, because it means that any discourse that would make the Other present in a positive sense runs up against not only conceptual, textual, and theoretical obstacles, but also cultural and political conflict with a broad sector. I have many reasons for rejecting this approach of total isolationism. For one thing, I believe that it is mistaken, from a Jewish perspective. This approach adds, on top of the exclusion derived from the covenant and the mission, the image of the Other as the enemy (Carl Schmitt),[20] as an element (unnecessary, in my eyes) for reinforcing the group identity. Nor it is moral. Finally, it is unrealistic. That is, it may be realistic to some extent for isolationist groups but cannot provide an existential solution for the public at large. Rejecting this path requires, of course, dealing with it.

To the second path I am even more strongly opposed than I am to the first way. Those who follow it are responsible for the emergence of conceptual dimensions that are divorced from the essential meanings of fundamental concepts such as "covenant" and "mission" as well as from the complex social reality. They have nothing but good intentions, but I cannot relieve them of their responsibility for strengthening the isolationist groups who hold to the first path. The typical themes of this second path are so out of touch and unacceptable that they leave many Jewish groups with no choice but to separate from and exclude the Other. Those who pursue the second way do not imagine, of course, that they are responsible for processes within the isolationist groups. From a superficial reading of

20. See note 5.

the sociological trends they believe that these groups relate directly to the non-Jewish Other. But a complex understanding of the process shows that the masses despise the universalist discourse of Jewish elites both because they cannot understand them and because it is a discourse that is oblivious to the most basic daily features of the culture of the public at large.

So I have chosen the third way: confronting the very real and very significant obstacles to dealing with the Other; examining the fortified wall for gates and drawbridges that were always intended to serve as a built-in passageway (and not something cobbled on later) within the existing systems of a particularistic culture and that are an integral part thereof.

I have identified three forms of the attitude toward the Other. The first model, Rabbi Akiva's, is a complex process at whose conclusion every Jew can make the Other, every non-Jewish human being, present in their own world. The advantage of Rabbi Akiva's model is that, despite its complexity, it is based on a realistic principle. It does not allow us to reject the Other with the assertion that accepting him would require sacrificing oneself or sacrificing another Jew. This model is constructed on a foundation of fulfilling our obligations toward ourselves, toward our family, and toward our people. It would be difficult even for isolationist groups to object to it, because it does not come "at their expense." The defect of this model may be that it leaves the Other faceless and unspecific. We need only declaim that he or she "was created in the image of God." That is, even though we are referring to some Other who is a specific individual, we accept him because Rabbi Akiva assigns him to the universalism of the faceless divine image; and in this sense he is no longer Other.

The second model is Rabbi Meir's. It challenges separation from the Other precisely when such isolation could be understood and even justified morally. Rabbi Meir shows a way to create discourse and dialogue with the ultimate Other, who seems to threaten his own path, who does not share his faith and does not observe the precepts. Rabbi Meir's attitude to *Akher* rests on an intellectual collaboration (study of the Torah), a shared culture (that of the House of Study), and mutual responsibility. He feels a responsibility to persuade *Akher* to return to the straight path and believes that severing all ties with him would be an irresponsible action. There is no danger that he himself will fall, because the Other — his teacher, Elisha ben Avuyah — also feels responsibility toward him, manifested in his unwillingness to allow Rabbi Meir to violate his principles and desecrate the Sabbath on his account. In this model, the Other retains his identity as Other and an individual, just as Rabbi Meir does not deviate

97

from his own path. The shortcoming of this model is that it fails the public test. For broad swaths of the community, who cannot discern all the fine points of the participants' conduct, Rabbi Meir crossed a red line and is plunging into the depths of oblivion. Only an apologetic defense arrests this fall and returns him to the warm bosom of the community consensus.

The third model is based on the seven Noahide precepts. This model creates an immediate collaboration between non-Jews and Jews in the mission — the observance of the precepts and even the covenant, if the non-Jews observe these precepts as divine commands. The advantage of this model is that it can be accepted by very broad sectors and that it is hard to dismiss. It is a very practical partnership that can easily be justified. It does not demand philosophical or theological depth and is not complex. The Jew remains a Jew. The Others remains Other, but at the same time they are partners in the observance of the divine injunctions and active on the same plane. Not only does this approach respect the particular and individual milieus of each group and of each individual within it, it even reinforces it. The consequence is that Otherness, however isolating and separating it may be, can at the same time be the basis for the existence of a genuine common denominator among human beings.

Covenant and Conversion:
The United Mission to Redeem the World

Shlomo Riskin

The word *hope* in English has a positive and optimistic connotation, as in "hope for the best." However, it does not suggest certitude of outcome. Much the opposite: I don't *hope* to graduate if I have passed all my exams and fulfilled all the requirements; I *know* that I shall graduate. On the other hand, I do *hope* to participate in my grandson's wedding, although he might not as yet have even chosen his fiancée.

In Hebrew, however, the word for hope *(tikvah)* contains the added nuance of *faith,* the anticipation of a blessed event that I know will occur because it has been guaranteed by God. This is the force behind Israel's national anthem, "Hatikvah," which glories in the fact that "our hope (faith) was never lost, our two-thousand-year-old hope (and faith) . . . that we will be a free nation in our land of Zion and Jerusalem." Indeed, it was this belief that faith can turn anticipated hope into cognitive certainty that kept the Jewish people alive as a committed, separate ethnic entity despite their two millennia of homeless peregrinations, persecutions, and pogroms.

Probably the best source for the identity of hope and faith is Psalm 27:

> To David: The Lord is my light and my salvation; whom must I fear? The Lord is the stronghold of my life, whom must I be afraid of? Although evildoers are near me, about to consume my flesh, and my enemies and foes are arrayed against me, they will falter and they will fall. . . . Have hope (*kavei,* faith) in the Lord, be strong and make your heart courageous, and have hope (*kavei,* faith) in the Lord.

When hope turns into faith because the outcome of your salvation is guaranteed by God, then you truly have nothing to fear — for your faith "in" God's word surely leads to belief "that" his guarantees will eventually be delivered.[1] Here the two topics of this theological project come together magnificently: Hope and Covenant as well as Responsibility and Mission. First, our optimistic hope (faith) for the realization of God's covenantal promise to Abraham that "through you all the families of the earth shall be blessed" (Gen. 12:3), that at the "end of the days, when the Temple Mount shall be established on the top of the mountains . . . all of the nations shall rush there; . . . nation will not lift up sword against nation and humanity will not learn war anymore" (Isa. 2:2-4); and then our responsibility to *"convert"* the world to the ideals of peace on earth as a result of universal moral principles (i.e., the seven Noahide laws) emanating from "the word of God from Jerusalem" that will move the process of messianic redemption forward. In this essay I will attempt to define the Jewish role in these endeavors, particularly our obligation to "convert the gentiles," bearing in mind that we must define precisely both what we mean by "convert" and who is included as "gentiles." I will then explain how Jews and Christians must join hands in hope and covenant as well as in terms of responsibility and mission.

Reasons for Despair

I begin with hope. Reading the newspapers or watching daily news programs is sufficient for one to logically conclude that the belief that we are moving towards a perfect human society, a messianic and redemptive endgame, is sheer naïveté and unworthy of a rational human being.

Look around at our world. Barely seven decades after the Holocaust the United Nations, which was created with the hope of ensuring world peace, time and time again gives a respected and well-publicized forum to the mad President of Iran, Mahmoud Ahmadinejad, for him to spew his hateful anti-Zionist and anti-Jewish venom; the United Nations refuses to enforce stringent economic sanctions that might prevent Iran's hell-bent purpose of developing nuclear weapons of destruction. North Korea flexes its nuclear muscles while thumbing its nose at the United States in front of a largely stunned but silent world. All of this is the backdrop to widespread and violent Islamist extremism, with terrorist suicide bombers preaching Jihad and death to any infidel who refuses to endorse their brand of reli-

1. Martin Buber, *Two Types of Faith* (Syracuse, NY: Syracuse University Press, 2003).

gious extremism. This extremism is not only taking over the Muslim world, but also threatens to engulf Europe and the West.

If the threat of nuclear self-destruction were not sufficient, global warming and the havoc we have wrought by polluting the air we breathe by our disregard for ecological concerns — all in the name of "progress" — will probably finish off any life that manages to survive the next world war. Indeed, Freud's id, expressing the dark, death-desiring, and destructive dimension of the human personality, appears to be far more powerful than the "portion of God from on High, the image of God" aspect of the human being that could lead us to salvation and world peace.

From this perspective, Europe's negative population growth, as well as the banner of gay parades and the advocating of alternative marital unions even for those finding sexual satisfaction in heterosexual relationships, seem like a more logical response to the world marching straight into doomsday than is a belief in a messianic era of human perfection — an ideal that is a unique gift that Jews bequeathed to Western civilization.[2]

The Jewish Messiah and Faith in Humanity

In defense of optimism and hope, I would like to analyze a curious aspect of biblical Judaism, a teaching that is *prima facie* quite strange. King David of the tribe of Judah — the progenitor of the Messiah according to the Jewish tradition — can only lay claim to a very problematic lineage. His great-grandfather, Boaz, was born (eight generations previously) from an act of incest between Judah and his daughter-in-law, Tamar, who posed as a harlot in order to have a child. Judah is father of the tribe from whom the Prince of Peace will one day emerge (Gen. 38–39:10; Ruth 4:18-22).

On David's maternal side was a disputed convert to Judaism, Ruth. She was a Moabite princess, and although the Bible forbade Moabite converts into the Jewish people (Deut. 23:4), the religious court of Boaz ruled nevertheless that the prohibition applied only to male Moabites, not to females. Moreover, Moab, Ruth's direct ancestor, was a result of incest between Lot and his elder daughter (Gen. 19:30-38). Apparently, Ruth,

2. See Matthew Arnold, "Hebraism and Hellenism," in Philip Goodman, *The Hanukkah Anthology* (New York: Jewish Publication Society, 1992); Leo Strauss, "Jerusalem and Athens," reprinted in *Jewish Philosophy and the Crisis of Modernity* (Albany: State University of New York Press, 1997), pp. 377-405; and Thomas Cahill, *Gifts of the Jews* (New York: Random House, 1999).

great-grandmother of the progenitor of the Messiah, stemmed from a questionable relationship! So, what is expressly Jewish in having the Messiah emanate from acts of adultery and incest?

The rabbinical sages of the *Midrash*[3] maintained that this messianic ancestry was purposely designed, their prooftext being the strange use of the word *zera* (seed), rather than *ben* (child or son), in reference to Boaz and Lot. When Boaz marries Ruth in the Scroll of Ruth, the Israelites bless the couple at the gates of the city of Efrat: "May your house become like the house of Peretz, whom Tamar bore to Judah, from the seed *(zera)* which the Lord gave you from this young woman *(na'arah)*" (Ruth 4:12).

Since it would be uncharacteristic for the text to refer to Ruth — a widow for at least a decade — as a young woman *(na'arah)*, when describing the incest between Lot and his daughter, the rabbis interpret the verse (Gen. 19:31) "And the elder daughter said to the younger. . . . 'Come, let us give wine to our father to drink, and let us lie with him, so that we may enable our father to give life to (his) seed *(zera)*'" as follows: "This (*zera* in the Scroll of Ruth) is part of the same *zera* that came from a strange other place (i.e., from Lot). From these seeds came King Messiah."[4]

Possibility for Change as a Source of Optimism

I understand this Jewish tradition to be teaching that despite the appearance that the belief in human perfectibility appears to be absurd, the notion that good may emerge from evil, that exalted and majestic sanctity can grow from the dregs of immoral sexuality, is built into the very ancestry of the Jewish concept of the Messiah. Just as the daughter of the cruel and flagrantly inhospitable Moab could be the loving, kind, and gracious Ruth, a generation of despair and disrepair can rehabilitate itself and bring a redeeming Messiah.[5]

---

3. The rabbinic literature explicating Hebrew Scriptures compiled from the first century CE.

4. Rabbi Tanhuma in the name of R. Yosi ben Pazi, *Midrash Rut Zuta;* Buber, *Two Types of Faith*, pp. 4, 12.

5. This may be the source for the unusual Jewish custom of eating dairy foods on the Festival of *Shavuot* when Jews publicly read the Scroll of Ruth. Despite the fact that Jewish law prescribes meat for Sabbath and festival meals, Jews eat milk products coming from animals to show that Jewish law recognizes how derivatives can differ from their source. Ruth can come from Moab and the Messiah can emerge from messiness.

My spiritual teacher, the most important Orthodox Talmudist and philosopher of the twentieth century, Rabbi Joseph B. Soloveitchik, read this very message and more into *Midrash,* insisting that this is precisely the lesson that Lot's daughter attempted to impress upon her younger sister. Commenting on Genesis 19:31, "The elder sister said to the younger, our father is old and there is no man throughout the land to come upon us (impregnate us) in the manner of all societies . . . ," another *Midrash*[6] suggests that "these sisters believed the entire world had been destroyed as in the days of the great flood," since the apparent earthquake that destroyed Sodom and Gomorrah seemed to them to have consumed the entire world. Hence, taught Rabbi Soloveitchik, the elder sister suggested that each in turn seduce their father to impregnate them to begin to repopulate the universe.

The younger sister demurs, expressing disgust at the act of incest; but more importantly, she sees no point in attempting to restart the universe. After all, God had attempted to establish a more perfect world, first in Eden with Adam and Eve, then again with Noah and the Covenant of the Rainbow (Genesis 9), and for a third time with Abraham. Each experiment ended in failure for a humanity that sank repeatedly into depravity. It would be absurd — and in this case of incest, immoral — to start humanity once more.

At this point the elder sister would not be silenced, contended Rabbi Soloveitchik. She argued that God would never have created the human being in the Divine Image, if evil were destined to emerge triumphant and if human civilization would destroy itself. No, she insisted, we must have faith in the possibility of repentance, of change, of human perfectibility. Because belief in the Messiah is predicated fundamentally upon faith in the possibility of human change throughout the world, an era in which all "spears will be turned into ploughshares and humanity will not learn war anymore," it is appropriate that the seed of the sexual relationship between Lot and his elder daughter be the sacred seed that ultimately led to messianic lineage.

God's Covenants with the World

From a biblical perspective, hope *for* and faith *in* the advent of a perfected world of peace and security is not dependent upon God alone. Not only

6. *Midrash Breishit Rabbah* (Vilna) Parasha 51, 8.

must humanity undergo a fundamental change, individual by individual, but there must be human catalysts who inspire them to want to change and who educate them how to change. A Yiddish adage has it, "humans must act, if God is to activate." The interface between hope (faith) in the divine promise and human responsibility to actively be engaged in making it happen is expressed in the biblical term "covenant," a two-way contractual and immutable relationship between God and human beings.[7]

The first of God's biblical covenants was with Noah (and derivatively with all humanity), in which God promises never again to destroy the world by flood. He stipulates at the same time that humanity must not destroy itself by violence. The rainbow is God's symbol of the divine side of the agreement (Gen. 9:9). The prohibitions against eating a limb or the blood of a living animal, against suicide and murder — and according to the talmudic sages, the remaining moral Noahide laws (not to steal, not to indulge in sexual licentiousness, not to worship idols, not to blaspheme God, to establish law courts) and the requirement to procreate were the responsibilities of humanity (Gen. 9:4-7).

God's First Two Covenants with the Hebrews

The Bible teaches that ten generations after Noah, when humanity had again descended into violence and immorality, God made a strategic decision to choose a nation to consecrate as his special agents to the world. God therefore elected Abram, commanding him to leave behind his land and birthplace of idolatry to become a great nation through whom "all the families of the earth shall be blessed" (Gen. 12:1-3). God then entered into two covenants with Abram and his descendants. In the first, God promised Abraham (Hebrew for "father of a multitude of nations") seed and a homeland (Genesis 15) — the necessary appurtenances of a nation, which is a family writ large. (Parents and children dwelling together in a place of habitation, a home, generally comprise a family.) The Bible strikingly explains for what purpose Abraham was elected:

> "Abraham will surely become a great and holy nation, and through him shall be blessed all the nations of the earth. I have loved, recognized and singled him out [all three verbs are legitimate translations for the He-

---

7. See Joshua Berman, "God's Alliance with Man," *Azure*, Summer 5766/2006.

brew root 'y-d-a' — SR] because he shall command his children and his household after him to keep the way of the Lord, doing compassionate righteousness *[tsedakah]* and justice *[mishpat]*, in order that the Lord might bring upon Abraham what He said about him." (Gen. 18:18-19)

In other words, *we can hope for and have faith in the eternal nation-hood of Israel, that the Jewish seed will never be destroyed and the Jewish people will become united with our homeland, as long as the children of Abraham fulfill their responsibility to imbue all future generations with compassionate righteousness and justice.*

The second covenant is with the Israelite nation on Mt. Sinai, wherein God added to Jewish national identity a distinct religious identity, the Ten Commandments of the divine revelation (Exodus 20), and according to normative Jewish tradition the entire legal structure of 613 commandments that serves as the Jewish national constitution (Exod. 21–24; Lev. 25:1-2). These laws serve to unite Jews wherever they may live on the globe, and provide moral, ethical, and ritual boundaries even when Jews are temporarily bereft of our homeland (Exod. 19:4-6). In other words, Jews have every right to hope for and have faith in their development as a unique and eternal religion connecting to God in a special way and even affecting the entire world.[8] However, the Jewish people has the responsibility to observe the laws if it expects them to work! Compassionate righteousness and justice are not sufficient; becoming a sacred nation requires at least the Ten Commandments, and the 613 Mosaic commandments given at Sinai, according to Jewish tradition.[9]

The Third Covenant

So God entered into a *covenant of nationality* with Abraham, and into a *covenant of religion* with the newly formed people of Israel when the Jewish people was freed from Egypt. The powerful message in this exquisite timing — revelation at Sinai having occurred seven weeks after the exodus — is that freedom requires ethical and moral responsibility.

It is generally not recognized that there is yet a *third covenant*, presented by God before the Jewish people entered the promised land of Israel.

8. See commentary of R. Obadiah Seforno on *Mamlekhet Kohanim*, Exodus 19:6.

9. "All 613 commandments are under the rubric of the Ten Commandments," *Midrash BaMidbar Rabbah* 13:16, cited by Rashi, Exodus 24:12.

This third covenant consists of twelve, not ten, commandments. It does not seem to include the other commands in the four chapters following the Decalogue (Exodus 21–24) or the other biblical commands throughout the Pentateuch, although it does reiterate other moral and universal biblical teachings. This covenant is to be written on stones taken from the River Jordan when it splits into dry land, allowing the Israelites to pass through on their way into the Promised Land after Moses' death (Josh. 3:4-18). The Bible stresses that it is to be "well clarified" *(be'er hetev)*, which rabbinic tradition interprets as the commandment to translate this covenant into the seventy languages of all the nations of the world.[10]

The Bible also delineates the punishments that will befall the Israelites if they disregard this covenant; at the conclusion of the litany, the Bible states: "These are the words of the covenant which the Lord commanded Moses to seal with the children of Israel in the land of Moab, aside from [in addition to] the covenant which He sealed with them at Horeb" (Deut. 28:69), emphasizing the unique nature of this third covenant.

What is the message of this third, additional covenant, especially since our other two covenants have already designated us as an eternal nation and an eternal religion? I submit that this is the Covenant of Universal Redemption, which can only come about if the nations of the world accept fundamental biblical morality. It is the covenant that squarely places upon the Jewish people the responsibility of teaching the moral truths of the Bible to the world. This explains why this covenant is sealed only when the Jewish people are about to enter the Land of Israel: Only a people that has its own homeland and is a nation amongst nations that must deal with problems of peace and war, economic and social gaps within society, poverty, crime, and minorities, can ever hope to influence and inspire other nations to accept an ethic of compassionate righteousness, justice, and peace. In this way, the third covenant links together in an indelible bind the two previous covenants of ethnic nationality and religious morality. It is important to note that the laws delineated in this third covenant are all directed to *"ish,"* the Hebrew generic term for "person" — as opposed to "Jews." They are universal in import:

"Cursed is the person *("ish")* who degrades his father or mother." . . .
"Cursed is the person who puts a stumbling block before the blind." . . .

10. B.T. *Sotah* 37b, cited by Rashi in his commentary to Deuteronomy 27:8.

"Cursed is the person who perverts the judgment of the widow and the orphan." . . .

"Cursed is the person who receives a bribe to slay an innocent person." (Deut. 27:15-26)

This also explains why the Sabbath and circumcision are not mentioned in this third covenant, although circumcision is an important aspect of the first covenant and the Sabbath is an important component of the Decalogue and Sinai covenant. Despite the fact that the first "curse" applies to "the person who will make a graven or molten image, an abomination to the Lord," recall that one of the seven Noahide commandments of morality was the prohibition against idolatry. Noahides are not obligated to believe in God, but they are prohibited from engaging in the cruel and immoral acts that idolaters performed in the names of the idols. Indeed, according to some rabbinic opinion, idolatry is defined by immoral acts rather than theological error.[11] It is interesting to note that virtually in every place that the Pentateuch deplores idolatry and forbids idol worship, it adds the reason "lest we learn from their practices" (Exod. 23:24; Deut. 7:5-11; 12:3-4, 30, 31; 18:9-13; 20:17-18).

This universal message of the third covenant may likewise be why, immediately after the content of the third covenant is delineated, the Bible records, "Not with you (Israelites) alone do I seal this covenant and this imprecation, but with whoever is here, standing with us today before the Lord our God, and also with whoever is not here with us today" (Deut. 29:13-14). The meaning of these words seems to be the inclusion of the gentiles as well as the Israelites: the gentiles who are not with us today will one day stand with us in acceptance of the fundamental laws of morality.

This is also why the sages of the Talmud saw fit to interpret the biblical *"be'er hetev"* (well clarified) to mean "translated into seventy languages of the world." Were these moral laws only meant for Jews, there would be no need to translate them into the languages of the gentiles or to position them on the twelve stones placed in Gilgal, at the point of entry and exit into Israel near the two great mountains of Gerizim and Eybal (Deut. 27:1-9). This locus of the twelve stones was Israel's gateway to the world, to where and from where Israelites and gentiles would come and go, read, and reflect upon whatever was displayed on those stones.

11. See Jacob Katz, *Exclusivism and Tolerance* (New York: Schocken, 1962), ch. 10; and Moshe Halbertal and Avishai Margolit, *Idolatry* (Cambridge, MA: Harvard University Press, 1992), pp. 204-9.

Which Torah Is to Be Taught to the Gentiles?

It is difficult to know precisely which text was to be written on the stones, as the verse declares, "and you shall write upon the stones all the words of this Torah (teaching), well clarified" (Deut. 27:8). I have assumed it refers to the "Torah" of the third covenant, the twelve moral laws on the twelve stones that are delineated in verses 15-26 — six blessings expressed by six tribes on Mt. Gerizim and six curses expressed by six other tribes on Mt. Eybal (Deut. 27:9-26). The medieval biblical exegete Isaac Abravenel interpreted "all the words of this Torah" to mean some parts of Deuteronomy, which can refer to the verses of "Cursed be," as I maintain. Another medieval commentator, Abraham Ibn Ezra, believes that "a number (or the number) of commandments . . . like warnings" were written on the stones. He well may be referring to the twelve imprecations (*azharot,* warnings), as well.[12]

However, Maimonides (ad loc) suggests that all 613 commandments were written on the stones, and the Aramaic Targumim[13] together with the majority of the biblical commentaries claim that the entire Pentateuch was somehow inscribed — with seventy translations — on those twelve stones (sic!). In truth, and perhaps in support of this latter view, the Book of Joshua records, "and (Joshua) inscribed there on stone a copy of the Torah of Moses" (8:32). However, I would argue that these Hebrew words may also be taken to mean the Deuteronomy of Moses or even a part thereof.

If I am correct in interpreting this third covenant to be a covenant for all the nations of the world, the implications of this debate are serious indeed. Are Jews covenantally responsible to teach gentiles only the seven Noahide laws and these twelve moral imprecations, or is the Jewish people duty bound to teach the world all 613 commandments to convert them to Judaism? I will analyze this question in greater depth before concluding this study. I add here that there are actually three possibilities: (1) Jews are responsible to teach gentiles only the universal laws of Noah and the twelve imprecations; (2) it would be salutary — but not necessary — for gentiles to learn and practice all 613 commandments, and hence Jews ought to expose them to the entire Torah but are not obligated to convert them; (3) Jews are obligated to teach gentiles and even attempt to convert them. However, Jews are only to coerce gentiles regarding acceptance of the Noahide laws.

12. See their respective commentaries on the Bible, ad loc.
13. The traditional Aramaic translation of the original Hebrew biblical text.

Conversion and the Jewish Responsibility to the World

We have seen that at the moment of the election of Abraham, God explicitly proclaimed, "Through you (Abraham), shall all the families of the earth be blessed" (Genesis 12–13). God repeats this universal directive immediately after the binding (and near-sacrifice) of Isaac at the place of the future Temple Mount, stating that "through your seed all the nations of the earth shall be blessed" (Gen. 22:14-18). God ordains this same mission for Isaac (Gen. 26:4), and then for Jacob: "And your seed shall be as the dust of the earth, and you shall spread out significantly westward, eastward, northward and southward, and all the families of the earth shall be blessed by you and by your seed" (Gen. 28:14). Hence from the inception of our faith Jews were ordained to be a blessing to the world, apparently by virtue of teaching the gentiles the message of Abrahamic ethical monotheism and to fulfill the biblical mandate to be "a kingdom of priest-teachers" (Exod. 19:6).

The third covenant reflects yet a third creation, the redemption of the world, "the last for which the first was made," the very goal of the initial creation. This is the new covenant in which God will place His Torah within us, will inscribe it onto our hearts. The Torah will not be foreign to us but will emanate from the portion of the divine within each and every human being, so "no one will have to teach about God, for everyone will know Him, all of humanity together" (Jer. 31:30-33). At that time "no one will injure or destroy in all My holy mountain, for the earth will be filled with the knowledge of the Lord as the waters cover the sea bed" (Isa. 11:9).

This third covenant reflects the truth that the Jewish people are "God's witnesses"[14] and affirms the Jewish covenantal responsibility to bear witness before all of humanity. The *Midrash* defines the Jewish obligation in a specific way:

> The Bible teaches, "a person is considered a sinner if he heard a false oath, and he is a witness either because he saw or knows the truth; if he does not give testimony, he must bear the guilt" (Lev. 5:1). "He is a witness" — this refers to Israel, as it is said, "You are My witnesses, says the Lord" (Isa. 43:13). "Either because he saw" — as it says, "You [Israel] have been shown in order to know that the Lord He is God" (Dt. 4:39) "and if he does not give testimony, he must bear the guilt" — if you [Is-

---

14. "You are My witnesses," says the Lord, "and I am God" (Isa. 43:13).

rael] do not declare My Lordship to the nations of the world, I shall exact punishment from you.[15]

Another *midrash*[16] emphasizes that the Torah was revealed in the desert rather than in the land of Israel to express the truth that the revelation at Sinai was intended for all peoples, not just for Jews:

> "They encamped in the wilderness" (Exodus 19:2). The Torah was given in a free place *(demos, parresia)*. For had the Torah been given in the Land of Israel, the Israelites could have said to the nations of the world, "You have no share in it." But now that it was given in the wilderness publicly and openly, in a place that is free for all, everyone wishing to accept it, could come and accept it.[17]

The Third Covenant Is Read Publicly before Rosh Hashanah

The Talmud records a striking and frightening prescription concerning when certain biblical texts are read in the synagogue:

> R. Shimon ben Elazar says, Ezra (the Scribe) enacted for the Israelites that they publicly read the Curses of the Book of Leviticus before Shavuot (The Feast of Pentecost, *atzeret*) and the Curses of the Book of Deuteronomy before Rosh Hashana. (B.T. *Megillah* 31b)

The two biblical texts known as "the curses" are Leviticus 26:14-46 and Deuteronomy 28:15-69. Each of these begins with the exile of the Israelites from the land of Israel, leading the medieval rabbinic authority Nahmanides to maintain that the Leviticus curses refer to the Babylonian exile after the destruction of the First Temple (586 BCE), while the Deuteronomy curses refer to the exile after Rome's destruction of the Second Temple in 70 CE.

Ezra the Scribe worked out the schedule for Jews to read specific biblical portions each week in synagogue, and he prescribed that they read the Leviticus punishments before the reading of the Sinai covenant and Ten Commandments on the Pentecost Festival that commemorates revelation

15. *Leviticus Rabbah* 6.
16. *Mekilta de R. Yishmael, Bahodesh* 1 (Lauterbach, ed.), p. 198.
17. Marc Hirshman, *Torah for the Entire World* (Tel Aviv: Kibbutz HaMeuchad, 1999), especially ch. 7.

of the Torah at Sinai — despite the fact that the Sinai Decalogue occurred chronologically well before the Leviticus punishments in the Bible. However, Jewish tradition decided that Jews not read the Deuteronomy curses as Ezra ordained, but two Sabbaths before, and it reserved the latter portion of Deuteronomy 29–30 for the Sabbath immediately before Rosh Hashanah, the Jewish New Year.

Why does Jewish practice today depart from Ezra's prescribed reading sequence? I maintain that the biblical portion of *Nitzavim* (Deut. 29:9ff.) is a direct continuation of the third covenant in the previous portion:

> You are standing today, all of you, before the Lord, your God, from the heads of your tribes . . . to the drawer of your water, for you to pass into the covenant of the Lord your God and into His imprecation. . . . Not with you alone do I seal this covenant . . . but with whoever is here . . . and with whoever is not here with Me today. (Deut. 29:9-14)

As I have interpreted, these last words refer to the gentile community, which was not yet standing together with the Israelites when they were poised to enter the Land of Israel close to four thousand years ago. Yet the third covenant was meant to include them, as far as the moral laws of the twelve imprecations.[18]

It is thus understandable why the talmudic sages prescribed the third covenant to be read before Rosh Hashanah, since it is the most universal Jewish holiday. The New Year's liturgy maintains that Rosh Hashanah is the day "on which the world was conceived, when the first human being was formed in God's womb." On that date Jews blow the *shofar* (trumpet)

---

18. My revered teacher Rav Soloveitchik offered another reason why *Nitzavim* is a continuation of *Ki Tavo;* the curses of Ki Tavo conclude with a promise of return just as was the case in *Behukotai,* yet not immediately. Jews must wait for the following biblical chapter of *Nitzavim.* It is there (Deut. 30:4, 5) that God promises "Even if you are scattered to the end of the heavens, from there the Lord your God will bring you to the land that your ancestors possessed and you shall possess it." Why is the promise not immediate? Because God tells us that in the instance of the Second Destruction, Jewish return will depend upon our repentance, and so the exhortation to repent and its historical occurrence must precede the promise to return (Deut. 30:1-10). "Return" involves a physical return to the Land of Israel as well as spiritual return to God's biblical teachings. Indeed, the two unique and revolutionary Jewish movements of this past century are 1) Zionism, a return to Israel initiated by the people rather than a passive waiting for a reluctant Messiah, and 2) the Ba'al Teshuvah (repentants) movement, bringing alienated Jews "home" to their traditional roots in a radical change of persona, à la Franz Rosenzweig. See Nahum Glatzer, *Franz Rosenzweig: His Life and Thought* (Indianapolis: Hackett, 1998).

of world redemption to anticipate the day "when all the inhabitants and dwellers of the earth will see the banner of God hoisted upon the mountains and will hear the sounds of the *shofar*," as Isaiah 18:3 insisted. Indeed, the central prayer of the day is the *Alenu* prayer, in which Jews are called "to perfect the world in the Kingship of the Almighty, when all children of flesh will call upon Your Name and all the wicked of the earth will turn towards You . . . when everyone will accept the yoke of Your Kingship and You will rule over them forever." Ten days later on Yom Kippur, the Fast of Universal Forgiveness, Jews repeatedly recite God's own prayer that, "My house (i.e., the Temple) shall be called a House of Prayer for all peoples" (Isa. 56:7). And the universal kingship of God is described by the High Holiday liturgy as the time when "All created beings will fear You and all creatures will bow down before You; everyone will unite in one bond to carry out Your will with a full heart."

The third covenant and the High Holiday liturgy both emphasize the Jewish responsibility for the world and thus the two experiences are conjoined. It is now not only clear as to why the curses are publicly read before Rosh Hashanah, and why the third covenant is known as the covenant of the responsibility *("berit arevut")*.[19] The Hebrew term *arev* denotes a cosigner, i.e., one who assumes legal responsibility for paying a loan when the debtor defaults. This third covenant, exhorting the Jewish people to teach ethical monotheism to the world, is crucially important for a free world to survive. In our global village where one extremist madman can set off a nuclear war and destroy humanity, without the universal acceptance of "Thou shall not murder an innocent person" no person is safe or secure. Each one of us — humanity in its entirety — is responsible for the other, co-signers for each other. We dare not "ask for whom the bell tolls"; it tolls for all of us together!

The Jewish covenantal mission is to teach the world ethical monotheism, as the term *kingdom of priest-teachers* (Exod. 19:6) suggests. If the Jewish people fail to fulfill this responsibility its onus is grave indeed. The Jewish people will suffer the consequences for the sins of the nations of the world. The nations will hate us because we gave them a divine moral order, but which they chose to dismiss. It is easier to shoot the messenger rather than refute the message. Hence we will become the first victims of hateful arrows and will be "the suffering servants," casualties of human immorality (Isaiah 53). This may be why the covenant was sealed in the

19. B.T. *Sotah* 23b-87b.

Plains of Moab. Ruth, the celebrated convert to Judaism, hailed from Moab, and according to the Bible she was destined to be the progenitor of the Messiah, the standard bearer for Judaism that fulfills its mission with world redemption.

Is There a Jewish Obligation to Convert?

Conventional wisdom is that Judaism is not a proselytizing religion and that we do not encourage — and perhaps that we are even legally mandated to discourage — proselytes to Judaism. I have argued that there is an undisputable Jewish obligation that Jews have largely abandoned since the Hadrianic persecutions in 135 CE: It is to actively proselytize gentiles to accept the seven Noahide laws of morality or the twelve imprecations of the third covenant. Maimonides' formulation of this obligation leaves no room for doubt:

> Moses our Master did not bequeath the Torah and the Commandments to anyone except to Israel, as it is written, "Moses commanded to us the Torah, a heritage for the Congregation of Jacob" (Dt. 33:4) as well as to those of the nations of the world who wish to convert, as it is written, "The Congregation (of Israel) shall have the same statute for you and for the convert who lives among you" (Num. 15:15). But one who doesn't wish to convert is not to be forced to accept the Torah and its commandments. Similarly, Moses our Master commanded Israel *to force* everyone to accept all of the commandments commanded to Noah.[20]

A beneficent social order is dependent on the acceptance of the fundamental principles of morality, and no human being is safe when another individual rejects these fundamental laws. Hence we have the right to coerce, if necessary, people to accept these universal laws of morality. Moreover, according to Maimonides once an individual accepts this ethical system and acknowledges its divine authority and hence its permanent validity, he is worthy of salvation and has a share in the world to come.[21]

---

20. *Mishneh Torah* (henceforth MT), Laws of Kings 8:10.
21. MT, Laws of Kings 8:11. For the scholarly discussion of this important passage and its implications, see Eugene Korn, "Gentiles, the World to Come and Judaism," *Modern Judaism* (October 1994).

Shlomo Riskin

Two Types of Commandments
and the Commandment to Convert

Is there a specific commandment for Jews to convert gentiles to Judaism? Since a life of commitment to the seven Noahide commandments is sufficient for non-Jews to secure a place in the world to come, it is clear to me that there is no *obligatory* commandment *(mitsvah hiyuvit)* upon a Jew to convert a gentile to all the Jewish commandments. There is, however, a type of commandment known as a *fulfillment* commandment *(mitsvah kiyumit)*. One is not obligated to act on this commandment, but if he/she chooses to do so of his/her own free choice, he/she then indeed fulfills a divinely desirable act. For example, no one is obligated to become a physician; if he does, however, and saves a person's life, he fulfills the divinely desirable act of saving lives. I maintain, therefore, that if the gentile *chooses* to convert, even though it is not necessary, he would then be fulfilling such a divinely desirable act. This is an important position, if only to ensure a welcoming attitude towards gentiles who display interest in becoming Jews.

The Talmud[22] ordains that when a would-be convert is circumcised for the sake of conversion, the Jew who oversees the act intones the blessing, "Blessed art thou, O Lord, King of the Universe, who has sanctified us with His commandments and has *commanded us to circumcise the converts* and to extract from them the blood of the covenant." The assumption of the Talmud may be that there is a commandment to convert.[23] Other biblical[24] and medieval rabbinic sources[25] suggest there is a commandment to convert also.[26]

22. B.T. *Shabbat* 137a.

23. Nahmanides concludes that the commandment to perform the act of conversion as symbolic of entry of the gentile into the covenant of Israel actually devolves upon the convert himself, even though he cannot yet be technically commanded since he is not yet Jewish (novella of Nahmanides on this passage in B.T. *Shabbat*); hence the blessing is to be made by the Jew overseeing the conversion process. See also B.T. *Yabamot* 47b and 48b, which imply that conversion is a commandment.

24. Genesis 12:25, in emulation of Abraham and Sarah, and Deuteronomy 10:9.

25. See commentary of Yosef of Barcelona on Deuteronomy 10:9; R. Yitzhak Perla, *Elucidations to the Book of Commandments of Rabbenu Saadeh Gaon,* Positive Commandment 19; Rabad of Posquierie, *Ba'alei Nefesh,* end of Gate of Immersion, 3 on Genesis 12:25; Maimonides, *Book of the Commandments,* Positive Commandment 3, on Deuteronomy 6:5.

26. Talmudic texts record both pros and cons of accepting converts. For texts supporting the recruitment of converts, see B.T. *Pesahim* 87b, B.T. *Nedarim* 32a, and *Sanhedrin* 99b. *Mishneh Avot* 1:12 also seems to support conversion. For texts discouraging conversion, see

To what extent these sources point to a commandment to convert gentiles to complete Judaism or merely to belief in one God, or to something in between, I will analyze further on in this essay. Suffice it to say at this point that the sages of the Talmud deemed it salutary to educate all of humanity to a religious commitment and understanding *beyond* the seven Noahide laws, which do not demand belief in one God. The obligatory obligation to convert applies only to the seven major moral commandments, because they are crucial for a free humanity to survive, but not to the formal entry into Judaism as a nationality and a religion.

Conversion of Gentiles in the Second Commonwealth

Prior to the Hadrianic persecutions, Jews actively proselytized. During the First Temple period, conversion by definition meant first and foremost to live in Israel; as Ruth says, "Wherever you shall go (the land of Israel), I shall go" (Ruth 1:16) and only afterwards adds, "Your nation shall be my nation, and your God shall be my God." During the Second Temple, when the majority of Jews lived outside of the land of Israel, geographic location ceased to be a criterion. The Book of Judith in the Apocrypha praises a proselyte who recognized all that the God of Israel accomplished, circumcised himself, and joined himself with the house of Israel "until this very day" (Judith 14:10). Yet the real population explosion of Jews due to conversion of gentiles didn't take place until the end of the Second Temple period.[27] The Sybilline Oracle (140 BCE) records that "it is the vision of the nation Israel that every land and every nation be filled with its prophecies" (3:271), and that "the nation of the Almighty God dwells all over, becomes strong, acts valiantly and teaches their way of life to all of humanity together" (3:194).

Even earlier, Plato recorded that Jews were exploding in population and were already inhabiting Egypt, Syria, Babylon, Asia Minor, and Europe. Josephus bears out this testimony:

> Through our hands the laws have been revealed to the rest of humanity.... The Hellenistic philosophers were the first...; in their life-style

---

B.T. *Yebamot* 109b and *Kiddushin* 70b. There is extended rabbinic discussion surrounding these texts on the desirability of conversion. The biblical Book of Ruth also highlights the benefits to the Jewish people and the world that are derived from converts to Judaism.

27. See Shmuel Safrai, "Conversion at the End of the Second Temple Period and in the Generations Following the Destruction," (Heb) *Maḥanaim* 92, pp. 82-87.

and their teachings they cling to Moses. . . . There is no city from among the Hellenic cities and no nation from among the Barbaric nations where the customs of resting (from work) on the seventh day, fasting on Yom Kippur, lighting the Sabbath and Festival candles and refraining from all forbidden foods have not spread. And how wondrous it is that they are keeping these (Jewish) customs not for the sake of personal gain. . . . It is the power of the Torah itself which moves them. Just as our God fills the entire world, so has His Torah spread out to encompass all human seed.[28]

Apparently proselytization continued even after the destruction of the Temple. Seneca (first century BCE) mocks Jewish fealty to the Sabbath, but concludes, "The customs of this wicked nation have been absorbed by the entire world; the conquered have caused their laws to be adopted by the conquerors."[29]

Within the talmudic literature, the sage Hillel went so far as to entice gentiles with study stipends to teach them Torah and to ease them into conversion. The Talmud (B.T. *Shabbat* 31) also records how Hillel converted virtually anyone who expressed a desire to do so, no matter what conditions the would-be convert demanded, confident that in *subsequent* lessons Hillel could disabuse them of their conditions. The Talmud likewise records traditions that the rabbis Shmaya and Avtalyon, Onkelos, Ben Bag Bag, and Ben Heh Heh were all proselytes, and that Rabbi Akiba and Rabbi Meir were born into families of proselytes. The *Tosefta* (*Pesaḥim* 6:15) recounts that when a large group of Roman legions converted the day before Passover, they ate of the Passover sacrifice that very night of the *Seder* in accordance with the view of the Academy of Shammai.

When interpreting Song of Songs 1:15, R. Yehudah the Prince expounded, "There is a type of dove which, when it's being fed, gives off a certain fragrance which attracts its friends to come to its dove-cote. A similar phenomenon occurs with Israel. At the time when the Elder sits and expounds Torah (to his disciples), many proselytes convert at that very time. . . ."[30] Finally, the blessing of the daily statutory prayer *(Amidah)*, which praises God for being a "support and security for the righteous," opens with the words: "Upon the righteous, upon the pious, upon the elders of your nation the House of Israel, upon the remnants of their Scribes

28. *Contra Apion* 2, 39.
29. Augustine, *De Civitate Dei* VI, II, 2.
30. *Midrash Shir HaShirim Rabbah* 1:15.

and *upon the righteous proselytes* may You rouse Your mercies, O Lord our God. . . ." It is likely that had conversion not been widespread, proselytes would not have been mentioned![31]

Conversion to Judaism or to the Noahide Laws?

Do the Bible and Talmud advocate converting the world to full Judaism, or merely to bring as many people as possible into the third covenant and the Noahide covenant with its seven fundamentals of morality? This question may be seen as a difference of opinion between the prophets Isaiah and Micah. Isaiah has a magnificent vision of the end of the days:

> When the mountain of the Temple of the Lord will be firmly established . . . and all the nations will stream to it, the multitude of nations will go and say, "Come let us go up . . . to the Temple of the God of Jacob, and he [Jacob] will teach us of his ways and we will walk in his paths." For from Zion will the Torah come forth, and the word of the Lord from Jerusalem. . . . They shall beat their swords into plowshares and their spears into pruning hooks; nation will not lift sword against nation and humanity will not learn war anymore. (Isa. 2:1-4)

These words may be taken to mean that everyone will convert to the complete Jewish tradition, that from Zion the entire Torah will come forth, and the "word of the Lord will extend from Jerusalem" to the world.

Micah 4:5 repeats this prophecy, yet he adds the following significant phrase: "For all the peoples will go forth, *each person in the name of his God*, but we shall go forth with the name of the Lord our God forever and ever." This suggests a pluralistic view, an acceptance of other faith communities with different names for God and other ritual customs, as long as those communities accept the basic moral principles of the Noahide laws, eschew war and bloodshed, and are committed to the God of peace.

As the foremost legal authority and philosopher in Jewish history, Maimonides' views on this question are critical to Jewish theology. As we have seen, Maimonides requires coercing humanity — if necessary — to accept the seven Noahide laws, but he does not require Jews to convert

---

31. See further B.T. *Rosh Hashanah* 31b, *Berakhot* 27b, and *Mishnah Yadayim* 4:4, which all deal with questions of proselytes after the destruction of the Temple, when they could not bring their "conversion" sacrifice.

moral gentiles to Judaism and its 613 commandments. He accepts every human being as a child of God and salvific in his/her own right as long as they accept the seven Noahide laws. Maimonides maintains, however, that in the messianic age, when true peace will reign and every individual will strive to know God to the greatest extent possible, "everyone will return to the true religion" *(dat ha'emet)*. The meaning of this term, *dat ha'emet* — and by implication whether Maimonides considers universal conversion to Judaism a theological ideal for today — is still unresolved. Scholars disagree whether Maimonides believes that (a) gentiles will accept all Jewish beliefs and commandments, (b) will fully accept only the Noahide commandments, or (c) will accept the Noahide commandments and belief in the God of creation and revelation. In other words, scholars disagree as to whether Maimonides believes that gentiles and Jews will remain separate and distinct religious bodies in the *eschaton*.[32] It is in MT, Laws of Kings, chapter 12:1 that Maimonides mentions *dat ha'emet*. The expression in question seems to refer to commandments beyond the seven Noahide laws and additional to belief in monotheism:

> Let it not enter your mind that in the days of the Messiah any aspect of the regular order of the world will be abolished or some innovation will be introduced into nature; rather the world follows its accustomed course. The verse in Isaiah, "The wolf shall dwell with the lamb, the leopard lie down with the kid" is an allegory and metaphor. Its meaning is that Israel will dwell in security with the wicked nations of the earth which are allegorically represented as wolves and leopards, as it says (Jer. 5:6) "The wolf of the desert ravages them; a leopard lies in wait by their towns." *Those nations will all adopt the true religion (dat ha'emet).* They will neither rob nor destroy; rather they will eat permitted foods in peace and quiet together with Israelites, as it says, "the lion, like the ox, shall eat straw."

One can argue that Maimonides maintained here that in the messianic age, everyone — Jew and gentile alike — will keep Jewish dietary laws, and

---

32. Menachem Kellner contends (a) that Maimonides believes gentiles will convert to Judaism; Chaim Rapoport believes (b) that Maimonides' texts indicate only that they will accept the Noahide laws. See Kellner, "Maimonides' True Religion: For Jews or All Humanity?" and Rapoport, *"Dat Ha-emet* in Maimonides' MT" in *Meorot* 7:1, *Tishrei* 5769, found at www.yctorah.org. Gerald Blidstein claims that Maimonides requires acceptance of Noahide laws and fundamental belief in God. See Blidstein, *Political Concepts in Maimonidean Halakah* (Ramat Gan, Israel: Bar Ilan University Press, 1983), p. 98, note 27 and p. 227.

by implication all other Sinaitic commandments. There are textual variants that support alternative interpretations.[33] Other writings of Maimonides stress the salutary quality of a gentile performing the commandments, even to the extent of his identification of *dat ha'emet* with conversion. In his "Epistle to Obadiah the Proselyte"[34] Maimonides describes a convert as "a person who left his father, his native land, his nation's realm (parallel to Abraham of Gen. 12) and, having gained inner understanding, came to join this nation (Israel) . . . and recognized and knew that their (Israel's) religion is a true and righteous religion *(dat emet va-tsedeq)*. . . . He came to recognize all this and sought after God, traversing the holy path and entering beneath the wings of the Divine Presence, embracing the dust at the feet of Moses our teacher. . . ."[35]

In *Guide of the Perplexed* (II:31) Maimonides refers to the Sabbath as a day when all humanity will rest, "ultimately as a universal day devoted to matters of the spiritual intellect." In his Responsa,[36] Maimonides declares that "it is permissible for Jews to teach Torah and commandments to Christians (but not to Moslems, since Christians accept the sanctity of our Scripture) in order to draw them closer to our truth," and he adds that "a Jew is permitted to circumcise a gentile if the gentile wishes to remove his foreskin, since a gentile receives reward for every commandment he performs" (II:31, section 148). To put it another way, Maimonides encouraged us to "bear witness" before gentiles, but did not believe that there is an obligation to convert gentiles.

Does this mean that Maimonides posited that in the *eschaton* all gentiles will accept the 613 commandments of the Torah and formally convert to Judaism? In his discussions of the *eschaton*, Maimonides never explicitly mentions conversion. Gerald Blidstein insists, however, that in Maimonides' vision gentiles will eventually accept more than the seven Noahide

33. Rapoport, "*Dat Ha-emet* in Maimonides' MT," p. 5, offers an alternative interpretation in the name of the Lubavitcher Rebbe, based on the textual version that includes the word *k'yisrael* ("like Israel" or "like Israelites") instead of "with" Israel. I respectfully disagree. *K'yisrael* indicates to me that Maimonides pictured a period when the differences in behavior between Jews and gentiles will largely disappear.

34. Responsa of Maimonides, ed. Freiman (Tel Aviv 5614, 1933-34), section 369.

35. Note the reference to Moses with regard to the convert, and not to Abraham. Maimonides described Abraham's discovery of monotheism as *derekh ha-emet*, because Abraham did not grasp and accept all of the commandments (MT, Laws of Idolatry, 1, 10). *Dat ha-emet*, the religion of truth, is apparently reserved for Moses and those converts who accept all the commandments.

36. I:149 (Blau edition).

laws or the twelve commandments of the third covenant.[37] Whether or not the gentiles will formally convert to Judaism in the *eschaton* is a difference of opinion within the Talmud (B.T. *Berakhot* 57b):

> One who sees a place from which idolatry was uprooted recites, "Blessed (be God) who has uprooted idolatry from our land: and as it has been uprooted from this place, so may it be uprooted from all places in Israel, and may You return the hearts of their worshippers to worship You." But outside the land of Israel there is no need to say "Return the hearts of their worshippers to worship You"; for the majority there are gentiles. R. Shimon ben Elazar says "Even outside the land of Israel one must say that, for (all the gentiles) are destined to convert, as it is written, 'then will I turn to the peoples a pure language, that they may all call upon the name of the Lord to serve Him with one consent'" (Zeph. 3:9).

The question whether the diaspora prayer should or should not include the request, "Return the hearts of their worshippers to worship You" hinges on whether or not Jewish theology maintains that eventually all gentiles will convert; the sages believe they will not, so the prayer in the diaspora is superfluous; R. Shimon ben Elazar believes they will, and so the prayer must be recited. R. Shimon ben Elazar has as his prooftext our citation from Zephaniah. Maimonides decides the law in accordance with R. Shimon ben Elazar, i.e., that we do recite the line in question in the diaspora, suggesting that everyone will eventually formally convert.[38] To buttress the view that all gentiles will convert to Mosaic Judaism in the messianic age, despite the fact that Talmud teaches that proselytes were neither accepted in the days of the kings David and Solomon, nor will they be accepted in messianic times (B.T. *Yebamot* 24b), Maimonides cites only the prohibition during the periods of the kings David and Solomon.[39] He pointedly omits the messianic era, apparently because he believes that gentiles will then convert and that they must be accepted in order for redemption to arrive.

Maimonides' position seems clear. He believed that Jews are enjoined

37. See Blidstein, *Political Concepts in Maimonidean Halakah*, pp. 228-35, who cites the sources mentioned here.

38. MT, Laws of Blessings, 10:9. This is significant, since Maimonides here departs from the normal legal protocol, deciding with the individual opinion of R. Shimon and against the majority.

39. MT, Laws of Forbidden Sexual Relations 13:15.

to coerce gentiles to accept the seven Noahide laws and the twelve commandments of the third covenant if necessary, because that acceptance is crucial for civilization to endure. We are not obligated to convert gentiles, and we surely do not coerce their conversion. When one's acceptance of Noahide moral principles is coupled with belief in a transcendent commanding God, this person has a share in the world to come (salvation) and is to be respected and loved as a child of God created in the Divine Image. We are however permitted — and perhaps even encouraged — to teach gentiles the Torah and its commandments, an act that Maimonides saw as part of the commandment for Jews to love God. Finally, Maimonides contended that in the *eschaton* all will convert because it will be rationally and morally compelling for them to do so.

There is historical confirmation of a gentile community that accepted universal natural law and monotheism, chose which of the ritual laws they desired to keep, and generally prayed in the synagogue, but did not formally convert. These "quasi or associate" Jews were nonetheless highly respected by the official Jewish community during the Second Commonwealth. Called *"yirei haShem"* or *"yirei Shamayim"* (God-fearing persons), they were involved in sundry Jewish practices but never converted:

> "They accepted without doubt faith in one God and the inter-personal commandments, but as far as the commandments between humans and God, they differed greatly from each other in practice." Many of them even attended synagogue — but they did not, and nor did they intend to, convert.[40]

Permit me a personal insight, one that is critical to the ground-rules of Christian-Jewish dialogue: I believe it is quite legitimate for any particular faith community to maintain that its revelation is the perfect one, and that ultimately (in the *eschaton*) all the others will convert to that faith. However, it is crucial that the members of each respective faith community respect the members of other faith communities as inviolable children of God even when they do not convert, as long as they subscribe to the ethical Noahide commandments.

---

40. Saul Lieberman, *Greek and Hellenism in Jewish Palestine* (Jerusalem: Bialik Institute, 1962), pp. 59-68. Lieberman titles this section of his book "Semi-converts, Semi-Gentiles." See also Psalms 115:13, 118:4, 135:20, which make positive reference to them as a separate and venerated group.

In Defense of Religious Pluralism and Ethical Absolutism

Maimonides adopted the Aristotelian monistic conception that led him to insist on absolute monotheism. This caused him to reject trinitarian Christianity as idolatry for both Christians and Jews.[41] However, Maimonides' is not the only Jewish perspective, neither from a study of the Bible nor from an investigation into the views of other rabbinical authorities and decisors of Jewish law, both early and late.[42] Nearly every time the Bible forbids idolatry, it is in the context of *immoral behavior:*

> Do not bow down to their gods and do not serve them; you must not do actions which are like their (the idolaters) actions. (Exod. 23:24)

> . . . Guard yourself . . . lest you seek out their gods. . . . Do not do that to the Lord your God, because every abomination to the Lord, which He hated, they do to their gods; they even burn their sons and their daughters in fire to their gods. (Deut. 12:30-31)

> . . . Do not learn to act like the abominations of those nations; let there not be found amongst you someone who passes his son or his daughter into fire. . . . (Deut. 18:9-10)

> . . . you shall surely destroy the Hittite and the Amorite; the Canaanite and the Perizite . . . in order that they not teach you to do in accordance with all their abominations which they did to their gods. . . . (Deut. 20:17-18)

The unmistakable concern of the Bible is correct behavior. This points to the profound difference between the Jewish outlook and the philosophical worldviews of Plato and Aristotle: Whereas the philosophers were mostly interested in correct thought (as is clear from Plato's "Theaetetus"), Judaism is primarily interested with moral action.[43] God chose Abraham

---

41. Commentary on *Mishnah, Avodah Zarah,* 1:3-4 and MT, Laws of Idolatry 9:4.

42. See Eugene Korn's masterful study, "Rethinking Christianity, Rabbinic Positions and Possibilities," in forthcoming *Jewish Theology and World Religions* (Littman Library of Jewish Civilization), from which this catalogue of early and late rabbinic authorities is taken. See also Halbertal and Margolit, *Idolatry,* and Jacob Katz, *Exclusivism and Tolerance,* ch. 10.

43. The fact that the Septuagint translates Torah as *nomos* (law in Greek), and that the Talmud concludes its argument as to what is superior — study or action — with the directive "Great is study because it leads to action" (B.T. *Qiddushin* 40b), buttresses this contention.

because he was committed to teaching succeeding generations *tsedakah u'mishpat*, "compassionate righteousness and justice" (Gen. 18:19) — rather than because he discovered or would teach pure monotheism![44] Perhaps the most important biblical verse that expresses emphasis on proper action as the cardinal principle of biblical faith is found in Jeremiah. Jews read this verse publicly on the ninth of Av, the fast day when they mourn the destruction of the Temple that Jeremiah foresaw:

> So does God say, "let the wise man not be praised for his wisdom, let the strong man not be praised for his strength, let the rich man not be praised for his riches"? Only in this regard shall one be praised:
>
>> "Be wise and know Me, for I am the Lord who does loving kindness, moral justice and righteous compassion in the land, because these are what I desire," says the Lord. (9:22-23)

Note well the prophet's words: proper knowledge of God is derived not from intellectual cognition, but from compassionate and moral conduct.[45] From this perspective, although Maimonides defines idolatry exclusively in theological and metaphysical terms,[46] R. Menahem Ha-Meiri defined idolatry in terms of the "disgusting immoral acts of the idolaters, whose paganism kept their adherents from accepting the moral norms of the Noahide laws or of the Third Covenant."[47] In addition to these two end positions, there are two intermediate positions held by the overwhelming majority of halakhic decisors. The first is based upon the talmudic statement (B.T. *Hullin* 13b) that "Gentiles outside of the land of Israel are not idolators but only follow the traditions of their fathers." This was the nor-

44. Although Maimonides portrays Abraham as philosopher, MT, Laws of Idolatry, 1:4.

45. This idea is also strikingly noted by the Talmud in a conversation between R. Hanina ben Teradion and R. Elazar b. Parta during the Hadrianic persecutions. The former says that he will be executed by the Romans and his colleague will be saved, since his colleague has both Torah knowledge and good works, whereas he has only Torah knowledge. He adds that someone who has only Torah knowledge but is devoid of good works is similar to someone who has no God! (B.T. *Avodah Zarah* 17).

46. Significantly, Maimonides ends his philosophic work *Guide of the Perplexed* by explaining the importance of Jeremiah's verse for Jewish theology. He maintained that when one attains a correct knowledge of God, he will then naturally act like God, performing loving-kindness *(hesed)*, justice *(mishpat)*, and righteousness *(tzedek)*.

47. *Bet HaBehirah*, B.T. *Sanhedrin* 57a, and B.T. *Avodah Zarah* 20a. See also Jacob Katz, *Exclusivism and Tolerance*, ch. 10; Moshe Halbertal, *Bein Torah L'Hakhma* (Jerusalem, 2000), ch. 3; and Halbertal and Margolit, *Idolatry*, pp. 204-9.

mative ruling held by all medieval rabbinic authorities living in Christian Ashkenaz, including R. Yitzhaki (Rashi) and R. Asher ben Yechiel as well as R. Yosef Karo in Turkey and Sefat. They considered trinitarian Christianity to be illegitimate theology, but ruled that Christians are not idolators.

The second of these intermediate positions maintains that while Christianity is illegitimate for a Jew, it is not so for gentiles. The Decalogue in the Book of Exodus forbade idolatry for Jews after idolatry had already been forbidden to all humanity in Genesis in the form of the seven Noahide laws of morality. Jewish exegetes inferred that apparently there was a specific addition to the prohibition in Exodus meant for the Jews alone, and this is the requirement of absolute monotheism.[48] As long as a religion worships the God Who is the Creator of the Heavens and the Earth as the ultimate moral Authority of the universe, it is not idolatrous for its adherents even if it appends other elements to the creator — as is the case with trinitarian Christians. This is the Jewish legal opinion of the majority of late rabbinic authorities *(aharonim).*[49]

Beyond this, R. Moshe Rivkis (seventeenth-century Lithuania) argued that Jews should pray for the welfare of our Christian brethren since they believe in the creation of the world and in the exodus from Egypt, and their intention is directed towards the Creator of heaven and earth.[50] R. Jacob Emden (eighteenth-century Germany) similarly praised Christians for having eradicated idolatry from the West and instilling a moral faith in consonance with the seven Noahide laws. Christians are instruments for the fulfillment of the prophecy that the knowledge of God will spread throughout the earth.[51]

A talmudic source for this last position can be found in the final Mishnah of chapter eight of the Tractate *Berakhot,* where the Jerusalem Talmud states that one should respond "Amen" to a gentile who blesses or praises

---

48. R. Joseph Saul Nathanson, *Shiel u'Meishiv* 1:26 and 51.

49. These include Rabbis Moses Isserles (Ramo, sixteenth-century Poland), Shabtai HaKohen (Shakh, seventeenth-century Bohemia), Moses Rivkis (Be'er HaGolah, seventeenth-century Lithuania), Jacob Emden (Ya'avetz, eighteenth-century Germany), and David Zvi Hoffman (nineteenth-century Germany). See Korn, "Rethinking Christianity," regarding this list of rabbinic authorities.

50. Gloss on *Shulhan Arukh, Hoshen Mishpat,* section 425:5.

51. Commentary on Ethics of the Fathers 4:13. See Eugene Korn, "The People Israel, Christianity, and the Covenantal Responsibility to History," in this volume for a fuller treatment of Rabbis Rivkis and Emden.

God. The same passage cites R. Tanhum as maintaining that "one must re-spond Amen to a gentile who makes a blessing in the name of the Lord, as it is written, 'Blessed shall You be by all the nations.'"[52]

I further suggest that Meiri's view — that idolatry is defined by ethical and moral abominations in the name of religion rather than by incorrect theological concepts — is strongly supported by the fact that a gentile *(ger toshav)* permitted to live in the land of Israel under Jewish religious sover-eignty is only required to conform to proper moral behavior. He need not believe in one God, and it is sufficient that he merely not practice idolatry.

The case for religious pluralism alongside ethical and moral absolut-ism is strengthened by the nature of the Noahide covenant, effectuated be-tween God and the new humanity that descended from Noah and his sons after the rest of the world was destroyed:

> And the Lord said, "This is the sign [symbol] of the covenant which I am giving between Me and between you and between all living beings who are with you forever: I am giving My bow into the cloud, and it shall serve as the sign of the covenant between Me and the earth." (Gen. 9:12-13)

The rainbow is the symbol of the covenant, signaling both the end of the rain and the Divine promise never to send another destructive flood upon the world again. The famous medieval Jewish commentator, Nahmanides, adds (ad loc) content to this symbolism: In ancient times, when two nations were at war with each other using bows and arrows, when one side held up an inverted bow it was a sign of surrender and peace. God's inverted bow symbolized God's commitment to never again go to war against humanity. Thus the rainbow is a divine sign to the world that God will never again attempt to destroy life on earth.

This may explain why God's sign of the rainbow is immediately pre-ceded by God's moral demands upon humanity, i.e., no drinking the blood or eating the flesh of a living animal, no suicide, and no murder: "One who sheds human blood shall have his blood shed by humans, since God made

---

52. R. Moshe Isserles established the normative ruling that one answers Amen to a gen-tile blessing when it is heard directly from the mouth of the gentile (gloss to *Shulhan Arukh Orah Haim* 215.2). *Mishnah Berurah* (12) explains that when the gentile uses the same term for God that a Jew uses, he does not intend the blessing to be for an idol. Biyur Halakhah adds that the Jew need not hear the blessing from the mouth of the gentile, and this became the later normative law as decided by the R. Elijah of Vilna (Vilna Gaon).

the human being in His image" (Gen. 9:4-6), which is the basis of the seven Noahide moral laws. The rainbow is a half circle, still an incomplete symbol. In effect, God said that He will never destroy humanity again. But having created humanity with free choice, God cannot guarantee that humanity will not destroy itself. The future of humanity can only depend upon the universal human acceptance of "Thou shall not murder."

R. Samson Raphael Hirsch provides additional content to the rainbow's symbolism: Gazing upon a rainbow, one sees seven dazzling colors: red, orange, yellow, green, blue, indigo, and violet. Yet, in reality there is but one color, white. When the rays of the sun shed their light upon the cloud, the white of the cloud refracts into the seven colors of the red, orange, yellow, green, blue, indigo, and violet. So it is also with human beings: Humanity seems separated into different peoples, with different skin pigmentations from black, to brown, to yellow, to white. In reality, however, we are all descendants of one human being, created in the image of the One Unique God. We all emerge from the divine womb and are all endowed with a portion of divine eternity.

Allow me to add to his symbolism. Can we not argue that, although we use different names, symbolic images, rituals, customs, and incantations by which we call and worship the Deity, everyone is speaking and praying to the same Divine Force who created and guides our world? Allah is another name for the one God *("El"* or *"Elohim"),* the Trinity is mysteriously considered a unity by Christians, all the physical representations of the Buddha are meant to express the All in the All that is the god of the Far East. Is it not possible that the real meaning of the credo of Judaism, the Sh'ma, is: "Hear O Israel, the Lord [who is known by our different names of different forces and powers], *Elohaynu,* is [in reality the] One [YHVH of the entire cosmos]"? Just as the white of the cloud is refracted into different colors, so the one God of love may be called by different names and different powers, but these all coalesce in the mind of the one praying and in the reality of the situation into the one all-encompassing Lord of the universe.

If this is the case, as long as humans are moral, they can call God by any name or names they wish since their true intent is the God of the universe. They may even be secular humanists, as long as they do not engage in the abominations of idol worship. The ultimate religious concern is that humans not destroy the world, and this can only be predicated upon the universal acceptance of ethical absolutes, compassionate righteousness and justice, the inviolability of the human being, and his/her right to live in freedom, peace, and security.

Epilogue

Our generation lives in an age of miracles. In addition to the return of the Jewish people to their covenantal home in the land of Israel and the in-gathering of the remnants of the Jewish people from the "lost" tribe of Dan in Ethiopia to the "lost" tribe of Menashe from India, there is the miracle of the rapprochement between Christianity and Judaism after nearly two thousand years of bitter enmity and Christian persecution of Jews.

Christianity sees itself as being grafted onto the Jewish covenant, God's covenant with Abraham. This is legitimate from a biblical and Jewish perspective, since Abraham, by his very name, is a patriarch of a multitude of nations. Christianity worships Abraham's God of compassionate righteousness and justice, and traditional Christianity surely accepts the seven Noahide laws as given by God. The return of the younger faith to its maternal roots was eased by leading theologians of most churches recognizing the permanent legitimacy of the Jewish covenant with God and the possibility of Jewish salvation on the merit of that covenant. The partnership between the daughter and mother religions is particularly important today in the face of the existential threat of Islamist extremism against which all who are committed to a hopeful future must battle — including moderate Muslims. The Bible records a loving reconciliation between Isaac and Ishmael, coming together in bringing their father to his eternal resting place (Gen. 25:9).[53] The God of Abraham as the God of love, compassion, and peace is the antithesis of Satan, who instructs violence against all those who do not accept his cruel prescription for world domination.

Yet our relationship goes beyond our mutual faiths in a God of love and our mutual struggle against religious violence. I have tried to show that Israel came onto the world scene, from the dawn of Abraham with a mission to the world, a responsibility to teach the compelling message of a God of love and morality. Until the Hadrianic persecutions, Jews attempted to fulfill that mission. With Hadrian, the Jewish people were forced to leave history. Jews were exiled from the state of historic actors, and perforce became insularly concerned with ethnic survival. We forgot — or were forced to forget — our world mission.

Thankfully, Christians took up this mission. Traditional rabbis like Maimonides and Jacob Emden understood that Christians brought the concepts of divine commandments, morality, messiah, and the God of love

53. See commentary of Rashi ad loc.

to the furthest corners of human civilization. Faithful Jews must be grateful for this.

Now that the Jewish people have returned to their homeland and to empirical history and now that Christians again recognize the legitimacy of the Jewish covenant, Jews and Christians must march together to bring the faith of morality and peace to a desperate but thirsting world. We dare not rest until we succeed and see "justice roll like the waters, and compassionate righteousness as a mighty stream" (Amos 5:24). This is our united mission, far more important than the legitimate and to-be-respected differences that divide us. And if the moderate, religiously pluralistic Muslims join us, we will all not only survive as free people created in the Divine Image. We will redeem ourselves and the entire world.

Judaism, the Political, and the Monarchy

Michael Wyschogrod

Preliminaries

Our topic is "Covenant, Mission, and Relation to the Other." There is hardly an aspect of Judaism and Christianity that does not interact with one or more of these concepts. Because of the richness and complexity of these categories, I have chosen to focus on a dimension that has not heretofore been at the center of my work, namely, Jewish political thought. The three terms under discussion are deeply theological. Covenant, for example, describes the relation between God and Israel. Instead of unilaterally imposing his will on Israel, God enters into a relation of mutual obligations with a people who becomes not only a servant of God but to some extent a partner of God, if such a relationship can be imagined between the King of all Kings and mortal humans. Similarly, mission flows out of covenant when this is understood as the obligations brought into being by covenant. The Other is the recipient of the obligations brought into being by the covenant. The Other is thus both God and fellow humans because, under the covenant, we owe obligations to both, and God in turn is not without obligations to his creatures. In short, although we may not realize it at first, we find ourselves sliding into a political-legal relationship.

Undoubtedly, some of us will be made uncomfortable by the injection of political-legal considerations into our relationship with God. We need only think of the criticism directed in the New Testament at the doctors of the law and the widespread impression in Christian circles that Jesus undertook to abolish the law even if he also undertook to fulfill it. In any case we must enter the realm of political thought, because however much emphasis we place on covenant and partnership between God and his human

creatures, the fact that God is referred to in the Bible and rabbinic literature as the King of all Kings perhaps more often than any other title makes
it clear that we are in a political situation, and specifically, the situation of a
monarch. We are subjects of a mighty King whose commands we must
obey. We must not permit the covenantal dimension of our relationship
with God to obscure the royal dimension of the King of all Kings.

There are three religious institutions and persons in the biblical polity that are divinely sanctioned: the king, the prophet, and the priest, particularly the high priest. Of the three, only the term *king* is routinely applied both to human beings and to God. This is particularly interesting
when we realize that of the three, prophet and high priest are the more religious categories, while king is the more secular. And yet it is precisely
king — the more secular of the three — that is so commonly applied to
God. God is never referred to as high priest or prophet, but is frequently
called king.

In the presence of a human king, Jews are instructed to recite the following blessing: "Blessed are You, Adonai, our God, King of the Universe,
Who has given of His glory to human beings." A human king thus partici-
pates in the glory of God. To see a human king is, in a sense, to see God. It
is probably for this reason that monarchy is so difficult for secularists and
should be so congenial to religious believers. A world without God is a
world without kings, a world in which nothing is hereditary, in which all
glory is temporary and republican, elected for a period of time and based
on policy agreements. God's election of Israel, which is in a way a royal
election, is based on none of these fleeting considerations, but is as permanent as the throne of David, the ultimate permanent throne sanctioned by God.

Sovereignty

The concept of sovereignty underlies both the republican and monarchical form of government. The dictionary defines "sovereign" as "free, independent, and in no way limited by external authority or influence: a
sovereign state." In a republic, the people are sovereign. They, or their representatives, are the authors of the law. The people elect all officers of government and no one can override the will of the people. Republican government is inherently secular, precisely because of the absolute
sovereignty of the people. Pure republicanism does not deal with the sub-

stance of the enactments of the people or their representatives but only with the procedures that constitute the legislative process. It is therefore theoretically possible for a law or policy to be profoundly flawed while procedurally exemplary.

In the monarchical model, the king is sovereign, and is often referred to as the sovereign because his will is the law and is not subject to review by any other person or body. It is thus theoretically possible for an absolute monarch to rule in a most authoritarian fashion by ignoring the will of his subjects and yet enacting laws that are profoundly just and in the true interest of his subjects. In short, procedure and substance must not be confused.

Until now I have drawn the embodiment of sovereignty either in the people or the person of the sovereign in rather absolute terms. In the political realm all kinds of compromises are possible. A constitutional monarch is theoretically sovereign but his powers can be limited in many ways. The Queen of England has in theory all the powers of a traditional absolute monarch but she chooses not to exercise them. All acts of Parliament are advisory to her but she chooses never to reject the advice of Parliament. Without her approval, no act of Parliament has any validity whatsoever, but her sovereignty remains untested because it is never exercised.

Parliamentary bodies are generally far more assertive than powerless monarchs because to many persons it is far more self-evident that the people and their elected representatives are sovereign than is a hereditary monarch. Nevertheless, the sovereignty of parliamentary bodies is usually also restricted. This becomes most apparent when the parliamentary body is subject to the rules spelled out in a written or unwritten constitution. A constitution almost always restricts the power of a future majority to enact the legislation it desires. Let us consider the simplest case where a constitution, itself adopted by a simple majority, requires more than a simple majority for constitutional change in the future. What right does a constitution-writing body operating by a simple majority have to frustrate a future majority that wishes to modify by majority vote the constitutional curb of majority rule? And even if a constitution-writing body adopts its anti-majority measures by more than a majority vote, it is still not obvious why any vote of the past should bind a majority of the present to require more than a majority. Suppose a majority of the present enacts a constitution that rules out any change forever. Or, suppose a constitution-writing body does not rule out any change for all eternity but requires a 98 percent vote of the future legislature to enact any constitutional change. Such an approach would not rule out all constitutional change *a priori,* but makes it all but impossible, practically speaking. I do not think many polities would accept such limitations on their sovereignty. It seems to me that the only basis for a polity accepting severe constitutional restrictions on its power to rule by majority vote is the conviction that the founding constitution is more than a human document. With the addition of this premise the indefensible becomes defensible and we find ourselves dealing with a theological state (in reference to Jews, a "Torah state") in which only one vote counts, namely that of God. Without such a theological foundation, a republic must feel itself bound by the rules laid down by its founders, who can dictate to subsequent generations the parameters of its liberties, particularly any changes in its constitution and the methods of amending the constitution by majority vote. A purely secular republic thus self-destructs because it cannot protect its constitution from a simple majority method of amendment.

Monarchy

What would a Torah state look like? How would it operate? Would it be compatible with a Jewish monarchy or would a Torah state governed by rabbinic scholars be incompatible with a monarchy? These are difficult questions that deserve careful thought. From 70 CE to 1948 CE, Jews did not live in a sovereign Jewish state, and it is therefore not surprising that fundamental issues of Jewish political thought have remained unexamined, a state of affairs that requires correction.

Interestingly, it is the method of governance adopted by the *Agudat Yisrael*[1] in the period after World War I that serves as a possible model of how a Torah state would function in modern times. *Agudat Yisrael* is governed by a Council of Torah Sages *(Moetzes Gedolei Hatorah).* It is not altogether clear how the members of the Council are chosen. It seems that to some extent new members are chosen by the older members of the Council. But there is also reason to believe that the professional leadership of *Agudat Yisrael* also plays an important role in selecting new members of the Council. Nevertheless, we are not dealing with an essentially elected body but an appointed one. The rationale behind this form of governance is that the great Torah scholars and authorities are the right peo-

1. The world organization of leading Orthodox rabbis, which was anti-Zionist.

ple to make the decisions that affect the whole Jewish people. Were this method of governance put into effect in Israel, it would cease to be a democratic state and become a Torah state governed by the great, leading, unelected Torah scholars of the generation. I suspect that this is the form of governance that the ultra-Orthodox *(Ḥaredi)* segment of the Israeli public prefers.

Was there ever a time when the people of Israel, living in a sovereign state of their own, were ruled by rabbinic scholars? It appears that this was never the case. Whether in the Babylonian exile or in medieval Europe, rabbis played an important role in guiding the lives of Jews, but this was almost always in the context of Jewish subordination to non-Jewish rulers, with the rabbis subject to the authority of such rulers. Jewish sovereignty existed in full measure only with the rule of Jewish kings, the first and most famous of whom were, of course, Saul, David, and Solomon. Saul was chosen by God in response to the demand addressed by the people to Samuel to "appoint for us a king to govern us, like other nations" (1 Sam. 8:5). This is a request that did not please God, who informed Samuel that "they have not rejected you, but they have rejected me from being king over them." It must be noted that God is not opposed to a monarchy. He is opposed to a human monarchy but supports the monarchy of God. Only after Samuel has outlined all the disadvantages that will accrue to the people when they are ruled by a human king and the people still demand a king does God reluctantly permit the appointment of a human king.

We can infer several things from this. First, human monarchy is not God's first choice for the governance of Israel. His first choice is the Kingship of God, who rules through the prophet as his spokesperson. Because God does not speak to the people directly, a prophet is required to transmit the word of God to the people. In this form of rule, exemplified by Moses' rule over Israel, God uses the prophet not only to communicate generalities to the people but concrete decisions, e.g., the request of the daughters of Zelophehad (Num. 27:1-11) for a portion of their inheritance as there were no male heirs. Moses presents the case to God, who rules that the daughters are to inherit on the same footing as their father's brothers. A more concrete form of divine monarchical rule can hardly be imagined. God is a royal sovereign and judge who rules over his people. While direct divine rule did not last very long, the fact that it is given as a viable option serves, among other things, to refute the view that after the revelation of the Torah to the Jewish people at Sinai, direct divine intervention is no longer possible or desirable.[2] Whatever subsequent forms of rule are depicted in the Bible, nothing can match direct divine rule which rules out the possibility of error.

When the law is interpreted by human beings, the possibility of error cannot be excluded, but when God issues specific decisions, error is not possible. The form of government under discussion can be termed Mosaic kingship because it is a form of monarchy in which God is the monarch who speaks through the prophet. The monarch is both king and prophet and rules in the context of a living dialogue with God, whom he can consult whenever the need arises. The Mosaic monarch combines in himself two partially contradictory qualities. On the one hand, Moses is the greatest prophet Israel has encountered because he speaks with God "face to face." On the other hand, it is precisely this proximity to God that diminishes Moses' authority because when in doubt, he consults God and receives the most reliable answer possible. Moses, it seems, does not need to acquire the art of legal reasoning. His questions are answered by the Holy One blessed be He, himself. It seems to me that the reason Moses is not generally referred to as a king is that he is not sovereign; it is God who is the sovereign king, with Moses his spokesperson. It follows that bestowing the title of king on God is not an honorific maneuver, as if the title of God were insufficient and another title were necessary. God is termed king because he is *the* king, the ruler from whom all decisions emanate and whom human kings resemble. That is why the blessing "who has given of his glory to human beings" is significant. The human king is created in the image of the Divine King, a statement we would not dare to make if it did not mirror the statement that human beings were created in the image of God.

More about Kings

It is widely thought that the attitude of the Bible to kings is ambivalent. This is largely based on 1 Samuel 8 where the people ask the aging Samuel to appoint a king over Israel so that the people of Israel will be governed "like all other nations." Needless to say this request is displeasing both to God and Samuel. God informs Samuel that this rebellion is not directed at

---

2. A famous passage in the Babylonian Talmud makes just this claim, maintaining that after Sinai, "It (the Torah) is no longer in heaven (but in the hands of the rabbinical majority)" — an ingenious interpretation of Deuteronomy 30:12. See B.T., *Baba Metsi'a* 59b.

Samuel, rather at God. Nevertheless, God grants the people's request and soon thereafter Saul is recognized as the legitimate monarch of Israel. To some extent these developments are foreshadowed in Deuteronomy 17:15, which can be translated either as God giving Israel permission to set a king over them or commanding them to do so. Maimonides reads Deuteronomy 17:15 as a commandment for Israel to appoint a king.[3] Why then, asks Maimonides, did God look with disfavor on the selection of a king? His answer is that the people asked for a king in a querulous spirit, motivated more by the desire to get rid of Samuel than a desire to fulfill the biblical command to place a king over Israel. As far as Maimonides is concerned, anointing a king over Israel is a positive biblical command that remains in place until the end of time.

What are the powers of a Jewish king? I shall focus only on one. Maimonides writes (Kings and Wars 3:8):

> The King is empowered to put to death anyone who rebels against him. Even if any of his subjects is ordered by him to go to a certain place and he does not go, or even if he is ordered to stay home and fails to do so, he is culpable, the king may, if he so decides, put him to death, as it is written "Whoever he be that shall rebel against thy commandments if he so decides, put him to death, as it is written: 'Whoever he be that shall rebel against thy commandment . . . shall be put to death'" (Josh. 1:18).

For Maimonides, the power over life or death is the very definition of a king. A king without this power is not a king.

But what about the requirement that a king of Israel be Torah-observant? Deuteronomy 17:18-20 requires the king to have a copy of the Torah written for him, which he is to read all the days of his life "so that he may learn to fear the Lord his God, diligently observing all the words of this law and these statutes." On the one hand, then, it is clear that a Jewish king is not a tyrant bound by no law greater then he. On the other hand, at least according to Maimonides, "the king is empowered to put to death anyone who rebels against him. Even if any of his subjects is ordered by him to go to a certain place and he does not go, or is ordered to stay home and fails to do so, he is culpable, and the king may, if he so decides, put him to death. . . ."

Maimonides adds (Kings and Wars 3:10):

---

3. *Mishneh Torah*, Laws of Kings and Their Wars 1:1.

If a person kills another and there is no clear evidence, or if no warning has been given him. Or there is only one witness, or if one kills accidentally a person whom he hated, the king may, if the exigency of the hour demands it, put him to death in order to insure the stability of the social order. He may put to death many offenders in one day, hang them, and suffer them to be hanging for a long time so as to put fear in the hearts of others and break the power of the wicked.

These are remarkable texts. On the one hand, the king is required to respect and obey the Torah with all its detailed instructions about almost all matters that could come before a Jewish king. On the other hand, he seems to be given *carte blanche* power to declare anything he wishes a capital crime for which the death penalty may be imposed. How are we to understand this?

The Danger of States

In the pristine "state of nature" there are no states because every person is sovereign. There is no structure above the individual that limits his or her freedom. The state of nature is thus a natural state of war in which every sovereign individual is exposed to the violence of the Other. Since no war is possible without an enemy, the state of nature is a state of war among natural enemies relating to each other as enemies. Once the Other is understood as an enemy, very few, if any, of the laws of peaceful coexistence apply to the Other. The key to this state of affairs is the dualities war/peace and enemy/friend. Once a state of war is declared, the basic mode of the being-in-the-world of the participants changes. Many actions that are forbidden in peace are permitted and even praised in war. One example is the role of snipers. In peacetime, it is a crime to shoot at and kill another with premeditation. Such actions are widely condemned and severely punished. Not so in war. Snipers are carefully trained to shoot and kill people who are unaware of the presence of snipers in the vicinity. At the end of the day, snipers return to their base with the knowledge that they have killed scores of people. These lives were extinguished by skilled marksmen who do not think of themselves as criminals because they have acted in the context of war rather than peace. Nor do their governments and their legal systems consider these snipers criminals. When they leave the arena of combat they leave the state of war for that of peace, and because they acted at the orders of their government most snipers feel little guilt. They obeyed their superiors and believe that this fact itself entitles them to a clear conscience.

The transformation of the state of war into the state of peace is a complex process at the heart of which is the social contract. In the state of war, as we have seen, all are vulnerable because no one is protected against the aggression of her neighbor. To escape from the condition of perpetual war, the members of the society in question enter into a contract the main provision of which affirms that they all give up their natural rights under the state of war and transfer these rights to the sovereign, who then becomes free to regulate the society over which he/she is sovereign as he/she sees fit. Naturally, this means that the sovereign cannot be criticized for any unjust measures because the sovereign is now heir to all the rights and privileges he/she has acquired from the citizens who transferred to the sovereign the rights they possessed during the state of war. The sovereign cannot be sued except with his/her consent, a doctrine that republics perpetuate with the claim that the state cannot be sued except with its permission.

Hegel and the State

Even this theory about the rights of the monarch or the sovereign republic does not go far enough. It was Hegel who developed a theological-metaphysical understanding of the state. The centrality of the state in Hegel's thought cannot be overestimated. For him, the state is nothing less than the embodiment of reason, particularly philosophic and moral reason. While there is a pragmatic element in Hegel's understanding of the state inasmuch as it is the state and only the state that stands between us and the state of war, even more fundamental is Hegel's claim that the state is the guarantor of religion and culture. The regulatory function of the state extends to all domains of culture. For Americans raised on an ideology of the separation of church and state, this is not easy to understand or accept. Should not the state stay away from interfering with sensitive spiritual issues that are best left to the judgment of theologians and artists, ones who should not be burdened with state regulation? The Hegelian philosopher of the state would reply that it is the state and only the state that can draw lines that must not be crossed. For example, the state might prohibit the teaching of hatred in the name of religion. There are activities of religious and artistic bodies that the state must evaluate, permit, or forbid.

137

Separation of church and state understood strictly would give religion and art *carte blanche* to act as they wished.

But even this somewhat pragmatic understanding of the state does not do justice to the Hegelian appreciation — if not worship — of the state. For Hegel the Prussian state was the most precious fruit of the Enlightenment. For Jews this meant that emancipation enjoyed the support of the Prussian state and therefore of most of the other German states, because the influence of Prussia in the German confederation was immense. Importantly, Kant welcomed Moses Mendelssohn into the fellowship of German culture. As a result of this broad Prussian acceptance, when an Eastern European Jew disembarked from the train bringing him from Warsaw to Berlin, he must have thought that he was witnessing the advent of the messianic era. That is how sharp the difference was between Jewish life under the Russian monarchy and Jewish life under the enlightened rule of the German states. Jews and gentiles alike believed deeply in the inevitability of progress and were convinced that the human condition could only improve with the passage of time. While temporary setbacks could not be ruled out, they would be temporary and could not reverse the overall movement toward an ever-improving world of justice and equal rights. Darkness was yielding to light and evil to good.

The State and Tyranny

At this point it is customary to contrast the Enlightenment world of eighteenth-century Germany with the Hitler era. It is not easy to grasp how the Third Reich could have evolved out of the enlightened Germany of Kant and Mendelssohn. If Carl Schmitt was right, then the liberal state of Kant and Mendelssohn had to generate an enemy and that enemy was the criminal state of Adolf Hitler. Schmitt does not explain why and how a particular group becomes the enemy, though it is not difficult to see that once an enemy is required, a group that does not fully blend into the culture of the dominant group is the natural candidate for that enemy role. The contribution of Schmitt is not so much that he discovered the need for a group to be designated the enemy of the state, but rather the insight into the enemy as a category that comes to dominate the atmosphere especially when the companion category of the enemy, i.e., war, begins to dominate the life of a society. Let us look once again at the power of the concept of war. This is a profound paradigm shift that constitutes a transvaluation of all values.

At this writing, the United States is involved in a difficult and painful debate about the treatment of terrorist suspects. Should they be awarded the protections of the Geneva Convention or can they be questioned with the aid of enhanced interrogation techniques that include procedures like waterboarding, which clearly constitute torture? In this discussion, a key role is played by a memorandum titled "The President's Constitutional Authority to Conduct Military Operations Against Terrorists and Nations Supporting Them" written by John Yoo, a Deputy Chief in the Justice Department's Office of Legal Counsel.[4] In the memo, among other things Yoo argues that the Founding Fathers meant to bestow on the President of the U.S. the powers of the British kings to wage wars. This is particularly true in time of war. Jane Mayer remarks:

> Wars have always aggrandized presidential powers in America's history. Some of the country's greatest presidents, including Abraham Lincoln and Franklin Roosevelt, trampled civil liberties in the name of safeguarding national security. Lincoln infamously suspended habeas corpus during the Civil War. Roosevelt interned 120,000 Japanese-American citizens. By comparison, President Bush's infringements of American's civil liberties during the war on terror have been modest.[5]

Carl Schmitt would, of course, be pleased to read the above passage. He would be particularly pleased to learn that the U.S. Supreme Court approved the internment of the Japanese Americans against whom not an iota of evidence of disloyalty was ever produced. States, it seems, play by another set of rules, particularly in time of war. Could this be one of the factors that led to the Holocaust?

Davidic Monarchy

"Throughout history," Michael Walzer writes, "the rule of one has been the most common form of government — also the most stable, at least in the sense that the 'one,' however his or her rule ended, was usually succeeded by another 'one.'"[6] The advantages of monarchy against a republican form

---

4. See Jane Mayer, *The Dark Side: The Inside Story of How the War on Terror Turned into a War on American Ideals* (New York: Anchor Books, 2008), p. 64.

5. Mayer, *The Dark Side*, p. 47.

6. Michael Walzer, Menachem Lorberbaum, and Noam J. Zohar, eds., *The Jewish Political Tradition*, vol. 1 (New Haven: Yale University Press, 2000), p. 109.

of government can be debated at length. There is little doubt that in modern times, particularly since the French Revolution, monarchies have been on the wane and republics on the increase. The reasons for this development are many, but the secularization of the modern world is surely one of them. The institution of monarchy is deeply tied to its religious roots. We must only recall that the coronation of the Queen of England some decades ago was held in Westminster Abbey and was rich in religious symbolism. The actual coronation was performed by the Archbishop of Canterbury. Kings and Queens rule not by election but by the choice of God, a consideration that plays almost no role in the symbolism of republican politics.

As we have seen, the term "king" is perhaps the most frequently bestowed title on God in the Bible. God is the supreme king, the king of all kings. I have said and I repeat now that a human king or queen is certainly not God and must be distinguished most sharply from God. Nevertheless, Jewish tradition prescribes a blessing that asserts that kings share in the divine glory of the King of the universe. It seems therefore, that there is a relationship of parallelism between God and a king. Some of God's glory rests on the king as the image of God rests on every human being. The authority of the king is not derived from the governed. This is perhaps the most difficult insight for the secular mind to grasp. For the secularist, nothing is more self-evident than the thesis that ultimately it is the people that is sovereign, and all those who rule the people derive their legitimacy from those they rule. But this is not how Judaism understands the matter. Ultimately, it is God and not the people that is sovereign. Rulers are chosen by God, and it is only to God and his Torah that they are responsible.

We cannot here deal in detail with the complicated history and theory of kingship in the Bible and Judaism. But a number of well-known facts bear repetition. As we have seen, 1 Samuel tells us that it is the people who demand of Samuel that he appoint a king over Israel. This does not please Samuel, presumably because he believes that God is Israel's true king. While God understands that the people's request for a king is directed against God and not Samuel, instead of simply turning down the request, God commands Samuel to anoint Saul king of Israel. Thus from the beginning of kingship in Israel there is a deep ambivalence. The true king is God and a human king is a second best. But the very fact that a human king is accepted and serves as a substitute for the Divine Monarch bestows on the human king a political and religious weight that no democratically elected politician can ever achieve.

We are left with two considerations that introduce us to the issue of Jewish kingship in the contemporary setting. Based on Deuteronomy 17:14-20, Maimonides, among many others, ruled that upon entry into the Holy Land, the appointment of a king is not optional but one of the positive commandments of the Torah. This king should be a descendant of David, and this is the reason that the New Testament (Matt. 1:1-16 and Luke 3:32) traces Jesus' descent to David. Summarizing a view he does not share, Gedalyahu Alon writes:

> The Pharisees were opposed to the monarchy generally, and especially because the throne belonged to the House of David. Hence, when the Hasmoneans proceeded to take the crown for themselves (and "they ate the Messiah"), they became unfit to rule, being completely disqualified. . . . Inevitably we must conclude that there is a distinction between everlasting kingship, which belongs to David, and temporary monarchy, which pertains to all Israel. . . .[7]

Maimonides writes (Laws of Kings and Wars 1:19):

> The kings of the House of David will endure forever, as it is written "And thy throne shall be established forever" (II Sam. 7:15). But in case of a king selected from any other tribe in Israel, the kingship will be wrested from his house, as it was said to Jeroboam: "and I will afflict the seed of David, but not forever. . . ."

It is thus clear that for Maimonides only a Davidic king is a fully legitimate and permanent king of Israel.

A Modest Proposal

Any view of Jewish sovereignty that is not based on the House of David is therefore not fully legitimate. I believe that it is necessary to inject Davidic royal legitimacy into the State of Israel. How can this be done? The crowning of an actual Davidic monarch would require prophecy to select the proper person, and in the absence of prophecy this is not possible. Yet Is-

---

7. Gedalyahu Alon, *Jews, Judaism and the Classical World* (Jerusalem: Magnes Press, 1977), pp. 2 and 5. I am grateful to Prof. J. J. Schacter for drawing my attention to the Alon volume.

rael can be declared a Davidic monarchy without a reigning king. Many monarchies have faced the situation in which there is no king or the king cannot rule because, for example, he is a minor. In such situations, a regent is appointed as a placeholder for a king. Such a placeholder can be appointed or elected or a combination of the two. The most important point is that Israel understands itself as a monarchy temporarily without a king.

There is only one basic reason for this proposal. It is the will of God that Israel be ruled by the House of David, and that is all we need to know. Once this is understood, collateral benefits might accrue. A contiguous neighbor of Israel with whom Israel has particularly good relations is a monarchy. Declaring Israel a Davidic monarchy would give content to the claim that Israel is a Jewish state, a claim that at this writing is advanced by Israel and rejected by the Muslim world. This proposal is not connected in any way with hawkish or dovish policies, nor have I defined the actual power of a Davidic monarch, which could range from considerable to mainly symbolic, such as the British monarchy.

My only purpose in offering this proposal is to give expression to the deep Jewish longing, expressed so frequently and with such deep emotion in our liturgy when we beseech God to see a ruler of the House of David on the throne of Israel. Finally, I would not underestimate the impact of a Davidic ruler of Israel on the emotions of countless Christians for whom Israel under Jewish sovereignty is already a nourishing source of their faith.

Hope and Responsibility for the Human Future

The People Israel, Christianity, and the Covenantal Responsibility to History

Eugene B. Korn

To be a member of God's covenant with the Jewish people — to be a *ben berit* — is to live in the unfolding of sacred history. The drama began at twilight of the sixth day, when God created Adam with a unique holiness, inscribing him with *Tzelem Elohim (Imago Dei)*. It progressed through Noah, Abraham, and the revelation at Sinai. It continues through today, and will end in the messianic era, when all persons recognize the reality of God and his[1] moral authority. And as the prophets Isaiah, Micah, and Zechariah taught, only when all the world lives in blessing and tranquility will the Jewish people fulfill the sacred covenant that God made with Abraham and his descendants. The call of the covenant is to be a partner with the Divine in completing creation and an essential actor in the story of humanity.

God's covenant with the Jewish people at Sinai would be meaningless without this historical mandate. A divine covenant with individuals whose purpose is personal redemption is possible without a historical dimension, but the God of history's covenant with an eternal people assumes purpose only if the covenantal people has an enduring mission over the sweep of time.

---

1. I use the masculine "his" in reference to God only as a linguistic convention, not implying any gender or gender preference to God. In the Jewish theological tradition God transcends gender, although in attempting to understand God it is helpful to ascribe to the Divine traits traditionally both associated with masculinity (e.g., authority and punishment) and femininity (e.g., compassion and nurturing). This has significant pedagogical implications: *Imitatio Dei* would demand that human beings also strive to develop a combination of personality traits as an ideal religious and ethical model. According to Jewish mystical thought, in the eschaton all these traits will merge into a perfect unity — both in God and his creatures.

Eugene B. Korn

The Covenant with Israel

Jewish covenantal theology has its roots in the Bible's account of the founding of the Jewish people and its spiritual destiny. Genesis (12:1-3) relates that God created a unique personal relationship with Abraham, calling upon him to break with his father's home, culture, and gods in pagan Mesopotamia and travel to Canaan. It is there that Abraham was to become "the father of a great nation," whose destiny is blessing. Upon arrival, Abraham and his descendants received eternal title to the land of Canaan, and Abraham immediately built an altar "to call out the name of the Lord" (12:7-9). These events are only the beginning of the intimate covenant between God and Abraham that is formalized soon thereafter in chapter 15. Like all contracts, each covenantal partner acquired benefits and assumed responsibilities: Abraham received blessing, fame, and land. In return, Jewish tradition understood that Abraham assumed the responsibility to function as the witness to God's presence in heaven and on earth.[2] A bit later, Abraham's responsibilities expanded to "teaching the way of the Lord, to do righteousness and justice *(tsedakah u-mishpat)*" (Gen. 18:19). This covenant was passed down to Isaac and Jacob through the generations as told in Genesis, and the family covenant blossomed into a *national* covenant between God and the entire Jewish people with the revelation at Sinai, where Jewish tradition has taught that God gave the Jewish people the whole of the written Torah and its 613 commandments.[3] Rabbinic tradition understands the Sinai covenant to be an extension of Abraham's covenant in Genesis, i.e., they are theologically and spiritually identical though varying in detail.[4] The

---

2. The early rabbinic interpretation (*Midrash, Sifre, Ha'azinu* 313) states that "before Abraham, God was called 'God of the heavens'; after Abraham, people called Him 'God of the heavens and the earth.'" That is, Abraham taught people that God was present in human affairs. The rabbis derived the *midrash* from the text of Genesis 24:2-3, in which Abraham requires that his gentile servant, Eliezer, swear "by the Lord, the God of heaven and earth." Since Christianity adopted this idea of religious purpose and popularized the term "witness," Jews have shied away from using it. However, neither God nor Isaiah hesitated to do so in reference to the Jewish people and its mission. Through Isaiah, God calls Israel "My witnesses" (Isa. 43:11-12).

3. Shlomo Riskin has creatively suggested that God established a third covenant with Israel, other than the "covenant of nationality" with Abraham and the "covenant of religion" at Sinai: the "covenant of the stones" described in Deuteronomy 27–28 established immediately before Moses' death and the entry of the Israelites into the Land of Canaan. This may be thought of as a formalization of the mission of Abraham that will be explicated later.

4. The verses in Exodus describing Jewish slavery in Egypt and Moses' deliverance of

revelation of the Torah at Sinai to Abraham's descendants was but a fuller expression of the original covenant with Abraham in Canaan.[5] In other words, in the rabbinic mind Abraham is Israel and Israel is Abraham.

Jews understand themselves theologically as a covenantal people. It is the Sinai covenant that provides the content, meaning, and commitment to the Jewish people's faith in God. The commandments are the covenantal terms that shape Jewish spiritual life. They are, in the language of Jewish liturgy, "our lives and the length of our days." And it is the experience of the Sinai revelation together with the definition and application of the Sinaitic commandments (Jewish law or *halakhah*) that form the foundation for daily Jewish religious intellectual endeavor and Judaism's religious worldview.

The covenant also establishes an intimate personal relationship between God and his people. Like all forms of intimacy, the covenantal relationship is particularistic and forms an exclusivist relationship between the partners. This is why the biblical prophets repeatedly use the metaphor of marriage to describe the covenant between God and the Jewish people. The sanctity of marriage lies precisely in the fact that husband and wife are devoted exclusively to each other. Because it is an exclusive relationship, the covenant's benefits accrue only to the Jewish people, and the responsibilities of the covenantal commandments do not apply to the rest of humanity in the eyes of normative rabbinic thinkers. Jewish theology was true to the biblical narrative and, unlike Christianity, did not try to universalize God's covenant with Israel. Quite the contrary, for the Talmud and Jewish law *(halakhah)* were suspicious of gentiles who studied Torah and followed the Sinai commandments, viewing them metaphori-

---

the Jewish people emphasize this continuity. "God remembered his covenant with Abraham" (2:24) and God is identified to the Jewish slaves as the God of Abraham . . . (3:15). The exodus is but a fulfillment of the promise to Abraham (6:3-8). Thus the religious dramas of Abraham and the theological events of the exodus and at Sinai are portrayed as being of one continuous cloth.

5. Though historically and textually difficult on a literal level, some talmudic and medieval rabbinic opinions tried to emphasize this point by claiming that Abraham kept all the Mosaic (and even later rabbinic) commandments. This is the opinion of mishnaic sage R. Nahorei, expressed in the last *mishnah* in tractate *Kiddushin* and the late second-century–early third-century talmudic sage Rav, in Babylonian Talmud, *Yoma* 28b. (The same talmudic text records an equally authoritative disagreeing opinion.) Rav derives this conclusion from his exegesis of Genesis 26:5. It is also articulated by the popular medieval biblical commentator Shlomo ben Yitshak (Rashi) in his commentary on that verse. As we shall see, this is a minority view, and one, I am convinced, that is made for pedagogical purposes only.

cally as third parties adulterously intruding on the intimate betrothal between God and Israel.[6]

This understanding of Israel's covenant exposes a literary problem in the biblical story, and it can easily lead to a deeper theological problem. As do all identity-forming relationships, the covenant erects boundaries, and thereby it creates an insider/outsider dichotomy. Jews are in the covenant under God's parental care; all else are "Other." If so, what are we to make of God's relationship with those outside our parochial covenant? The Bible seems to reinforce this challenge since, once Abraham appears in the biblical narrative, Hebrew Scriptures become almost an exclusively Jewish story. From Genesis 12 through Chronicles, the Bible is a history of the successes, failures, and journeys of the people of Israel. If gentiles appear at all, they are in the background. With the arrival of Abraham, then, the original grand cosmic drama of creation piercing the farthest corners of heaven and earth shifts with shocking discontinuity to a local family narrative.

On the theological level, God's singular concern with his covenantal people severely narrows divine involvement with his cosmic creation. Throughout the Bible, both covenantal partners are so lovesick with each other that they appear to leave the universe behind; those outside the covenant merit neither prolonged divine nor Jewish concern. Abraham's travel from Haran to Canaan transformed not only Abraham, but also his divine partner. Sometime during Abraham's journey to Canaan, the majestic all-caring Creator of humanity voluntarily diminished himself and became a demanding and protecting Father of this nation alone. Where is the Author of creation, the God of resplendent holiness, whose glory fills the entire universe and whose concern extends to all his children? God, it seems, has "gone ethnic."

Living the covenant faithfully requires intense focus on performing the *mitsvot*, the behavioral commandments that connect the Jewish people to their God and individual Jews to their kin. As a result, Jews can easily interpret the covenant as demanding that they be a people "who dwells apart, not reckoned among the nations" (Num. 23:9), in splendid isolation from the rest of the world.[7] And certainly the Jewish historical experience

---

6. Babylonian Talmud (henceforth BT), *Sanhedrin* 59a, Maimonides, *Mishneh Torah* (henceforth *MT*), Laws of Kings 8:10 and 10:9-10. Although Maimonides says in 10:10 that gentiles may perform commandments for their utilitarian value, he states in 10:9 that they should not do so *qua* commandment, i.e., as a covenantal obligation, without conversion to Judaism and thus joining the Jewish people.

7. In his essay in this volume, Naftali Rothenberg offers a well-articulated illustration of

in exile amongst the nations conduces toward this withdrawal theology. Today Jews are a traumatized people. The deep wounds inflicted by the harsh historical oppressions of Rome, the Church, the Tsars, the Nazis, the Communists, and the current widespread Muslim hostility to Israel easily lead some religious and nationalist Jewish thinkers to idealize isolation from world affairs. It seems that whenever Jews engaged with the world, Jewish blood ran in the streets. Thus it is quite natural for the Jewish people to turn inward and to elevate survival to its primary religious value.

This inward gaze is expressed poignantly by a central part of the daily Jewish liturgy:

> My God, guard my tongue from evil and my lips from deceitful speech. To those who curse me, let my soul be silent; may my soul be to all like the dust. Open my heart to Your Torah and let my soul pursue Your commandments. As for all who plan evil against me, swiftly thwart their counsel and frustrate their plans. Act for the sake of Your name; act for the sake of Your right hand; act for the sake of Your Torah. That Your beloved ones may be delivered, save with Your right hand and answer me. May the words of my mouth and the meditation of my heart find favor before You, Lord, my Rock and Redeemer. May He who makes peace in His high places, make peace for us and all Israel — and say: "Amen."[8]

This is the final paragraph of the eighteen blessings-prayers that religious Jews recite three times daily as they formally stand before God. As such, it represents the culmination of a Jew's personal petition to God. Note its major aspirations:

(1) personal piety
(2) individual and national deliverance from hostile enemies
(3) personal observance of the divine commandments (Torah)
(4) peace for all Israel

The prayer's spiritual vision is cautious and restricted. The penitent sees the outside world not as a blessed manifestation of God's creation, but as wholly Other: an existential threat to him and the Jewish people ("Your

---

this understanding of the covenant. He assumes *ab initio* that Torah and the Jewish covenant necessarily create an obstacle for Jewish relations with all others.

8. *The Koren Siddur*, American Edition (Jerusalem: Koren Publishers, 2009), p. 134.

beloved"). The fervent plea is for God to act as the deliverer of the Jewish people and carrier of peace to Israel, not the Father of all humanity. The religious dream is personal piety unconnected to its impact on the world. Indeed, God's infinite creation as the arena of religious wonder and covenantal challenge has been left behind.

Blessing and Mission

Maimonides is foremost among Jewish rationalist theologians, all of whom insist that God's commandments are rational.[9] Rational human action is behavior directed toward a desired end. Similarly, for God's commandments to exhibit rationality each must have a purpose and be commanded with a constructive end in mind. The God of Genesis who created a world characterized as good cannot be arbitrary when he commands his children. To argue that the divine commandments have no rational purpose diminishes the Creator, making him a whimsical dictator who orders his children around simply to parade his authority over them.[10]

If this is true of individual commandments, so it must be with the system of commandments as a whole. If God is a benevolent Father, the covenant must be part of the divine rational economy with an overarching purpose that transcends the fulfillment of the individual commandments. It is precisely this *telos* that provides coherence to the Bible's cosmic account of creation alongside its particularistic account of the Jewish people, and it is this *telos* that gives the covenant theological significance beyond Israel itself. It endows the Jewish people with a universal purpose in sacred history, redeeming their covenantal life from tribalistic limitation.

Not merely rational theology but the Bible itself testifies to this covenantal *telos* and Israel's universal religious purpose. Indeed in the very text that establishes God's particular covenant with Abraham, God preserves the divine concern for all his children when he articulates the theological imperative for Abraham to interact with humanity: "You shall be a blessing. . . . Through you [i.e., Abraham], all the nations of the earth shall be blessed" (Gen. 12:2-3). Abraham and his descendants — the Jewish people — are challenged to play a role in universal human history. God's covenant

9. Maimonides, *Guide of the Perplexed* III: 25-26; see also Sa'adia Gaon, *Book of Beliefs and Opinions* III: 1-3.

10. In *Guide* III: 31, Maimonides implies this diminution of God by people who ascribe no rational purpose to divine commandments.

demands that the Jewish people be neither a parochial nor a ghetto people relegated to an insignificant footnote in the larger drama of humanity. God's covenantal people is to be a central actor — *the* central actor — in the grand human story. This broad covenantal mission is so important to God's plan for Israel that the Bible reiterates it four more times, twice when God reaffirms the covenant with Abraham, once when it is passed to Abraham's son, Isaac, and once when it is bequeathed to Isaac's son, Jacob.[11] Thus the divine paradox of sacred history: God shows a special love to Abraham that extends to his particular descendants functioning in a particular land for the purpose of bringing God's blessing to humanity everywhere. (Christianity understood this paradox, for if Christian thought claims that redemption and the divine love of humanity come through the particular sacrifice of Jesus on the cross, it is possible only because Jesus is the climax of the process that began with the particular election of Abraham.)

It was Michael Wyschogrod who cogently revealed the universalist implications of God's particular election of Abraham and Israel. For him, only God's preferential love for Abraham could guarantee the possibility that every individual person can have a genuine personal relationship with God: "Chosenness expresses to Jew and Gentile alike that God also stands in relation with them in the recognition of their uniqueness." In other words, it is God's choosing of Abraham the individual that ensures that God relates personally to each individual, not merely to humanity as an impersonal collective. Moreover, "when we grasp that the election of Israel flows from the fatherhood that extends to all created in God's image, we find ourselves tied to all men in brotherhood, as Joseph, favored by his human father, ultimately found himself tied to his brothers."[12]

The particular/universal paradox plays out on a third level, that of geography: In the biblical vision, the Jewish Temple restricted to the particular locale of Jerusalem is the source of God's Word radiating outward to touch all people everywhere: "My house shall be called a house of prayer for all nations" (Isa. 56:7).

The Bible does not spell out explicitly the nature of the blessing that Abraham's children are to bestow upon the nations, but both classical and modern Jewish thinkers have given it content. The consensus is that Abra-

11. Genesis 18:18; 22:18; 26:4; 28:13-14.
12. See Michael Wyschogrod, *Body of Faith* (Lanham, MD: Rowman & Littlefield, 1996), and Meir Y. Soloveichik, "God's First Love: The Theology of Michael Wyschogrod," *First Things*, November 2009.

ham's children are to emulate Abraham by spreading knowledge of God[13] and teaching divine moral values to the world as fundamental to human welfare.[14] This is achieved actively through teaching or more passively by acting as role models for the successful moral life, as witnesses to God and his moral law.[15] According to the biblical history, God charged Abraham to reteach humanity what it lost in its spiritual descents from Adam and Noah and from Noah and Abraham.[16] The covenantal task of Abraham's children is to partner with the Divine in bringing the nations of the world to their spiritual and moral fulfillment. This is the covenant's purpose in sacred history and the "mission" of the covenantal people, although Jews tend to eschew "witness" and "mission" language since these terms were so widely appropriated by Christian thinkers.[17] Nevertheless, this is exactly

13. See commentaries of Isaac Abravanel and Menachem Ricanati on Genesis 12:2, Maimonides, *MT,* Laws of Idolatry 1:3 and *Guide of the Perplexed* III: 29, and Yehudah Leib Alter, *Sefat Emet, Sukkot* 5664. This interpretation is supported by the numerous passages in Genesis where Abraham "calls on the name of the Lord" (Gen. 12:8; 13:4; 21:33). Isaac does the same in 26:25. Gerald Blidstein claims that Maimonides "points to Israel's universalistic mission of the Jewish people as instructors of humankind in the worship of God," when he codifies in *MT,* Acts of Sacrifices 19:16, that Jews may teach gentiles how to offer sacrifices to God. See Blidstein's "Maimonides and Me'iri on Non-Judaic Religion," in *Scholars and Scholarship: The Interaction Between Judaism and Other Cultures,* ed. Leo Landman (New York: Yeshiva University Press, 1990), p. 31, n. 12.

14. This also has biblical support in Genesis 18:19. See also Maimonides, *MT,* Laws of Kings 10:11, who states that the Noahide laws with their requirement of a legal order were given to humanity to help ensure that "human society is not destroyed."

15. Deuteronomy 4:6-7 articulates how the model life constitutes a living "proof" to the nations of God's existence, wisdom, and morality: "Observe them [i.e., divine commandments] faithfully, for that will be proof of your wisdom and discernment to other peoples, who on hearing all these laws will say, 'Surely that is a wise and discerning people.' For what great nation is there that has a god so close at hand as is the Lord our God whenever we call upon him? Or what great nation has laws and rules as perfect as all this Torah that I set before you on this day?" Also Zechariah 8:23: "In those days it will happen that ten men of all the [different] languages of the nations, will take hold, they will hold the corner of the garment of a Jewish man, saying, 'Let us go with you, for we have heard that G-d is with you.'"

16. This is how Maimonides understands pre-Abrahamic history, although in Maimonides' account, Abraham discovered God rather than God commanding Abraham. See *MT,* Laws of Idolators 1:1-3.

17. Christianity appropriated this definition of mission exactly: "The term mission, in its proper sense, is referred to conversion from false gods and idols to the true and one God, who revealed Himself in the salvation history with his elected people" (Walter Cardinal Kasper, then president of the Vatican's Commission on Religious Relations with the Jews, May 2001, quoted in Mary Boys, "Does the Catholic Church Have a Mission 'with' or 'to' Jews?" *Studies*

the way rabbinic thinkers have understood Abraham's behavior and his children's spiritual purpose.

The Bible also articulates the purpose of the Sinai covenant and its commandments with the children of Israel: "If you will faithfully obey Me and keep My covenant, you shall be My treasured possession among all people. All the earth is Mine, but you shall be for Me a kingdom of priests and a holy nation" (Exod. 19:5-6).

The function of a priest is to bestow God's blessings upon others:[18]

> Thus shall you bless the people of Israel: May the Lord bless you and keep you.
> May the Lord deal kindly and graciously with you.
> May the Lord bestow His favor upon you and grant you peace.
> Thus they shall link My name with the people of Israel and I will bless them. (Num. 6:22-27)

Yet if all Israel is to be a "kingdom of priests," it must be the gentile nations who are the community that Israel is called upon to bless. Mirroring God's charge to Abraham to "be a blessing," Jewish theologians identified the Sinaitic priestly function as spreading blessing by teaching the world about God and divine ethical values.[19] Indeed, this is the meaning of the Sinai election, the reason for Israel's covenantal existence. One modern rabbinic authority went so far as to claim that in establishing the covenant with Israel at Sinai, God completed his plan for all of creation that began in Genesis.[20] Israel is the culmination of creation, not because Jews are the center of the universe, but because Sinai charged the Jewish people to be humanity's teachers, instructing all people of God's authorship of creation and his moral rules for continuing the human social order. Israel was created for the world, not the world for Israel.

---

in Christian-Jewish Relations 3 [2008]: 6, found at http://ejournals.bc.edu/ojs/index.php/scjr/article/view/1482/1335).

18. See commentary of R. Tsadok ha-Kohen (nineteenth-century Poland) on Deuteronomy *Parshat Ki Tavo*, 4. Indeed, this is the very formulation of the rabbinic interpretation found in the *Midrash Aggadah* (Buber, ed.) on Genesis 12:3, which saw Abraham as functioning as a priest to the community around him.

19. See the commentaries of Rabbis Obadiah Seforno (*Torah Chaim Humash* [Hebrew] [Jerusalem: Hamakor Press, 1986]) and Samson Raphael Hirsch (*Hirsch Commentary on the Torah* [Judaica Press, 1989]) on Exodus 19:6.

20. See R. Naftali Tsvi Yehudah Berlin (Netsiv), commentary on Pentateuch *(Ha-Emeq Davar)* (New York: Friedman, 1977), Introduction to the Book of Exodus.

In God's name, Isaiah poetically expresses this same covenantal calling of Israel:

> I have called you in righteousness, and will hold your hand and keep you. And I will establish you as a covenant of the people, for a Light of the Nations. . . . Behold, darkness shall cover the earth, and a thick darkness the nations. But God will shine upon you. Nations shall then go by your Light and kings by your illumination. (42:6; 60:2-3)

The disparity between Genesis 1–11 and the rest of Hebrew Scriptures is now closed by God's paradox of sacred history: A particular people, a tiny people is tasked with the mission of bringing God's blessing to all of humanity and the light of divine morality to every corner of creation.

The Noahide and Abrahamic Covenants

As indicated, the Sinai covenant is particularistic, restricted to the Jewish people.[21] This is in marked contrast to the church's "new covenant," whose domain is in principle universal. Yet this is not the end of the Jewish view of God's covenants with his children.

From at least as early as the talmudic era (200-500 CE), Jewish thinkers found a way to establish God's enduring relationship with gentiles and grant them theological legitimacy. Judaism has long subscribed to "double covenant theology": The rabbis of the Talmud believed that Jews stand obligated to God through the Sinai covenant and its 613 commandments, while gentiles stand under another divine covenant containing seven commandments that promote moral values essential for a flourishing human social order: the six prohibitions of murder, theft, sexual immorality, idolatry, excessive cruelty, and disrespect for life indicated by eating the limb of a live animal and blasphemy against the God of the universe who is a transcendent moral authority, as well as the one positive injunction to set up courts of law that justly enforce these six prohibitions.[22] These are

---

21. Judaism has taken much unkind and unfair criticism for the parochial nature of its covenant, but, as I have argued elsewhere, it is precisely this limitation in the Sinai covenant that provides a logical opening for acknowledging non-Jewish religious forms and conceptions, that is, limited theological pluralism. See my "A Jewish Conception of Theological Pluralism," in *Two Faiths, One Covenant?* ed. Eugene B. Korn and John T. Pawlikowski (Lanham, MD: Rowman & Littlefield, 2005), pp. 151-60.

22. *Tosefta Avodah Zarah* 8:4 and Maimonides, *MT*, Laws of Kings 9:1.

known as the seven Noahide commandments, and the talmudic rabbis attempted to locate sources for these moral commands in the biblical history of humanity from Adam to Noah.[23]

While gentiles who do not accept the moral Noahide commandments are considered unworthy pagans, all gentiles who live under these basic laws of civilization are considered to be worthy Noahides, or *benei Noah* in Jewish theological parlance.[24] It is crucial to stress that according to this double covenant theology, each covenant is valid for its respective adherents and there is no theological need for Noahides to convert to the Jewish covenant. Noahides participate in an independent and authentic covenant that defines a separate and religiously valuable way of life. In rabbinic tradition they are accorded positive status — even to the extent that gentiles who faithfully keep the Noahide commandments are regarded as more beloved by God than Jews who violate the fundamentals of their covenant of 613 commandments.[25] Normative Jewish tradition paid some of these gentiles the ultimate theological compliment by teaching that "righteous gentiles have a share in the world to come."[26] Hence (and again in contrast to Christianity), there was never a theological urgency for gentiles to convert to Judaism and observe the Sinaitic commandments.

It may be fruitful to reconsider the patriarch Abraham and God's covenant with him. Was Abraham a Jew or simply a righteous Noahide? For most Jews schooled in the biblical genealogy of Abraham through Moses and in traditional rabbinic interpretation *(midrash)*, the answer is clear: Abraham is the first — perhaps the paradigmatic — Jew. Yet we can ask the question differently in legal and theological terms: Did Abraham stand under the 613 Sinaitic commandments given to Israel or only under the seven Noahide commandments? When we pose the question this way, it becomes apparent that the majority of rabbinic exegetes did not see Abra-

---

23. See BT, *Sanhedrin* 46b.

24. Maimonides, Laws of Kings 8:10.

25. R. Jacob Emden, *Seder Olam Rabbah*, cited in translation by Oscar Z. Fasman, "An Epistle on Tolerance by a 'Rabbinic Zealot,'" in *Judaism in a Changing World*, ed. Leo Jung (New York: Oxford University Press, 1939).

26. BT, *Sanhedrin* 105a and Maimonides, Laws of Repentance 3:5 and Laws of Kings 8:11. For an extended discussion of the topic of salvation for righteous gentiles, see Eugene Korn, "Gentiles, the World to Come and Judaism: The Odyssey of a Rabbinic Text," *Modern Judaism*, October 1994.

ham as an Israelite, since they believed that he was not obligated in, nor did he observe, the Sinaitic commandments.[27]

But Abraham was no mere Noahide. To be precise, according to most Jewish biblical authorities *Abraham was a theological Noahide:* He observed the fundamental moral Noahide laws as well as a few other individual behavioral commandments, such as circumcision. Abraham's uniqueness lay in his recognition of the One Creator of Heaven and Earth, in his understanding of the theological foundation for the Noahide laws,[28] and in his giving public witness to these beliefs. This is the meaning of Abraham repeatedly "calling the Name of the Lord." This gesture was testimony to all around him that God exists, and it was a public prayer that proclaimed God's continuing involvement with his children.[29] The Abrahamic covenant, then, was the seed for the covenant at Sinai, but was far from identical with it.

Jewish Theology and Christianity

How can Jewish theology understand Christianity in covenantal terms? Are there authentic grounds for a new *theological* relationship in which Jews see Christians as participating in a common covenant with them? If

27. See commentaries on Genesis 26:5 by Rabbis David Kimḥi (Radak), Obadiah Seforno, Moses ben Naḥman (Naḥmanides), Abraham Ibn Ezra, Samuel ben Meir (Rashbam), and Chizkiya bar Manoach (Ḥizkuni). All found in *Torah Chaim Humash* (Hebrew) (Jerusalem: Hamakor Press, 1986). See also Maimonides, *MT*, Laws of Kings 9:1. For a contemporary expression of this position by a traditionalist rabbinic authority, see Rabbi Joseph B. Soloveitchik, *Abraham's Journey*, ed. David Shatz, Joel B. Wolowelsky, and Reuven Ziegler (Jersey City, NJ: Ktav, 2008), p. 58. These interpretations comport well with the biblical text, which indicates that the patriarchs violated some of the Sinai commandments, and they eliminate the need for historical anachronism. (How could Abraham observe Passover in commemoration of the exodus from Egypt, which was yet to occur?) They have no reason to ascribe prophetic powers to Abraham to enable him to know later biblical or postbiblical Jewish history. As such, they are more rational than the minority view of the talmudic sages R. Nahorei (*Kiddushin* 82a) and Rav (*Yoma* 28b) and the medieval commentator, Rabbi Shlomo ben Isaac (Rashi). See note 5.

28. None of the Noahide commandments require a positive theological commitment.

29. According to the talmudic sages and later authorities Abraham established the practice of (morning) prayer. See BT, *Sanhedrin* 26b, and Maimonides, Laws of Kings 9:1. This is also the way that medieval rabbinic biblical commentators understood "calling the name of the Lord." For Rashi, it was an act of prayer and for Naḥmanides it was public proclamation of God's existence. (See their respective commentaries on Gen. 12:8.)

so, what are the boundaries of this commonality? The answers to these questions may well determine whether Jews and Christians can understand each other with greater theological appreciation and forge an active partnership to build a better future together on the basis of a common religious mission.

Because of the painful historical experience that Jews endured with Christianity almost since its inception, most rabbinic authorities have lacked an incentive to view Christianity as a positive phenomenon. Yet over time there was a perceptible shift in the rabbinic understanding of Christianity. One can plot four stages in the evolution of rabbinic thinking about Christianity in different historical eras:[30]

(1) In the first and second centuries, Jewish Christians were a tolerated sect in the community and then came to be regarded as heretics or apostates from Judaism. Belief in Jesus as messiah and the "new covenant" were considered illegitimate and illicit doctrines, i.e., *avodah zarah* ("foreign worship," often connoting idolatry).

(2) During the Middle Ages, when Jews lived in small communities in Christian Europe and were dependent on economic interaction with Christians, most medieval rabbis in Germany, France, and Italy ruled that gentile Christians were not the same as the idolators of the Bible or the Talmud.[31] Nevertheless, because of the doctrines of the trinity and the incarnation, many rabbinic authorities still considered Christianity to be an illicit form of worship (*avodah zarah,* often connoting idolatry). Under this conception, Christians were considered observing Noahides who — for technical reasons — did not violate the prohibition against idolatry.

(3) In the late Middle Ages and early modernity, the majority of rabbis living in Christian Europe *(aḥaronim)* did not consider Christianity to constitute *avodah zarah* for gentiles. They ruled that while Jews were obligated to believe in absolute monotheism, gentiles were not so obligated by the terms of the Noahide covenant. Hence Christianity became a valid belief system for gentiles.

30. For extensive details of this evolution and the logical map of rabbinic opinions regarding Christianity, see my "Rethinking Christianity: Rabbinic Positions and Possibilities," in *Jewish Theology and World Religions* (London: Littman Library of Jewish Civilization, 2012).

31. That is, the biblical and talmudic legal restrictions on commercial and social interactions with idolators did not apply to Christians.

(4) From the seventeenth century through the twentieth century, when Christian toleration of Jews grew,[32] a number of rabbinic authorities began to appreciate Christianity as a positive historical phenomenon and an unobjectionable theological system for gentiles because it spread many fundamental principles of Judaism (e.g., existence of God, *creatio ex nihilo*, Noahide morality, and the fact of Sinai revelation) and thus advanced the Jewish religious mission.

Here are some examples of this fourth category of opinions expressing a new theological recognition of Christianity:

R. Moses Rivkis (seventeenth-century Lithuania):
The gentiles in whose shadow Jews live and among whom Jews are dispersed are not idolators. Rather they believe in *creatio ex nihilo* and the Exodus from Egypt and the main principles of faith. Their intention is to the Creator of Heaven and Earth and we are obligated to pray for their welfare.[33]

Rabbi Jacob Emden (eighteenth-century Germany):
The Nazarene brought a double goodness to the world. . . . The Christian eradicated *avodah zarah,* removed idols (from the nations) and obligated them in the seven *mitsvot* of Noah so that they would not behave like animals of the field, and instilled them firmly with moral traits. . . . Christians and Moslems are congregations that (work) for the sake of heaven — (people) who are destined to endure, whose intent is for the sake of heaven and whose reward will not be denied.[34]

---

32. Jacob Katz (*Exclusivism and Tolerance* [New York: Schocken, 1962]) advances the causal thesis that it was the budding Christian tolerance during this period that significantly influenced the development of a positive halakhic attitude toward Christians held by traditionalist Orthodox rabbis of the time: "The first signs of tolerance toward Jews . . . gave rise to corresponding attitudes on the part of Jews to Christians" (p. 166). It is evident from the statements of Rivkis, Emden, and Ya'ir Bacharach (to which Katz is referring) that this positive attitude referred not only to Christians, but also to Christianity *qua* religious belief system.

33. Gloss on *Shulhan Arukh, Hoshen Mishpat*, section 425:5.

34. *Seder Olam Rabbah* 35-37; *Sefer ha-Shimush* 15-17. For a fuller explanation of R. Emden's position, see Harvey Falk, "Rabbi Jacob Emden's Views on Christianity," *Journal of Ecumenical Studies* 19, no. 1 (Winter 1982); and Moshe Miller, "Rabbi Jacob Emden's Attitude Toward Christianity," in *Turim: Studies in Jewish History and Literature*, vol. 2, ed. M. Shmidman (New York: Touro College Press/Ktav, 2008), pp. 105-36.

The goal of [Christians and Muslims] is to promote Godliness among the nations . . . to make known that there is a Ruler in heaven and earth, Who governs and monitors and rewards and punishes. . . . We should consider Christians and Moslems as instruments for the fulfillment of the prophecy that the knowledge of God will one day spread throughout the earth. Whereas the nations before them worshipped idols, denied God's existence, and thus did not recognize God's power or retribution, the rise of Christianity and Islam served to spread among the nations, to the furthest ends of the earth, the knowledge that there is One God who rules the world, who rewards and punishes and reveals himself to man. Indeed, Christian scholars have not only won acceptance among the nations for the revelation of the Written Torah but have also defended God's Oral Law.[35]

Rabbi Samson Raphael Hirsch (nineteenth-century Germany):

Judaism does not say, "There is no salvation outside of me." Although disparaged because of its alleged particularism, the Jewish religion actually teaches that the upright of all peoples are headed toward the highest goal. In particular, they have been at pains to stress that, while in other respects their views and ways of life may differ from those of Judaism, the peoples in whose midst the Jews are now living [i.e., Christians] have accepted the Jewish Bible of the Old Testament as a book of Divine revelation. They profess their belief in the God of heaven and earth as proclaimed in the Bible and they acknowledge the sovereignty of Divine Providence in both this life and the next. Their acceptance of the practical duties incumbent upon all men by the will of God distinguishes these nations from the heathen and idolatrous nations of the talmudic era.[36]

Before Israel set out on its long journey through the ages and the nations, . . . it produced an offshoot [Christianity] that had to become estranged from it in great measure, in order to bring to the world — sunk in idol worship, violence, immorality and the degradation of man — at least the tidings of the One Alone, of the brotherhood of all men, and of man's superiority over the beast. It was to teach the renunciation of the worship of wealth and pleasures, albeit not their use in the service of the

35. *Commentary on Ethics of the Fathers* 4:11.

36. *The Collected Writings*, vol. 7: *Jewish Education*, "Talmudic Judaism and Society" (New York: Feldheim, 1984), pp. 225-27.

One Alone. Together with a later offshoot [Islam] it represented a major step in bringing the world closer to the goal of all history.[37]

Note that these later rabbinic authorities judge Christians positively because of their beliefs. That is, unlike the early medieval rabbis, these early moderns appreciated Christians *because* of the influence of Christianity on their behavior and belief. Implicitly then, these authorities are making theological statements regarding Christianity, not merely Christians.

On the Christian side, Catholic and Protestant theologies have always insisted that Christianity is the heir to the Jewish covenant:

> There is neither Jew nor Greek, there is neither slave nor free, there is neither male nor female — for all of you are one in Christ Jesus. If you belong to Christ, then you are Abraham's descendants, heirs according to the promise. (Gal. 3:28-29)

The church is part of the unfolding history of Israel — indeed, it is "*the* new Israel."[38] Unfortunately, for many Christians this means replacement of the old Israel. Christians see themselves as the contemporary recipients of the divine blessing given to Abraham and members of the covenantal chain from Abraham to Moses that culminated in the new covenant established with the blood of Jesus.[39] In other words, Christians see themselves as the contemporary chosen people, not merely *b'nai Noah,* or people following the Noahide covenant.

This is an unacceptable thesis for Jewish theology, and traditional Jewish thinkers have consistently maintained that Jews and Christians do not share any covenant. (Of course, both are obligated by the Noahide covenant, but Jews do not identify themselves as Noahides.) Jews have resisted acknowledging the Christian claim for historical and theological reasons to be discussed in the next section. Yet the matter cannot remain settled

37. *Nineteen Letters on Judaism,* edited and annotated by Joseph Elias (Jerusalem: Feldheim, 1995).

38. Unfortunately, for many Christians this means replacement of the old Israel, but apparently not for Paul. See Romans 11:17-24, 29. I thank my colleague Gerald McDermott for pointing my attention to this text. More on replacement theology and supersessionism later in this essay.

39. This is the formulation of Irenaeus of Lyon, in *Heresies* III.11.8, found in *Irenaeus of Lyons,* trans. Robert M. Grant (New York: Routledge 2007), p. 132. More recently, Cardinal Dario Castrillon Hoyos put it this way: "Abraham is the father of faith, but in a chain of salvation in which the Messiah is expected. And the Messiah has arrived." See Boys, "Does the Catholic Church Have a Mission 'with' or 'to' Jews?" p. 9.

with this denial, for it is clear that Christianity is closer to Judaism in history, mission, and content than, for example, an Asian religion that might fulfill the Noahide commandments. For whatever reasons, God has closely intertwined Jews and Christians historically, and Judaism and Christianity theologically. For Judaism, then, Christians cannot be mere Noahides. Christianity must stand theologically somewhere between the Noahide religion and the Judaism of the Sinai covenant.

When we combine the above-cited modern rabbinic appreciation of Christianity with the recent sympathetic Christian theologies toward Judaism, we open up fresh possibilities for rethinking a Jewish covenantal relationship with Christianity and for fashioning new Jewish-Christian cooperation in pursuit of common values.

We have seen that medieval and modern Jewish biblical commentators understood Abraham's covenantal mission as teaching the world about God and bearing witness to his moral law. And in the philosophic eyes of Maimonides, spreading the knowledge of the One God of Heaven and Earth throughout the world was the primary vocation of Abraham.[40] It is interesting to note that this understanding of Abraham's mission is exactly the mission and historical impact of Christianity according to Rabbis Rivkis ("[Christians] believe in *creatio ex nihilo* and the Exodus from Egypt and the main principles of faith. Their intention is to the Creator of Heaven and Earth"); Emden ("The Christians removed idols (from the nations) and obligated them in the seven *mitsvot* of Noah so that they would not behave like animals of the field, and instilled them firmly with moral traits. . . . The goal of [Christians and Muslims] is to promote Godliness among the nations . . . to make known that there is a Ruler in Heaven and Earth"); and Hirsch ("The peoples in whose midst the Jews are now living [i.e., Christians] have accepted the Jewish Bible of the Old Testament as a book of Divine revelation. They profess their belief in the God of heaven and earth as proclaimed in the Bible and they acknowledge the sovereignty of Divine Providence. . . . Their acceptance of the practical duties incumbent upon all men by the will of God distinguishes these nations from the heathen and idolatrous nations of the talmudic era. . . . Judaism produced an offshoot [Christianity] . . . in order to bring to the world — sunk in idol worship, violence, immorality and the degradation of man — at least the tidings of the One Alone").[41]

---

40. *MT*, Laws of Idolators 1:3; Book of Commandments, positive commandment no. 3; *Guide of the Perplexed* III: 51.

41. It is because Hirsch believed that the fulfillment of God's covenant as spreading the

In effect, these rabbis viewed Christianity as playing a role in the covenant of Abraham. If so, Jews can view Christians as partners in that covenant.[42] This may be a common assumption in Christian theology, but it is a new claim for Jewish theology. It means that Christianity qualifies as an Abrahamic religion covenantally, not merely historically.[43] Jewish thinkers have always assumed that gentile nations could be genealogically descended from Abraham, but no gentile could be within the particular covenant that God made with Abraham. That was reserved for the Jewish people alone.

If this is so, then Jews and Christians can see each other as sharing Abraham's covenant. They can understand themselves to be working toward the same spiritual goals of sacred history, but under different systems of commandments and with differentiated functions.

The Problematics of Sharing the Covenant

There are two principal reasons why Jews have rejected the Christian claim to be included in the covenant of Israel. The first problem was the exclusive and supersessionist character of traditional Christian theology. Christianity's claim to the same covenantal promises God made to Israel was the very source of intense theological rivalry, the de-legitimization of Judaism, and Christian persecution of Jews over the course of Jewish-Christian history.

---

reality of God throughout the world constituted the *telos* of sacred history that he could claim that Christianity [and Islam] "represented a major step in bringing the world closer to the goal of all history." See his commentary on Exodus 19:6.

42. The contemporary Jewish theologian Steven Schwarzschild and the noted contemporary Maimonides scholar Menachem Kellner have argued that Maimonides believed that some theologically advanced gentiles were included in the designation "Israel" as "Israel of the Mind." See Kellner's *Maimonides' Confrontation with Mysticism* (London: Littman Library of Jewish Civilization, 2006), ch. 7. This idea strengthens the idea that non-Jews could also be members of the same covenant God made with the Jewish people. Of course, however, Maimonides would not have included Christians in that category because of their belief in the trinity, a belief tantamount to idolatry for Maimonides.

43. Old-new problems remain with this claim, foremost among them that circumcision was an obligatory sign for members of Abraham's covenant. How uncircumcised Christians could be members of the covenant needs to be addressed. Title to the land of Canaan, which was promised to Abraham's covenantal descendants, is less problematic, as that can be understood as limited to the biological descendants of Isaac (see Gen. 21:10-12).

"Hard" supersessionism[44] (i.e., the doctrine that the new covenant replaced the Jewish covenant and that after Jesus, God rejected the Jews in favor of the church) was the longstanding Christian teaching regarding Judaism and Jews. The "new Israel" has invalidated the "old Israel," and the new covenant of the spirit rendered the Mosaic covenant limited temporally, i.e., during the time the Jerusalem Temple stood. The concurrent validity of the Mosaic covenant and the new covenant (i.e., "soft" supersessionism," the doctrine that the church has been grafted onto the living tree of the Jewish people, but the new covenant is the ultimate fulfillment of the still-living Jewish covenant) with its implication that there could be concurrent validity to both the Mosaic and the new covenants, was entertained by only a few early Christian thinkers, but ultimately rejected by early normative Christian theology, which was so heavily shaped by Augustine's hard supersessionist understanding of covenantal history.[45] With the advent of the new covenant of the spirit, the Mosaic covenant became meaningless, even an obstacle to future salvation history. And as Galatians 3:28 seems to indicate, there is no room left for the continued distinct existence of the Jewish people or its independent covenantal mission.[46]

Thus according to hard supersessionism, if Christianity is true, post-Temple Judaism must be false — or at least dead. The rival claim to the same covenant was a theological duel to the death, and since Jews were never inclined toward physical or spiritual suicide they have consistently rejected the Christian claim.

The second obstacle to Jews seeing Christianity sharing a covenantal identity with Judaism is rooted in the doctrines of the trinity and the incarnation, both of which posed formal problems for Jewish legal authori-

---

44. David Novak makes the useful distinction between "hard supersessionism" and "soft supersessionism" in "The Covenant in Rabbinic Thought," in *Two Faiths, One Covenant*, ed. Korn and Pawlikowski, pp. 65-80.

45. See Steven McMichael, "The Covenant in Patristic and Medieval Christian Theology," in *Two Faiths, One Covenant*, pp. 49-51.

46. A number of contemporary Christian scholars (e.g., Krister Stendahl, *Paul Among the Jews and the Gentiles* [Minneapolis: Augsburg Publishers, 1976] and *Final Account: Paul's Letter to the Romans* [Philadelphia: Fortress Press, 1995], and Mark Nanos, "The Myth of the 'Law-Free' Paul Standing between Christians and Jews," online at Nanos's website, http://www.marknanos.com/Myth-Lawfree-12-3-08.pdf, 6) have argued that Paul wanted Jewish followers of Jesus to continue to observe Torah, as he himself does, and hence Jewish Christians would follow Jesus in a way that is different from gentile followers. John Gager ("Reinventing Paul") also argues that Paul's audience in Galatians is entirely gentile. If so, popular supersessionism may have obscured this reading of the New Testament.

ties and theologians. Jews understand the second of the Ten Commandments, "There shall be no other gods for you besides Me" (Exod. 20:2),[47] as demanding absolute monotheism that excludes a trinitarian concept. Any denial of God's absolute unity would violate the divine essence. Moreover, Jews understood that the incarnation violated the second half of that same commandment: "You shall not make for yourself a sculptured image, or any likeness of what is in the heavens above or on the earth below or in the waters under the earth" (Exod. 20:3). The Creator of the material world could never become a human (or any being) with a physical form. Philosophically inclined Jewish theologians saw these two restrictions as logically identical, for to predicate any division of God is to imply that God is physical, limited, and imperfect, i.e., is not God at all.[48] Thus, prior to the sixteenth century, most Jewish thinkers understood Judaism and Christianity as worshiping different gods, and if so, Jews and Christians could hardly share membership in the same divine covenant.

Today, however, we have the means to overcome these problems. The change in Christian thinking about Jews and Judaism that occurred after the Holocaust has significant implications for the Jewish understanding of Christianity and its relationship to the covenant. This is possible because Jewish theology is neither dogmatic nor derived exclusively from theoretical "first principles." Jewish theology is vitally influenced by the experiences of the Jewish people through history. As God's living witnesses, Jews understand God and divine providence mediated through their experiential reality as a people.

After the moral and physical devastation of the Holocaust, a number of Christian thinkers understood where the traditional hard supersessionist teachings led: directly to Christian complicity in the Final Solution and indirectly to Auschwitz.[49] Christians developed more tolerant

47. Interestingly, it was the literal reading of this verse that opened up the logical possibility for many early modern rabbinical authorities to consider Christianity nonidolatrous for gentiles, while remaining idolatrous for Jews. They understood that the prohibition "There shall be no other god *for you* . . ." was addressed exclusively to the Jewish people at Sinai ("for you"), and thus the Christian concept of a trinitarian deity that included the one Creator of the universe along with other associations with the Creator to be permitted to gentiles. This became known in Jewish legal and theological parlance as *"shituf"* (partnership or associationism) and is based on the commentary of the Tosafists on the Babylonian talmudic tractate *Sanhedrin* 63b, s.v. *"assur."*

48. Maimonides, *Guide of the Perplexed* I: 50.

49. See Mary C. Boys, *Has God Only One Blessing? Judaism as a Source of Christian Self-Understanding* (New York: Paulist Press, 2000), ch. 4; James Carroll, *Constantine's Sword*

teachings about Jews and Judaism in soft supersessionist teachings maintaining that God's covenant with the Jewish people was never revoked, that Judaism continued to occupy a role in salvation history, and that Jews were not a rejected people.[50] This seems to be the dominant position today of the Catholic Church as a result of *Nostra aetate* and the theological approach to Judaism that has grown out of the Second Vatican Council. Major Protestant churches have followed suit, and a number of Evangelical theologians make a similar argument.[51] In most of their views, however, Christianity and the new covenant remain the highest fulfillment of the old covenant, and Jewish conversion to Christianity is still a theological desideratum — for God, the church, and for Jews themselves. Yet soft supersessionism, which now appears to be normative in many official Christian theological circles, decreases the urgency and imperative nature to convert Jews.

One version of soft supersessionism is "eschatological supersessionism" — evidently the position of Cardinal Josef Ratzinger, now Pope Benedict XVI: "Sinai is indeed superseded . . . but theological unification (i.e. the conversion of Jews to Christianity) is hardly possible within our historical time, and perhaps not even desirable."[52] In this version, Christianity remains the highest fulfillment of God's word to all on earth, but the full return of Jews to the church is a matter for God at the end of time.

Finally, some Christian theologians deny any form of supersessionism whatsoever and assert an unqualified two-covenant theology: Judaism is salvific for Jews, equal in validity for Jews as Christianity is for Christians, and therefore attempts at converting Jews to the church are theologically unacceptable.[53] Rightly understanding that Christians are closer to Juda-

---

(Boston: Houghton Mifflin, 2001); Edward Flannery, *The Anguish of the Jews* (New York: Paulist Press, 1985); Malcolm Hay, *Europe and the Jews* (Chicago: Academy, 1992); Jules Isaac, *Jesus and Israel* (Austin, TX: Holt, Rinehart & Winston, 1971) and *The Teaching of Contempt: Christian Roots of Anti-Semitism* (New York: Holt, Rinehart & Winston, 1965); Joshua Trachtenberg, *The Devil and the Jews* (Philadelphia: Jewish Publication Society, 1984); Robert Wilken, *John Chrysostom and the Jews: Rhetoric and Reality in the Late Fourth Century* (Eugene, OR: Wipf & Stock, 2004).

50. *Nostra aetate* (1965) is the most famous articulation of this soft supersessionist teaching. For Protestant statements, see Boys, *Has God Only One Blessing?*

51. Documented in Boys, *Has God Only One Blessing?*

52. Josef Ratzinger, *Many Religions, One Covenant: Israel, the Church and the World* (San Francisco: Ignatius, 1999), p. 109.

53. See "Reflections on Covenant and Mission," Consultation of the National Council of Synagogues and the Bishops Committee for Ecumenical and Interreligious Affairs,

ism than are Noahides, the prominent nonsupersessionist Catholic theologian, Mary Boys, has suggested to me that Christians should somehow be seen as having stood with Jews at Sinai. Yet it is difficult to see how Jews (or even contemporary nonsupersessionist Christians) can logically understand Christians as partners in the Sinaitic covenant when they are not obligated to observe all the Sinaitic *mitsvot,* without at least part of the Sinai covenant being superseded.[54] As obvious illustrations, the Sinaitic Decalogue prohibits making images of God and requires Sabbath observance on the seventh (and not the first) day of the week — two commandments that Christianity does not observe.

Churches long ago lost their temporal power and their capacity for physically threatening the Jewish people, and the recent emergence of soft supersessionist, eschatological supersessionist, and nonsupersessionist theologies renders Christian theology less threatening to Judaism and to Jewish covenantal integrity. These recent Christian theologies remove or at least significantly lessen the Christian theological attack on the continuing integrity of the Jewish covenantal mission in history. Understanding this, Jews need not be defensive about adopting a positive new theological approach to Christianity. Jewish and Christian theologies are no longer engaged in a theological duel to the death, and Jews need not fear a sympathetic covenantal understanding of Christianity that is true to the Bible, Jewish thought, and values.

It is important to note that this new covenantal understanding does not require either Jews or Christians to give up their eschatological convictions. Both soft supersessionism and eschatological supersessionism still maintain that Christianity is the highest fulfillment for everyone, including Jews, and that all will join the church when truth is revealed at the end of time. Orthodox Jews, too, are free to continue "believing with great passion in the ultimate truthfulness of our views, praying fervently for and expecting confidently the fulfillment of our eschatological vision

---

United States Conference of Catholic Bishops, August 12, 2002, found at http://www
.jcrelations.net/en/?item=966. This claim elicited strong dissenting reactions from a number
of traditionalist Catholic and Protestant theologians. A prime example is Avery Dulles,
"'Evangelization and the Jews,' with a Response by Mary C. Boys," in Philip A. Cunningham
and John T. Pawlikowski, *America* 187, no. 12 (21 October 2002): 8-16. See also Dulles's "The
Covenant with Israel," *First Things,* November 2005, pp. 16-21.

54. Indeed, Josef Ratzinger (Pope Benedict XVI) asserts the supersession of the Sinai
covenant in the very same passage in which he insists on Christian participation in that covenant. See Ratzinger, *Many Religions,* pp. 70-71.

when our faith will rise from particularity to universality,"[55] should they wish.

The new covenantal relation does require, however, that Christians and Jews give up intense rivalry in their pre-eschaton activities and that they begin to view each other as partners in carrying out God's covenant instead of striving in the here and now to triumphantly convert the other.[56] Surely in our pre-eschaton days, God has more than enough blessings to bestow upon each of his covenantal children.

The second formal theological problem of the unacceptable status of the trinity and incarnation according to Jewish law has also been resolved by the late rabbinic distinction between what Jews are required to believe about God (absolute monotheism) and what is permitted for gentile belief (belief in the One Creator of the universe with additional associated elements). I have argued elsewhere that this difference in legal requirements leads to a philosophic problem and points to the avoidance of theology by formal *halakhah*,[57] but the significant covenantal point for us is that this distinction allows acceptance of legitimate differing Jewish and Christian beliefs about God, and that it is consistent with Jews and Christians retaining their differences in worship, their fidelity to their respective faith communities, and their viewing each other as mutual partners in God's covenantal mission. Lastly, it is crucial to note that under this distinction there are limits to theological pluralism. Christianity and Christian belief remain strictly off-limits for Jews.

---

55. Joseph Soloveitchik, "Confrontation," *Tradition: A Journal of Orthodox Thought* 6, no. 2 (New York: Rabbinical Council of America, 1964), p. 25.

56. It seems that the Roman Catholic Church is still working out how this dialectic can be achieved in practice, and is caught in what some scholars have called a "contradictory pluralism" and a "bipolarity of tendencies" entailed by its soft supersessionism, and its struggle to work out a coherent theology about Jews and the need for their conversion to the Church after *Nostra aetate* and the Second Vatican Council. See Boys, "Does the Catholic Church Have a Mission 'with' Jews or 'to' Jews?" Boys documents the "bipolarity" of official Catholic documents and statements regarding the need for converting Jews. The issue has become even more controversial since 2008, with the 2009 statements of the USCCB on this issue regarding evangelization toward Jews and its place in Catholic-Jewish dialogue and relations. See USCCB's "Note on Ambiguities of RCM" and USCCB's subsequent revision of "Note."

57. See my "Rethinking Christianity: Rabbinic Positions and Possibilities," in *Jewish Theology and World Religions* (London: Littman Library of Jewish Civilization, 2012).

The Meaning of Abraham's Covenant
in the Twenty-First Century

Reconsideration of Abraham's covenant offers a rich theological agenda and new practical challenges and for Jews and Christians. Jews will need to learn how to successfully navigate between their commitment to their exclusive Sinaitic covenant and the more open covenant with Abraham. And if they share covenantal membership with Christians, what will be the theological and practical borders of this partnership that will ensure the enduring particularism of the Jewish people and their mission?

I suspect that Christians will still have to grapple with the issue of supersessionism, but in a new form: Has Christianity superseded Abraham's covenant? If not, how does Abraham's more open covenant relate to traditional Christology and ecclesiology, both past and contemporary? And of course, the conundrum of the universality of the church coexisting with the continuing validity of the particular Jewish covenant still cries out for resolution. Is it a virtuous divine mystery that is cause for humble reflection and celebration,[58] or a vicious logical inconsistency to be eliminated?

If we are true to the biblical account of Abraham and his covenant, we will admit that the Bible does not portray Abraham as a theologian, but as a man of faith, action, and morality. His covenant, then, should above all entail a commitment to practical action in sacred history. And it is precisely today that the practical teachings of Abraham's covenant assume particular urgency.

At the dawn of the twenty-first century, human beings face awesome and terrifying possibilities. We have the tools to improve and protect human life as never before, as well as the means to destroy all human life and God's creation. Civilization as we know it stands on the edge of a precipice. Our values, choices, and behavior will be the difference between a future of blessing or the world descending into its primordial chaos. After witnessing the Holocaust, the genocides, and the democides of the twentieth century, any naïveté or complacency on our part are religious sins, for these horrors should have taught us that radical evil was a reality then and remains an ever-present potentiality for today and the future. As covenantal partners,

---

58. See Richard Sklba, "New Beginnings: Catholic-Jewish Relations After 40 Years," *Origins* 35, no. 31 (19 January 2006): 509-14, who argues that the tension between the universal theological claim of Christianity and the enduring particular validity of the Jewish covenant is a mystery to be appreciated.

the moral imperative needs to be foremost in both our behavior and theology, and there is no justification for any teleological suspension of the ethical — be the *telos* theological, political, financial, or personal.

A number of powerful troubling signs dominate our contemporary cultural and political landscapes. Postmodern secularism has created a pervasive value-orientation whose foundations contain the seeds from which destructive forces can again grow. Hedonism drives much of contemporary life and ethos. Violence saturates our media and popular culture, sometimes appearing as merely another justified form of pleasure. This contributes to the evisceration of moral concern and the numbing of individual conscience, both essential to securing human welfare and dignity. Moral utilitarianism has also made a comeback in contemporary academia and high culture. In this ethic human life is devoid of intrinsic value and individual human life too often becomes a commodity to be traded and sometimes discarded. This moral philosophy shares the Nazi denial of the axiom of Judeo-Christian ethics, namely that all persons are created in God's image, and hence that each person's life has nonquantifiable sacred value.

Because relativism has become one of the most accepted moral theories in our time, objectivity and moral absolutes are under ferocious attack and are on the cultural defensive. The belief that there is no objective bar by which to measure human actions easily slips into the belief that there is no bar at all for valid moral judgment. And from there, it is but a small step to the denial of ethics entirely. In the political theater, a radical and intolerant Islamist monism has grown into a common threat to Judaism and Christianity and to moderate Muslims as well. It denies Jewish and Christian legitimacy in the Middle East and by implication tolerance of all religious diversity. Finally, irrational religious extremism has become a potent force in both world politics and religious identity. Although the twenty-first century is in its infancy, we have already seen too much violence and mass slaughter committed in the name of God. All these phenomena are frightening dangers and call Jews and Christians to joint action.

Jews and Christians play an essential role in God's sacred plan for human progress in history — indeed for the survival of humanity. As partners in Abraham's covenant, we are spiritually obligated to heed the divine call of bringing blessing to the world. We can do this together by publicly bearing witness to God's covenantal values to the world:

1. There is a spiritual center to the universe because the world was created by a loving God, who is intimately involved in human lives and who yearns to redeem his children. Jews and Christians should be unembar-

rassed about teaching this reality, as was Abraham who made God known as the "God of Heaven and Earth."

2. As Creator, God is the transcendent authority over human life, and establishes the validity of moral values. Although sometimes difficult to apply, moral values are neither relative nor human conventions, but intrinsic parts of the universe and essential for human flourishing. The fundamental Noahide moral values must remain primary to all human endeavors.

3. All persons are created in the image of God, and each person has intrinsic sanctity that derives from this transcendent quality. All persons therefore possess inherent dignity and must be treated as such. Because human life has this transcendent character, human worth cannot be measured solely in utilitarian or materialistic terms. The spiritual essence of each person ensures that individual human life is not a process of biological decay toward death but a journey of spiritual growth toward life. And because every person is created in the Divine Image, any assault on innocent human life is an assault on God that diminishes the Divine Presence in the world.

4. Abraham learned from the binding of Isaac that God loves human life and abhors death. Thus Abraham's covenantal children must teach that killing in the name of God is contrary to the God of Abraham, and all forms of religious violence[59] are idolatries that the world must reject.

5. As Abraham defended and taught justice and righteousness before the destruction of Sodom and Gomorrah, his children are duty bound to teach social justice and display individual righteousness. It was Abraham's moral protest to God and concern for the moral treatment of others that distinguished his righteousness from the self-righteousness of Noah, and that earned him the privilege to be the father of the covenant. Our commitment to justice and righteousness for all human creatures is the test of our fidelity to God's covenant that is designed to bring peace and harmony to the world.

6. As faithful Christians and Jews believing in messianic history, we must teach the eternal possibility of human progress and moral reform as part of human history. We cannot fall prey to pessimism, nihilism, or a Malthusian acceptance of war, disease, and oppression as permanent features of human destiny. Hope in the possibility of a peaceful humanity is the meaning of our messianic belief.

Can the long story of Jewish-Christian enmity be transformed into covenantal partnership? Critical theological differences must remain be-

59. I exclude from this category capital punishment, which draws its justification from biblical and theological sources according to many religious theories of legal justice.

tween Judaism and Christianity, yet both faiths demand belief in messianic history and action to make a place in the world for God to enter. We share the covenantal task to make the world a better place, one where each person possesses infinite value because we are all created in God's sacred image, where moral values are real, where human affairs reflect a spiritual center to the universe and where every human life is endowed with meaning.

God asks us to repair his world through the covenant, whose full realization even Maimonides — Judaism's harshest critic of Christianity — admitted required Christian help.[60] He offers a beautiful vision of this repaired world, the eschaton, in the final words of the *Mishneh Torah*, his magisterial code of Jewish law:

> At that time, there will be neither hunger, nor war; neither will there be jealousy, nor strife. Blessings will be abundant and comfort within the reach of all. The single preoccupation of the entire world will be to know the Lord. Therefore there will be wise persons who know mysterious and profound things and will attain an understanding of the Creator to the utmost capacity of the human mind, as it is written, "The earth will be filled with the knowledge of God, as the waters cover the sea" (Isa. 11:9).[61]

Micah also offers a stunning description of that world, the messianic culmination of human history.

> Come, let us go up to the mountain of the Lord and the God of Jacob, that He teach us His ways, and we will walk in His paths. . . . Let the peo-

---

60. *MT*, Laws of Kings 11:4 (uncensored edition). Although repairing the world *(tikkun olam)* is sometimes dismissed by traditionalists and scholars as an inauthentic popular invention, in this passage Maimonides insists on the human responsibility to repair the world *("l'takken ha-olam")* as essential to sacred history.

61. *MT*, Laws of Kings 12:5 (according to the Yemenite manuscript). Most printed texts include the word "Israel" to qualify those who will attain ultimate knowledge of the divine. This qualification is inconsistent with the earlier, more accurate manuscripts. See the Shabse Frankel edition of *Mishneh Torah* (New York: Congregation Benei Yosef, 1998). It is also inconsistent with the earlier emphasis on the universal nature of messianic blessing ("The single preoccupation of the entire world . . ."). See Menachem Kellner, *"'Farteitsht un Farbessert':* Comments on Tendentious 'Corrections' to Maimonidean Texts," in *Be-Darkei Shalom: Iyyunim be-Hagut Yehudit Mugashim li-Shalom Rosenberg (In the Paths of Peace: Topics in Jewish Thought in Honor of Shalom Rosenberg)*, ed. B. Ish-Shalom (Jerusalem: Bet Morashah, 2006), pp. 255-63 (Hebrew). For English translation, see *"Farteitsht un Farbessert"* (On Correcting Maimonides), *Meorot* 6, no. 2 *(Marheshvan 5768)* at www.yctorah.org.

ples beat their swords into plowshares and their spears into pruning hooks. Nations shall not lift up sword against nation, nor shall they learn war anymore. Let every man sit under his vine and under his fig tree; and no one shall make him afraid. . . . Let all the people walk, each in the name of his God; and we shall walk in the name of the Lord our God for ever and ever. (4:2-5)

If Jews and Christians can become partners after nearly 2000 years of theological de-legitimization and physical conflict, then peace is possible between any two peoples anywhere. That peace would be our most powerful witness to God's presence in human history and to our covenantal responsibility to carry God's blessing to the world. It is the very stuff of which the messianic dream is made.

The Antinomian Threat to Human Flourishing

R. R. Reno

The Empire of Desire

It's easy to feel disoriented in the contemporary West. Tomorrow, a man can wake up and say, "Enough! I'm tired of fighting against my innermost feelings. I've always felt myself to be a woman, and I'll be damned if I'll let myself go on like this." Medical professionals stand ready at hand; psychologists are prepared to help. If he has generous and expansive insurance coverage, then the way is clear. Hormones are administered, surgeries performed, wardrobes changed, and eventually co-workers are informed that Charlie is now Charlene.

The sex change itself does not upset me. Who can be surprised that people will turn to the promise of modern technology for solutions to the afflictions of inner unhappiness? And who among us with a scintilla of life experience can be shocked that people harbor all sorts of strange, urgent desires? *The Golden Ass,* written by Apuleius in the second century, tells a ribald tale of human depravity and excess, showing us that Michael Jackson was hardly a uniquely modern phenomenon. The human psyche is extraordinarily unstable and diverse, and, like water finding its way downhill, our intense wants and urgent desires seek paths toward satisfaction.

What does shock me, however, is our present cultural sensibility, a pervasive mentality of therapeutic affirmation that most of us participate in, however half-heartedly. It is a plain fact that Charlie can not only become Charlene, but he can also feel entirely justified in demanding that everyone around him accept his decision and accommodate the fulfillment of his desires. And his demanding voice finds sympathetic ears. We may snicker inwardly, and roll our eyes in unguarded moments. But for the most part we fall in line and do our best to make Charlie's transformation seem like any other personal decision — a lifestyle choice, as we often say.

Richard Weaver once wrote: "Every man participating in a culture has three levels of conscious reflection: his specific ideas about things, his general beliefs or convictions, and his metaphysical dream of the world."[1] At the level of specific ideas and general convictions, our age has settled into a pragmatic affirmation of any number of social constraints. Most recognize the ongoing need for economic discipline to promote productive behavior, as well as social norms to censure and control disruptive, violent tendencies. So, we accept policing, the punishment of criminals, and bureaucratic regulation, as well as a vastly expanded array of social norms designed to improve health and facilitate social cooperation. No-smoking signs, calorie-counting and resumé-building high achievers, exhortations to save for retirement and use condoms, anxious efforts to reduce environmental impact, sharp rebukes for off-color remarks, to say nothing of the tremendous social pressure to be tolerant and nonjudgmental: all this and more testifies to the ongoing and powerful role of behavior-shaping norms.

Yet, at a deeper level, the postmodern West cultivates an antinomian sensibility. Our age judges the laws of behavior to be fundamentally extrinsic to human flourishing, and we tacitly believe that humanity more fully realizes itself as the need for norms is minimized. Thus we affirm the countless little disciplines to ensure health, productivity, success, and social harmony, and all the while we push social mores, discipline, and restraint to the margins of the soul, creating the existential freedom to craft a vision of life tailored to our own judgments about what we most want and imagine we need. What makes for happiness and fulfillment — and here we enter into the metaphysical dream that defines our era — is an Empire of Desire, a regime of life in which the existence of norms is justified only by their service to the greater goal of the maximal satisfaction of individual desires. We celebrate the rock star and rap artist, a guy who, however well muscled from time in the gym, however enriched by astute financial dealing, however prudent in his relations with others, nonetheless symbolically gives the finger to social convention as he steps out of the limo with a sultry girl on his arm. Therein lies the cultural crisis of our time: not that there should be such men (for there always are and always will be), but that we should find them so alluring, so exemplary, so worthy of imitation.

---

1. Richard Weaver, *Ideas Have Consequences* (Chicago: University of Chicago Press, 1948), p. 18.

Culture, Brown, and Freud

Norman O. Brown gave clear expression to this new metaphysical dream. Born in 1913, Brown came to maturity during two great crises of the twentieth century: the Great Depression and World War II. Like many others, his response was to ally himself with progressive causes. However, in the aftermath of World War II and as the Cold War deepened and American society turned away from anything that suggested revolutionary politics, Brown became demoralized by what he took to be a spirit of complacency. This led him to seek a deeper analysis of what he took to be the profound and potentially life-destroying problems of social existence. In 1959, he published *Life Against Death: The Psychoanalytical Meaning of History,* an effort to provide "a wider general theory of human nature, culture, and history" that will allow us "to reappraise the nature and destiny of man."[2] It was a reappraisal that gave expression to a general trend of sentiment in the middle of the twentieth century, a sentiment that came to suspect and critique the soul-shaping power of culture, shifting the dreams of our age toward the Empire of Desire.

Brown argues that we need to turn to Sigmund Freud in order to get a true picture of human nature and its relation to culture. By Freud's way of thinking, the human person is caught in a painful bind. The psychic energy for life comes from archaic instinctual drives, the so-called Id. Freud never settled on a stable description of these primitive drives. Initially, he distinguished between a sexual or pleasure-seeking instinct and a survival or self-preserving instinct. Later, he pictured a dichotomy between Eros, the energizing life instinct that is epitomized by (but not limited to) sexual desire, and Thanatos, the death instinct that seeks rest and release from the exhausting urgency of life. However characterized, it is important to recognize that we do not experience these drives as raw psychological facts. On the contrary, Freud's psychoanalytic theory posits the existence of the Ego, the structured reality of our conscious lives that emerges from the way in which the instincts are shaped and redirected by culturally mediated repressions that we internalize.

Freud offered many speculations about the emergence and inner workings of this process of internalized repression in his theories of subli-

---

2. Norman O. Brown, *Life Against Death: The Psychoanalytical Meaning of History* (Middletown, CT: Wesleyan University Press, 1959), pp. ix and xi. Subsequent page references to this work are given in parentheses in the text.

mation, the superego, and taboo, none of which have survived as scientifically serious options for explaining human psychology or the origins of culture. Yet the overall picture has remained extraordinarily influential, in part because it reflects some enduring assumptions about the permanent sources of the human predicament.

As Aristotle observed, the natural self is unformed because it is dissipated by undisciplined impulses. Aristotle assumed that our goal should be to train and habituate this natural self so that our desires can become focused and coordinated. We should culture the self with the pruning arts of repressive disciplines, he argued, which allows us to realize the true potential and purpose of our inborn and instinctual desires. Both the Christian and Jewish traditions presume a similar vision of the perfecting role of soul-shaping disciplines. As the classic formulation in Thomistic theology puts it, grace perfects nature.

Unlike Aristotle and traditional Jewish and Christian thinkers, Freud held out no hope that our instinctual desires can be brought into a deeper, more satisfying harmony by way of the repressive project of internalized discipline. As Philip Rieff observes in his unsurpassed account of the larger significance of psychoanalytic theory, *Freud: The Mind of the Moralist*, the therapeutic goal is not to achieve a resolution of conflict between Id and Ego but rather its humane, scientific management. As a doctor, Freud sought the best interests of his patients, which in many cases required therapeutic strategies to soften the internalized, repressive attack of guilt and shame. But as a social theorist he accepted the relentless sacrifice of instinctual satisfactions to the narrowing, inhibiting dynamics of repression. "He was more a statesman of the inner life," writes Rieff of Freud and his psychoanalytic approach, "aiming at shrewd compromises with the human condition, not its basic transformation."[3] The formation of the Ego in the crucible of repressive limitation is the fundamental condition for civilized life, and our fate is to live in the irreconcilable tension between instinctual desires and their culturally mandated denial.

Brown deemed Freud's acquiescence to the inevitable and interminable necessity of self-attacking repression intolerably pessimistic. We should not be satisfied, he thought, with the grim project of trying to manage the unending Cold War between the vigilant Ego and the all-desiring Id. In order to avoid this outcome, Brown reads Freud against himself, developing an account of psychoanalytic theory that promises to guide us to-

---

3. Philip Rieff, *Freud: The Mind of the Moralist* (New York: Anchor Books, 1961), p. xx.

ward a unified, self-reconciled mode of existence. Our humanity is not perfected by socially mandated traditions of discipline, as Aristotle would have it. Nor does Brown turn in the direction of modern humanism, which envisions a regime of autonomy — the internalized application of a self-realizing law that disciplines and therefore ennobles the unruly realm of immediate, instinctual desire. Instead, Brown preaches antinomianism. We should renounce law in all its repressive, soul-shaping forms, thus allowing us to live in the timeless immediacy of desire.

Brown's basic move turns on a perceptive insight into the metaphysical implications of Freud's analysis of the human condition. Freud faced a puzzling fact: What would seem to be the most natural and urgent dimensions of the soul — instinctual desires — are always and everywhere dominated by moral ideals and cultural norms. Where do these norms gain their power? Because he was a scientist committed to a naturalistic explanation of all dimensions of conscious life, including moral ideals, a paradox emerged. Our natural selves, that is to say our instincts, must somehow provide the explanation for their own repression.

Insofar as they purport to be scientific, all modern theories of morality and culture face this paradox. In general, the solutions appeal to versions of a utilitarian calculus. The repressive limitations on instinct somehow constellate to allow for their more enduring satisfaction. Sociobiologists, for example, formulate just-so stories that claim to show how the collective flourishing of the human genome miraculously transmits psychic energy to moral and cultural forms that repress individual instinctual impulses. Freud was interested in unpacking this transmission of psychic energy rather than simply assuming it. In his clinical experience, he saw neurotic patients whose degree of repressive self-discipline seemed oversupplied with moral energy. This led him to hypothesize that the self-limiting imperatives of the Ego are energized by the very instincts they repress. According to Freud's theory, therefore, culture attains its power over us because our unconscious selves are constantly refreshing and renewing its psychic potency. An epiphenomenon of our instinctual selves, culture is engorged with erotic desire. Thus energized, culture circulates desire back upon itself.

In view of the fact that instinct provides the energy that drives the economy of repression, Brown recognizes that Freud could give no deep justification for the lordship of the Ego over the Id: "The essence of man consists, not, as Descartes maintained, in thinking, but in desiring" (p. 6). As a nineteenth-century rationalist with a bad conscience, Freud equivocated, recognizing the primacy of desire, but remaining loyal to reason.

Brown seeks to force the issue, insisting that we should not be satisfied with therapeutic self-management that tries to negotiate between desire and duty. Our goal should be to live in accord with our essence, and our real inner being is found in the timeless flux of instincts and desires, which Brown refers to as "the body." Instead of shuttling back and forth between the free spontaneity of instinct and the rigid repressive laws of the ego, we should remain fully and finally loyal to instinct. The revolutionary and distinctively postmodern agenda of *Life Against Death* flows directly from this exaltation of desire to metaphysical primacy.

It is important to see the significance of this shift and its break with the main lines of modern humanism. Kant's ideal of autonomy gave clear and influential expression to the humanistic ideal that largely defined the modern era. Kant articulated what he took to be the universal moral law for all rational creatures, and he thought this critical principle able to transform external commandments into an internal law that the person can accept as his own. The later Romantics were uneasy with Kant's absorption of individuality into a universal humanity defined by reason, and they placed an accent on feelings of authenticity. The deepest moral law is to be true to oneself. Nonetheless, the larger modern consensus remained intact. There is a law, form, or pattern that, once recognized, gives shape and meaning to our lives. In this sense, modern humanism may have rejected the sacred authority of Sinai, but it preserved the pronomian structure of command and obedience. For all modern figures, human flourishing arises when a freshly minted, human-oriented set of self-imposed norms corrects or supplants the inherited norms of traditional life. A law that somehow emerges from within the self — from reason, experience, or a lightning flash of self-possession — replaces the law that had been sanctioned by a theological substructure that traces the authority of tradition back to an even deeper divine authority.

In Brown's view, modern ideals of autonomy and authenticity offer no real alternative to old-fashioned loyalty to transcendent authority. Both Kant and Moses, and for that matter Wordsworth, endorse a repressive attack on the plenary scope of instinct and desire. Although Moses speaks for God's commandments, while Kant speaks for a morality discerned by reason, both want to subordinate the raw modalities of the soul to the shaping and disciplining power of law, and in so doing, thinks Brown, they doom the human person to perpetual alienation — the conflict of life ("the body") against death ("repression"). Even the imperative of authenticity becomes suspect. "The body," as Brown rightly recognizes, is a transpersonal reality. The notion of authenticity requires fixing the ever-changing flux of desire into a stable Ego to which one can remain loyal, and this denies the ever-changing flow of desire. Thus, by Brown's way of thinking, modern notions of autonomy and authenticity are not nearly as revolutionary as we often imagine. They are but two forms of the alienating law of the self that retain a desire-repressing form, and therefore remain opposed to "the body."

The fact that Kant, and even Sartre, merges so easily into the Mosaic role of lawgiver shows us how profoundly Brown breaks with prior assumptions about human flourishing. His goal is not to replace a corrupt set of cultural norms with another, not even with the nebulous norm of authenticity. He does not set out to transform a distorted, unjust system into a more just one, nor does he want to supplant an old theological vision of culture with a new, humanistic approach. Instead, civilization *itself* becomes the great enemy of humanity, representing, Brown asserts, a collective neurosis. The goal of a true humanism, therefore, should not be to encourage Kant's ideal of self-legislating reason, nor, as Freud would imagine, should we fall back on the more modest goal of carefully managing the perpetual struggle between the legislative goals of the Ego and the rebellious desires of the Id. According to Brown, we must be loyal to desire in all its primitive, polymorphous perversity. The repressive form of law, whatever its source, must be destroyed, which in the Freudian frame of reference means destroying the very possibility of culture.

Brown grasped and affirmed the anticultural implications of his antinomian vision. "The unrepressed animal," Brown writes, "carries no instinctual project to change his own nature" (p. 106). Against the great bulk of the moral tradition in the West, Brown draws the conclusion that it is precisely the impulse to change and shape our natures that corrupts human life. We should forsake the repressive, habituating project of culture and embrace "that simple health that animals enjoy" (p. 311). The destruction of civilization — "the abolition of repression" — becomes the great imperative against imperatives. No longer forming life in accord with the projects of progress, competition, and domination that empower the Ego, in a postcultural world we can live in "the mode of unrepressed bodies," cultivating a "Dionysian or body mysticism" that simply seeks and finds satisfaction as an undifferentiated biological mass, "the body" (pp. 307-10). The abolition of repression, Brown promises in rapturous phrases that nonetheless show an acute metaphysical imagination, will free us from "history," which is all about *doing*, allowing us to enjoy the simple *being* desired by instinct, "the Sabbath of Eternity" (p. 93). An unmitigated loyalty to our essence as instinct-driven animals will usher in the End of History, trigger "the resurrection of the body," and establish the timeless, unchanging, antinomian Empire of Desire.

It's easy to make fun of Brown. His appeals to the "dialectical metaphysics of hope" can sound hopelessly jejune: "Only if Eros — the life instinct — can affirm the life of the body, can the death instinct affirm death, and in affirming death magnify life" (p. 109). The hymns to the great humanizing power of "the body" remind us of the easy platitudes of the 1960s: "Make love, not war!" He envisioned the transformation of society and the inauguration of freedom, cooperation, and world peace, all guided and energized by the chrysalis of life-affirming instincts ready to burst from the hard cocoon spun by millennia of repressive culture. These dreams have remained remote: there has been no "resurrection of the body." Today, the process of globalization has extended economic disciplines even more deeply into everyday life; bureaucratic, regulatory authority has expanded; therapeutic self-regulation is widespread. The martini-drinking company man and cigarette-puffing suburban housewife of the 1950s can easily seem to be lax hedonists compared to the gym-toned muscles and carefully planned careers of our present-day high achievers.

Nonetheless, Brown's mobile metaphysical imagination allowed him to recognize the larger implications of modern conceptions of culture, and he drew the obvious conclusions in bold, prophetic strokes. Today we no longer take Freud very seriously, but we nonetheless tacitly accept his basic analysis of culture and its relation to desire. For the most part, postmodern men and women submit to all sorts of social disciplines with the deeper assumption that the cultural pressures that shape our personalities are evolved forms of the very instincts and desires that are being repressed. Indeed, it is the fundamental principle of all postmodern cultural theory that social norms and cultural ideals are nothing more than the extruded, solidified manifestations of the primitive primeval dimensions of the human psyche: sexual desires, will-to-power, a lust for domination, and so forth. Even our selfish goals — to look thin or dress for success — are analyzed as social constructs energized by manipulative advertising designed to stimulate our erotic or egocentric desires for the sake of satisfying a capitalist desire for profit. Under this assumption, every law, including those we impose on ourselves, slowly sinks into an alien, endless, and conceptually more primary circulation of desire.

This tacit reduction of all forms of culture to instinct and desire should not surprise us, for the metaphysical primacy of desire is broadly characteristic of late-modern social theory. As soon as one lets go of the dialectical teleology in Marx's historical materialism, his social analysis ends up treating culture solely in terms of its sources: power and class interests. Not all find the Marxist categories persuasive; yet, though debates can be passionate, most twentieth-century social theorists agree that some form of primitive interest or desire drives history. They presume that culture is a historically elaborated and institutionalized form of the past desires of the powerful that intrude and organize our present desires. In short, the reigning assumption is that we live in an Empire of Desire, and the only real question is whether the Empire will be ruled by my desires or the desires of others — or in the case of liberal political theory, some imagined harmony or equilibrium of desires that is dignified by the name of justice.

Max Weber's concept of charismatic authority, the strange inexplicable eruption of soul-commanding imperatives, may seem an exception. But the difference is not as great as it seems at first glance. According to Weber, charismatics are anomic figures, strange interlopers who bring into the social sphere new possibilities for organizing the human psyche. However, this charismatic power can only endure and influence culture by way of the process of institutionalization, which involves giving law-like form to the original, anomic source of inspiration. As a result, charisma becomes routinized and domesticated. Once again, as is the case throughout so much of the intellectual history of the late nineteenth and twentieth centuries, culture and its disciplining function rotates into position as the enemy of the true sources of human vitality. Weber ends up indirectly affirming Brown's conclusion, which is but a blaring pronouncement of the often-unspoken assumptions of modern social theory. The antinomian brings life; culture encloses us in an iron cage.

By my reading of the last century, this increasingly articulate and explicit consensus about the life-destroying significance of culture distinguishes postmodern culture from its modern antecedent.[4] In spite of the

---

4. The ascendancy of anti-bourgeois rhetoric offers a convenient way to plot the historical transition from modern to postmodern. In most cases, late nineteenth- and twentieth-century uses of "bourgeois" function as a synecdoche for the repressive function of culture. By the end of the nineteenth century, an anti-bourgeois sentiment largely defined the European *intelligentsia,* and midway through the twentieth century this sentiment became so widespread that it ended up shaping the consensus among the bourgeois about themselves. John Lukacs has written suggestively about this transformation. Among his many books, see

fact that we encounter a great deal of prudential self-discipline, our age seems to have become anticultural in the antinomian sense Brown endorses (as have countless others in recent decades, most of whom lack Brown's metaphysical clarity). Instead of carrying forward something like the Kantian project of renewing law by critique and reformulation according to reason or authenticity, the postmodern West now opts for an antinomian vision. We serve the human person and promote human flourishing — or so we imagine — by diminishing the power of law itself. It is true that this antinomian project includes the simulacra of law. The Empire of Desire endorses imperatives of health, economic growth, and social stability, which lead to a great deal of regulation, limitation, and exhortation in matters of health, economic growth, and social stability. The Empire of Desire has a bureaucratic rationality of the soul, as all empires must. But we should not be deceived by the new postmodern regimes of discipline, for they are justified solely by calculations of utility that affirm rather than contradict Brown's metaphysical decision in favor of the primacy of desire.

Although our age does not lack for urgent moral imperatives that impose disciplines on our desires — environmentalism, animal rights, opposition to war, anti-globalization, et al. — these ideals tend to propagate harmlessly in the Empire of Desire. Global warming may be a matter of moral importance, but various schemes for reducing one's carbon footprint involve "lifestyle changes" that lack the scope, depth, and soul-shaping power of religious or cultural traditions. Indeed, the Empire of Desire strongly encourages us to politicize our moral convictions, which transforms the commandments of traditional morality into society-changing agendas. A moral censure of greed, for example, becomes a critique of capitalism and private property. The corporeal works of mercy are translated into commitments to progressive causes. Here as elsewhere it is easy to be misled by the enduring rhetoric of moral urgency in postmodern society. The human soul craves commanding truths, and in the Empire of Desire we are entertained by circuses of moral earnestness and *ersatz* visions of discipline.

If we turn away from social observation and toward intellectual

---

especially *The Passing of the Modern Age* (New York: Harper & Row, 1970) and *A Thread of Years* (New Haven: Yale University Press, 1998). On the importance of anti-bourgeois rhetoric in literary and artistic movements, see Peter Gay, *Modernism: The Lure of Heresy* (New York: W. W. Norton, 2008).

trends, the picture is clearer. The theoretical gestures that have predominated over the last forty years are unified by a metaphysical abhorrence of law and preference for spontaneity. Terms such as "metanarrative," "univocity," "foundationalism," and "presence" suggest determinative principles and authoritative truths. Not surprisingly, these pronomian terms are consistently used to refute, denounce, or discredit. In contrast, terms such as "difference," "heterogeneity," and "absence" cut against enduring principles and stable truths, and they are always deployed to evoke positive alternatives. "Marginality" is bathed in luminous light. "Alterity" serves as a liberating force. I can think of no postmodern theoretical gesture that does not reflect the broad shift in the West toward the antinomian ideal. Something like Brown's goal of ending repression animates and gives high moral purpose to postmodern theory.

After Christianity?

Gianni Vattimo offers a useful summation of the logic of postmodern analysis in *After Christianity*.[5] "Philosophy, today," he writes, "conceives of Being as event and as destiny of weakening" (p. 44). Like the death-of-God theologians of the 1960s, Vattimo's goal is to show that secularization and the disenchantment of cultural authority is the fulfillment of the gospel promise of life. The collapse of Christianity as the source of law for the self and society seems like a failure, but it is in fact the realization of Christianity's true spiritual genius. We are heading, he prophesies, "toward emancipation by diminishing strong structures (in thought, individual consciousness, political power, social relations, and religion)" (p. 91). Indirectly (and unknowingly) evoking the rich tradition of liberal Protestant theology, Vattimo suggests that this antinomian trajectory is "a transcription of the Christian message of the incarnation of God, which Saint Paul also calls *kenosis* — that is, the abasement, humiliation and weakening of God" (p. 91). Here we find a wonderfully pure expression of the metaphysical dream of our era: God himself is an antinomian. Christ does not fulfill the law of Moses; instead, he undercuts Moses and evacuates the law of all normative power. Sinai becomes the anti-Christ.

Few contemporary academics have Vattimo's flair for metaphysical

5. Gianni Vattimo, *After Christianity*, trans. Luca D'Isanto (New York: Columbia University Press, 2002). Page references to this work are given in parentheses in the text.

rhetoric. However, the practice of cultural study over recent decades has been given over almost entirely to what Vattimo calls "weakening." Norman O. Brown has a long chapter devoted to showing that "money is excrement." The effect, clearly desired by Brown, is to disenchant the social norms of bourgeois society. I doubt that Michel Foucault ever read Brown, but his intellectual life was devoted to detailed studies of cultural norms oriented toward the same goal. Every gimcrack cultural theorist today has internalized this mode of analysis: what seems like a noble cultural ideal or elevating vision of the good life is, in fact, the intellectually sublimated form of a desire for domination, or a class interest, or the metaphysics of presence. Thus the critical platitude of our postmodern age: culture is an artificially solidified, socially sanctified, and rhetorically disguised expression of the desires of the powerful.

This presumption about culture is so widespread that it has become an item of almost unconscious conviction. In *Harper's Magazine*, writer and literary scholar Mark Slouka launches a sally against what he regards as the crushing dominance of economic rationality in contemporary higher education.[6] "We are," he writes, "hypnotized by quarterly reports and profit margins." Against this show-me-the-money mentality, Slouka pleads for the importance of culture, hoping to revitalize "the deep civic function of the arts and the humanities" (p. 33). Yet, the way in which this would-be humanist frames the surpassing role of culture is telling: "I believe that what rules us is less the world of goods and services than the immaterial ones of whims, assumptions, delusions, and lies" (p. 32). The dark turn is typical of our era. Culture isn't really "immaterial" in any metaphysical sense. Instead, what we take to be cultural ideals and norms for living a humane life are disguised and deluded expressions of. . . . Slouka doesn't fill in the blank, but as we know from the most casual acquaintance with contemporary literary and cultural theory the answer is clear. Cultural artifacts are etherealized expressions of our material, instinctual desires for pleasure and domination.

Slouka's plea for humanistic study cannot succeed, because he cannot conceive of an alternative to the Empire of Desire. We default to GDP, because, as his own cynicism shows, our metaphysical dreams are dominated by images of desire: desires expressed, satisfied, sublimated, repressed, re-

6. Mark Slouka, "Dehumanized: When Math and Science Rule the School," *Harper's Magazine*, September 2009, pp. 32-40. Parenthetical page references in this paragraph are to this article.

directed, imposed, and reified. Therefore students, educators, politicians — that is, all of us to one degree or another — draw the sensible conclusion. As long as we cannot imagine anything real and lasting and true other than primitive instincts, we might as well concentrate our minds on the economic, medical, and psychological factors that promise to maximize our satisfaction. If we are fated to be ruled by desire, then we ought to acquaint ourselves with the logic of its circulation and adopt our postmodern roles as bureaucrats, therapists, managers, and other well-groomed functionaries trained to analyze and maintain the pneumatic systems of the Empire of Desire.

Christianity, Judaism, and the Human Future

The greatest threat we presently face is not Islamic terrorism, global warming, nuclear proliferation, genocide, or poverty, pressing as these problems may be. The antinomian revolution in the postmodern West poses a deeper, more fundamental and profound existential threat to the human future, because it erodes the cultural capital necessary for a morally robust response to these challenges and others. The richest and most powerful countries in the world are dominated by an elite that, however individually well intentioned and personally influenced by inherited moral traditions, cannot collectively conceive of a transcendent law as the source of human flourishing. Indeed, as the implicit metaphysics of modern social theory becomes explicit in postmodern cultural analysis, this elite is being trained to regard everything that poses as a transcendent law as simply the desires of others covertly seeking dominion. The end result, as Brown recognized and championed, encourages animal existence.

In his apocalyptic reveries, Brown failed to see the practical upshot of his hoped-for "resurrection of the body." Instead of life abundant, we are sliding toward a world of barbarized masses overseen by cynical elites who are reconciled to amoral techniques of governance appropriate to human herds animated by raw lusts and fears. Today we see the first-fruits of this antinomian world. Social theorists with an interest in the common good recommend carefully designed cattle prods with calibrated dials that range from the soft setting of economic incentives to the harsh options of lethal force. The bureaucratic instruments of social management necessarily increase in importance, justified by philanthropic benevolence and palliated with a therapeutic empathy. Legal regulation of personal behavior, family

life, and social interactions expands in order to take over the ordering, har-
monizing function once performed by an unofficial but deeply internalized cultural *nomos*. Thus runs a soulless world that has lost its capacity to
dream of the ennobling possibility of life animated by a transcendent law.

This ascendant Empire of Desire exposes a pronomian vision that uni-
fies Jews and Christians who have been at odds with each other for centuries. "Choose life," Moses urges the Israelites in the book of Deuteronomy.
The choice requires the full commitment of a person to the project of obedience: "You shall love the Lord your God with all your heart, and with all
your soul, and with all your might" (Deut. 6:5). Christianity quarrels with
Judaism about the content of the law to be inscribed on the hearts of those
who believe, but it shares the same broad outlook. When Paul writes to the
Galatians, "For freedom Christ has set us free" (5:1), he does not envision
an antinomian "resurrection of the body." Instead, Christ frees his followers from the law of sin and death, and thus freed, they obey the law of
Christ without reservation. As Paul says of his own life: "It is no longer I
who live, but Christ who lives in me" (Gal. 2:20). Fullness of life comes
from allowing oneself to be governed by the law of Christ.

One of the most effective Christian affirmations of the vivifying role
of law in recent years came in August 1993, when John Paul II published
Veritatis splendor, an encyclical designed to resist the Empire of Desire.
This long encyclical is multifaceted, and the main sections address technical questions in moral theology: the notion of intrinsically evil acts, the
role of conscience, and the relation between faith and moral choices.
Nonetheless, as a writer and thinker, John Paul II had an astute sense of the
age in which we live. He knew that the scandal of moral truth is not
epistemological, as if our present tendencies toward moral relativism stem
from insufficient exposure to traditional natural law arguments, and he
was aware that technical questions of moral theology are largely remote
from the minds of most Christians.

John Paul II frames the problem very broadly: "At the root" of our
alienation from moral truth, he writes, "is the more or less obvious influence of certain currents of thought which end by detaching human freedom from its essential and constitutive relationship to truth" (para. 4).
Moral truth commands with the invading force of "thou shalt" and "thou
shalt not," and this invasion invariably conjures images of aggression and
attack in the minds of many, even in those who want to submit themselves
to God's commandments. What can be done to allay these fears? John
Paul II saw that one does not argue with nightmares. Therefore, the encyc-

lical begins and ends with biblical meditations, passages of reflection that are better understood as elaborations of the metaphysical dream of faith and obedience than exercises in technical exegesis or systematic theology.

The encyclical begins with a long discussion of Matthew 19:16-22, the story of a rich young man who came to Jesus to ask for spiritual guidance. "What good deeds must I do," he asks, "to have eternal life?" Jesus answers quite simply: "Keep the commandments," a response that could serve as the coda for the entire encyclical and its trenchant defense of the inflexible authority of moral truth. The young man continues, asking Jesus which commandments are necessary, and Jesus responds by enumerating the second table of the Ten Commandments, summing them up with the Levitical commandment to love your neighbor as yourself.

John Paul II treats this summation as the hinge of the encounter, for as the New Testament emphasizes in many places, the commandment of love is all-invading, all-consuming. The rich young man seems insensitive, however, and he claims to have done all these commandments. He presses for still more: "What do I still lack?" In his final response, Jesus says: "If you would be perfect, go, sell what you possess and give to the poor, and you will have treasure in heaven, and come, follow me." Human fulfillment will require "giving up one's wealth and very self," as John Paul II glosses, and in an elaboration of the Pauline vision of freedom in Christ, he continues by observing that this renunciation will free us to partake of Christ's "life and his destiny, sharing in his free and loving obedience to the will of the Father" (para. 19).

After Jesus exhorts him to abandon his wealth — and through his wealth, his deepest love, therefore his will — the rich young man does not follow. Instead he leaves very much saddened, for he will not abandon himself to Christ's authority. It's an altogether realistic response, one most Christians know firsthand, because it is so often our own. It is only in the much briefer, concluding meditation that John Paul II offers a positive image of perfect obedience: the Virgin Mary, who accepted her role as the mother of the Incarnate Word. John Paul II adds a further dimension to this picture of the young Virgin who accepted a vocation she could not fathom or understand. In the Gospel of John, the wedding revelers have exhausted the supply of wine, and the Virgin Mother calls upon Jesus to provide for what is lacking. Securing the necessary assistance, she mobilizes the servants and exhorts, "Do whatever he tells you" (John 2:5).

By John Paul II's reading, this hypernomian imperative ("Do *whatever* he tells you") is directed outward from the gospel story to address everyone who calls Jesus Lord. The image is striking. The Virgin Mother, an inexhaustible source of compassion, gives voice to a hypernomian exhortation, and she does so in her role as one who cares for the flourishing of others. She embodies a metaphysical dream utterly at odds with the antinomian fantasies of the present postmodern era: the joyful triumph of divine law, its happy conquest of the human heart.

William James once made an astute observation about the fragility of our convictions: "The greatest enemy of any one of our truths may be the rest of our truths."[7] The theological concepts of law and commandment have a difficult, confusing history in Western Christianity, and this history tends to mute the effectiveness of Christian witness on behalf of the pronomian structure of human flourishing. Paul's polemics against circumcision and other forms of legal observance have often been read as rejections of the fundamental role of law in the divine plan of redemption. During the Reformation, this reading of Paul became a convenient way for Protestants to demonstrate what they took to be the fatal Catholic error of works righteousness. Over the last two centuries, Protestants and eventually Catholics found themselves attracted to an antinomian reading of Paul, because it provided the theological tools for reconciling Christianity with an increasingly autonomous secular world that was unwilling to allow itself to be governed by divine authority. The true gospel, this way of thinking concludes, commands nothing; indeed, the very form of commandment is antithetical to the teachings of Jesus. As we have seen, Gianni Vattimo completes that train of thought (as have many modern theologians in less direct and cheerful fashion): The modern world and its rejection of divine law actually reveals rather than contradicts the true gospel. Many contemporary Christians find this conclusion reassuring.

The effectiveness of John Paul II's defense of the commanding authority of moral truth suffers from this history of Christian antinomianism. For example, in his account of the story of the rich young man, an account that so richly suggests the redemptive pattern of commandment and obedience, John Paul II speaks of the need to "transcend a legalistic interpretation of the commandments" (para. 16). Because the concept of law has acquired so many dark, negatives connotations in recent Christian theologies, this warning against legalism, however nuanced in John Paul II's mind, bears an uneasy and ill-defined relation to his robust affirmations of obedience. In another instance, when John Paul II makes the

---

7. William James, *Pragmatism* (New York: Longmans, Green, 1912), p. 78.

traditional claim that Christ fulfills the Torah and thus becomes "a living and personal Law," the same legacy of Christian antinomianism blocks our comprehension. In numerous Protestant theologies, and some modern Catholic ones as well, the ambiguities surrounding the concept of law dissolve into an unfortunate clarity. Law becomes the antithesis of grace, salvation, and fullness of life. As a consequence, most contemporary Christians find it difficult to comprehend a positive equation of Christ with the law.

Christians will not agree with Jews about the application, or even content, of the Law given on Mount Sinai, but Christians can learn from Jews how to revitalize and renew the concept of law as a foundational category for describing the conditions for human flourishing. For example, in his evocation of the project of Torah observance in *Halakhic Man,*[8] Joseph Soloveitchik develops theological and phenomenological categories that can enrich Christian reflection. Is the intensification of the Decalogue that Jesus so clearly teaches in his dialogue with the rich young man (and John Paul II emphasizes) akin to the notion of *ḥiddush,* the creative, innovative interpretation of legal requirements that Joseph Soloveitchik understands as the primary mechanism for fulfilling the divine plan in creation by extending the dominion of law? Is Soloveitchik's image of the cognitive immersion in the law — "swimming in the sea of the Talmud" — an evocation of a specific set of practices that could help Christians give day-to-day content to the Pauline exhortation that we put on the mind of Christ? Is law the ideal instrument for concretizing the divine will, and therefore analogous to the notion of Incarnation? Does the future-creating power of prescriptive language help us understand the eschatological drama of the kingdom of God? After all, it is the miracle of commandment that a past and present "Ought" can energize and direct the obedient will to effect a future "Is." Freedom without law has no such history-making power, as the metaphysical genius of Norman O. Brown recognized and embraced.

Answers to these questions and many more would be intrinsically enriching. But more immediately, answers would leaven the Christian theological outlook with a more robust confidence in the language of law. We need such confidence today. Our postmodern mentality, defined by an antinomian sentiment, envisions life as fated to slump into the endless, pointless circulation of desires and instincts. In this Empire of Desire, it is

---

8. Joseph Soloveitchik, *Halakhic Man* (New York: Jewish Publication Society of America, 1984).

very difficult to imagine that obedience to moral and religious commandments ennobles and sanctifies life.

Perhaps, therefore, our most important contribution to the collective
hopes of a demoralized West rests in renewing the pronomian imagination. Of the ideal Jewish personality, Soloveitchik writes, "We do not have
a directive that imposes upon man obligations against which he rebels, but
delightful commandments which his soul passionately desires."

This is a vision of the kingdom of God shared by Christians, however
differently we understand the way in which God sets about to secure the
triumph of his will in the renovation of the human heart. It is, moreover, a
vision much needed today, that of a Dominion of Law in which our desires
are neither affirmed in their untutored immediacy nor repudiated as irre-
mediably wanton, but instead transformed and fulfilled as they are trained
to love and serve a greater truth.

God, Hope, and Human Flourishing

Miroslav Volf

In a Christian sense, hope is love stretching itself into the future.

When I hope, I expect something from the future. But I don't hope for everything I expect. Some anticipated things — like a visit to the dentist — I face with dread, rather than welcoming them in hope. "I speak of 'hope,'" wrote Josef Pieper in his *Hope and History*, "only when what I am expecting is, in my view, *good.*"[1] And yet, even all good things that come my way are not a matter of hope. I don't hope for a new day to dawn after a dark and restful night; I *know,* more or less, that the sun will rise. But I may hope for cool breezes to freshen up a hot summer day. In our everyday usage, "hope" is, roughly, the *expectation of good things that don't come to us as matter of course.*

Christian faith adds another layer to this everyday usage of "hope." In *Theology of Hope* Jürgen Moltmann famously distinguished between optimism and hope. Both have to do with positive expectation, and yet the two are very different. Optimism has to do with good things in the future that are latent in the past and the present. The future associated with optimism — Moltmann calls it *futurum* — is an unfolding of what is already there. We survey the past and the present, extrapolate about what is likely to happen in the future, and if the prospects are good, we become optimistic. Hope, on the other hand, has to do with good things in the future that come to us from "outside," from God; the future associated with hope — Moltmann calls it *adventus* — is a gift of something new.[2] We hear the

---

1. Joseph Pieper, *Hope and History: Five Salzburg Lectures,* trans. David Kipp (San Francisco: Ignatius Press, 1994), p. 20.

2. Jürgen Moltmann, *Theology of Hope: On the Ground and the Implications of a Chris-*

word of divine promise, and because God is love we trust in God's faithfulness, and God brings about "a new thing" — aged Sarah, barren of womb, gives birth to a son (Gen. 21:1-2; Rom. 4:18-21); the crucified Jesus Christ is raised from the dead (Acts 2:22-36); a mighty Babylon falls and a New Jerusalem comes down from heaven (Rev. 18:1-24; 21:1-5). More generally, the good that seemed impossible becomes not just possible but real.

So hope is the expectation of good things that come as a gift from God — and that is love, too, projecting itself into our and our world's future. For love always gives gifts. It is itself a gift, and inversely every genuine gift is an expression of love. At the heart of the hoped-for future, which comes from the God of love, is the flourishing of individuals, communities, and our whole world. But how is our God of love, "who gives life to the dead and calls into existence things that do not exist" (Rom. 4:17), related to human flourishing? And how should we understand human flourishing if it is a gift of the God of love?

Human Flourishing

Consider with me a prevalent contemporary Western understanding of human flourishing, how it differs from some previous understandings, and what its consequences are.

Satisfaction

Many people in the West today have come to believe — to feel in their gut, is a colloquial but more accurate way of putting it — that a flourishing human life is an experientially satisfying human life. By this they don't mean only that the experience of satisfaction is a desirable aspect of human flourishing, so that, all other things being equal, people who experience satisfaction flourish in a more complete way than people who do not. Energetic and free of pain, for instance, we flourish more than when enveloped in sadness and wracked with pain — even if it is true that pain can be a servant of the good and exhilaration can be deceptive. Though some an-

---

tian Eschatology, trans. Margaret Kohl (San Francisco: HarperSanFrancisco, 1991). For a brief summary see also Jürgen Moltmann, *The Coming of God: On Christian Eschatology,* trans. Margaret Kohl (Minneapolis: Fortress Press, 1996), p. 25.

cient Stoics believed that one can flourish equally well on the torture rack
as in the comfort of one's home, most people from all periods of human
history have thought that experiencing satisfaction enhances flourishing.

In contrast, many in the West believe that experiencing satisfaction is
what their lives are all about. Satisfaction does not merely enhance flourishing, it defines it. Such people cannot imagine themselves as flourishing
if they do not experience satisfaction, if they don't feel "happy," as the preferred way of expressing it goes. For them, flourishing *consists* in having an
experientially satisfying life. No satisfaction, no flourishing. The sources
of satisfaction may vary, ranging from appreciation of classical music to
the use of drugs, from the delights of "haute cuisine" to the pleasures of
sadomasochistic sex, from sports to religion; but what matters is not the
source of satisfaction but the fact of it. What justifies an activity or a given
lifestyle or activity is the satisfaction it generates — the pleasure. And
when they experience satisfaction, people believe that they flourish. As
Philip Rieff noted in *The Triumph of the Therapeutic*[3] some decades ago
(1966), ours is a culture of managed pursuit of pleasure, not a culture of
sustained endeavor to lead the good life, as defined by foundational symbols and convictions.

Love of God and Universal Solidarity

Contrast contemporary Western culture and its default account of human
flourishing with the two dominant models in the history of the Western
tradition. The fifth-century church father Augustine, one of the most influential figures in Western religion and culture, represents well the first of
these two accounts. In his reflections on the happy life in his major work
The Trinity, he writes that "God is the only source to be found of any good
things, but especially of those which make a man good and those which
will make him happy; only from him do they come into a man and attach
themselves to a man."[4] Consequently, human beings flourish and are truly
happy when they center their lives on God, the source of everything that is
true, good, and beautiful. As to all created things, they too ought to be
loved. But the only way to properly love them and fully and truly enjoy

3. See Philip Rieff, *The Triumph of the Therapeutic: Uses of Faith after Freud* (New York: Harper & Row, 1966), pp. 232-61.
4. Augustine, *The Trinity,* XIII, 10.

them is to love and enjoy them "in God." Augustine readily agrees with
what most people think, i.e., that those are happy who have everything
they want, but he immediately adds that this is true only if they want
"nothing wrongly,"[5] that is, if they want everything in accordance with the
character and will of their Creator whose very being is love. The supreme
good that makes human beings truly happy — in my terminology, the
proper content of a flourishing life — consists in love of God and neighbor
and enjoyment of both. In the *City of God*, Augustine defines it as a "completely harmonious fellowship in the enjoyment of God, and each other in
God."[6]

In the eighteenth century a different account of human flourishing
emerged in the West. It was connected with what scholars sometimes describe as an "anthropocentric shift" — a gradual redirection of interest
from the transcendent God to human beings and their mundane affairs
and a birth of a new humanism. This new humanism was different "from
most ancient ethics of human nature," writes Charles Taylor in *A Secular
Age*, in that its notion of human flourishing "makes no reference to something higher which humans should reverence or love or acknowledge."[7]
For Augustine and the tradition that followed him, this "something
higher" was God. Modern humanism became exclusive by shedding the
idea of human lives centered on God.

And yet, even as the new humanism rejected God and the command
to love God, it retained the moral obligation to love neighbor. The central
pillar of its vision of the good life was a universal beneficence transcending
all boundaries of tribe or nation and extending to all human beings. True,
this was an ideal that could not be immediately realized (and from which
some groups, deemed inferior, were *de facto* exempt). But the goal toward
which humanity was steadily moving was a state of human relations in
which the flourishing of each was tied to the flourishing of all and the
flourishing of all tied to the flourishing of each. Historically, Marx's vision
of a communist society, encapsulated in the phrase "from each according
to his abilities, to each according to his need,"[8] was the most influential
and most problematic version of this idea of human flourishing.

5. Augustine, *The Trinity*, XIII, 8.
6. Augustine, *City of God*, XIX, 17.
7. Charles Taylor, *A Secular Age* (Cambridge, MA: Harvard University Press, 2007),
p. 245.
8. Karl Marx, *Critique of the Gotha Program*, in *Essential Writings of Karl Marx* (St. Pe-
tersburg, FL: Red and Black, 2010), p. 243.

Another shift occurred in the late twentieth century. Human flourishing increasingly came to be defined as experiential satisfaction (though, of course, other accounts of human flourishing remain robust as well, be they derived from religious or secular interpretations of the world). Having lost earlier reference to "something higher which humans should reverence or love," it now lost reference to universal solidarity, as well. What remained was only concern for the self and the desire for the experience of satisfaction. Of course, it is not that individuals today simply seek pleasure on their own, isolated from society. It is also not that they don't care for others. Others are very much involved. But they matter mainly in that they serve an individual's experience of satisfaction. That applies to God as well as to human beings. Desire — the outer shell of love — has remained. Yet love itself, by being directed exclusively to the self, has been lost.

Hope

One way to view the three phases in the conception of human flourishing — love of God and neighbor, universal beneficence, experiential satisfaction — is to see them as a historical diminution of the object of love: from the vast expanse of the infinite God, first tapered to the boundaries of the universal human community, and then radically contracted to the narrowness of one's own self. A parallel contraction has also occurred with the scope of human hope.

In the book *The Real American Dream*, which Andrew Delbanco wrote at the turn of the millennium, he traced the diminution of American hope. I am interested in it here because America may be in this regard symptomatic: it is possible to trace an analogous diminution of hope in most societies or their elites, which are highly integrated into globalization processes. A glance at the book's table of contents reveals the main point of his analysis. The chapter headings read: "God," "Nation," "Self." The infinite God and the eternal life of enjoying God and one's neighbors (at least some of them!) was the hope of the Puritans who founded America. American nationalists of the nineteenth century, notably Abraham Lincoln, transformed this Christian imagery, in which God was at the center, into "the symbol of a redeemer nation." In the process, they created a "new symbol of hope."[9] The

9. Andrew Delbanco, *The Real American Dream: A Meditation on Hope* (Cambridge, MA: Harvard University Press, 1999), p. 77.

scope of hope was significantly reduced,[10] and yet there still remained something of immense importance to hope for — the prospering of the nation that itself was a "chosen people" called upon to "bear the ark of the Liberties of the world," as Melville put it.[11] In the aftermath of the combined hippy and yuppie revolutions in the 1960s and 1980s, "instant gratification" became "the hallmark of the good life." It is only a minor exaggeration to say that hope was reduced "to the scale of self-pampering."[12] Moving from the vastness of God down to the ideal of a redeemer nation, hope was narrowed, argues Delbanco, "to the vanishing point of the self alone."[13]

Earlier I noted that when the scope of love diminishes, love itself disappears; benevolence and beneficence mutate into the pursuit of self-interest. Something similar happens to hope. This is understandable if hope is love stretching itself into the future of the beloved object, as I suggested at the beginning of this essay. So when love shrinks to self-interest, and self-interest devolves into the experience of satisfaction, hope disappears as well. As Michael Oakeshott rightly insisted, hope depends on finding some "end to be pursued more extensive than a merely instant desire."[14]

Unsatisfying Satisfaction

Love and hope are not the only casualties of placing the experience of satisfaction at the center of human striving. As many have pointed out, satis-

10. The claim that the scope of hope was reduced when it was directed away from God and toward the nation can be contested. Delbanco himself maintains that the national ideal is lesser than God. In his review of Delbanco's book, Richard Rorty protests: "Why, one can imagine Whitman asking, should we Americans take God's word for it that he is more vast than the free, just, utopian nation of our dreams? Whitman famously called the United States of America 'the greatest poem.' He took narratives that featured God to be lesser poems — useful in their day, because suitable for the needs of a younger humanity. But now we are more grown up" (Richard Rorty, "I Hear America Sighing," *New York Times Book Review* [November 7, 1999], p. 16). The dispute about which dream is bigger — the dream of a nation or of God — must be decided in conjunction with the question of whether God in fact exists. For only under the assumption of God's nonexistence can God be declared lesser than the nation, however conceived.

11. Herman Melville, *White-Jacket; or, The World in a Man-of-War* (1850), ch. 36.

12. Delbanco, *The Real American Dream*, pp. 96, 103.

13. Delbanco, *The Real American Dream*, p. 103.

14. Michael Oakeshott, "Political Education," in *Rationalism in Politics and Other Essays* (Indianapolis: Liberty Press, 1991), p. 48.

faction itself is threatened by the pursuit of pleasure. I do not mean simply that we spend a good deal of our lives dissatisfied. Clearly, we are dissatisfied until we experience satisfaction. Desire is aroused, and striving begins, goaded by a sense of discontentment and pulled by the expectation of fulfillment until satisfaction is reached. Dissatisfied and expectant striving is the overall state, fulfillment is its interruption; desire is eternal, satisfaction is fleetingly periodic.[15]

More importantly, almost paradoxically, we remain dissatisfied in the midst of experiencing satisfaction. We compare our "pleasures" to those of others, and begin to envy them. A fine new Honda of our modest dreams is a source of *dissatisfaction* when we see a neighbor's new Mercedes. But even when we win the game of comparisons — when we park in front of our garage the best model of the most expensive car — our victory is hollow, melancholy. As Gratiano says in Shakespeare's *Merchant of Venice*, "All things that are, are with more spirit chased than enjoyed."[16] Marked as we are by what philosophers call self-transcendence, in our imagination we are always already beyond any state we have reached. Whatever we have, we want more and different, and when we have climbed to the top, disappointment clouds the triumph. Our striving can therefore find proper rest only when we find joy in something infinite. For Christians, this something is God.

Second, we feel melancholy because our pleasure is truly human and therefore truly pleasurable only if it has meaning beyond itself. So it is with sex, for instance. No matter how enticing and thrilling it may be, it leaves an aftertaste of dissatisfaction — maybe guilt, but certainly emptiness — when it does not somehow refer beyond itself, when it is not a sacrament of love between human beings. So too with most other pleasures.[17]

---

15. Offering a particularly bleak version of this point, Arthur Schopenhauer writes that in human existence, there is only "momentary gratification, fleeting pleasure conditioned by wants, much and long suffering, constant struggle, *bellum omnium*, everything a hunter and everything hunted, pressure, want, need and anxiety, shrieking and howling, and this goes on in *secula seculorum* or until once again the crust of the planet breaks" (*The World as Will and Representation*, trans. E. F. J. Payne [New York: Dover, 1969], vol. 2, p. 354).

16. Act II, Scene VI.

17. This observation fits with one of the central conclusions of the Grant Study — a study of well-adjusted Harvard sophomores begun in 1937, which, after more than seventy years of following its subjects, remains one of "the longest running, and probably most exhaustive, longitudinal studies of mental and physical well-being in history." In an interview in 2008, its longtime director, George Vaillant, was asked, "What have you learned from the Grant Study of men?" His response was that "the only thing that really matters in life are

When we place pleasure at the center of the good life, when we decouple it from the love of God, which is the ultimate source of meaning, and when we sever it from love of neighbor and hope for a common future, we are left, in the words of Delbanco, "with no way of organizing desire into a structure of meaning."[18] And because we humans are ineradicably meaning-making animals, the surd desire to satisfy self-contained pleasures always remains deeply unsatisfying.

Accounts of Reality and Conceptions of Flourishing

For the sake of the fulfillment of individuals, the thriving of communities, and of our common global future, we need a better account of human flourishing than experiential satisfaction. The most robust alternative visions of human flourishing are found in the great faith traditions. It is to them — and the debates between them regarding in what human flourishing truly consists — that we should turn for resources to think anew about human flourishing. In the following, I suggest contours of human flourishing as contained in the Christian faith, or more precisely one strand of that faith.

Centrality of Human Flourishing

Concern with human flourishing is at the heart of the great faiths, including Christianity. True, you cannot always tell that from the way faiths are practiced. When surveying their history, it seems on occasion that the goal of faiths were simply to dispatch people out of this world and into the next — out of the vale of tears into heavenly bliss (Christianity), out of the world of craving into nirvana (Buddhism), to give just two examples. Yet for great religious teachers, even for the representatives of highly ascetic and seemingly otherworldly forms of faith, human flourishing has always remained central.

Abu Hamid Al-Ghazali, one of the greatest Sufi Muslim thinkers, is

---

your relationships with other people" (Joshua Wolf Shenk, "What Makes Us Happy?" *The Atlantic* [June 2009], p. 36). Applied to the question of satisfaction, this suggests that relationships give meaning to pleasure; pleasure hollows itself out without them.

18. Delbanco, *The Real American Dream*, p. 103.

one example. "Know, O beloved, that man was not created in jest or at random, but marvelously made and for some great end," he begins one of his books. And what is that great end for a being whose spirit is "lofty and divine," even if its body is "mean and earthly"?

> When in the crucible of abstinence he [man] is purged from carnal passions he attains to the highest, and in place of being a slave to lust and anger becomes endued with angelic qualities. Attaining that state, he finds his heaven in the contemplation of Eternal Beauty, and no longer in fleshly delights.

These lines come from the introduction to Ghazali's book, which is all about "turning away from the world to God." As a consequence you might not think that his concern is human flourishing. And yet its title is *The Alchemy of Happiness.*[19] Precisely by talking about turning away from the world to God and purging oneself from carnal passions, the book is about flourishing in this world and the next.

Or take one of the greatest Jewish religious thinkers, Moses Maimonides. At the beginning of *The Guide of the Perplexed* he writes that the image of God in human beings — that which distinguishes them from animals — is "the intellect which God made overflow into man."[20] To underscore this point, Maimonides ends his work by stating that intellect is "the bond between us and Him."[21] True human perfection consists

> in the acquisition of the rational virtues — I refer to the conception of intelligibles, which teach true opinions concerning divine things. This is in true reality the ultimate end; this is what gives the individual true perfection, a perfection belonging to him alone; and it gives him permanent perdurance; through it man is man.[22]

19. Abu Hamid Al-Ghazali, *The Alchemy of Happiness,* trans. Claud Field (Gloucester, UK: Dodo Press, 1909), p. xii.

20. Moses Maimonides, *The Guide of the Perplexed,* trans. Shlomo Pines (Chicago: University of Chicago Press, 1963), I: 2 (p. 24).

21. Maimonides, *The Guide of the Perplexed* III: 51 (p. 621).

22. Maimonides, *The Guide of the Perplexed* III: 54 (p. 635). Though prevalent, this "intellectualist" reading of Maimonides' account of human perfection has not remained unchallenged. For an alternative reading that emphasizes not just human apprehension of God but human love of God as well as human "return" to the world as a being transformed by the knowledge of God "to participate in the governance of one's society according to the principles of loving-kindness, righteousness, and judgment," see Menachem Kellner, "Is Mai-

The nature of ultimate reality, the character of human beings, the meaning of their lives, and the most worthy of their pursuits all cohere. The whole religious system is connected with human flourishing.

Contemporary fellow Muslims or Jews might quarrel with al Ghazali's or Maimonides' account of human flourishing, most likely deeming them too ascetic or intellectual. Indeed many internal debates within a religious tradition concern the question just what is it that constitutes properly understood human flourishing. Christians might do so as well (though many Christian sages and saints have understood flourishing in strikingly similar ways[23]). They might also disagree with them about the best means to achieve it (noting especially the absence of Jesus Christ in their accounts). My point in invoking al Ghazali and Maimonides is not to offer a Christian assessment of their thought, though a respectful critical conversation among great faiths about human flourishing is important. It is rather to illustrate that the concern for human flourishing is central to great religious traditions and is one of their defining characteristics.

Not so long ago human flourishing was also central to the institutions of higher learning in the West. They were largely about exploration of what it means to live well, to lead a meaningful life. They were less about how to be successful at this or that activity or vocation, but about how to be successful *at being human.* In my terms, they were about human flourishing. This is no longer so. In his book *Education's End,* Anthony Kronman tells a compelling story of how the ideal of a "research university" and fascination with "postmodernism" in culture and theory colluded in making colleges and universities give up on exploring the meaning of life.[24] Today, he writes, "If one wants organized assistance in answering the question of life's meaning, and not just the love of family and friends, it is to the churches that one must turn."[25]

As a self-confessed secularist, Kronman is critical of the way religious traditions go about giving answer to the meaning of life. He believes —

---

monides' Ideal Person Austerely Rationalist?" *American Catholic Philosophical Quarterly* 76, no. 1 (2002): 125-43 (quote on p. 134).

23. Indeed, it has been a widespread Christian *critique* of Islam in the Middle Ages and Renaissance that it is "founded on pleasure," as Pope Pius II expressed in his letter to the Ottoman Sultan Mehmed II (Aeneas Silvius Piccolomini, *Epistola Ad Mahomatem II (Epistle to Mohammed II)*, ed. and trans. Albert R. Baca (New York: Peter Lang, 1990), p. 91.

24. Anthony T. Kronman, *Education's End: Why Our Colleges and Universities Have Given Up on the Meaning of Life* (New Haven: Yale University Press, 2007).

25. Kronman, *Education's End*, p. 197.

wrongly, I think — that faiths are inherently inhospitable to responsible pluralism and always demand a sacrifice of intellect. As a person of faith, I think that a secular quest for the meaning of life is likely to fail, and that the viable candidates for the meaning of life are all religiously based. Yet whatever position one takes in the debate between secular humanism and religious traditions, both share a concern for human flourishing and stand in contrast with a pervasive cultural preoccupation with experiential satisfaction in Western societies today.

Fit

Ghazali's *The Alchemy of Happiness* and Maimonides' *The Guide of the Perplexed* illustrate not only the centrality of human flourishing to religious traditions. They also highlight one significant way in which religious accounts of human flourishing differ from the contemporary propensity to see flourishing as experiential satisfaction. The difference concerns a fit between how the world, including human beings, is constituted and what it means for human beings to flourish. The central chapters of Ghazali's book deal with the knowledge of the self, of God, of this world, and of the next world.[26] To know what it means to reach happiness, you need to know who you are and what your place is in the larger household of reality — created and uncreated.

In this regard Ghazali is not unusual. As illustrated by Maimonides, most religions and most significant philosophies are based on the idea that there is a fit — maybe a loose fit, but some kind of fit nonetheless — between an overarching account of reality and a proper conception of human flourishing. And most people in most places throughout human history have agreed that there should be such a fit. They have done so mainly because their lives were guided by religious traditions. Let me fill out this notion of a fit by stepping away from religious figures such as Augustine and Ghazali for a moment and looking briefly at two philosophers, one ancient and one modern: Seneca and Nietzsche.

Seneca and the ancient Stoics (who have benefited from something of a comeback in recent years) coordinated their convictions about the world, about human beings, about what it means to live well, and about the

26. See Ghazali, *The Alchemy of Happiness*, pp. 1-26.

nature of happiness.[27] They believed that god is Cosmic Reason, spread throughout creation and directing its development completely. Human beings are primarily rational creatures; they live well when they align themselves with Cosmic Reason. They are happy when, in alignment with Cosmic Reason, they achieve tranquil self-sufficiency and are not subject to emotions such as fear, envy, or anger, no matter what the outward circumstances might be. Thus, Stoic accounts of the world and of human flourishing cohere.

My second example, Friedrich Nietzsche, was a modern thinker radically opposed not only to Christianity but also to the ancient Stoics.[28] He was an anti-realist thinker suspicious of all systems, but even he was not able to abandon the idea of a fit between an intellectually responsible understanding of the world and what it means for human beings to flourish within that world. He believed that the whole Western tradition of morality should be rejected, not just because it is to blame if "man, as a species, never reach[es] his highest potential power and splendor."[29] The Western tradition of morality is inappropriate primarily because it does not fit who human beings actually are. Contrary to the assumptions of Western moral traditions, human beings are (1) not free in their actions, but are governed by necessity; (2) not transparent to themselves and others in their motivations, but opaque; (3) not similar to each other and therefore subject to the same moral code, but each different. Conversely, Nietzsche's own advocacy of the "will to power" of "higher humans" fits precisely these features of human beings and makes possible the maximization of the excellence of "higher humans."[30] His "will to power" is simply the tendency of all beings — humans included — not just to survive, but to enlarge and expand — to flourish, so to speak, even at the expense of others. Though completely different from the Stoics, Nietzsche's account of human flourishing also fits his account of reality as a whole.

---

27. For the purposes of this essay, I am following the discussion of Seneca and Stoics in Nicholas Wolterstorff, *Justice: Right and Wrongs* (Princeton: Princeton University Press, 2008), pp. 146-79.

28. See Friedrich Nietzsche, *Beyond Good and Evil,* p. 9.

29. Friedrich Nietzsche, *On the Genealogy of Morality,* ed. Keith Ansell-Pearson, trans. Carol Diethe (Cambridge: Cambridge University Press, 1994), Preface 6.

30. This last point stands even if it is true that Nietzsche cannot give rational reasons for preferring his noble morality to Western slave morality because he did not believe that there are objective facts about what is morally right and what is morally wrong. See Brian Leiter, http://plato.stanford.edu/entries/nietzsche-moral-political/.

Absence of Fit

In contrast, those among our contemporaries who think that flourishing consists in experiential satisfaction tend not to ask about how this notion of flourishing fits with the character of the world and of human beings. The reason is not simply that, for the most part, they are ordinary people, rather than philosophers (like Seneca or Nietzsche) or great religious thinkers (like Augustine, Ghazali, or Maimonides). After all, over the centuries and up to the present, many ordinary people have cared about aligning their lives with the character of the world and of ultimate reality. No, the primary reasons have to do with the nature of the contemporary account of flourishing and the general cultural milieu prevalent in today's Western world.

As I have already noted, satisfaction plays the key role in many contemporary accounts of human flourishing. Satisfaction is a form of experience, and experiences are generally deemed to be matters of individual preference. Everyone is the best judge of their own experience of satisfaction. To examine whether a particular experience fits into a larger account of the world is already to risk relativizing its value as an experience. If those who understand human flourishing as experiential satisfaction happen to be religious, their faith sheds its power to orient people, and is reduced to a servant of experiential satisfaction, which is a major malfunction of faith. From being revered as the "Creator and the Master of the Universe," who by that very identity defines who human beings are and how they should live, God is then transformed into something like a combination of "Divine Butler" and "Cosmic Therapist."[31]

This sort of transformation of faith is in line with the pervasively anti-metaphysical tenor of contemporary Western culture. "In post-Nietzschean spirit," writes Terry Eagleton, "the West appears to be busily undermining its own erstwhile metaphysical foundations with an unholy mélange of practical materialism, political pragmatism, moral and cultural relativism, and philosophical skepticism."[32] In his book *The Meaning of Life*, Eagleton notes that many contemporary intellectuals, unsurprisingly, tend to dismiss serious reflection on "human life as a whole as disreputably 'humanist' — or

31. On God as Divine Butler and Cosmic Therapist among American teenagers, see Christian Smith, *Soul Searching: The Religious and Spiritual Lives of American Teenagers* (New York: Oxford University Press, 2005), p. 165.

32. Terry Eagleton, "Culture and Barbarism: Metaphysics in a Time of Terrorism," *Commonweal* 136, no. 6 (2009): 9.

Miroslav Volf

indeed as the kind of 'totalizing' theory that led straight to the death camps of the totalitarian state." In their view, there is "no such thing as humanity or human life to be contemplated";[33] there are only various culturally conditioned and individually inflected changing life projects. If each person is an artist of her own life, aiming to achieve experiential satisfaction unconstrained by moral norms reflective of a common human nature, then it is superfluous to ask how the stream of ever-new artistic self-creations aimed at experiential satisfaction fits within the larger account of reality.

My point is not that it would be impossible to offer a plausible interpretation of reality — "plausible," I write, not "true"! — into which an account of human flourishing as experiential satisfaction could nestle comfortably. It is that many today would not care whether they live with or against the grain of reality. They want what they want, and that they want it is a sufficient justification for wanting it. Arguments about how their desires fit with the more encompassing account of reality — how they relate to "human nature," for instance — are simply beside the point.

Creator and Creatures

It is a mistake — a major mistake — not to be concerned about how well our notion of flourishing fits the nature of reality. If we live against the grain of reality, we cannot experience lasting satisfaction, let alone be able to live fulfilled lives. That is what the Christian tradition (as well as other great religious and philosophical traditions) has always insisted. The great Christian saints, theologians, and lay leaders of the past believed that accounts of human flourishing had to cohere with ideas about God as the source and goal of all reality.

But how should they be made to cohere? At the outset, we can eliminate one option. We cannot start with a preferred account of human flourishing and then construct an image of God to go with it, designing the fit between God and human flourishing the way we might look for a jacket to match our slacks. We would then be consciously enacting Nietzsche's devastating critique of the emergence of Christian morality and Christian

33. Terry Eagleton, *The Meaning of Life* (Oxford: Oxford University Press, 2007), p. 35. For a parallel critique of the impact of postmodernism on the engagement with the question of the meaning of life in educational institutions of higher learning, see Kronman, *Education's End*, pp. 180-94.

204

faith as a whole. According to Nietzsche, Christians had designed false beliefs about God in order to legitimize their preferred values. If we were to start with an idea of human flourishing and subsequently "build" God to match our values, then the only difference between Nietzsche's version and ours would be that Nietzsche dismissed those values themselves as being perverse, while we uphold them as healthy. More importantly, by constructing an image of God so as to fit already-given notions of human flourishing, we enact one of the most troubling malfunctions of faith — divesting faith of its own integrity and making it only an instrument of our own interests and purposes.

Let's return once more to Augustine. We may sum up his convictions about God, the world, human beings, and human flourishing in four brief propositions. These are tailored to highlight the relation of his position to that of Stoics, Nietzsche, and many contemporaries. First, he believed that God is not an impersonal Reason dispersed throughout the world, but a "person" who loves and can be loved in return. Second, to be human is to love; we can choose *what* to love but not *whether* to love. Third, we live well when we love both God and neighbor, aligning ourselves with the God who loves. Fourth, we will flourish and be truly happy when we discover joy in loving the infinite God and our neighbors in God.

For Augustine, convictions about God, human beings, and human flourishing all cohered. That's the positive side of the fit: It specifies what is in, so to speak, when it comes to human flourishing. But the fit also specifies what is out. If we share Augustine's convictions about God and human beings, we have to reject some interpretations of reality and some accounts of human flourishing. Let us again consider from an Augustinian perspective the Stoic, Nietzschean, and contemporary Western accounts of flourishing.

If we believe that God is love and that we are created for love, the Stoic ideal of tranquil self-sufficiency will not do. Instead of caring for our neighbor's well-being to the extent that we care about living our lives well, as Stoics did, we will care for our neighbors' well-being — including their tranquility — for their own sake, not just our own. Our concern will then be not just to lead life well ourselves. Instead, we will strive for life to go well for our neighbors and for them to lead their lives well, and acknowledge that their flourishing is tied deeply to our flourishing.[34]

---

34. I owe the idea that human flourishing consists formally in a combination of life being lived well and life going well to Nicholas Wolterstorff, *Justice: Right and Wrongs*, p. 221.

Similarly, if we believe that God is love and that we are created for love, we will be disinclined to believe that the Nietzschean noble morality designed to further the excellence of the "higher humans" is a proper road to human flourishing. Compassion and help for those whose lives do not go well — for the vulnerable, the weak — will then be an essential component of leading *our* lives well.

Finally, if we believe that God is love and that we are created for love, we will reject the notion that flourishing consists in being experientially satisfied. Instead, we will believe that we will be experientially satisfied when we truly flourish. When is it that we truly flourish? When is it that we lead our lives well, and our lives are going well? We lead our lives well when we love God with our whole being and when we love neighbors as we (properly) love ourselves. Life goes well for us when our basic needs are met and when we experience that we are loved by God and by neighbors — when we are loved as who we are, with our own specific character and history and notwithstanding our fragility and failures. Echoing Augustine's comment on the contrast between Epicurean and Christian visions of happiness, instead of our slogan being, "Let us eat and drink" (or a more sophisticated version of the same that privileges "higher pleasures"), it should be "Let us give and pray."[35]

Loving God, Loving Neighbor

What I have written about the relation between God and human flourishing is but a theological echo of two central verses from the Christian Scriptures: "God is love" (1 John 4:8) and "You shall love the Lord your God with all your heart, and with all your soul, and with all your strength, and with all your mind; and your neighbor as yourself" (Luke 10:27).[36] In conclusion, I would like to apply this notion of human flourishing, together with its undergirding convictions about God, to the proper functions of faith in human life.

Every prophetic religion, including the Christian faith, has the following two fundamental movements: the ascent to God to receive the prophetic message, and the return to the world to bring the received message to

35. Augustine, *Sermons*, 35.
36. The sources of this passage in Luke are Deuteronomy 6:5 and Leviticus 19:18 in Jewish Scriptures.

bear on mundane realities. Both movements are essential. Without ascent, there is nothing to impart; without return, there is no one to impart to.

Most malfunctions of faith are rooted in a failure to love the God of love or a failure to love the neighbor. Ascent malfunctions happen when we don't love God as we should. We either love our interests, purposes, and projects, and then employ language about God to realize them (we can call this "functional reduction"); or we love the wrong God ("idolatrous substitution"). Return malfunctions happen when we love neither our neighbor nor ourselves properly; when faith either energizes or heals us, but does not shape our lives to our own and our neighbors' benefit, or when we impose our faith on our neighbors irrespective of their wishes.

The challenge facing Christians is ultimately very simple: Love God and neighbor rightly, so that we may both avoid malfunctions of faith and relate God positively to human flourishing. And yet, the challenge is also complex and difficult. Allow me to highlight three aspects:

First, we need to *explicate* God's relation to human flourishing with regard to many concrete issues we are facing today — from poverty to environmental degradation, from bioethical issues to international relations, from sex to governing. Without showing how Christian notions of God and human flourishing apply to concrete issues, these notions will remain vague and inert, with little impact on the way we actually live.

Second, we need to *make plausible* the claim that the love of God and of neighbor is the key to human flourishing. For centuries, nonbelievers have not simply called into question God's existence, but railed against God's nature, against the way God relates to the world, and consequently against theistic accounts of how humans ought to live in relation to God. Sometimes it seems that they would not have minded God existing if they could have believed that God is good for us. And this underscores how difficult it is to make plausible to nonbelievers the connection between God and human flourishing. For the notion of what is "good for us" — and not just the existence and character of God — is highly contested.

Finally, maybe the most difficult challenge for Christians is to actually *believe* that God is fundamental to human flourishing. And it is not sufficient for us to believe it as we might believe that there may be water on some distant planet. We must believe it as a rock-bottom conviction that shapes the way we think, preach, write, and live. Charles Taylor tells the story of hearing Mother Teresa speak about her motivation for working with the abandoned and the dying of Calcutta. She explained that she did the hard work of tending them because they were created in the image of

God. Being a Catholic philosopher, Taylor thought to himself, "I could have said that, too!" And then, being an introspective person and a fine philosopher, he asked himself, "But could I have *meant* it?"

That, I think, is today's most fundamental challenge for theologians, priests, ministers, and Christian laypeople: to *really mean* that the presence and activity of the God of love, the God who enables us to love our neighbors as ourselves, is our hope and the hope of the world — that that God is the secret of our flourishing as persons, cultures, and interdependent inhabitants of a single globe.

Hope and Responsibility:
The Assembly with the Promise of God

Douglas Knight

What can we say about the future? What confidence can we have that humankind has one? It is surely better to say something about it, even if unverifiable or banal, than to concede that the future is too difficult an issue to tackle. One community is obliged to speak about the future, since when it does so the question of the future exists for all mankind.

The community that has been addressed by God has hope. God has made a covenant with Abraham and his seed forever and so has brought Israel into covenant with himself. He has spoken, made promises, raised expectations, and so put himself under an obligation. We may talk about the future by considering this community, and doing so in terms of the future to which it is oriented.

Two things must be said about this covenant. First, Israel's covenant with God is for Israel's sake. There is no further rationale than the love of God for Israel. Second, Israel confesses that the God who raises the possibility of a future for them is the true God, and therefore the God of all men. Since Israel is in covenant with the God of all humankind, this covenant is the truth of all humanity, and there is no humanity for which some other kind of existence is true.[1]

Israel's covenant with God is both for Israel's own sake and for the sake of the world. Israel is in the world — of the gentiles — as the presence of God with man, as the witness of God to man and the embodiment of man's proper recognition and worship of God. Since Israel is covenantal, humankind is covenantal. Each human is in relationship, fundamentally and immediately, with God and, through God, with every other human being.

---

1. Karl Barth, *Church Dogmatics* IV/1 (Edinburgh: T. & T. Clark, 1956), pp. 3-54.

Humans are in relationship because God has made them so. God calls us into existence so that we may come into *communion* with him and with one another: communion is the purpose of existence. We do not exist first and enter an initial relationship at some later date.

Man is made for his fellow. God brings each of us before others; we may recognize that other as a bearer of the image of God, and each of us hopes that the other can discern that image and glory in us. Since we are called before those who are not ready for us as well as those who are, we have to wait for their recognition, and suffer when it does not come. Through encounter with each particular person we hope to enter the communion with all humanity and with God. But since not all humankind is ready for it, this covenant with God obliges Israel to wait for humankind.

Israel

God has made man his covenant partner. He has done so by making one particular man, Abraham, and the particular people descended from him, Israel, his partner. "Covenant" is not a general truth or a universal right but a specific communion, membership of which is by invitation. The covenant of God is with man through this people only; it is exclusive. But it is inclusive too. It is simultaneously with Israel and for all mankind, *particular* and only thus *universal*. It is good news for all mankind that God loves Israel, for Israel is the truth of *Man with God* and the future of mankind, held out by God to man.

Israel is *"Knesset Israel"* — the *assembly* of Israel. This assembly of Israel worships, from the beginning and forever, before the throne of God. The "church" *(ecclesia)* is the second assembly called into being around the first assembly that is Israel: Israel is the center around which the church gathers. We baptized gentiles worship the Lord with Israel and we see him surrounded by the whole company of the patriarchs, the prophets, and all his people, as Christ.[2] The church is present only where the Scriptures of Israel are read, the patriarchs and prophets heard, and the worship of heaven reaches down to earth.

The one divisible testament of God makes itself heard in the sequence

---

2. Liturgy of Saint Basil: "Grant that we may obtain mercy and grace, together with all the saints which have been since the world began, with our forefathers and fathers, patriarchs, prophets, apostles, evangelists . . . and every righteous spirit in faith made perfect."

of readings "Old Testament-Psalm-Epistle-Gospel" of every service of Christian worship. The New Testament is not the antithesis of the Old Testament, but simply the one testament of God opened *to* the gentiles. Christians refer to this one testament in its twofold form as Old and New simultaneously: "old" because it is the original, unchanging testimony of God, and "new" since it makes all things new.[3] Christians worship the Lord as "Christ," anointed (*christ*-ed) and surrounded first by Israel, and then by all mankind and all creatures who participate in his glory. Without them Christ would be without his kingdom, and so would be no *Christ*. Christians' conception of the simultaneously plural and unitary nature of the *ecclesia* enables them to ask whether the plurality of this assembly also informs the deepest logic of Jewish thought.

To the outsider, Jewish thought appears to point in two directions. On the one hand is the Law, which some contributors to this volume reserve to Israel. Israel is in an exclusive relationship in which the gentiles have no part, they suggest, so that Christians have no more to say about this private relationship than any other gentiles. On the other hand, Jewish thought is committed to the discourse of philosophy. Since philosophy represents an engagement with gentile wisdom, this indicates a requirement to make sense of the gentiles, wrestle with them, and perhaps offer them whatever wisdom they are able to accept.

What about the *exclusivity* of the covenant of God with Israel? Is this covenant solely a private affair, or is it also missional? Israel is the community that correctly identifies God. By identifying him so, Israel identifies all else as *not*-God, and calls excessive devotion to anything else idolatry. Such idolatry is the way that gentiles give themselves to what-is-not-God, and lose themselves by doing so. Their false orientation and the misdirection of their passions sets them against one another, making the world a violent place. They are enslaved and in misery. The gentiles give themselves away in worship to every creature, and are captive to the tyrannies that result; but since they cannot help themselves, Israel may be moved to have compassion on them.

Israel is given to the world, that is, to the gentiles. By its worship Israel witnesses that the true goal of man's life is God, and all other ends are false. The true God is our proper orientation, by which alone man may be at peace with himself, with his neighbor, and with all other creatures. Simply by worshiping God, and refusing to give worship to any other being, Israel

---

3. Irenaeus, *Against the Heretics*, 2.9.1-2, 3.6.4.

is the witness of God to all. The holiness of Israel is not achieved through removing herself from the gentiles, but by remaining holy in their midst, so that they can marvel at this holiness and even desire it for themselves. Jews are here to resist the world, not capitulate to it. As long as Jews are holy and inviolable, gentiles will discover that to throw themselves against Israel is to throw themselves against God, and against their own true orientation, which Israel's God alone secures.

For long periods of history Israel must bear foreign masters, even lawless and violent ones. The "harsh historical oppression" (Eugene Korn, in this volume) that Israel suffers begins with Egypt, not with Rome. Every subsequent regime — Assyria, Babylon, Persia, Greece, medieval European Christendom, modern European nationalisms — is a continuation of "Egypt." Egypt is not only outside us but also within; the passions, resentment, and rage that bubble up within us are, until we can master them, as dangerous as any external power.[4] Israel is confronted by, often subjugated by, the nations, but must never imitate them or be suborned by them. But equally, Israel can only be threatened by them because they appeal to the violence that is yet to be mastered within each man.

Israel identifies God in its worship. The gentiles gathered in the church are able to identify God because they identify Israel in the person of Christ as the true worshiper of God and therefore as his witness. They have taken Israel as their guide and teacher, expectations have been created, and they have learned to hope. With the gathering of the church, the gentile acknowledgment of Israel, and with it her vindication, has begun.[5]

Israel will not be extracted from the gentiles, or they from her; she will be raised over them and they, gathered around her, will be her glory.[6] Without an account of the extrinsic purpose of the covenant, and thus of the responsibility for the world that attaches to it, Israel's testing relationship with the gentiles is surely incomprehensible. Without a doctrine of

---

4. Philo, *Allegorical Interpretation* II, xxv-xxvi (99-103).

5. Evensong Canticle *Nunc Dimittis* (Book of Common Prayer): "For mine eyes have seen thy salvation, which thou hast prepared before the face of all people; to be a light to lighten the Gentiles and to be the glory of thy people Israel." In the Liturgy of Saint John Chrysostom: "For thou only, O Lord our God, has dominion over heaven and earth, who art borne by the cherubim on the throne, who art Lord of the Seraphim and King of Israel, who only art holy."

6. For an account of resurrection as the vindication of Israel see Jon D. Levenson, *Resurrection and the Restoration of Israel: The Ultimate Victory of the God of Life* (New Haven: Yale University Press, 2008), pp. 201-16.

election that understands that this witness is its purpose and this vindication its climax, it is hard to see why God subjects Israel to what must otherwise appear pointless cruelty. If Jewish thought makes these connections between covenant and purpose and between worship and public witness at all, it makes them in such a minor key that God seems unready to help or to care. Could this be why theodicy, apostasy, and atheism are such prominent options for Jewish thinkers?

Gentiles are without the Law. In their misery, they harm themselves and lash out at one another. They give themselves away to the wrong gods and murderous behavior results. But gentile violence also laps against Israel, occasionally identifying Israel as uniquely the one they must lash out against. When Israel is persecuted and suffers she cannot but wish to tell the gentiles that it is only their failure of true orientation and ignorance of true worship that creates the misery that drives their rage. Israel can also point out that there is release from this self-destruction through conversion to true worship. For gentiles, salvation means deliverance from false to true worship and orientation; whereas for Israel salvation means that God does not let the gentiles prevail against her, but vindicates her before them. Nonetheless, the gentiles are the storm that Israel has to walk through, for life with man without God is the task to which the man with God is called. The mission of Israel is intrinsic to its worship of God, not additional to it.

In the assembly of Israel we see humankind with God. The truth about God concerns us gentiles because it gives us our own proper orientation and therefore the truth of our existence. The future, and with it *our* future, is there in that assembly around the throne of God. But presently for the gentiles it appears as promise and as question: we are not compelled to acknowledge or receive it, but simply invited to do so. From the future the Lord God has sent this assembly back to us in one person. The many individual epiphanies that make up the history of Israel are appearances of this future assembly, recapitulated for the gentiles in this person. Christ is the epiphany, the decisive view, of the whole. He is the eschaton, making itself diffidently available in a single moment of our space and time, so that we may receive it or refuse it in freedom. The gentiles are brought to the edge of this worshiping assembly by this one member of Israel.

Jesus is the Jew who is not on the run from gentile violence. He goes through all that the gentiles hurl at him, unmoved by our rage, without reviling; thus he is the person of Israel victorious and vindicated. In this person Israel is planted and established in the world through all generations, withstanding all assaults, worshiping the true God and no other. The gentiles may see this and wonder at it.

Israel worships the God who has committed himself to man, specifically to Abraham and his children; the God who has *not* done so is an untruth. And idolatry, that is, the substitution of a false image, is to the detriment of man who is the true image of God. That God makes himself one person among the many created persons of the world does not diminish him. For our sake, so that we may come to acknowledge him, God does not come to us without creation; whether as "fire and cloud" or "garments of flesh," he clothes himself with what is created, for how else may we know him? God is faithful to Israel. Since this means that gentile violence will not overcome her, it is also good, indeed it is salvation, for the gentiles that God is so.

Philosophy and Theisms

Israel is this witness in the face of the gentiles. Gentiles can only withhold their worship from the God of Israel by giving themselves to another divinity. They may believe that the unconcerned and disengaged God is higher and more compelling than the covenanted, and thus concerned and engaged God who has made himself known to Abraham and who shares his fortunes with Israel. But they pay an awful price for such theism, or the atheism to which it gives rise, because for better or worse, our conception of God shapes our conception of our own identity and place in the world.

Philosophy — gentile wisdom — has determined that God is not interested in man. What comprehension can the philosophers, imitators of Plato, have of the God who engages with the vulgar assembly, enables man to worship him, and so allows a foretaste of heaven to reach earth so that it is renewed? What can these elective Hellenists make of a world that exists in time, yet is not dissolved but renewed by it? The Jewish thought that is unwilling to let Israel's worship shape its wisdom, or the inner aspect of the covenant shape the outer, admires a deistic conception of the God who disdains to take any interest in man.

In such a negative theology God is so vanishingly distant that nothing can be said about him. This concedes too much to gentile refusal to acknowledge that Israel has been addressed and her prayers heard. Philosophy is a coy expression of a deism that believes that any indication of God's concern for man arises from an immature religious consciousness. Could it be that, when Jewish thought is reluctant to let Israel's Scriptures frame the dialogue with gentile wisdom, a doctrine of a disengaged, noncovenantal God appears between this "Law" and "Philosophy"? If we have an unconcerned God it makes no difference whether or not he exists. Such theism or a-theism sets what is *not* personal above the living person, putting what is lifeless above life. The God of the philosophers is indistinguishable from Death.

Monotheisms are not inevitably allies. The theism in which "God" cannot tolerate what is not God is simply a *monism:* such a "God" is confronted by creation as by something alien. The oneness of God is not a doctrine about number, for the revelation to Israel is not solely that there is an underlying unity, but also that the true God has made *something that is not himself,* and that he loves what he has made. Alongside unity therefore is a duality, of God and the world, and therefore of God and man. On the basis of this unity-and-duality the human being may also be in relationship with what *is* not himself. Each of us is both ourselves and open to another.

Israel may point out the fears and compulsions of modernity. Moderns imagine themselves as individuals alone in the world, and conceive of others as units similarly without intrinsic relation, each a threat to be shunned. Each is a dark star, unknowable to others or to himself. They impose on one another obligations that, over time, develop into ideologies and cults, so that the world of modernity is gripped by its own "gods," every individual his own. Israel can ask whether modernity is a manifestation of an Other-phobia, a failure to come to terms with the fact that we are not ourselves without our fellow man. Only through Israel may we discover that true knowledge of God releases us from the ideology and cult of this monad, enabling us to discover the truth of our neighbor's claim on us, and with it our own proper identity.

The high view of Israel in Christian doctrine of God may represent unwelcome attention, but it surely means that, for Israel, Christians are not the enemy. The suggestion that Israel has been supplanted in the affections of God is sometimes termed "supersessionism"; from the first the church identified this as the heresy of Marcion.[7] Christianity is entirely dependent on the witness of Israel; it does not attempt to displace it, but defers to it, indeed bows before it. This is not to deny that individual Christians and churches have spoken and acted against Israel, but this is the pagan within speaking, in defiance of the gospel. When this occurs the universal church

---

7. Irenaeus, *Against the Heretics,* 1.27.2-4.

must hold out to these Christians the oxygen mask from which they can draw deep drafts of the Scriptures, to return them to lucidity.

It is modernity that is opposed to any understanding of covenants, and of Israel's covenant in particular, and which is therefore unable to concede the distinctiveness of this people. Ideological moderns are committed to a metaphysics of unity over plurality, which wants to reach the universal through the reduction of particularities. Modernity is antagonistic even to its own origins; it attempts to separate itself from its origins in the Christian gospel, and thus from the worshiping assembly of Israel to which the church points. A monist conception deforms the modern conception of man as much as of God.[8]

In particular it is the concept of the will unconstrained by covenant that determines the account of man in that society. If in our conception God also is simply a will, each human is bound to fight this different will. It makes no great difference whether the monist account takes the form of furious assertion of the rights of God against man (ideological primitivism) or of the (deist or theist) distance and irrelevance of God to man, or even the (atheist) nonexistence of God, represented by modernity.

Two forms of monism are appalled at Israel as a fundamental theological fact. The explicitly theist monism of the ideological primitivism that characterizes the Middle East is the counterpart of the ostensibly atheist and nonreligious monism that dominates the West. Each is an articulation of the gentile form of life, of man-without-God shrunk to a unit of will, and unable to affirm creation and his fellow creature as good. Confronted by the world he did not make and cannot love, the monist "god" turns his frustration against one particular people. Karl Barth pointed out that when they shake off the restraining influence of Christian culture, gentiles end by lifting their hand against the Lord's anointed.[9] Identification of Israel as the peculiar enemy is the self-harming of gentiles without hope, so we should take contemporary antagonism towards Israel as warning of cultural decay in Western societies.[10]

---

8. Jean Bethke Elshtain, *Sovereignty: God, State and Self* (New York: Basic Books, 2008).

9. Karl Barth, *Dogmatics in Outline* (London: SCM, 2001), pp. 67-68. "The attack on Judah means the attack on the rock of the work and revelation of God, beside which work and revelation there is no other. . . . A nation which — and that is the other side of National Socialism — chooses itself and makes itself the basis and measure of everything — such a nation must sooner or later collide with the truly chosen people of God."

10. I am indebted here, and on several other points in this essay, to David Goldman's columns in *First Things* and as "Spengler" in *The Asia Times*.

Without a concept of covenant, we are left with man baffled by the world and by his neighbor, and unwilling to commit himself to the disciplines by which he could develop relationships with them. In the modern version, our present selves will even be reluctant to make concessions to our future selves, much less be willing to regard children as any form of second self.

The Human Covenant

Against this autistic account of man, Israel may hold up its high, "covenanted" view of man. The covenant of God with man in Israel gives a complex account of man in which, as persons, each of us is both a unique being and fundamentally committed to all others. Since God is with each human, a man may be truly known only as the person loved by God: the Lord brings each of us before the other so that we may wonder at the image of God that each presents us. We must seek one another's recognition and wait to receive it. We may seek other persons, and demand their wisdom, judgment, and approval. We may hope that neighbors and successors will find our projects good and wish to pursue them when we are gone, so that our efforts do not come to an end. We may term this a metaphysics of promise, or an eschatological ontology, which means simply that we may live in hope, indeed, in faith, hope, and love.

Man flourishes as he knows he is loved, and is enabled by love to give his service to his neighbor. All communities and societies are entities of love: love aspires to permanence, we desire its growth and not its breakdown. Love aspires to greater self-control, so that it becomes more lasting. Each society must seek its own continuation, and thus hope for a generation that will recognize it as good. No generation can be sufficient to itself: it can only receive this affirmation from another. Our present existence therefore requires that we pass on both life and the culture by which those who come after us can affirm that life as good. If we live as though there is only this present, and deny existence to that new generation who could give us the affirmation that we seek, we are our own enemies. We must live in such a way that the long-term can emerge, for if we live as though nothing will come after us, our present life will be of no value.[11]

---

11. Robert Spaemann, *Persons: The Difference between 'Someone' and 'Something'* (Oxford: Oxford University Press, 2006), p. 123. "Only the affirmation of the future perfect makes the present tense fully real."

Fundamental to the concept of hope is the prospect of new generations to continue the human race. The covenant of God orients Israel to its
future: the obligation to parents is honored by presenting them with another generation by which the life of this people will continue.[12] Light
from the covenant of God with Israel helps us see that the life of humankind is sustained by further covenants. Each society consists of two covenants, one that holds together the present generation as a functioning society; the other of which takes place between one generation and another,
and sustains that society through time.

Let us look at the *intragenerational covenant* first. Man is a covenanted
being because humanity is not unisex, but sexed and so dual. We are *either*
man *or* woman and so may give ourselves to another being as man to
woman or woman to man. Each may desire the one who is not like themselves, and in love give themselves to that other, for good. Marriage is the
covenant in which each partner recognizes the lasting uniqueness of this
single other person. Marriage is then public recognition by society, that
these two make a single unit, and that such units are themselves new little
societies, each as fundamental as society itself, each of which serves society's renewal. This covenant exists first for these two people and then for
those outside.[13] Their relationship is *exclusive,* and it recreates and renews
society as a whole only because it is so; what we have said about the exclusive and inclusive nature of Israel's covenant holds good here too. It is good
for society that two people make this fundamental identification of one
another as good, not relatively or provisionally, but finally and unchange-
ably. When marriage is not understood as covenant, aloneness is promoted
over life together. When we fail to sustain our own covenants, which we
enter freely, we become dependents of that other covenant that we have
not entered freely, the state.[14]

Marriage acknowledges the possibility that a new third party may
come into existence through our love. Children may arrive. Marriage pro-

12. Michael Wyschogrod, *The Body of Faith: God in the People Israel* (Northvale, NJ:
Aaronson, 1996), p. 253. "The Jewish family is thus the space in which the future membership of the *Knesset Israel* is prepared. . . . The bond of the Jewish parent to his child reflects
the faith that the Jews of future generations are already members of the house of Israel and
that redemption will come to humanity through them."

13. Robert P. George and Jean Bethke Elshtain, eds., *The Meaning of Marriage: Family,
State, Market, and Morals* (Dallas: Spence, 2006).

14. Patricia Morgan, *The War between the State and the Family* (London: Institute of
Economic Affairs, 2007).

vides children with the security in which their own readiness to enter covenants and start families may develop.[15] The recognition of the irreducible particularity of persons secured by marriage has the long-term effect of creating the culture in which persons are understood as irreducible, and are ready for the commitment to others that will generate new covenants and give that society a future.

The continuation of society rests on an understanding that the present is not self-sufficient, but oriented towards a future out of its sight. The present must give itself away so that something other than itself can come into existence. Self-giving and a readiness to invest without immediate reward are essential to any society's transgenerational continuity. Each generation has a debt to all previous generations, which it honors as it bears children to present to its own parents. The human economy is about the transfer of life from one generation to another, while the material economy is the flow of goods and services that enables this intergenerational transfer of life. Thus there is a covenant between this and subsequent generations and so between the present and the future. We need the covenanted community of Israel, along with those gentiles added to her, to say so.

In recent decades the intergenerational covenant seems to have weakened in Western societies. The expectation of parents that their children will, when adult, present them with grandchildren and thus keep their society in business, has dwindled. As a consequence there is a less certain orientation to the future.[16] Since we are less confident of our future, we are less willing to receive our reward in the long-term and implicit currency of recognition by our contemporaries, so we insist on receiving recognition in that immediate and explicit currency that is money.

By insisting that payment in money is finally the only valid form of public acknowledgment, we enforce this single medium on one another, replacing particular relationships and actual plurality with universal *relationship-stuff.* If everything can be adequately denominated in the single medium of money, all obligations may be met, differences equalized, and relationships concluded. We may all be paid off and have no further reason for human communication or existence. As we opt out of our particular covenants and relationships, the market and state expand to fill the

15. Jonathan Sacks, *Faith in the Future: The Ecology of Hope and the Restoration of Family and Faith* (Macon, GA: Mercer University Press, 1997), p. 23. The family is "the best means we have yet discovered for nurturing future generations."

16. Mary Eberstadt, "How the West Really Lost God: A New Look at Secularization," *Policy Review* 143 (June/July 2007).

gap. Unable to account for the motivation of man to serve a generation that does not yet exist, the modern state and modern economics are unable to concede the long-term economic function of the household in the production of the next generation. The market attempts to assimilate the household, with the effect that the short-term erodes the motor of the long-term.

If all particular relationships are made interchangeable and commensurable by market and state, all ends and purposes can be made present to us, here and now, without loss; we have no reason to look forward to any other time or future, so the present generation begrudges leaving anything to future generations. No personal relationship has ultimate status, all are fungible; the universal is permanent, we its merest epiphenomena. Each of us will be finally extinguished as a particular being. It is the responsibility of the one God-worshiping assembly to identify as "gods," idols, and forms of captivity, the various ways in which the man of modernity subjects himself to the monad, the undeclared god of modernity.

The large public square of the West is the result of the long presence of the community that acknowledges the God who gave his name and promise to Abraham. The assembly that worships this God, in its twofold form of the Jewish and Christian communities, practices the skills and virtues of self-examination, and from them Western societies have learned the art of self-judgment that has made them open societies.[17] We can assess Christianity by the extent to which its presence ameliorates our own intrinsic warrior culture through the, at best partial, conversion of any society.

Since it is a faith, Christianity is not the permanent possession of any society: when the Christian tide goes out it simply reveals more of the pagan beneath. When Western culture does not deign to hear from the Jewish and Christian communities, it is baffled by the question of the permanence of the human person. It will not continue to be secular, but descend into the various forms of collectivization, totalitarianism, and tribalism from which it once emerged. The cultural self-abjuration that is directing public policy against the faith that generated our inherited culture comes from a great ingratitude and self-reviling. Once again, it is only the assembly of Israel and the baptized gentiles added to her who give this warning.

The society with no conception of this covenant will suffer a crisis of confidence that manifests itself as cultural and demographic crisis, which

---

17. Oliver O'Donovan, *The Desire of the Nations* (Cambridge: Cambridge University Press, 1996), pp. 146-57.

appears as specific political and economic crises, but is fundamentally always the same crisis of man in paralysis before the summons of God. The greatest favor that the God-worshiping assembly can do for any society is to remain holy, while still a public part of that society, and for the sake of the future hold out against the all-demanding present. Made confident by the covenant of God with man, this assembly can say that God sets us before one another and invites us to look for his image in one another and so makes us the future-oriented people. To say that we are the people summoned by God to be his witnesses is the single constructive thing we can do for our society and for the human future.

Messianic Hope

Alan Mittleman

Hope, as Emily Dickinson famously wrote, is a thing with feathers. But, to continue the avian metaphor, it is also a thing with claws. Hope enables our imagination, moral and otherwise, to take flight. It lifts us above immediacy and fills our expectation with confidence. Without hope, we are consigned to fate. We acquiesce in the status quo; we repudiate our partnership with God to advance the good that resides in creation. But hope also pinions us to our dreams. It undercuts or complicates our rational assessment of possibility, rendering us vulnerable to fantasy and illusion. Hope can be injurious and false. True hope, whatever that might mean, ennobles us. False hope can distract and debase. With hope comes risk.

Like faith, hope is a complex interplay of reason and imagination, of cognition and emotion. It begins in desire and yearning and arcs into images and symbols of fulfillment. It is stirred by the travail and want of the present; it intends the fullness and completion of the future. Hope is expectation colored by a mysterious confidence that expectation has good grounds. True hope is not mere wishful thinking; it is arduous and not idle, as Aquinas says. It senses that the desire and yearning from which it springs spring themselves from something deep and true. This is the source of its mysterious confidence. The object of desire is an object that *ought* to be. The *ought* indicates transcendence; that which *is* not but which beckons. Thus, hope often arises from our sense of justice, from our experience of the outrage of injustice. When it intends the dominion of justice — of law, right, desert, and recompense — hope seeks to affirm a transcendent dimension of human affairs. *Ought* supervenes on *is*. To hope is to affirm an ideal based on an intuition about the goodness of life. Hope asserts what is felt to be truth. When its objects are high and worthy, this is what separates it from wishes and dreams. Hope entails a radical axiology rather than a spurious wishfulness.

But wishes and dreams, the flights of the imagination, are nonetheless often implicated in acts of hope, particularly as those acts are articulated in cultural patterns across spans of time. In the Jewish tradition, eschatology is a prominent locus for the hopes of our savaged people. The endless injustices of history will be made right at a consummation of history. The ideal pattern of a just society, limned by the laws of the Torah, will be enshrined in an eschatological polity. In place of tyranny there will be accountable rule. In place of poverty — plenty. In place of degradation, dignity; in place of humiliation, respect. The way the world is will give way to the way it ought to be.

The hope for a definitive dominion of the good is rooted in the earliest memories of the Israelites. That God entered history to declare an end to the injustice of slavery, that he miraculously liberated his people, gave them a model law, and brought them to a promised land, all set the pattern of expectation. Injustice can be repaired; it is not a decree of fate. Society can be bent to the demands of a just law. Political life in a fertile, lovely land can be fair and humane. The Israelite experience had traces, foretastes, fabled memories of these blessings. That real experience fell tragically short of these blessings could not cancel the transcendent normativity of the blessings themselves. On the contrary, it strengthened their appeal. Imagination embroidered the memories of liberating acts, righteous kings, and justice-seeking norms into scenarios of eschatological resolution and consummation.

In his essay on the messianic idea in Judaism,[1] Gershom Scholem distinguished between different modes of the eschatological imagination. In some texts, the emphasis is restorative: eschatological hope focuses on a return to imagined conditions of holiness, purity, and justice at the beginning. The orientation is conservative. What was once right will be restored. This is an orientation highly compatible with Jewish law, which projects an ideal that is not so much rooted in the past as it is available in the present. Were the law to be practiced with full devotion, were it to fill and shape the souls of its devotees, the saintliness of persons and the justice of society would themselves constitute the eschatological fulfillment. The days of the Messiah grow naturally out of the norms of *halakhah* (Jewish law).

1. Gershom Scholem, *The Messianic Idea in Judaism* (New York: Schocken Books, 1972), p. 7.

In other texts, the emphasis is apocalyptic: eschatological hope posits a complete break with nature and history as we know them to date. The end will be nothing like the beginning or the middle. Eschatology is a "theory of catastrophe," in Scholem's words. Nothing we can do can bring about the end. It does not matter whether we strive to improve the world through moral exertion or abandon it to irresponsibility. It will all come crashing down. God will bring the end in his time irrespective of our action or inaction. The future eon will not develop out of the present order, but will supplant it in ways that exceed our most fervent hopes. Imagination is given a free range here. Heaven and earth mingle. Death itself will die as the tombs open and the dry bones are knit together in life again.

These two tendencies, the restorative-conservative and the apocalyptic-utopian, are not wholly distinct from one another in actual cases of Jewish messianic thought. They are ideal types, relative emphases. Nonetheless, in the tradition that I want to explore here, the medieval and modern rationalist tradition, the restorative tendency predominates. Apocalyptic, utopian, and fantastic elements are minimized, if not entirely extirpated. The rationalist emphasis stresses the continuity of the laws of physics, as it were, and of the patterns of history. It focuses on the amelioration of the world as it is, on the perfection of creation and culture through the exercise of human intellect, ethics, and law. It sees the end in the beginning: the Torah's blueprint for an ideal society will be actualized. The talmudic and medieval expressions of this kind of view do not assume, as we modern ones do, a doctrine of progress. Nonetheless, all expressions of this view prize human action, guided by right reason, as the crucial lever for moving history forward. The passivity of apocalypse is rejected, as are its extravagantly imaginative features. Yet imagination cannot be banished, because hope is impotent without imagination.

The rationalist views accept this, but they domesticate imagination to a naturalistic and normative framework. In what follows, I will assay several contributions to this rationalist framework and raise critical questions as to their coherence and plausibility. My aim here is not to carp or quibble with searching and earnest thought, but to drill down into a basic problem. I accept without question the superiority of a naturalistic and normative — what I call a "realist" — account of messianism over an apocalyptic and indulgently fictive one. A realist account represents the sum of what we can hope for as public men and women, as communal, political, and economic beings. Such an account could orient our politics and ethics, could give us confidence in our collective, human future. Yet it can only do so if it is more than merely edifying. It must be nonfictive in a strong sense; not only realist in temper but realizable in principle. Do realist messianic programs actually pass this test? In particular, do they make sense from the point of view of political economy? How far can these programs be carried forward without paradox or paralyzing internal contradiction?

Historical Background

The restorative view, which I call "realistic messianism," has roots in the Bible and rabbinic literature. The ultimate biblical source is what the Harvard scholar Jon Levenson refers to as the "Zion covenant."[2] By this he means the divine selection of and covenant with King David, which both founds righteous kingship in Israel and, eventually, a physical locus for the divine presence, the Temple. On this view, the "Sinai covenant" founds a path of individual and communal sanctification that stands outside of history. The Zion covenant engenders an ongoing engagement with history through political life. It is of utmost importance that the Temple is destroyed by historical agents, can be rebuilt by other historical agents, and will be restored again through realistic action at the consummation of history. Eschatology in general and messianic thought in particular take rise from the Zion tradition with its emphasis on history and politics. The postexilic prophecies of Haggai and Zechariah emphasize the need for realistic human action, effected through politics, to bring about the final consummation of history. Haggai expresses the divine demand to complete the rebuilding of the Temple (Haggai 1) after which God will restore some form of righteous rule to Judah (2:21-23). Zechariah bids the people to "speak the truth to one another, render true and perfect justice in your gates. And do not contrive evil against one another, and do not love perjury . . ." (Zech. 8:16-17), after which the messianic king will come to Jerusalem (9:9). These events are already incipient (Zech. 4:4-6). There is continuity between present circumstances and the idealized future. (The opposite view, which holds that the end is completely detached from the present — that the end is beyond the process of history altogether — is found in the prophecies in Isaiah 24–27 and Ezekiel. God will enter history and reveal his presence, which all will acknowledge [Isa. 25:6]. He will de-

---

2. Jon D. Levenson, *Sinai and Zion: An Entry into the Jewish Bible* (San Francisco: HarperSanFrancisco, 1987).

stroy not only the rule of the wicked, but death itself [Isa. 25:8]. In a transhistorical manner, the dry bones of the House of Israel will rise to life [Ezek. 37].) Texts such as Ezekiel are foundational to the apocalyptic-utopian expression of eschatology. Texts such as Haggai and Zechariah buttress the tradition of realistic messianism.

The Talmud and *Midrash* (Jewish rabbinic interpretation) are heir both to the restorative-realistic and to the apocalyptic tendencies. Foremost among the expressions of realistic messianism is the statement in Babylonian Talmud *Berakhot* 34b (with parallel in *Sanhedrin* 99a) where the sage Samuel asserts that "[t]here is no difference between this world and the days of the Messiah except [that in the latter there will be no] bondage to foreign powers, as it says: For the poor shall never cease out of the land (Deut. 15:11)."[3] This statement takes the Torah's word in Deuteronomy that the poor shall never cease from the land to extend even into the days of the Messiah. It thus concludes that the difference between the messianic time and the present will be minimal, although highly significant. Israel's liberation from servitude to alien political power is a crucial shift, albeit within the bounds of a stringent realism. There is danger inherent in this realism: If the difference between the messianic age and the present age is only a matter of degree and if human action can precipitate the messianic age, then it is always possible for human beings to imagine that they can do something "to force the end." The rabbis, especially after the disastrous Bar Kokhba episode of 132-135 CE, accordingly played down the importance of messianism altogether. A famous (and highly realistic) statement is "[i]f there is a plant in your hand, and you are told: 'Behold, the Messiah is here,' go plant the plant, and (only) then go forth to welcome him" (*Avot de-R. Nathan*, xxxi, 33b-34a).[4] This statement assumes that essential features of the world will remain so unchanged by the advent of the Messiah that one might not notice his arrival while one is at work in the field. Nor should one interrupt one's work to investigate whether the Messiah has arrived.

To be sure, there are innumerable rabbinic texts that have a much more imaginative and metaphysically inflated projection of the messianic age than the realist view enunciated by Samuel. There was enough of realism, however, for medieval thinkers such as Maimonides to develop a

---

3. Cited in Ephraim Urbach, *The Sages*, trans. Israel Abrahams (Cambridge: Harvard University Press, 1994), p. 308.

4. Cited in Urbach, *The Sages*, p. 667.

highly rationalistic picture of the messianic age. In his legal code, the *Mishneh Torah,* Maimonides writes:

> The Messiah will arise and restore the kingdom of David to its former might. He will rebuild the sanctuary and gather the dispersed of Israel. All the laws will be reinstituted in his days as of old. . . . Do not think that the Messiah needs to perform signs and miracles, bring about a new state of things in the world, revive the dead, and the like. It is not so. . . . Rather it is the case in these matters that the statutes of our Torah are valid forever and eternally. Nothing can be added to them or taken away from them. And if there arise a king from the House of David who meditates on the Torah and practices its commandments like his ancestor David in accordance with the Written and Oral Law, prevails upon all Israel to walk in the ways of the Torah and to repair its breaches, and fights the battles of the Lord, then one may properly assume that he is the Messiah. If he is then successful in rebuilding the sanctuary on its site and in gathering the dispersed of Israel, then he has in fact proven himself to be the Messiah. He will then arrange the whole world to serve only God, as it is said: "For then shall I create a pure language for the peoples that they may all call upon the name of God and serve him with one accord" (Zeph. 3:9). Let no one think that in the days of the Messiah anything of the natural course of the world will cease or that any innovation will be introduced into creation. Rather, the world will continue in its accustomed course (Laws of Kings: chapters 11–12 [selections]).[5]

Maimonides proceeds to explain that the typically utopian view of Isaiah 11:6 ("The wolf shall dwell with the lamb, the leopard lie down with the kid") and all similar passages must be understood as parables. Israel is the vulnerable animal that will dwell securely among the heathen nations, which will be depleted of their violence by their conversion to the worship of the one, true God. Maimonides confirms his realist view by citing the famous talmudic dictum of Samuel noted above.

Maimonides' realist view was taken up and given currency by Rabbi David Kimchi ("Radak," d. 1235).[6] But it also immediately provoked dissent.

5. Cited in Scholem, *The Messianic Idea in Judaism,* pp. 28-29.

6. Cf. Radak, Isaiah 11:6, where Radak follows Maimonides' de-mythologizing interpretation but affirms that, although the beasts will not change their nature and cease to kill and eat prey, righteous Israelites living in the land of Israel will nonetheless not be attacked by them in the days of messiah. The popular, if not uncontroversial, commentary of Radak helped to "mainstream" Maimonides' rationalistic interpretation.

227

A contemporary commentator on the *Mishneh Torah*, Rabbi Abraham ben David of Posquières ("Ravad," d. 1198), rejected the assertion that nature will remain the same. Does the Torah not promise that dangerous beasts will be banished from the land? The promise contradicts the postulate of an unchanging nature.[7] Even Maimonides, however, cannot sustain a purely realistic presentation of the days of the Messiah. He endorses symbols of the traditional poetic imagination. For example, in the days of the Messiah, the Holy Spirit will rest upon Israel and the Israelites will once again know to which tribes they belong (*Mishneh Torah*, Laws of Kings 12:3). Indeed, they will also know much else. They will be able to devote their days to the knowledge of God, untroubled by famine, competition, and war, and know as much of God as it is possible for human beings to know.

Maimonides' realism leads him into a set of internal contradictions that he cannot overcome. Consider his claim that choice goods *("ma'ada-nim")* will be as common as dust — in other words, that great prosperity will prevail.[8] People, however, will not care for these goods. (Can we also read the text to imply that people will treat them as dust?) All of their attention, their business, will be devoted to God. Indeed, Israel yearns for the days of the Messiah not in order to enjoy such prosperity or to rule over the nations, but solely in order to be able to devote themselves, in leisure and freedom, to the Torah and its wisdom.[9] But how can a prosperous economy be sustained by a race of contemplative saints? How can the markets be full of desirable goods if no one desires them or desires them so little that there would be no incentive for producers to supply them? Presumably a nation of saints or, minimally, of persons striving for holiness, would be content with a very modest level of goods and services, with a static economy. The opportunity cost of consuming more would be communing less, which is too high a price to pay. Without the desire for affluence underwriting a competitive market economy capable of generating it, the economic activity of a messianic society would decline. Without a certain enduring venality — a persistent "evil inclination" — demand would diminish and production would contract.[10] In terms of its

7. On Ravad's (R. Abraham ben David) view, the beasts will actually change their nature in the land of Israel but will not change in other nations. In regard to the world at large, therefore, the text should be understood, as Maimonides does, allegorically. In regard to Israel, it should be understood in the straightforward, nonallegorical *(pshat)* sense.

8. *MT*, Laws of Kings 12:5.

9. *MT*, Laws of Kings 12:4.

10. The rabbis of Talmudic times had a good grasp on the view that "economic progress

political economy, the messianic age would be an altogether poorer and meaner affair than the present age. Yet this is no one's idea of a messianic age. It is unclear then, within the limits of realistic messianism, how it would be possible to lift an economy above a subsistence level, without the endurance of those human traits that militate against a more cooperative, pacific, and satisfied society. Unless Maimonides were to import an overt supernatural agency to drive the economy, it is unclear how an affluent society could be generated or maintained. Realistic messianism faces a quandary.

Perhaps for reasons such as these, Maimonides cautions his readers not to dwell on the symbols and images of the messianic age: "Therefore a person should never occupy himself a great deal with the legendary accounts nor spend much time with the *midrashim* dealing with these and similar matters. He should not regard them as of prime importance since devoting himself to them leads neither to the fear nor to the love of God" (*Mishneh Torah*, Laws of Kings 12:2).[11] Maimonides does not want us to indulge in eschatological fantasies. Perhaps he sensed as well the tensions or contradictions that inhere in the very project of a realistic messianism and did not want us to dwell on the problematic details. These contradictions remain unresolved in his rationalist successors. Even more so, they are amplified by our greater awareness of the dynamics of political economy.

Hermann Cohen

Hermann Cohen was a theologically minded philosopher who saw in the messianic idea the highest realization of the implicit promise of monotheism.[12] Cohen fused elements of Maimonides with an idealist interpretation of Kant. He adopted Kant's progressive reading of the trajectory of hu-

---

will be enhanced if free play is given to the pursuit of selfish ends. The vice of selfishness will spur each individual on to maximize his or her gains, thereby contributing to the growth of the wealth of a society." See Roman A. Ohrenstein and Barry Gordon, *Economic Analysis in Talmudic Literature: Rabbinic Thought in the Light of Modern Economics* (Leiden: E. J. Brill, 1992), p. 41. Cf. Rodney Wilson, *Economics, Ethics and Religion* (New York: New York University Press, 1997), p. 52. For rabbinic sources, see BT *Yoma* 69b, BT *Sanhedrin* 64a, *inter alia*.

11. Cited in Scholem, *The Messianic Idea in Judaism*, p. 29.

12. This treatment of Hermann Cohen is drawn from Alan Mittleman, *Hope in a Democratic Age* (Oxford: Oxford University Press, 2009), pp. 206-13.

man history and crowned it with the Jewish concept of the messianic age. The one humanity, created by the One God, will recover its oneness in the fullness of the future through its hopeful and persistent practice of ethics in the present. When directed to society as a whole, Cohen's religion of ethics has no option other than morally grounded socialist politics.[13] Human action, realized in politics, is the strategy of messianism.

For Cohen, Israel's central philosophical insight is that God is unique. "Hear, O Israel, the Lord our God, the Lord is One!" (Deut. 6:4) does not assert that there is one God as opposed to many gods, in a mere numerical sense.[14] Rather, it asserts the uniqueness of God: God is wholly unlike everything in his creation. For Maimonides, who shared this central insight, the uniqueness of God has primarily metaphysical and epistemological consequences. For the neo-Kantian Cohen, the uniqueness of God — the distinctiveness of God as against all existent things — served to correlate the *idea* of God with the *idea* of ethics.[15]

The concept of the one God also correlates with the concept of one humanity. The factual pluralization of humanity into nations, however, requires that the idea of a unified humanity be kept alive and available in another form: the concept of the one people, Israel. Israel is not just another *Volk*; it is a people that has not come into being in a *natural* way but whose very existence is constituted by an *ethical* calling. That calling is to exemplify and effectuate for humanity the future messianic reappropriation of its normative conceptual oneness. Until the actual achievement of the messianic age in history via ethical-political action, the Jews are required to retain their exemplary oneness as a sign, symbol and, tragically, as a provocation to the nations. The Jews — one people in all the earth — are made to suffer with sufferings of divine love for the messianic cause, which flows from the deepest logic of monotheism.

---

13. For a thorough study, see Steven S. Schwarzschild, "The Democratic Socialism of Hermann Cohen," *Hebrew Union College Annual* 27 (1956): 417-38. In Schwarzschild's words: "The messianic belief is primarily the belief in the ethical norm of a united humanity created by the moral endeavors and history-shaping actions of men. . . . Messianism is thus only the religious term for socialism" (pp. 427-28). For the original source, see Hermann Cohen, *Ethik des Reinen Willens* (Berlin: Bruno Cassirer, 1904), p. 528: *"Ihrer Politik nicht anders ist, als was wir heutzutage Sozialismus nennen."* (Their [i.e., the Hebrew prophets'] politics is nothing other than what we today call socialism.)

14. Hermann Cohen, *Religion of Reason Out of the Sources of Judaism,* trans. Simon Kaplan (Atlanta: Scholars Press, 1995), p. 35.

15. Cohen, *Religion of Reason,* p. 67.

Cohen reconfigured the question of theodicy from the metaphysical problem of *evil* to the human problem of *suffering*. Exemplary suffering furthermore is to be found not in the natural fact of mortality but in the moral scandal of poverty. In Cohen's view, the real suffering of humanity is sociological, not metaphysical. As such, it can be ameliorated. As he saw it, the entire prophetic enterprise is directed toward the amelioration of society — toward making it a world worthy of God's creatures — through the relief of suffering. The prophets equate the just man with the suffering, impoverished man. The knowledge of God, through which we recognize the one next to us *(Nebenmensch)* as our fellow *(Mitmensch)* whom we are to love, issues into moral knowledge and moral commitment. Ethics is the praxis of social love. Israel, as the suffering people par excellence, is charged with putting the love of humanity into practice in the social-political domain.[16]

The prophets discovered the idea or ideal of a unified humanity — hitherto unrecognized in human thought — made in the *imago Dei*. This insight gives rise to the emotion, indeed, the Hebraic virtue, of compassion *(Mitleid)*. Compassion goes a long way toward recognizing as our *Mitmensch* the poor, the widow, the orphan, the marginal one unlike ourselves. But compassion cannot go the whole way. To make compassion effective as an engine of social justice, one needs science. One needs, in Cohen's idiom, both the prophets and Plato. Cohen trusted that the modern sciences of sociology, politics, and economics, fueled by prophetic compassion, could buttress a scientifically based socialism that could work toward the holy task. Cohen's is a religious socialism, articulated politically along Social Democratic lines. It is in this sense that Cohen embraces a political messianism as the principal object of hope:

> [H]ope is the product as well as the expression of faith in divine providence. And divine providence means neither a concern, first and foremost, with the individual nor exclusively with one's own people, but rather with all mankind as the children of God. Hope for one's own well-being is conducive to vanity. Hope for the well-being and continued existence of one's own people, though possibly conducive to the development of courage and a sacrificial spirit, easily engenders pride as well. And when one's own country experiences a prolonged period of distress, all

---

16. For Cohen's way of interpreting biblical law as a praxis of humanitarian social ethics, see especially *Religion of Reason*, ch. 9, pp. 144-64.

hope seems to be in vain, adding merely to one's sense of frustration and dejection. But man's hope is transformed into faith when he no longer thinks of himself alone, that is, of his salvation here and now, or of his eternal salvation (the latter, if I may say so, with calculating sanctimoniousness). Hope is transformed into faith when man associates the future with the emergence of a community whose concerns will reach beyond its everyday concrete reality. Such a community will not be composed merely of man's immediate circle of friends or family nor will it include only those who share his own cherished beliefs; indeed, it will even cut across the borders of his own country because it will represent the community of mankind. As faith in mankind, Israel's faith is hope. And it is this epitome of Israel's prophetism, this hope in mankind's future, that comprises the substance of the Messianic idea.[17]

Hope is a correlate of a rational faith in God. It culminates in the messianic idea of a united humanity living together in peace and justice. The path to this eschaton, the messianic praxis, is social ethics realized through socialism.

By socialism Cohen meant a just social order in which poverty is eliminated, people rule themselves in a democratic manner, education is universal, and compassion drives public policy. Cohen did not fill out the details of a socialist politics. He takes it for granted that democratic socialism, as it was articulated in Germany in the nineteenth century, is the most just form of political order.[18] Such a socialism would entail a politics of complete equality between human beings. There would no longer be ruler and ruled — Cohen vigorously faulted Plato's static division of his republic into a philosophical governing class and the nonphilosophical masses. All would participate as equals in a self-governing society.[19] The ever-growing progress toward the achievement of such an order would constitute (an approximation of) the messianic age.

Cohen's philosophy is the leading modern expression of Jewish rationalism, and it struggled mightily to wed Kant's theory of knowledge and of ethics to traditional Jewish faith, as exemplified by earlier demythologizing Jewish rationalists such as Maimonides. Yet Cohen, who stood much far-

---

17. *Reason and Hope: Selections from the Jewish Writings of Hermann Cohen,* trans. Eva Jospe (New York: W. W. Norton, 1971), pp. 123-24.

18. For a bit more detail, as well as a defense of Cohen's demurral on detail, see Schwarzschild, "The Democratic Socialism of Hermann Cohen," pp. 432-33.

19. Jospe, trans., *Reason and Hope,* pp. 74-75.

ther than Maimonides from traditional faith, wagered more on realistic human action than did his medieval predecessors. For Cohen, democratic socialism was both praxis and *telos*. The commandments of the Torah, reconceptualized along purely ethical lines, must suffice to bring about the messianic age. In fairness to Cohen, his view must be stated correctly: *The messianic age is always approaching but will never fully arrive.* The tasks of ethics are infinite; the end is approached as an asymptote, a line infinitely approaching, yet never intersecting, a curve. We will move, if we will it, toward an axis of perfection, but we will never intersect it. Nonetheless, progress is real; social amelioration can occur; ever-higher levels of political and economic justice can be achieved. Like Kant, Cohen believed that history must be interpreted as a narrative of progress. This has less to do with description than with orientation: We must believe that our moral and political acts improve the world in order to sustain our hope for it. Without that confident teleology, no commitment to ethics could be sustained. Let us defer a critique of Cohen until we consider his twentieth-century protégé, Steven Schwarzschild.

Steven Schwarzschild

This neo-Kantian view was carried on and developed by the late twentieth-century rationalist Steven Schwarzschild, an explicit devotee of Cohen. Schwarzschild gave a precise formulation to Cohen's view that the Messiah cannot on principle arrive: "The eternal futurity of the Messiah, translated into operational language, asserts that no smallest time-unit nor any smallest space-unit in the universe is as yet, or will ever have been, redeemed. Indeed, what is asserted is that the universe is always infinitely different from what God wants it to be and what we must, therefore, make it, insofar as this lies within and perhaps beyond our power."[20] Schwarzschild acknowledged that the view that the Messiah cannot come but "will always be coming" is a "radical assertion." He made it for two reasons. First, the infinite postponement of the Messiah militates against mythologizing him, a temptation "to which, above all, Christianity has fallen prey."[21] More important for our purposes is the second reason: "It makes humanity's ethical (and, indeed,

---

20. Steven Schwarzschild, *The Pursuit of the Ideal*, ed. Menachem Kellner (Albany: State University of New York Press, 1990), p. 211.

21. Schwarzschild, *The Pursuit of the Ideal*, p. 212.

scientific) tasks not an interim obligation but a perpetual (if you please, metaphysical) destiny."[22] The eternal delay of the messianic advent gives rise to an "eternal moral striving." "The striving toward total human morality on earth ('the messianic kingdom') continues beyond any and all individual human lives: This is what we call 'history' and it consists of the infinite and therefore never-completed spiritualization of the human universe. The regulatively postulated completion of that infinite historical process of spiritualization is what is called 'the coming of the Messiah.'"[23]

Following in the footsteps of Cohen, for Schwarzschild Jewish messianism is a Kantian regulative idea; it is a *telos* that orients moral striving. The Messiah cannot come because the Messiah is an ideal, a fictive depiction of a norm. Furthermore, the concept of the Messiah is not only a normative goal, it is a normative ground. Schwarzschild argued that "messianism in fact operates . . . as a direct producer of moral values and as an intermediate criterion of proper action in any and every situation."[24] Just as for Kant the (quasi-messianic) Kingdom of Ends is to be the regulative ideal for practical reason, so for Schwarzschild, the (unreachable) end of the messianic age should launch and orient moral action. The unbridgeable logical gap between "is" and "ought" necessitates an insuperable historical gap between our age and the messianic age. But if the messianic age is incapable in principle of arriving, what sense is there in referring to it as an "age" at all?

Unlike Cohen, Schwarzschild was willing to let theological views resist complete assimilation to philosophical rationalism. God's grace can close the gap that human action cannot. "God's saving hand may force the end at any time that He determines. . . . The final upshot, then, of the dialectic of grace and ethics in Jewish eschatology is this: salvation may come about by works or by grace, but, in the first place, grace is indispensable to works themselves, and, in the second place, salvation by grace alone would be such a horrifying experience — morally atrocious and experientially painful — that humanity will not choose it as the way to the goal: 'May he [the Messiah] come, but let me not see it!' Thus, ethics remains the only actionable course."[25] Schwarzschild thus admitted that God, through grace, could bring the messianic age, could close the otherwise perdurable

---

22. Schwarzschild, *The Pursuit of the Ideal*, p. 212.
23. Schwarzschild, *The Pursuit of the Ideal*, p. 215.
24. Schwarzschild, *The Pursuit of the Ideal*, p. 218.
25. Schwarzschild, *The Pursuit of the Ideal*, p. 225.

gap, but that such a miraculous eruption would be "horrifying." Precisely why it would be horrifying he did not say; he relied only on the rabbinic belief in the "birth pangs of the Messiah." Schwarzschild cited here the twice-repeated saying in *Sanhedrin* 98b of sages who hope for the Messiah to come but do not wish to be alive in those days. The saying assumes the apocalyptic tradition, which postulates great travail prior to the coming of the Messiah. But surely more is going on in his usage of this doctrine than the assumption of its literal truth, in which one doubts he actually believed. That human beings would choose the way of ethics over the way of grace, of ethics albeit itself infused by grace, suggests an economy of desert. It would be "horrifying" to be given a world one is unworthy of receiving. How could less-than-moral persons live in a fully realized moral world? Unless that world, however asymptotically, be achieved through human moral performance, humans could not inhabit it without destroying it. Hence the imperative of realism over apocalypticism. Accordingly, ethics remains the only plausible option for messianism. Judaism, he concludes categorically, is "actionable messianism."[26]

In commenting on his Cohenian understanding of messianism shortly before his death, Schwarzschild wrote that "infinite ideals rather than empirical expectation are, or ought to be, the incentive to human life and history."[27] Faith in infinite ideals, he implies, ought to supplant hope for specific empirical outcomes. Accepting the task of bringing the Messiah is more worthy than cultivating the hope for him. The task has the full dignity of ethics; the hope breathes the air of fantasy. Messianism as infinite task precludes the false hope that typifies utopianism. Schwarzschild argues that Jewish messianism, conceived along realist lines with the proviso of infinite deferral, escapes the critique of utopianism tendered by Reinhold Niebuhr, Karl Popper, Hannah Arendt, and others. Yet it is hard to see why it should. Schwarzschild's realist messianism remained proudly activist; it did not content itself with constraining the *summum malum* via a democratic politics. It fully embraced the task of achieving the *summum bonum*. Yet it affirmed, non-negotiably, that the *summum bonum* cannot be achieved; it can only be ever more finely approximated. On this ground alone Schwarzschild's view evaded the criticism that it is a utopianism. But does it also render itself incoherent?

For Schwarzschild, messianism as an infinite task cannot be falsified.

---

26. Schwarzschild, *The Pursuit of the Ideal*, p. 219.
27. Schwarzschild, *The Pursuit of the Ideal*, p. 254.

It has the immaculate aloofness of the categorical imperative. But is this coherent? Can one maintain faith in ethical ideals and assert at the same time that they are permanently unrealizable? Isn't this a labor of Sisyphus? This is less a question of moral psychology than of logic. On Schwarzschild's account, obligation entails a vicious circularity. It ends in itself: "Ought" implies "can't." We ought to bring the messianic age, which we cannot do. We ought to do what we can't do. "Ought" hangs in the air. Like Cohen's, Schwarzschild's view was highly Platonic. Ideals by definition cannot be realized. Our local instantiations of the Good necessarily fail to capture the full, ideal amplitude of value. There is no ethics without ontology and the ontology of value is always otherworldly. Value is but another name for "what Plato called the idea of ideas, the good, God."[28] Our likeness to God permits — indeed requires — that we act ethically. Our unlikeness requires that our ethics falls short. It is only a Platonism that refers ethics to another realm that keeps Schwarzschild's view of ethics from becoming incoherent. The threat of incoherence lies in Schwarzschild's commitment to the Kantian principle, "ought implies can." But, as we have seen, if one can never respond to an "ought" satisfactorily, then ought implies can't. Like Kant of the *Critique of Practical Reason*, Schwarzschild requires a quasi-theological apparatus to guarantee the coherence of ethics.

Schwarzschild's and Cohen's Platonism was fully at work in their adulation of socialism as well. The poor performance of actual socialist economies, the tension between socialism and democratic governance, the complete unwillingness to consider the failures of *real existierende* socialism, would constitute grave flaws for anyone other than a Platonist. But even on a purely theoretical level it is hard to conceive of how a messianic socialist economy could possess all of the desirable features of a real economy with none of its tradeoffs and costs. Schwarzschild, describing the putative messianic age, wrote that "it would seem to have certain necessary features: economic abundance, economic equality, the abolition of private property in land and of the market economy, the universal rule of Jewish monotheism, theocratic democracy, universal truth, justice and peace."[29] But exactly how one gets to abundance without a market is nowhere addressed.[30]

---

28. Schwarzschild, *The Pursuit of the Ideal*, p. 251.

29. Schwarzschild, *The Pursuit of the Ideal*, p. 108.

30. For important criticisms of Jewish (and Christian) economic ethics see Paul Heyne, *"Are Economists Basically Immoral?" and Other Essays on Economics, Ethics, and Religion*, ed. Geoffrey Brennan and A. M. C. Waterman (Indianapolis: Liberty Fund, 2008), esp. pp. 171-212.

Unless everyone is to be economically self-sufficient, there will have to be trade; for trade there will have to be markets. Even if everyone deals fairly and justly with everyone else in the market, there will still be prices. (What would fairness and justice mean without reference to prices?) Who will set these prices? Will the Messiah be wise enough to second-guess his "theocratic democratic" citizen-subjects? Is any central agency more adept at setting prices than the supply-and-demand mechanism of the market? Would the Messiah preside over a command economy? That could not be squared with either freedom, presumably an important feature of the democratic half of the governing structure, or with abundance. And what about the tensions between democracy and theocracy? That was not a problem for Maimonides, with his strong monarchism, but it is obviously a problem here. Even to raise these questions indicates the grave inadequacies of both Cohen and Schwarzschild's views. Their insufficient attention to basic aspects of political economy renders their views just slightly less fantastic than the apocalyptic messianism they mean to supplant.

Lenn Goodman

Lenn Goodman's project of realist messianism attends to these basic aspects more closely than did either Cohen or Schwarzschild. Goodman focuses closely on the means to the messianic end; he sees the Torah and the ways in which the rabbis operationalize its principles as vehicles for the refinement and eventual perfection of human nature. The Torah's gradualist program of refinement leads to an achievable — not, *pace* Cohen and Schwarzschild, an infinitely deferred — messianic age. Indeed, in fidelity to Maimonides' vision, this program leads beyond the fulfillment of moral virtue to a yet higher level, the intellectual perfection of humanity. This highest level is what the rabbis portray as *"olam ha-ba,"* the world to come, which for both Maimonides and Goodman is not an afterlife but the teleological consummation of human intellectual, moral, and spiritual potential. The messianic age is thus an intermediary state where humanity becomes morally refined but not yet transfigured by intellectual perfection.[31]

31. Lenn E. Goodman, *On Justice: An Essay in Jewish Philosophy* (Oxford: The Littman Library of Jewish Civilization, 2008), p. 164. (This second, paperback edition with new Introduction is identical in pagination to the original edition, published by Yale University Press in 1991.)

"Accordingly, social justice is not a remote ideal but a present demand, not to be striven for but to be lived up to. The Torah does not presuppose but aims toward the transformation of human nature and institutions, their gradual perfection and ultimate reform — perfecting the soul. The goal does lie beyond all past achievements of humanity. But the means toward it, the laws themselves, rest on the givens of the human condition."[32] The Torah's project is the gradual refinement of individual and society such that an age of "fellowship and respect" and "universal peace and justice" can be achieved. Goodman rejects Cohen and Schwarzschild's nonadventist messianism. The Torah aims at instilling in us the moral and intellectual virtues to live life well, both individually and in community. "The messianic age as we envision it, then, is in and of this world, yet it sees the world transformed."[33]

Cohen and Schwarzschild both seek to guard the transcendence of Jewish ethics, doing so by projecting ethics onto a future that is always out of reach. Transcendence is regulative; it is a logical condition for normativity. In contrast, Goodman takes the transcendent ground of Torah, here comprised by a richer tissue of teaching and practice than is captured by "ethics," to be present and actual. The world as an act of God bears within it "the seeds of the perfection of human relations in accordance with the standards of God's justice."[34] Unlike Cohen or Schwarzschild, Goodman is a normative realist who ensconces ethics in the deserts of beings; he roots moral normativity in nature and in the claims that nature makes on existence.[35] Informed by a far richer understanding of nature than the Jewish Kantians, Goodman sees normativity incipient in the processes of the world and described by the physical and the life sciences in a way that

32. Goodman, *On Justice*, p. 160.

33. Goodman, *On Justice*, p. 162. For a concise statement of Goodman's Maimonidean messianic realism, see his gloss on Laws of Kings 11:1: "Nothing more is intended by our messianism than is implied in the biblical expectation of a world reformed through the fulfillment of the Law. Symbolic and projective visions of a supernatural end to history are mere surrogates of the moral changes by which alone the transhistoric goal is brought about and made lasting. Without moral transformation, cosmic cataclysms would be mere pyrotechnics" (p. 170).

34. Goodman, *On Justice*, p. 165.

35. "Value," Goodman writes, "is intrinsic in all of being, not merely in subjects or in objects of desire. Value, in fact, is identical with the being of things, dynamically considered — that is, with regard for their prospects and potentials. It follows that justice amounts to giving beings their deserts and that deserts are the claims of beings, their positive self-affirmations, as scaled against those of all other beings" (*On Justice*, p. 27).

would be disagreeable to Cohen. Yet nature on its own is a necessary, but not sufficient, condition for moral normativity. There is also the "infinitude of God and the inviolability of the principles of his law" — the highly abstract concept of perfection — which the Torah and the rabbis represent in vivid mythopoeic ways in order to address ordinary human beings.[36] Divine Transcendence ultimately grounds the law. It seems that something stronger is meant here than a Cohenian correlation of moral conscience and the "the spirit of holiness."[37]

The figure of the Messiah is de-personalized and thus demythologized, and the messianic age develops from the pursuit of a doable good, from an ever more devoted acceptance of the Torah's moral tutelage. We grow in the direction of greater moral awareness; our communities become more just, more merciful, more *gemeinschaftlich*, less *gesellschaftlich*. Yet this is no Marxist utopia where alienation is finally overcome and the human condition made permanently right after the travails of the revolution. The messianic age is not a "robotic utopia" — persons remain free and capable of choice, so backsliding into incivility and disrespect remains in principle possible. Virtue can be lost. Nonetheless, Goodman envisions the Torah-informed social order as a "virtuous circle," in which institutions are placed

> in the service of our moral and intellectual growth, enhancing our capabilities for freedom and judgment and promoting the social integration that in turn strengthens humanity, not only materially but morally and intellectually. Justice is made stable and dynamic by the progressive strengthening of an ethos of respect for deserts. This is the virtuous circle I cited in arguing that our Law is not utopian. The stability of the messianic age rests not on ever more repressive sanctions against individuality but on the support provided for a thoughtful ethos through the fulfillment of the commandments of the Law, and on what that ethos in turn creates to raise the sights of our humanity still higher.[38]

Goodman's vision is social but not fully political, that is, it assumes that a principal thrust of the Torah's purpose is to reform society toward a

36. Goodman, *On Justice*, p. 163.
37. The fullest statement of Goodman's philosophical theology is found in his *God of Abraham* (New York: Oxford University Press, 1996). A consideration of his doctrine of God cannot be attempted here.
38. Goodman, *God of Abraham*, p. 190.

more just, more communal direction. Indeed, Goodman convincingly interprets the laws of the Torah, in their civil, criminal, and economic dimensions, as implementations of "Thou shalt love thy fellow as thyself" (Lev. 19:18).[39] Fellowship (*"re'ut"* in Hebrew) becomes the animating principle of the good society. It corrects the harshness of pure self-interest, of the exiguous economic rationality of market relations, as well as of xenophobia toward outsiders. (The stranger, the "Egyptian," is also our fellow [Deut. 10:19; 23:8].) But missing from this account, unlike from its Maimonidean inspiration, is any constitutional design in the political sense of a frame of government. The Torah entertains a number of civil constitutions. Although constitutional monarchy wins pride of place, it is more symbolic than normative. Any regime type that secures public justice and allows for a common life of Torah observance will suffice. Under diasporic conditions, the leading Jewish political tendency has been republican. The point is not to specify and elaborate a constitution; it is that the Torah *entails a political dimension* that must be taken into account. The laws of the Torah, although separable and vital from a Jewish state, *contra* Spinoza, retain an urge toward instantiation in a Jewish state, specifically in a *medinat ha-Torah,* a state governed according to the laws of the Torah. And there is at least a tension between this political thrust of Jewish law and the norms of liberty assumed to be authoritative in a democratic polity. Should the Torah not require a sanctified political framework for its person- and society-shaping project, then there is no tension between the messianic age and what Tocqueville called "the ages of equality." But if the Torah's project does entail a constitutional design, as the history of Judaism suggests, then there is a tension. It is unclear how Goodman would resolve it. A messianic society with less liberty, with the lack of a "right to be wrong" in moral, intellectual, and religious matters, would be unattractive. Yet a society conceived along the lines of Berlin's "negative liberty" or Oakeshott's *societas* would not necessarily be compatible with the Torah's vision. (In a Torah-ordered society, one could not, for example, just shrug at a public Sabbath desecration.) How would liberal toleration, let alone the positive good of religious liberty, be reconciled with a *medinat ha-Torah,* however liberally constituted? This is not a problem for Maimonides, who seamlessly embeds the entirety of Jewish law into a constitutional monarchic order. But it is a problem for demo-

39. Goodman, *God of Abraham*, p. 6. See also Lenn E. Goodman, *Love Thy Neighbor as Thyself* (New York: Oxford University Press, 2008).

crats whose democracy is ordered by some of the normative gains of a secular age. Realist messianism, I suggest, needs to pay further attention to Judaism's political dimensions.

How does Goodman's vision stand with the economic dimension of a good society? The Torah aims at "the maintenance and enlargement of the sphere of respect and concern rather than of interest and advantage." It does not intend that we transcend the world of the market, only that the alleged autonomy of the mercantile sphere be dispelled and that economic relations be re-moralized:

> Biblical legislation, the locus of an alternative paradigm to that of pure civility, restricts market contractual relations in numerous ways, from the reservation of gleanings and the corners of the field for the poor to the prohibition of land ownership by priests and ordination of a fallow period for the land. The nisus of the Law tends to deflate the notion of the omnisufficiency of economic welfare — for example, in the demand that even when we grow prosperous we should present ourselves at regular intervals before a God who expects more of us than mere prosperity and who will not accept "the hire of a whore or the price of a dog."[40]

Only the most orthodox free market devotee would argue that *any* Torah rules regulating competition or resource allocation are wrong in principle. There are always constraints on markets. The more interesting analysis is how particular Torah rules affect market relations in particular circumstances. Did rabbinic attempts to break up monopolies on a vital good or service in a medieval Jewish community *(kehillah)* increase market access and drive down prices, or did they discourage producers? How workable were rabbinic strictures about "fair and reasonable" profits? Did they ensure equity or inhibit growth (or both)? Goodman's vision tries to straddle a realistic appreciation of the wealth-generating potential of markets with an attention to the underlying and contextualizing moral relations that make markets possible. This is very much in line with philosopher-economists such as Amartya Sen or Daniel Hausman. For example, Sen argues that the orthodox interpretation of Adam Smith as an unreserved advocate of self-interest is both a misreading of *The Wealth of Nations* and a refusal to integrate the latter with *The Theory of Moral Sentiments*. Smith was concerned to order self-interest (which for him was itself ordered by the richer Stoic concept of self-command) to social concerns such as "humanity, justice,

40. Goodman, *On Justice*, p. 42.

generosity, and public spirit."[41] Hausman interrogates the moral assumptions behind economic concepts such as preference-satisfaction as the criterion of welfare. Like Sen's, his thrust is to expose the poverty of economic thought *qua* philosophical anthropology and ethics.[42] Goodman reacts, quite properly, against the twentieth-century de-moralization of economics, a path undertaken in its attempt to achieve scientific rigor. Whether his full re-moralization of economic life in conformity with the ideal of *re'ut* would also be compatible with growth is an open question. Although preferable to Cohen and Schwarzschild's unrealistic socialism, Goodman's sketch of a messianist market economy invites further exploration.

Conclusion

The difficulties I have tried to describe indicate the conceptual limits of realistic messianism. It cannot remain aloof from the paradoxes and tradeoffs of the human condition, especially those ensuing from the fundamental problem of scarcity. It need not be the case that in relations "between man and his fellow" *(bein adam l'havero),* let alone between man and God *(bein adam l'makom),* commitments always entail costs. To pursue one good, say friendship or fidelity, need not, tragically, undermine the pursuit of another. Life can grow in a virtuous circle. There is no finitude to friendship and fidelity, other than the finitude that marks individual human lives. In principle, friendship is not a scarce resource.

Yet that is not the case with material goods. In the world of limited resources that we actually inhabit, economic transactions entail consequences, some of which are not benign. The rising prosperity of China, India, and Brazil, for example, accelerates environmental degradation. There is a cost paid in climate change, and there will always be tradeoffs of this kind. A realist messianism wisely promises no utopia where there are no costs to be paid and where all contradictions are resolved. It promises a future where contradictions can be minimized, where blessings for some do not necessarily entrain curses for others.

The realist messianist tradition is neither tragic nor ironic, neither Augustinian nor Niebuhrian. It represents the endurance of a form of po-

41. Amartya Sen, *On Ethics and Economics* (Oxford: Basil Blackwell, 1988), p. 23.
42. See, for example, Daniel M. Hausman and Michael S. McPherson, *Economic Analysis and Moral Philosophy* (Cambridge: Cambridge University Press, 1996).

litical hope, born in the biblical and Hellenic past, yet active today. It is an ancient politics that still aspires to achieve the *summum bonum* in this world through moral, legislative, and governmental means. This politics was most memorably framed by Plato and Aristotle, their differences notwithstanding. The Torah and rabbinic tradition fully complement, enrich, and complicate that politics. As messianism, rather than Hellenic political philosophy, Jewish biblical and rabbinic tradition represents an important strain of Jewish hope. It is hope in a doable good. For some, such as the many contemporary Jews who talk of *tikkun olam* (repairing the world), this vision orients normative conduct and thought. For others, perhaps those most impressed by the "crooked timber of humanity" and the mounting threats to democratic ways of life, this is no more than a dream. There are no blessings without curses. To believe that messianism is realistic implies that the contradictions on which all human institutions and practices rest can be expunged. It entails, to use the economist's term of art, that choices are possible without opportunity costs. In a world of finite resources in which minds with finite knowledge must choose, there will always be costs. To remain oblivious to them is mere wishful thinking, not the profound and sober hope that scales itself to the possibilities inherent in the real world. Let us leave the business of messianism to the Messiah, such skeptics might say, and concentrate, without illusions, on restraining the evil in the world. For some, the idea of a realistic messianism is the lynchpin of Judaism; for others it is a distracting fantasy.

What should we hope for? Kant would say, not to be happy, but to be deserving of happiness. This may be too little, but it contains something true. We may well remain skeptical of the grand goals that religious reason-*cum*-imagination sets before us. But we ought to remain true to the rightness and the goodness of the norms that fund those goals. Whether our actions bear fruit in some vast, messianic way is less important than that we continue to act with fidelity toward what we know to be right, toward what we know promotes the good. Whether that good finds its ultimate realization in our world is not wholly in our hands, despite whatever efficacy our deeds ultimately may have.

To hope for a world not happy but deserving of happiness is hope enough.

Moral Agency, Sin, and Grace:
Prospects for Christian Hope and Responsibility

Darlene Fozard Weaver

Abundant evidence shows that the world is largely inhospitable to our plans and purposes. Experience testifies that even well-intentioned efforts to improve human life and culture eventually prove misguided, self-serving, and (in)culpably at odds with what others really require. Doesn't hubris easily dog those bent on ensuring moral progress, including their own? Considering how limited our prospects are, how powerless we often feel in the face of complex problems and incorrigible persons, doesn't hope sometimes feel like a burden instead of sustenance?

Of course, sometimes we underestimate the power that we do have to change situations and lives, to protect and enhance the lives of others and the world around us. Sometimes complacency lulls us into accepting the way things are as the way things must be. Sometimes we falsely believe a situation or environment or other persons must change before we can act, without realizing that we may and should change first. Sometimes we fall prey to the illusion that the only things worth doing are those that yield immediate, visible results.[1] Sometimes, perhaps often, we shirk responsibility for doing what clearly does lie within our power. Sometimes we hope for too little.

It would seem, then, that our sense of responsibility for the human future needs to be calibrated by a truthful, realistic apprehension of our prospects and limits as agents. If the question is how best to construe human responsibility between the poles of presumption and despair, how responsibility might be truthfully and realistically understood and willingly

---

1. Thomas Merton, "Blessed Are the Meek: The Christian Roots of Nonviolence," in *The Nonviolent Alternative*, ed. Gordon Zahn (New York: Farrar, Straus & Giroux, 1980).

taken up and exercised, then the answer centrally concerns the moral phenomenon of hope. The virtue of hope strikes a mean between presumption and despair. It morally informs reason and orients our will so that we are empowered to act on a truthful understanding of the scope and aims of our endeavors.

I offer here six theses about the conditions for, character, and aims of Christian hope and responsibility.[2] Taken together they outline a constructive theological ethical argument about the scope of moral agency given, on the one hand, the pervasive influence and complexity of structural violence, and on the other hand, the power and sufficiency of grace. I argue that Christian hope is a realistic, penitent appetite that God's will be done. It is grounded in faith in Jesus Christ and bears fruit in a love that does justice. Along the way I will note that this account shares some affinities with the Jewish understanding of responsibility and hope offered by Rabbi Jonathan Sacks.

First Thesis: Structural violence/social sin threatens our sense of hope and responsibility.

Structural violence refers to the systemic, institutional, and cultural shape that human violence acquires in organized society.[3] Human beings harm and oppress each other through institutional and cultural mechanisms. They establish and sustain hierarchical relations that unduly limit some persons' access to basic resources, render certain groups vulnerable to direct forms of violence or assault, and obstruct their participation in social, economic, political, and cultural life. Examples of structural violence include racism, sexism, heterosexism, ageism, and economic oppression. Structural violence is socially constructed. Individual and collective choices create and sustain systems that organize access and participation, distribute social status, and engender vulnerability. Structural violence is therefore a product of human freedom. This means that the mechanisms that instantiate and transmit structural violence are subject to change, that social life could be organized more justly.

Structural violence extends the reach of our agency so that our choices

---

2. The first and second thesis are condensed versions of an argument I develop in chapter 4 of my book *The Acting Person and Christian Moral Life: Involvements with God and Goods* (Washington, DC: Georgetown University Press, 2011).

3. For a treatment of structural violence see Paul Farmer, *Pathologies of Power: Health, Human Rights, and the New War on the Poor* (Berkeley and Los Angeles: University of California Press, 2003). Religiously informed accounts can be found in various liberation theologies.

affect more people, many of whom are otherwise far removed from us. In a globalized market, for example, the mundane decision to buy food involves me in a complex web of economic and environmental relations across geographic and cultural boundaries. Structural violence also attenuates our agency. It does this by making it more difficult to act knowingly, obscuring basic information about the circumstances surrounding our choices: Who grew my food and where? Were they paid a just wage and provided with safe working conditions? How was this food distributed and with what environmental effects? Structural violence also undercuts our responsibility by dispersing it through the social structures that mediate our interactions with and impact upon other persons. Moreover, because structural violence occurs in given or standing features of society and culture, the mechanisms and value judgments that make up structural violence can appear benign, unavoidable, and even necessary. It therefore can be difficult to recognize these structures and conventions as violent. Structural violence lulls us into believing that change is not possible, that current ways of organizing society and distributing social and material goods are more or less the way things must be. And even though structural violence results from human freedom and therefore is subject to change, as Sacks notes, the social and institutional arrangements that do violence are so vast, complex, and seemingly intractable that we understandably question whether we can impact them at all.[4] We require an accurate sense of the scope of our responsibility, something we will consider by contrasting modern understandings of responsibility with Christian and, briefly, Jewish perspectives.

Another way to name structural violence is "social sin." The terminology of social sin emerged in Latin American liberation theology in the 1960s and 70s, though Scripture long before named unjust patterns of social organization sinful. As a manifestation of sin, structural violence involves more than systemic mediation of human conflict and oppression. It expresses our radical, fundamental alienation from God. Understood properly, social sin names more than institutional structures built "atop" human freedom. Social sin names the alienating processes by which we become selves in relation to others.

We receive the means for acting in a manner capable of moral evaluation (i.e., freely) through the processes of social reproduction. But these

---

4. Jonathan Sacks, *To Heal a Fractured World: The Ethics of Responsibility* (New York: Schocken Books, 2005), p. 7.

processes are themselves distorted by sin, and so we receive the distortions of our situation alongside — or, rather, at the very heart of — our personal being. We do not therefore enter the stage of personal action with a clean slate, morally in neutral as it were, but already infected with the pathologies of our situation, alienating us from God and the good. We stand already, prior to any action on our part, in a pathological relationship to God — in sin. Furthermore, through our subsequent, active participation in corporate sin, we ourselves contribute to the building up of a distorted and distorting common life, which passes these distortions on to others.[5]

Thus sin distorts the very conditions of our moral agency — reason, freedom, and desire.[6] This distortion affects us in relation to the very ground of our being, i.e., God, who is our good. Any realistic hope must reckon with the radical depth and breadth of sin. Any fitting sense of responsibility must acknowledge that we depend utterly on a solution beyond our own making. Moreover, since social sin simultaneously discloses our mutual implication in one another's sinful alienation, and points to our impotence to redeem this social economy through our own efforts, any fitting sense of responsibility needs to encompass our indebtedness to all of creation and our dependence on a gracious and redeeming intervention in this economy.

Second Thesis: Human responsibility is more complex than modern understandings of autonomy allow.
According to Gerald McKenny, responsibility involves three modes: "*imputability* (that actions can be ascribed to one), *accountability* (that one is answerable to someone), and *liability* (that one is answerable for something or someone)." McKenny claims the concept of responsibility is actually a modern one, expressing something traditional concepts can't capture. That something is a more intense and expansive sense "in which a matter of morality or the whole thereof is 'up to us.'" The emergence of responsibility is "correlative to the modern withdrawal of God from the world."[7] As God exits the scene, our perceived field of action expands;

---

5. Alistair McFadyen, *Bound to Sin: Abuse, Holocaust, and the Christian Doctrine of Sin* (Cambridge: Cambridge University Press, 2000), pp. 36-37.

6. Feminist theologies of sin speak to this point.

7. Gerald P. McKenny, "Responsibility," in *The Oxford Handbook of Theological Ethics*, ed. Gilbert Meilaender and William Werpehowski (Oxford: Oxford University Press, 2005), p. 237.

more and more of the world falls under our power. Sacks makes a similar point regarding a sense of "space" in which human responsibility emerges. Importantly, the Jewish mystical doctrine of divine contraction *(tsimtsum)* does not mean that God withdraws from the world or exits the scene. Rather, Sacks claims that "Judaism has distinctive beliefs, not the least of which is the way in which God empowers us to exercise our freedom, under his tutelage, to create a social order that, by honoring human dignity, becomes a home for his presence."[8] Divine contraction rules out hard determinism of human behavior in favor of metaphysical and moral space for human responsibility. Accordingly, the overarching question of "how much is up to us" will depend upon the conditions for imputing actions to us (i.e., whether we act freely or from necessity), whether or not we are accountable to anyone beyond ourselves, and the claims and consequences for which we must answer. As we will see, since "what is up to us" depends upon convictions about "what is the case," our agential prospects for hope and responsibility appear quite different when examined in light of faith. Christianity and Judaism entail beliefs regarding God's presence and activity in history, in addition to God's appointment of his covenant partners. In neither tradition is human responsibility fittingly understood as inversely proportional to God's presence and activity in the world.

Modernity prizes human freedom understood as autonomy. Autonomy is first and foremost freedom from external determination. This is freedom of choice. It is self-determining choice inasmuch as nothing outside the self is understood to determine the will's capacity to choose from among available objects or options, but not in the sense of developing an agential history that internally conditions or disposes one's freedom. Autonomy is thus episodically exercised, lacking a personal history of cumulative self-determination. Autonomous freedom is also an individualistic freedom. The person exists prior to relationships, community, or society, and remains capable of transcending these sufficiently so that freedom remains intact.

Freedom as autonomy leads to a "strong" view of moral responsibility. Strong theories of responsibility "give a more ambitious account of the necessary and sufficient conditions for imputing actions, requiring that these actions be not only voluntary (uncoerced) but also free (spontane-

---

8. Sacks, *To Heal a Fractured World*, p. 12. The account of responsibility Sacks offers is more robust than the one I develop here given my concern to explore the impact of social sin on our moral agency.

ous).["9] A strong sense of responsibility means we are responsible for our choices and actions only when we have the ability to do otherwise. Only on this condition are actions legitimately imputed to us. McKenny notes that other strong versions of responsibility construe it as "the act of a subject who makes himself responsible or asserts responsibility. . . . Responsibility is an act of self-assertion by which one posits or constitutes oneself as a subject over against what is other."[10]

This narrow understanding of responsibility obscures important aspects of human willing, like the way it is socially, culturally, and historically situated and just so conditioned, the way freedom emerges within an economy of sin and thus is always already disoriented. It sets the bar unrealistically high with regard to the necessary conditions for *imputing* responsibility. Moreover, if we are *accountable* to anyone other than ourselves it is because we elect to be so, and that accountability depends on our ongoing willingness to make ourselves such. Further, *liability* for the actions of others is difficult to square with a strong theory of responsibility. We would only be liable for persons or things in our care if we consented to such responsibility. If the actions of others can be traced causally to us and the conditions for imputability are satisfied, we might be liable for the actions of others. For instance, we might hold a manager responsible for the actions of his employees when they follow his workplace policies.[11] But this notion of liability stops well short of the mutual implication in sin discussed in the previous section.

On the terms of a modern account of responsibility, one can acknowledge the pervasive presence and complexity of structural violence yet espouse a strong theory of responsibility by asserting the possibility of opposing or resisting its influence. People sometimes express such a view when public discussion of gratuitous sex and violence occurs ("Just because I play video games/watch movies with sexual or violent content doesn't mean I go out and act on it") all the while missing the fact that sexual objectification or violent dehumanization of others is not an object of choice presented to an otherwise neutral will but is built into the perceptions and value judgments that structure reason and will. Moreover, because responsibility here is moral self-constitution "over against what is

9. McKenny, "Responsibility," p. 243.
10. McKenny, "Responsibility," pp. 243-44.
11. Faith in autonomy would require us to emphasize our freedom to do otherwise (albeit with consequences) or admit considerations (like fear of being fired) that weaken our autonomy.

other," a modern understanding of moral agency assumes that our separation from one another is more real than our interdependence. Opposition rather than relationality is basic to responsibility.

McKenny contrasts this modern view of freedom and responsibility with "weak" theories of responsibility, like those he finds in Augustine. For Augustine, the "will enjoys a neutrality of independence neither from the desires of the agent nor from the attractive power of the good; hence neither is it arbitrarily self-motivating and self-moving. It is always 'in gear,' as it were . . . drawn towards that identified as the good."[12] Since sin preconditions freedom, since it involves an internal disorientation prior to action, our will is properly understood as operative but not free, bound but not incapacitated.[13] Weak theories allow actions to be imputed to an agent even given the influence of desire, inclination, habit, and so forth, so long as "the action originates in the agent's power to act or not act."[14] For McKenny, in weak theories of responsibility the "ability to act otherwise" simply means the absence of external coercion; apart from this the agent acts freely, and thus is responsible for her action, even if internally she is bound to act sinfully. William Schweiker offers a more nuanced account. He identifies Augustine's understanding of freedom as "evaluative" and contrasts it with the voluntarism of autonomy. An evaluative account of freedom sees the will as divided in its attraction to conflicting apparent goods. Schweiker says that on this view the "ability to do otherwise" refers not to choice but the evaluation and formation of our wants. "An evaluative theory argues that an agent is free if and only if she or he acts on what is most basically valued, what really matters to her or him, and not simply what is desired or wanted. . . . The fact that what we value might be shaped by social roles, conventional beliefs, natural desires, and needs does not negate moral freedom if we come to endorse those values."[15] Here, too, the person constitutes herself as a moral agent. The difference is that she does so in relation to something identified as good or valuable. Instead of solitary choice in a neutral field of action, moral selfhood emerges responsively in a world independently imbued with value. Notice, however, that evaluative freedom requires some sort of voluntarism; in order to act on "what is most basically valued" humans must morally transcend their conflicting values, desires, and commit-

12. McFadyen, *Bound to Sin,* p. 179.

13. McFadyen, *Bound to Sin,* p. 110.

14. McKenny, "Responsibility," p. 242.

15. William Schweiker, *Responsibility and Christian Ethics* (Cambridge: Cambridge University Press, 1995), p. 146.

ments. The truth latent in the voluntarism of modern autonomy is that self-constitution as an agent is linked to a capacity to transcend influences sufficiently so as to endorse some and resist others.

At this point we need to return to the effects of social sin. Not only does social sin constrain and disorient our willing, but social sin also blocks our moral self-transcendence. By engaging us in distorted patterns of relationship, by striking down into the conditions for moral agency, by alienating us from the very ground and good of our being, sin obstructs our access to normative reference points that would enable us to evaluate these patterns differently. Therefore, our capacity to evaluate our conflicting wants, to endorse ones that matter most to us certainly should not be understood as a reservoir of freedom untouched by sin. By sharing himself in creation, in history, in interpersonal human bonds, God empowers our moral self-transcendence. Grace replaces the social processes by which we emerge as selves in relation to others. As a share in God's own life, grace reconciles us to the ground and good of our being and incorporates us into a new economy of relations with others and the world.

For his part, Sacks argues on behalf of collective responsibility, but without pressing the point I make regarding sin's distortion of the very grounds of our agency. Sacks notes that initially "it is far from obvious that if you sin, I should bear part of the blame and punishment," though upon reflection we realize that physical proximity and a shared political structure bind us together in relationships of mutual responsibility.[16] In spite of the destruction of the Second Temple and the geographic dispersion of the Jewish people, Jews remained a nation "bound by a covenant of mutual responsibility."[17] The basis for this responsibility is the Sinai covenant, which sustains collective responsibility in the absence of physical proximity and shared political structure. As Sacks puts it, "Bound to God, they were bound to one another."[18] Moreover, Jewish responsibility, like human responsibility in general, is ontologically grounded in God, the Other "beyond nature" to whom we are accountable.[19] Our God-given freedom to choose makes this responsibility personal while the reality of God and our co-humanity set moral limits on what we may choose.[20] Jewish responsibility as *covenantal* responsibility emphasizes God's initiative in creating

16. Sacks, *To Heal a Fractured World*, p. 88.
17. Sacks, *To Heal a Fractured World*, p. 92.
18. Sacks, *To Heal a Fractured World*, p. 92.
19. Sacks, *To Heal a Fractured World*, p. 144.
20. Sacks, *To Heal a Fractured World*, p. 145.

space for human initiative. While Sacks appears more interested in recovering a robust sense of human agency (note his appreciation for cognitive therapy and positive psychology)[21] than attending to sin's agential debilitation, we will see that his account of responsibility, like the Christian account crafted here, credits divine action on behalf of human beings and faith in the God who so acts by establishing the conditions in which we may and should hope as responsible actors.

Third Thesis: Christian hope is principally a matter of appetite liberated and reoriented by faith, such that the Christian hopes that God's will be done.

The strong version of responsibility considered above would imply that hope may be mustered at will, that it is warranted by one's perennially intact capacity to transcend given features of one's situation and fashion a new future. On this account hope consists in the confidence in one's power to project desired outcomes onto the world. One hopes to achieve some state of affairs by hoping in one's own powers to achieve that end.

Christian hope is grounded in Jesus Christ rather than confidence in human power. This hope depends upon faith that God has decisively acted in history through Jesus to free us from sin and that the Holy Spirit is acting in our lives and world to sanctify us and it (Rom. 5:1-5). Christian hope thus reckons with the bondage of freedom and disorientation of desire. As John Webster puts it, "Hope is a correlate not of freedom (understood — degenerately — as radical self-government) but of nature (that is, of the reality which the work of the triune God establishes and which the gospel announces with joy). The Christian who hopes is one whose being is enclosed, determined, and protected by Jesus Christ our hope."[22] Hope, then, entails faith-informed convictions about reality. Furthermore, whereas the strong version of responsibility that modernity offers lends itself to a hope that one can always make a new future, Christian hope anticipates a future of God's making.

Hope is an operation of the will, a desire for some state of affairs. Thomas Aquinas says that "hope denotes a movement or a stretching forth of the appetite towards an arduous good."[23] In hope we are oriented toward a good identified as our good, that is, as good for us. This orientation implies a current lack; we do not hope for what we already have, thus hope's orienta-

---

21. Sacks, *To Heal a Fractured World*, pp. 184-85.
22. John Webster, "Hope," in *The Oxford Handbook of Theological Ethics*, p. 300.
23. Thomas Aquinas, *Summa Theologiae* II/II, q. 17, a. 3.

tion is toward the future. Moreover, if the object of our hope were easily obtained, says Aquinas, we would simply desire it. Hope arises when the object of our appetite is difficult to obtain. Yet hope is not longing for something unrealistic, not wishful thinking. Rather, we hope for a good that is possible for us to obtain.[24] Because sin confuses reason and disorients our wills, hope requires the reorientation of our appetites toward God our true good.

Hope is properly understood as a theological virtue, as a gift of grace infused in us. The Holy Spirit liberates and reorients our wills by incorporating us into an alternative economy of relations, one that is reconciling us to our true good.

> The Spirit does not illuminate the good so that we may then decide whether to pursue it from a position of neutrality; rather the Spirit instills love of God and therefore of the good. This makes the will good. That is to say, the will is reoriented *internally*. . . . Although the will's independent and unaided power is insufficient to do and will the good, the action of the Spirit empowers and reorients the will so that subsequent willing and acting do not happen without the will's own (aided) power and active engagement. The power of an individual will is a necessary but insufficient condition for good willing and action.[25]

Because this reconciliation with God our good is not yet complete, we have the status of wayfarers. We hope for a future good. In the knowledge of our forgiven sins that faith provides and with our freedom yet unfinished, we know this good to be possible yet our path to it arduous. Indeed, as a theological virtue hope directly relates us to God precisely in our wayfaring status. "While hope by definition never attains its object, the act of hoping possesses a suitable perfection in itself, qualifying it as a truly virtuous activity."[26] Aquinas understands that perfection to consist in the believer's reliance upon God. When we hope "for something as possible to us precisely through God's help, such hope, by reason of its very reliance upon God, reaches God himself."[27]

According to Sacks, Jewish hope differs from optimism. The former has grounds to warrant it, namely the terms of God's covenant with Israel.

24. See Romanus Cessario, OP, "The Theological Virtue of Hope (IIa IIae, qq. 17-22)," in *The Ethics of Aquinas,* ed. Stephen Pope (Washington, DC: Georgetown University Press, 2002).

25. McFadyen, *Bound to Sin,* p. 176.

26. Cessario, "The Theological Virtue of Hope," p. 234.

27. Aquinas, *Summa Theologiae* IIa IIae, q. 17, a. 1.

It is also warranted by the open-ended character of the covenantal relationship, by the freedom of God and human beings alike. This hope is certainly not the belief that all will go well, but that mistakes and sins are forgiven, that present and future action can be efficacious. Faith in the God
who covenanted with Israel affects how Jews see the world, interpret
events, and imagine the possible. In these ways faith alters the conditions
for responsible action. Indeed, Sacks argues that Judaism entails the *"principled rejection of tragedy in the name of hope."*[28] For both Jews and Christians hope is "principled" because it rests on faith in God. For both, hope is
also ordered by moral responsibility toward others. My own account of
Christian hope specifies that "ordering" in explicit relation to God's will to
reconcile the world, while Sacks's Jewish account emphasizes the wide
"space" God creates in which what to do is "up to us."

The Christian hopes that God's will be done, which is to say that the
Christian hopes as Jesus taught us to pray (Matt. 6:10; Luke 11:2). To hope
that God's will be done presupposes trust in the providence of God. It requires humility regarding our own best understandings of the world
around us and the historical processes through which God is reconciling
everything unto himself. In her meditation on the "Our Father," Simone
Weil says this regarding the specific petition that God's will be done:

> We are only absolutely, infallibly certain of the will of God concerning
> the past. Everything that has happened, whatever it may be, is in accor-
> dance with the will of the almighty Father. That is implied by the notion
> of almighty power. The future also, whatever it may contain, once it has
> come about, will have come about in conformity with the will of God.
> We can neither add to nor take from this conformity. In this clause ["thy
> will be done"], therefore, after an upsurging of our desire toward the
> possible ["thy Kingdom come"], we are once again asking for that which
> is. . . . We are asking for the infallible and eternal conformity of every-
> thing in time with the will of God. . . . We have to desire that everything
> that has happened should have happened, and nothing else. We have to
> do so, not because what has happened is good in our eyes, but because
> God has permitted it, and because the obedience of the course of events
> to God is in itself an absolute good.[29]

28. Sacks, *To Heal a Fractured World*, p. 178 (emphasis in original). Tragedy can have no
ultimate triumph.

29. Simone Weil, "Concerning the Our Father," in *Waiting for God* (New York: Harper
& Row, 1973), pp. 218-19.

Hope that God's will be done is a deliberate endeavor to will what God wills — to make this "want" the one that defines our identity, the one that orders all other wants. Hope that God's will be done positions us to be attentive, expectant, ready to be surprised as God reveals himself in unexpected ways, open to fresh revelations of the forms our resistance to his will can take, the places it can hide. Yet Weil presses the point uncomfortably — to hope that God's will be done is "to desire that everything that has happened should have happened, and nothing else." How can we desire this when what has happened includes war and famine, the Holocaust, terrorism and slavery, domestic abuse and exploitation of vulnerable populations? Granted, Weil says that what has happened may not be good in our eyes. We are to desire the course of events that God has permitted because we trust that "that which is" is a course of events leading to the coming of the Kingdom.

Nonetheless, Weil's interpretation of the petition that God's will be done compromises the integrity of human freedom, undercuts the possibility of sin being a real human rejection of God, and misconstrues divine providence, particularly with regard to the meaning of evil and suffering. Weil fixates on God's power such that God's permitting something to happen becomes an instantiation of divine control over creation rather than God's creative self-limitation in order to bring into being and sustain something (creation itself, we humans in particular) genuinely other. God's providence becomes conscripted by a sense of necessity — if God permitted it to happen it needed to happen in order for God to direct history toward the coming Kingdom. What does the death and resurrection of Jesus mean on this count? Acquiescence to suffering for the sake of obedience? What becomes of the moral imperative to alleviate suffering and oppose injustice?

Jesus' death and resurrection is instead God's irruption into a human situation of alienation that creates new possibilities for human life in relation to God and one another. It is protest that effectively renders human bondage as "past." Jesus' death and resurrection make sin a *felix culpa* only by inverting its meaning so that the site of our alienation from God becomes an opportunity to apprehend the liberating presence of God who enters into our desolation precisely to deliver us from it. "That which is" includes the presence of Jesus who has already inaugurated the kingdom of God in his own person. In short, hope that God's will be done indexes our activity to God's purposes. In Judaism and in Christianity those purposes appear centrally in God's liberating action toward those who suffer. This speaks directly to the question of how much is "up to us" and brings us to my next thesis.

Fourth Thesis: Our responsibility for the future is not to fix a world that is broken but to learn to share it in ways that permit God to heal it and us. As Christians translate hope into action they unavoidably confront the question of how much is "up to us." What sort of action is consistent with hope in Christ? What is the scope of our agency given the eschatological tension in which we live? How ought we to confront sin and suffering while desiring "that which is"?

Since hope is the virtue in which one relies on God's help, that reliance "constitutes the basis for establishing the proper measure or rule" for virtuous action.[30] If responsibility for improving the future of human life is construed in terms of this reliance, the sort of attitudes and actions that correspond to this responsibility will differ from an account of responsibility built upon modern notions. Whereas modernity envisions freedom as a matter of arbitrary choice, the Christian account of freedom being crafted here envisions freedom in relation to the attractive power of God our good. Whereas modernity envisions the world as a neutral field of action, Christian faith recognizes the world as God's creation, laden with value and entrusted to our stewardship. Modern understandings of responsibility emphasize our moral self-constitution against what is other than us. Even versions that grant that cultural forces and social relations influence us posit some reservoir of freedom that enables us to transcend this influence. Hence, our opposition to everything and everyone else is taken to be more real than our interdependence. This paper posits no such reservoir of freedom. Instead, human moral self-constitution is a matter of incorporation into an economy of relations. As a gift of grace, hope is our reliance upon the ground and good of our being, the ground and good of everything and everyone. Hence, human interdependence is more real than opposition to what is other than us.

Reliance upon God orders our attitudes and actions so that they do not aim to fix a broken world but to share it. This does not mean that we bide our time or wait in some passive quietism for God to manage the world's affairs without us. Pope Benedict XVI captures the point when he says that in hope Christians learn "what they have to offer the world and what they cannot offer."[31]

---

30. Cessario, "The Theological Virtue of Hope," p. 234.

31. Pope Benedict XVI, *Spe Salvi*, 22. The encyclical is available online at: http://www.vatican.va/holy_father/benedict_xvi/encyclicals/documents/hf_ben-xvi_enc_20071130_spe-salvi_en.html.

We *can* ameliorate human suffering in the form of removing (partially and temporarily) or diminishing some of its causes. We are able to utilize our capacities and talents, material resources and time, personal energies and prayers to make concrete improvements in human lives. Through good stewardship of our time, talent, and treasure we participate in the creative work of God. Indeed, we are called to be co-workers with God (1 Cor. 3:9).[32] Our collaboration is itself a taste of the reconciled relationships God is establishing.

We *cannot* offer a human future secured by just social structures. As Benedict argues, social structures alone, no matter how good they are, cannot guarantee "the right state of human affairs." Indeed, "the Kingdom of good will never be definitively established in this world."[33] Benedict makes this claim not simply because of human finitude but on account of human freedom. "Freedom must constantly be won over for the cause of good." Every generation therefore must "search for the right way to order human affairs . . . [and] make its own contribution to establishing convincing structures of freedom and of good."[34]

Hope orders our attitudes and actions so that we respond to human suffering well. Rather than trying to "fix" the world, we seek to share it in ways that permit God to heal it and us. "Fixing" is characteristic of responsibility as a moral self-constitution over against that which is other. Such an approach involves trying to dominate that which we want to fix. We set a course of action in which, rather than engage persons as fellow subjects, we act on them as passive objects; rather than discern whether the fitting response is to accept or let go or embrace the way things are, we get caught up in trying to manipulate it. By contrast, sharing the world in a way that permits God to heal it and us means recognizing our own complicity in the causes of human suffering, our brokenness and alienation in sin, our limitations and shortcomings. If we share the world with others we recognize the world as a place given to us to be held in common. We enter into relationships of solidarity with others.

Indeed, we are always, by God's grace, able to offer ourselves. As we are incorporated into God's own life we are drawn into relationship with others. "Our relationship with God is established through communion with Jesus . . . , the one who gave himself as a ransom for all (cf. 1 Tim. 2:6).

---

32. Here is a point of contact with the Jewish concept of *tikkun olam*.
33. Benedict XVI, *Spe Salvi*, 24.
34. Benedict XVI, *Spe Salvi*, 24-25.

Being in communion with Jesus Christ draws us into his 'being for all'; it makes it our own way of being."[35] By sharing ourselves we imitate and participate more fully in the self-giving love of God. In this way we can let go of misgivings we might have about our own brokenness or our insufficiency for those we would serve or release from suffering. We can overcome fear or discomfort in the face of those who suffer and respond to them in freedom and self-giving.

The sort of chastened but efficaciously reconciling action I am describing resonates with Sacks's use of the Jewish mystical concept of *tikkun olam,* mending a fractured world.[36] Sacks is clear that *tikkun olam* is a mystical idea, but one he considers a useful metaphor for responsible action.[37] My actions, though limited, help to mend a fractured world, contributing to an order that is disrupted but gradually being healed through my and others' efforts. According to Sacks, God redeems, but does it through our initiative.[38] *Tikkun olam* "is an expression of the faith that it is no accident that we are here, in this time and place, with these gifts and capacities, and this opportunity to make a positive difference to the world. . . . Where *what I can do* meets *what needs to be done* — there is God's challenge and our task."[39]

Hope leads us to offer what we can in a fashion marked by penitence and charity. Before we consider this, it is worth asking what the distinction between fixing and sharing the world might mean for Weil's injunction "to desire that everything that has happened should have happened, and nothing else." There are two points we can make in response. First, while theodicy questions understandably arise, we are mistaken if we think they set the terms for hope. Webster rightly notes that "a theology of hope does not hang upon a satisfactory answer to the question of theodicy (satisfac-

35. Benedict XVI, *Spe Salvi,* 28.

36. There may be general differences between Christians and Jews regarding the proper place, if any, for acceptance in the face of suffering and injustice. It is important to note that a number of Christian theologies (liberation theologies in particular) resist interpretations of Jesus' death used to encourage the suffering to tolerate or even embrace their lot. My attempt to delineate a moral difference between "fixing" and "sharing" is not meant to minimize human responsibility to alleviate suffering and oppose injustice but to point to qualitative differences whereby we (1) attempt these things in ways that injure those we would help by our hubris, presumption, manipulation, self-referential need for control, etc., and (2) acknowledge that sharing ourselves is itself one way to alleviate suffering and oppose injustice.

37. Sacks, *To Heal a Fractured World,* p. 78.

38. Sacks, *To Heal a Fractured World,* p. 77.

39. Sacks, *To Heal a Fractured World,* p. 72, emphasis in original.

tory to whom, and to what ends?), but vice versa: only on the basis of faith's confession of the God of hope, of his ways with the world in the history of fellowship in which we now live and for whose consummation we wait, is it possible to develop anything like a responsible Christian theodicy."[40] Second, the desire that everything that has happened should have happened needs to be understood as a matter of "asking for that which is." Again, Webster helps to make the point: "Hope enables the Christian moral agent to clarify and act out a way of life within the historical character of created existence — that is, existence in time. To exist in Christian hope is to trust that in all its dissipation, complexity, and misery, human history is by the mercy of God on the way to perfection. . . . Emerging from the promises of God, hope shapes the actions of Christian fellowship by instructing it about its true condition."[41] To hope is to ask for and act out of confidence in "that which is," namely, that God be reconciling us and the world unto himself.

Fifth Thesis: Accordingly, Christian hope is penitent.

Responsibility requires dying to one's old self in its alienated and alienating relations and emerging as a new creation in a divine economy of grace. Christian hope is penitent because it simultaneously involves honest awareness of our sinfulness and confidence that grace justifies us and will supply what we require to reach fullness of life with God. Christians join Jews in affirming that, as Sacks puts it, "We are here because of an act of supreme love on the part of the author of being. Despite the wrong we do, he does not relinquish faith that we will change. . . . For in his word he has given us the map, the guide, the way of return."[42]

Repentance is not another name for guilt or remorse, though guilt and remorse are affects that typically accompany repentance. Repentance is itself a change of heart, a redirection of our longing, a setting of our wills against sin and in favor of a new manner of life. At the center of repentance is the firm resolve to amend our lives, to be drawn by God into a future which is secured by grace. As Sacks puts it, human repentance for and divine forgiveness of sins together express our freedom vis-à-vis sin. Sin does not produce an inexorable fate.[43] So the summoning or gathering of

---

40. Webster, "Hope," p. 299.
41. Webster, "Hope," p. 292.
42. Sacks, *To Heal a Fractured World*, p. 200.
43. Sacks, *To Heal a Fractured World*, p. 179.

oneself, the assumption of responsibility that is constitutive of moral agency, takes the form of faith's trust in, hope's reliance on, and love's singular devotion to God.

As grace illumines our reason with the truth and reorients our wills toward what is truly good, we come to perceive better the ways we can avoid cooperating with social sin and forge more just relations. We also come to perceive better how we are unavoidably embroiled in sinful forms of social organization.[44] As we seek greater integrity our limited options and dirty hands will pain and frustrate us. Yet hope allows us to abide in the tension between what God already has accomplished and the fullness of redemption that is not yet ours. Hope retains an inescapably penitent character because that which we hope for by definition is not fully in our possession. Indeed, as we better perceive the value of others and the goodness of God's creation, our sense of sin and repentance will increase. Confronted by the value and fragility of God's creatures, our sense of accountability and liability expands. Accordingly, we lower the bar with regard to the conditions that must be met in order to impute responsibility to us. On a modern account we would only repent over sins "legitimately" imputed to us, that is, actions we performed when we could have done otherwise. When we understand responsibility as a matter of interdependence, sin names social processes in which we are all complicit, an ironically intimate mutual alienation. I therefore repent not only for those sins that could be imputed to me on the basis of a modern "ability to do otherwise." I repent a way of being and becoming myself in relation to others. Thus, my "evaluative freedom" is exercised by the power of grace, the pull of attraction exerted by God, my good who shares himself with me and draws me into a reconciling relationship with him, by which I become a new self in relation to him and others.

Sixth Thesis: Hope bears fruit in just love for ourselves and fellow creatures.

Faith informs us of our need for hope and that we may hope. Hope reorients our wills toward God our good. Love conforms us to God. As an infused virtue love is a gift by which God brings us to share more deeply in his own life. Love undoes the alienated and alienating dynamics of sin.

---

44. Alan Mittleman makes a similar point in his essay in this volume when he cautions against a messianic hope that believes "the contradictions on which all human institutions and practices rest can be expunged."

Love relates us rightly to our fellow creatures so that we come to love what God loves and in proper measure.[45]

Love does justice by relating us properly to God and God's creation. In that regard just love depends upon faith's truthful apprehension of the noncontingent goodness of God's creation. Human persons possess an inherent value that is independent from my decision to value them. And yet because God creates us to be in relation with him and one another, others' flourishing as creatures is intimately yoked to my own. As hope sets my heart upon God our good, I willingly endorse the sense of obligation or answerability that is awakened in me when I apprehend God's creation in the light of faith. To do justice in love to God's creation, I must attend to the concrete reality of those whom and that which I love.

Love for God's creation correlates with a range of behaviors. How we enact it depends on whether and how we are appointed or authorized to act and on the particular scope of action available to us. Love, for example, might in one situation call for a defensive protection of human life, and in another situation call us to suffer with another in solidarity. How to enact love in a particular situation is a question of justice answered through the work of practical reason under the guidance of the virtue of prudence. While we cannot pursue that line here, we can note that in order for love to do justice to the concrete reality of the beloved and the demands of a particular situation, it needs to be a creative love.[46] This does not mean that morality devolves into situation ethics. The point is that love drives us into a world given by God, already laden with value and already unfolding in a history governed by the divine will. So love's creativity is not a matter of manufacturing value or devising a moral order out of neutral material, but an encounter with a world that has its own integrity in relation to God. Specific sorts of actions will find their moral measure in relation to this integrity. This work of discernment is central to the responsibility God calls us to exercise. Hope emboldens us to undertake this work in the confidence that we are appointed as stewards under a good and sovereign Lord who is reconciling the whole world unto himself.

Concepts of stewardship, discipleship, covenantal partnership, and mission can capture the vital importance of assuming responsibility for improving human well-being without the mistaken correlate that the

45. Aquinas, *Summa Theologiae* II/II, q. 25.

46. This idea is not unique to Paul Tillich, but he does describe agape as creative justice in his book *Morality and Beyond*.

scope or degree of human responsibility is inversely proportional to God's presence and activity on the scene. Efficacious human action is a creative participation in God's ongoing care for and in the world. In the light of faith Christians and Jews understand themselves as obligated to act in imitation of the One who summons and empowers them, the One who shows himself to be power placed in the service of finite life.[47] Our own power as agents, then, is directed in the service of promoting and protecting the well-being of fellow creatures, to love in a way that does justice to their integrity as such.

Christian and Jewish approaches to hope and responsibility are not uniform, of course, and are sufficiently distinctive in terms of theology, ethics, and religious psychology. As indicated above, the approach Sacks takes relies on a more expansive sense of human initiative than the approach I take here both with regard to its agential springs and the moral latitude the natural order permits. Although a more detailed consideration of his worthy project is beyond the scope of this paper, there is no missing the fact that faith in the God of Abraham, who takes initiative on our behalf, grounds both human responsibility and hope.

Conclusion

This essay principally examines the ground and scope of Christian responsibility between the poles of presumption and despair and in light of the realities of sin and grace. After analyzing the way social sin impacts the very springs of human agency, we were able to contrast a modern understanding of responsibility with a constructive Christian account. Christian faith recalibrates one's sense of "what is up to us," for one can only determine this as one learns what one can and cannot offer in the world God gives and is reconciling. This means being instructed about the true condition of "that which is" and coming to desire with one's whole heart that God's will be done. The reconciliation of one's will with God's is the work of grace over a lifetime. But as a wayfarer the Christian can enter freely and wholly into the present while anticipating the good future God promises, for "by his great mercy he has given us a new birth into a living hope" (1 Peter 1:3).

47. See William Schweiker, *Responsibility.*

Zionism as Jewish Hope and Responsibility

Deborah Weissman

Will we destroy ourselves with nuclear bombs or with man-made plagues? Or will we survive as a precarious planet where a small affluent elite perches fearfully on the top of three continents of hungry peons? Or will we all end up in a subhuman world of efficiently lobotomized robots?

When we honestly ask ourselves whether we can have such a life-affirming world, we must move beyond mere optimism or pessimism, for the empirical evidence is either mixed or unfavorable. But we can hope. Hope in the religious sense rests in part on non-empirical grounds. Christian hope suggests that man is destined for a City. It is not just any city, however. If we take the Gospel images as well as the symbols of the book of Revelation into consideration, it is not only a City where injustice is abolished and there is no more crying. It is a City in which a delightful wedding feast is in progress, where the laughter rings out, the dance has just begun, and the best wine is still to be served.[1]

Sadly, Harvey Cox's questions from 1969 seem no less relevant four decades later. Added to his litany of problems could be the crisis of post–Cold War capitalism, global terrorism, and irreparable damage to the environment. The question of the possibility of hope is perhaps even more pertinent now than it was then. Can we still hope? And if so, in what? Before analyzing the

1. Harvey Cox, *The Feast of Fools: A Theological Essay on Festivity and Fantasy* (New York: Harper Colophon, 1969), p. 162. The "City" to which Cox refers is characteristic of "the secular city," about which he had written in 1965.

issue, permit me to recount a personal anecdote: One of my friends is the Palestinian Lutheran Bishop of Jerusalem, Dr. Mounib Younan. We often speak on the telephone to greet each other before our respective religious festivals, a practice we began during the bleak years of the Second Intifada (2001-2005). When I had almost plunged into the depths of despair, Mounib reminded me: "As long as you believe in a Living God, you must have hope." Faith and hope can be seen as responses to despair, but are they useful responses? What is the relationship between hope and responsibility? For me personally, I must be more specific: How do these questions relate to Zionism and Jewish life in the State of Israel today?

Strategies for Sustaining Hope

The theologians in our research group have noted that hope for redemption is not the same thing as the belief in progress. We sometimes hope because of reality, but we sometimes hope *despite* reality. Yet I still think it would be counterproductive to "de-couple" hope from reality entirely. People often feel a need for concrete experience as evidence that their hope is well placed. A primary example of this is the Jew who hopes for redemption, while on a weekly basis experiencing *Shabbat* (the Sabbath) as a foretaste of "the world to come." The appealing description in Harvey Cox's above statement actually occurs every Friday night in a traditional Jewish home: feasting, singing, laughter, the best wine, and so on. Without the weekly taste of *Shabbat,* it might have been difficult for Jews to sustain a messianic hope throughout two millennia of diaspora life.

In addition to periodically experiencing what the ideal future could be like, another way of sustaining hope is by reexperiencing the past:

> [H]ope is linked with memory. If memory shows that, for better or worse, the present is not like the past, then, again for better or worse, the future can be different from at least one of them.[2]

During Jewish festivals, time is experienced as spiral — cyclical, with an upward thrust. Events are not only commemorated as having simply occurred in the past, but are also relived, with a message for the present and the future. The traditional liturgy of the Passover *Haggadah* states that

2. Bernard Dauenhauer, quoted in Jayne M. Waterworth, *A Philosophical Analysis of Hope* (New York: Palgrave Macmillan, 2004), p. 64.

"in every generation, a person should see himself/herself as if he/she had (personally) gone out of Egypt." Modern Israeli slang includes an expression that fits in well with these ideas. Using the notion that memory and historical perspective can indeed offer a more hopeful outlook, Israelis say in Hebrew, "We endured Pharaoh; we can endure this, too."

As Rabbi Irving Greenberg has so eloquently put it,

> The overwhelming majority of earth's human beings have always lived in poverty and under oppression, their lives punctuated by sickness and suffering. . . . Most of the nameless and faceless billions know the world as indifferent or hostile. Statistically speaking, human life is of little value. The downtrodden and the poor accept their fate as destined; the powerful and the successful accept good fortune as their due. Power, rather than justice, seems always to rule.
>
> The Jewish religion affirms otherwise: Judaism insists that history and the social-economic-political reality in which people live will eventually be perfected; much of what passes for the norm of human existence is really a deviation from the ultimate reality. How do we know this? From an actual event in history — the Exodus. . . . The freeing of the slaves testified that *human beings are meant to be free.*[3]

Thus the celebration of the Passover *Seder* is not simply a commemoration of a historical event, important as it may have been. It is also an active expression of hope for a different and better future. Many of the other Jewish festivals can be analyzed in this way as well.

Hope has been characterized as not just an emotion, but an activity.[4] Moreover, it is not only an activity in and of itself; it is also a requisite component of many other activities — indeed, of human agency in general. Without hope, we might not be able to act. On the other hand, acting with hope does not imply any certainty as to the outcome of our actions. Jayne Waterworth claims that "[u]ncertainty is a central feature of hope, whereas perceiving matters as certain is a central feature of despair."[5] Acting in the face of uncertainty is characteristic of a number of biblical figures — most prominently, perhaps, Queen Esther.[6]

---

3. Rabbi Irving Greenberg, *The Jewish Way: Living the Holidays* (New York: Summit Books, 1988), pp. 34-35. Emphasis is in the original.
4. Waterworth, *A Philosophical Analysis of Hope*, pp. 65-68.
5. Waterworth, *A Philosophical Analysis of Hope*, p. 31.
6. Esther 4:15-16.

Deborah Weissman

Zionism and Its Traditionalist Opponents

In this short paper, I will consider Zionism as a form of translating the traditional Jewish *hope* for redemption into human agency, through the assumption of *responsibility* for the Jewish people's destiny. Interestingly, a challenge to translators posed by Psalm 27 exemplifies the issue in a concrete way. In verse 14, the Hebrew reads as follows:

קַוֵּה אֶל ה׳ חֲזַק וְיַאֲמֵץ לִבֶּךָ וְקַוֵּה אֶל ה׳.

Although the Hebrew first word of the verse can be rendered as "hope in . . ." or "put your hope in . . ." (the Lord), many English editions published under either Jewish or Christian auspices translate the verse as: "Wait for the Lord; be strong and take heart and wait for the Lord." The difference between the two translations — hoping and waiting — is critical and explains much of the *Sturm und Drang* in modern Jewish history.

Reaching back into the classical Jewish past, a formative text for the passive approach in the diaspora is the Babylonian Talmud *Ketubot* 110b-111a. The two main protagonists are Babylonian sages of the third century CE. R. Zera was a student of Rab Judah, who headed one of the important *yeshivot* (talmudical academies) of Babylonia.

> R. Zera was evading Rab Judah because he desired to go up to the Land of Israel while Rab Judah had expressed [the following view]: Whoever goes up from Babylon to the Land of Israel transgresses a positive commandment, for it is written in Scripture, *They shall be carried to Babylon, and there shall they be, until the day that I remember them, saith the Lord.*[7] And [for] R. Zera?[8] That text refers to the vessels of ministry.[9] Thus Rab Judah [countered]: Another text also is available: *"I adjure you, O daughters of Jerusalem, by the gazelles, and by the hinds of the field, [that ye awaken not, nor stir up love, until it please].*"[10] And [for] R. Zera? — That [verse] implies that Israel shall not go up [*en masse* as if

7. Jeremiah 27:22.

8. What was his response to his teacher's bringing the verse as a prooftext?

9. Zera countered that the verse refers to the vessels that were used in the Holy Temple. In other words, the verse should not be used against people who want to go up to the Land.

10. Song of Songs 2:7. His interpretation of the verse — predicated on the reading of Song of Songs as an allegory of love between God and Israel — is that the Jews in Babylonia should remain there patiently and not try to return before it pleases God to bring them back.

surrounded] by a wall.[11] And [countered] Rab Judah: Another *"I adjure you"* is written in Scripture.[12] And [for] R. Zera? — That text is required for [an exposition] like that of R. Jose son of R. Hanina who said: "What was the purpose of those three adjurations? One, that Israel shall not go up [all together as if surrounded] by a wall; the second, that whereby the Holy One, blessed be He, adjured Israel that they shall not rebel against the nations of the world; and the third is that whereby the Holy One, blessed be He, adjured the idolaters that they shall not oppress Israel too much." And Rab Judah? — It is written in Scripture, *"That ye awaken not, nor stir up."*[13] And [for] R. Zera? — That text is required for [an exposition] like that of R. Levi who stated: "What was the purpose of those six adjurations? — Three for the purposes just mentioned and the others, that [the prophets] shall not make known the end,[14] that [the people] shall not[15] delay[16] the end, and that they shall not reveal the secret[17] to the idolaters."

By the gazelles, and by the hinds of the field.[18] R. Eleazar explained: The Holy One, blessed be He, said to Israel, "If you will keep the adjuration, well and good; but if not, I will permit your flesh [to be a prey] like [that of] the gazelles and the hinds of the field."

This is a text rich in theological meaning, and an in-depth analysis would take us far afield. I offer only a few observations that are relevant to the general theme of this paper:

1. It is clear from the story related in the text that disputes about the centrality of the Land of Israel and its implications for Jewish life are not a

11. The verse is a warning against the organization of mass *Aliyah* ("ascent" to Israel). Individuals, however, may go back.

12. Actually, the verse appears in three separate places in the Song of Songs — 2:7, 3:5, and 5:8. The implication is that each instance carries a different significance.

13. Thus, if each of the three adjurations contains two separate warnings, there must, in fact, be six oaths, rather than three.

14. In other words, the timing of the end of the Exile and the beginning of the Messianic Era.

15. By their misdeeds.

16. An alternate reading says "shall not regard the end of Exile as being too far off, and thus lose hope . . ." or even "force the coming of the end, by engaging in excessive prayer."

17. One approach identifies the secret with the intercalation of the Jewish calendar; another, with the reasons for the commandments; still a third suggests that the Oral Torah is not to be taught to gentiles. (In this essay, I am clearly violating the third interpretation.)

18. From the verses quoted from Song of Songs.

recent development. Most of the contemporary positions in the dispute have their ancient parallels.

2. Later in the same tractate *(Ketubot)*, it is revealed that R. Zera acted upon his convictions and emigrated to the Land of Israel — called *"Aliyah"* in Hebrew, the traditional term for "ascent" to Israel. He was one of the great role models for a deep love of the Land of Israel. Nevertheless, he cannot be called a Zionist, as he concurred with Rav Judah in his opposition to an organized movement. Love of Zion and Zionism itself, while related, are not synonymous.

3. They also both agreed that the Jewish community should not rebel against their subjugation to the other nations of the world. This passive acceptance of life in exile was seen by many of the early Zionists as a negative condition that had to be radically changed.

4. The "three oaths" or adjurations mentioned in this passage form the core of the anti-Zionist stance of the Satmar Ḥasidim, as outlined in the book *VaYoel Moshe* written by Rabbi Joel Teitelbaum in 1958. To this day, the book is a central text for ultra-Orthodox theological anti-Zionism.[19]

5. The last passage raises the possibility that if the Jewish people violate their oaths, they will be punished. It was used as a prooftext by Rabbi Teitelbaum to support his claim that the Holocaust was a divinely ordained punishment for the sin of Zionism — a double violation of the oaths, in that the Zionists both organized mass *Aliyah* and called for a rebellion against the powers of Exile. Some Orthodox critics of Satmar have countered that the nations of the world had violated *their* oath, by making the Exile too harsh — namely, the Holocaust — and therefore in the post-Holocaust world cooperation with the Zionists was permitted. Thus within the ultra-Orthodox world, we find both anti-Zionists and non-Zionists. The latter are often willing to cooperate with the Zionists, even sitting in the Zionist Israeli Knesset (parliament) and government.[20]

Regarding the last point, I believe it would be both too cynical and simplistic to attribute the willingness of the Orthodox non-Zionists to cooper-

19. See Aviezer Ravitzky, *Messianism, Zionism, and Jewish Religious Radicalism* (Chicago and London: University of Chicago Press, 1996), pp. 63-66, 211-34.

20. Following the tradition of *Agudat Yisrael* in Poland, which had its own representatives in the Polish Sejm. See Gershon Bacon, *The Politics of Tradition: Agudat Israel in Poland, 1916-1939* (Jerusalem: Magnes Press, 1997).

ate with the Zionists as just a way of receiving government allocations for their communal institutions. To be sure, political and economic considerations play a role, as they do with other segments of society, but the issue is far more complex. The longer and more intensely they are involved in the life of the State of Israel, the more some non-Zionists begin to identify with it.[21] To some extent, there has been a blurring of the boundaries between what we might call the left wing of the non-Zionists and the right wing of the religious Zionists. I hope to make this more evident as we continue.

Most of the early Zionists were secular Jews who were in rebellion against not only the external conditions of Jewish exilic existence. Their rebellion was directed as well internally, against the exilic characteristics of what they saw as the *"Golus"* or *"Galut"* [the negatively valenced "diaspora"] Jew, depending on whether they were speaking Yiddish or Hebrew. As the rebels saw it, one of these characteristics of exilic condition was passivity, lack of human agency, and waiting quietistically for a messianic redemption. The great secular writer and Zionist thinker Joseph Hayyim Brenner called to his Jewish brothers and sisters, "Let us rise up and live without a Messiah!"[22] Indeed, one of the goals of the Zionist educational enterprise in Palestine was to create a "new Jew," radically different from his forebears in various ways, including a lack of passivity and an adoption of human agency.[23] The new Jew would be virile, muscular, a farmer and a fighter. Most of all, he would be assertive, not only vis-à-vis the non-Jews around him, but also vis-à-vis the exilic conditions of his existence. An interesting case study in what some Zionist thinkers have called "the transvaluation of values"[24] is evident in the newly renewed celebration of Chanukah. Throughout history, the festival of Chanukah had been a minor festival. Going back to the Talmud, the themes of the traditional celebration had largely emphasized the divine miracle of a small cruse of oil lasting for eight days,[25] and the continuity of Jewish life through rejecting Greek culture and

---

21. Menachem Friedman, "The State of Israel as a Theological Dilemma," in *The Israeli State and Society: Boundaries and Frontiers,* ed. B. Kimmerling (Albany: State University of New York Press, 1989), ch. 7, pp. 165-215. Rabbi Aaron Lichtenstein has also described this phenomenon.

22. Ravitzky, *Messianism, Zionism, and Jewish Religious Radicalism,* p. 35.

23. See Marc Rosenstein, *The New Jew: The Connection to Jewish Tradition in General Zionist Secondary Education in the Land of Israel, from Its Beginning to the Establishment of the State,* unpublished doctoral dissertation, Hebrew University, 1985.

24. Arthur Hertzberg, *The Zionist Idea* (New York: Atheneum Books, 1969), p. 292.

25. *Shabbat* 21b.

emphasizing the study of Torah. In the twentieth century, Zionists turned it into a major celebration of human agency through armed struggle.[26]

Most of the Orthodox Jewish world initially opposed the Zionist movement. One of the reasons for the intense opposition was this very question of waiting or not waiting for the Messiah. For example, the Lithuanian-born Rabbi Joseph B. Soloveitchik (1903-1993), who was an outstanding American rabbi and philosopher of the twentieth century and who supported Zionism, said that the Zionists were like the followers of Shabbatai Zevi, the seventeenth-century false Messiah.[27] Throughout Jewish history, the false Messiahs have been perceived in very negative ways, but perhaps the most influential was Zevi. His movement was enormously disruptive to Jewish communities throughout Europe and the Levant. In 1666, he and thousands of his followers gathered at the court of the Sultan in Constantinople. The legendary account of the incident says that Zevi went into the palace wearing a Jew's hat and emerged wearing the fez, symbolizing his conversion to Islam. Many of his disciples were disillusioned; other Jews concluded that they must follow suit and adopt Islam. To this day, in Turkey and parts of Greece there are remnants of a sect called the "Donmeh," syncretists who merge Jewish and Muslim practices.[28] To compare the Zionists to the Sabbateans, as did Soloveitchik, is to besmirch them with a major condemnation.

The Possibility of Human-Divine Partnership

Similarly, Rabbi Menachem Schneerson (1902-1994), the ḥasidic Lubavitch *Rebbe* at the turn of the twentieth century,

> . . . combines two classical messianic tenets — the requirement of human passivity and the quest for perfection — and makes them interdependent. Zionism is the antithesis of both these principles; it represents both activism and the acceptance of partial fulfillment. . . .[29]

26. Peretz Rodman, "A Zionist Hanukkah: Modern Hebrew Culture Made of Hanukkah a Celebration of the New, Self-Reliant Jew," on-line at Myjewishlearning.com, accessed May 14, 2009.

27. Ravitzky, *Messianism, Zionism, and Jewish Religious Radicalism*, p. 13.

28. Gershom Scholem, *Major Trends in Jewish Mysticism* (New York: Schocken Books, 1941), pp. 287-324.

29. Ravitzky, *Messianism, Zionism, and Jewish Religious Radicalism*, p. 17.

He thus concluded that Zionism was antithetical to traditional Jewish theology and he opposed it vigorously. We will return shortly to the question of partial fulfillment. But one could make a case that human agency, rather than just passivity and quietism, had been part of the classical Jewish tradition as well. If we take the three major themes of Creation, Revelation, and Redemption, we can see how each of these may be viewed as a process of partnership between God and his human creatures.

1. Rabbi Joseph B. Soloveitchik, basing his statement on longstanding rabbinic *midrashic* traditions, extolled the potential of human creativity: ". . . man is bidden by the principle of *Imitatio Dei* to create, to be a *shutaf* (partner) in creation, fashioning form out of chaos."[30] For Soloveitchik and other modern Jewish thinkers, the human partnership in creation often involves the advancement of science, medicine, and technology for the betterment of the world.

2. The famous and oft-cited story[31] of the rabbinic dispute over the ritual purity of a certain kind of oven relates to the human role in revelation. In that story,

> . . . Rabbi Joshua will not be moved — even if heaven tells us differently, the human process of interpretation is what matters. "The Torah is not in heaven," he quotes. . . . Human agency, *even at the expense of "truth,"* is what really matters.[32]

This text dramatizes how the Jewish traditions of the Oral Torah, human rabbinic commentary, interpretation, and even heated debate lie at the core of how Jews understand revelation and what Gods asks of them.

3. Finally, with regard to redemption, Jewish tradition contains a variety of sources, offering different approaches. Some sources stress human agency, as per the following:

> This is what the Sages mean when stating (in *Mishna Avot*) "All the people of Israel have a portion *to* the world to come," and not stating, "*in* the world to come," whose conventional meaning would be that the world to come is ready from the moment of Creation as a

30. Abraham R. Besdin, *Reflections of the Rav: Lessons in Jewish Thought* (Jerusalem: Dept. for Torah Education and Culture in the Diaspora of the WZO, 1979), p. 26.

31. Babylonian Talmud, *Baba Metzia* 59b.

32. Barry W. Holtz, *Finding Our Way: Jewish Texts and the Lives We Lead Today* (New York: Schocken Books, 1990), p. 21.

separate, self-contained entity, so that in acting justly a person would be given a portion of that pre-existing world to come as a consequence. But the truth is that the world to come is man's very handiwork *itself*, having broadened, expanded and restored a portion for himself in his deeds.[33]

Not only is human agency a theme in many traditional Jewish sources, but also the notion of associating life in the Land of Israel with the assumption of human responsibility echoes rabbinic *midrashim* that discuss the desert phenomenon of the manna.[34] While in the desert, the Israelites were like infants or small children whose every need is met by their parents. When they entered the Land, they were forced to fend for themselves as farmers. Engaging in agriculture involves the storage of food, which can lead to its unequal distribution and the creation of a society divided into social classes, haves and have-nots. All of this involves assuming types of responsibility that were unknown during the desert experience.[35]

Thus, some of the themes of Zionist activism were not foreign to traditional Jews. The national anthem of the State of Israel and the pre-State Zionist movement is *"Ha-Tiqvah"* — the hope. The Russian Jewish poet Naftali Hertz Imber wrote the anthem's words based on the well-known biblical passage in Ezekiel 37, known as "the Vision of the Valley of Dry Bones." Where the biblical text included the words, "Our bones are dried up, our hope is lost . . ." (v. 11), Imber wrote, "Our hope is not yet lost." Zionism held out a promise of hope for the Jewish people, particularly during the period when they most needed it, the Holocaust. Zionism in its mainstream submovements held out a promise of hope for the general human future as well. Except for certain fringe groups, which more recently have become far more dominant,[36] many, if not most, Zionists saw

33. This is from the eighteenth-century Lithuanian work, *Nefesh Ha-Hayyim* (literally, "The Soul or Spirit of Life"), written by Rabbi Hayyim of Volozhin (1749-1821). I thank Dr. Steve Copeland for bringing it to my attention.

34. Exodus 16:4-35.

35. See: www.netivot-shalom.org.il, esp. *Beshalach* 5762, accessed on May 17, 2009.

36. See Anita Shapira, *Land and Power: The Zionist Resort to Force, 1881-1948* (Oxford: Oxford University Press, 1992), pp. 143, 202-7, 248-49; Shlomo Avineri, *The Making of Modern Zionism: The Intellectual Origins of the Jewish State* (London: Weidenfeld & Nicolson, 1981), p. 166. See also Anita Shapira, "Reality and Ethos: Attitudes toward Power in Zionism," in *Vision Confronts Reality: Historical Perspectives on the Contemporary Jewish Agenda*, ed. Ruth Kozodoy, David Sidorsky, and Kalman Sultanik (Rutherford, NJ: Fairleigh Dickinson University Press, 1989), pp. 68-119.

the national redemption of the Jewish people as a step on the way to universal redemption.[37]

One of the main differences between the traditional Jewish belief in waiting for the Messiah and what Arthur Hertzberg characterized as "secular Messianism"[38] was precisely this point: Zionists took Jewish destiny into their own hands. Simply waiting and praying were not enough; there had to be practical human action, whether in the diplomatic, philanthropic, agricultural, or educational realms, or sometimes in combination. Even the religious Zionists predicated their involvement in the Zionist movement on a certain acceptance of human autonomy. If they weren't in fact bringing the coming of the Messiah, at least they were paving the way for his coming.[39]

Two Types of Messianism

In an important essay titled "Toward an Understanding of the Messianic Idea in Judaism,"[40] the historian of Jewish mystical and messianic movements Gershom Scholem distinguished between two chief ideal constructs in the study of Jewish messianism. The first of these is apocalyptic, utopian messianism, in which the arrival of the Messiah will be precipitated by catastrophic extra-natural events. The coming of the Messiah will engender a totally different world order. According to Scholem, this view reached its climax in the nineteenth century under the leadership of a colorful ḥasidic *rebbe,* Yisrael of Rizhin. The latter suggested that the messianic world "will be a world without images," in which the image and its object can no longer be related, "which apparently means that a new order of being will emerge which cannot be pictorially represented."[41] Not all utopian messianism was as radical as this, but generally involved some type of historic discontinuity.

There was another type of messianism, whose most significant exponent was undoubtedly Moses Maimonides. In his late twelfth-century legal

---

37. See, for example, Theodor Herzl, *Zionist Writings,* vol. 1 (New York: Herzl Press, 1973), pp. 127-28, and Golda Meir, *My Life* (New York: Dell, 1975), pp. 308-9.

38. Hertzberg, *The Zionist Idea,* especially pp. 16-22.

39. See Avineri, *The Making of Modern Zionism,* pp. 52-55.

40. In Scholem, *The Messianic Idea in Judaism* (New York: Schocken Books, 1971).

41. Scholem, *The Messianic Idea in Judaism,* p. 35.

work, *Mishneh Torah,* in the section, "Laws Concerning Kings and Their Wars," Maimonides wrote,[42]

> Let no one think that in the days of the Messiah anything of the natural course of the world will cease or that any innovation will be introduced into creation. Rather, the world will continue in its accustomed course.... The Sages said: "The only difference between this world and the Days of the Messiah is the subjection of Israel to the nations."[43]

This type of messianism can be characterized as rational, continuous with natural history, noncatastrophic and nonutopian. However, some of its proponents prefer not to use messianic language at all when referring to modern political Zionism.

A Jerusalem-based rabbi has summarized what is basically a non-utopian approach to Zionist ideology in the following manner:

> The Jews are primarily a nation, and not a religious confession or church, as these words are generally understood.... Many young Jews abandon their Jewishness because of the confusion over this point, be-cause they fail to understand the simple and historically obvious but seemingly paradoxical point that many of the best Jews have been athe-ist, or at least agnostics.... The corollary of this is that, as a nation, the Jews have a history; and, third, that the time has come for the Jewish people to return to history as actors, and not as passive objects depen-dent upon the good graces of others. That, in a nutshell, is the essence of the ideological revolution wrought by Zionism.[44]

It is noteworthy and interesting that an *Orthodox* rabbi would summa-rize the essence of Zionism in this way, which is actually close to the ap-proach of certain classic religious Zionist thinkers, most notably Rabbi Isaac Jacob Reines (1839-1915). Reines was a Lithuanian rabbi and the founder of the *Mizrahi* religious Zionist movement. An essential differ-ence between Reines and some of his successors in the religious Zionist movement is that he did not associate modern political Zionism with the

---

42. As cited in Scholem, *The Messianic Idea in Judaism,* pp. 28-29.

43. *Sanhedrin* 91b. This was definitely the approach espoused by the late Professor Isa-iah Leibowitz, whose thought ranges far beyond the scope of this essay.

44. *Hititizei Yehonatan* — Year X: Rambling with Rashbi (Zohar) Yom Ha'atsma'ut, "Are We Still Zionists?" Sent to me via e-mail, April 28, 2009, by the author, Rabbi Yehonatan Chipman.

fulfillment of the traditional messianic aspirations of the Jewish people.[45] At the Sixth Zionist Congress in 1903 held in Basel, Herzl raised the possibility of a solution to the Jewish problem in Uganda. It is perhaps not widely known that many delegates from the *Mizraḥi* movement actually voted in favor of the plan, agreeing with the secular ideologue Max Nordau that Uganda would be a temporary way-station to solve the immediate physical problems of the persecuted Jews of Eastern Europe.[46] Thus Zionism could be divorced — at least on a temporary basis — from the messianic hope of return to the Land of Israel.

However, the mainstream of religious Zionism later became imbued with messianic fervor. This was due largely to the contribution of the single most important figure in the history of the movement, Rabbi Abraham Isaac Ha-Kohen Kook (1865-1935). In his work there was

> a systematic attempt to integrate the normative centrality of the Land of Israel within the religious tradition into a radical and revolutionary reinterpretation of the political and practical activity of Zionism and the resettling of Palestine. . . . Rabbi Kook is the one who finally presents a comprehensive Zionist religious-national philosophy, and thus the gap between religious Judaism and modern Jewish nationalism could be closed.[47]

Years before the establishment of the state, Kook had used the phrase "State of Israel" and had seen the future state in a utopian messianic perspective, as the fulfillment of biblical prophecy. But it was actually his son, Zvi Yehudah (1891-1981), head of the influential and still existent *Merkaz Ha-Rav Yeshiva* in Jerusalem, who more fully developed this approach. Kook the son saw not only the establishment of the State in 1948, but also its near-miraculous victory in the 1967 Six-Day War. During those heady days, the Jewish world was gripped by a euphoria that had not been known in a long time. From that point on, Kook and his followers proclaimed the State to be "the pedestal of God's throne in this world."[48] When criticized for this messianic fervor, Kook justified it by saying, "It is not we who are forcing the End,[49] but the End that is forcing us!"[50]

45. Ravitzky, *Messianism, Zionism, and Jewish Religious Radicalism*, pp. 33-35.
46. See: www.herzl.org/english/Article.aspx?Item=543, accessed on May 17, 2009.
47. Avineri, *The Making of Modern Zionism*, p. 188.
48. Ravitzky, *Messianism, Zionism, and Jewish Religious Radicalism*, p. 83.
49. See footnote 14.
50. Ravitzky, *Messianism, Zionism, and Jewish Religious Radicalism*, p. 80.

Let us reconsider the Orthodox critique that suggests that Zionism in general, and messianic religious Zionism in particular, are a form of *false* messianism. We should consider what the blessings and the pitfalls are of seeing historical events in redemptive terms. Once you have declared something to be "the beginning of the flowering of our redemption" (using as many qualifiers as you like), what practical significance does that have? Does it call upon us to behave differently? As Gershom Scholem put it, "What is the price of Messianism?"[51]

In a situation perceived as messianic, there is reluctance to engage in practical compromise like giving up any of the Land of Israel, as well as a kind of mystical fervor that beclouds issues of *realpolitik*. A primary example is the Israeli disengagement from Gaza in 2005, which many settlers refused to believe would happen at all. In this messianic euphoria, the actions and policies of the State can become sanctified and assume a cosmic meaning. And the enemy becomes a *cosmic* enemy. Seventeenth-century Sabbateanism spawned an even more radically antinomian movement called Frankism in the eighteenth and early nineteenth centuries. In a trend reminiscent of these false messianic movements, some contemporary Jewish settlers condone violent actions, including the rise of a Jewish underground in the early 1980s and more recent developments that have been no less violent.

There is even a new kind of religious-social-cultural identity that has arisen in Israel — "Ḥardal,"[52] which combines certain features of the religious Zionist community and certain features of the Ḥaredi (ultra-Orthodox) world. These Jews are ultra-nationalist, serve in the Army, often condone the use of violence against their Arab neighbors, and reject many features of modernity including democratic values.[53] They lack two elements that serve as a curb on violence — the Ḥaredi, non-Zionist commitment to quietism, and the mainstream religious Zionist commitment to cooperation with the secular authorities, which itself emerges from a basic commitment to the democratic process.

Aviezer Ravitzky, who was one of Israel's most significant public intellectuals until his debilitating accident in 2006, used to say that the challenge of Israel is that it doesn't fit into the two categories by which Jewish

---

51. Ravitzky, *Messianism, Zionism, and Jewish Religious Radicalism*, p. 3.

52. The word itself literally means "mustard." But it is not necessarily derogatory and may be used by spokespeople of the group for self-identification.

53. Shlomo Fischer, "Israeli Modern Orthodoxy: Fundamentalist or Romantic Nationalist?" (2004), accessed through Wikipedia.org/wiki/Hardal on May 19, 2009.

history was traditionally understood: it is neither Exile nor Redemption.[54] Sober Zionists today need to develop new categories to describe our situation. Ravitzky was very critical of Messianists. They are in some ways like the anti-Zionists, since both groups believe in determinism with regard to the future of the State of Israel. The future of Israel is not subject to our intervention, for good or ill. Ravitzky writes:

> [T]he notion of "the revealed End"[55] also restricts the human role, for it implies that we are only responsible for the beginning of the process (of return, settlement, and struggle), whereas its successful outcome will be guaranteed by Divine Providence.[56]

Ravitzky prefers to see the present situation of the State of Israel not as a redemptive reality, but as a redemptive opportunity. Its outcome depends on human actions. Ultimately, we will be able to designate a specific situation as having been the beginning of redemption solely *ex post facto* (*"b'di-avad"* in classical Hebrew). We hope that Zionism and the State of Israel will be proven to have been not only an episode in history, but the beginning of a positive process for all of humankind, to create a world of justice and peace. That depends, first and foremost, on human beings assuming responsibility for the future. And we cannot know it *a priori*.

In line with the common adage that "the perfect is the enemy of the good," sometimes the very prophetic messages that inspire us to work for peace in the long run get in the way of actually achieving some modicum of peace in the short run. Many of the utopian Messianists who talk about peace are referring to some ideal peace as described in the prophetic visions of the End of Days, when "the lion will lie down with the lamb."[57] It is difficult to reconcile these prophecies with the kind of partial, fragmented reality represented in the actual, yet-to-be-redeemed world in which we live in the present. One exceptional Orthodox rabbi in Israel today, a former member of the Israeli parliament and sometime-member of the government's cabinet, Michael Melchior, has suggested that we should be striving for a "piece of peace."[58]

---

54. Ravitzky, *Messianism, Zionism, and Jewish Religious Radicalism*, especially pp. 208-9.

55. See footnote 14.

56. Ravitzky, *Messianism, Zionism, and Jewish Religious Radicalism*, p. 131.

57. Isaiah 11:6.

58. In a presentation to the U.S. Senate Committee on Foreign Relations, Subcommittee

Deborah Weissman

Many of us likely find the concept of a "divine state" problematic. Having said that, however, the State of Israel is not devoid of religious and theological meaning for a religious Jew. I would like to explore some of the implications of Zionism in terms of hope and responsibility, without the burden of the utopian messianic perspective.

Zionism as Jewish Hope and Responsibility

One could suggest that Zionism represented the collective decision of the Jewish people to reenter history, in a return to the quintessential Jewish place. For most Jews in the world, the State of Israel represents any or all of the following: an ethnic second home, where they can "feel at home"; a refuge in case of danger ("Home is the place where, when you have to go there, they have to take you in"); the promise of Jewish survival and Hebrew cultural creativity; a "living laboratory" for Jewish values; the possibility of a modern society run according to Jewish law; an opportunity for intense spiritual experiences; a fascinatingly multicultural society where Jews from over a hundred different diaspora communities now live.

Perhaps the most rudimentary form of Jewish identity is a sense of connection between the Jewish past, present, and future. Nowhere is that connection more palpable than in the State of Israel, the only Jewish community in the world today with a positive birthrate. On the one hand, it is easier to live a Jewish life in Israel — kosher food is readily available, the Sabbath and Jewish festivals are the national days of rest, etc. On the other hand, it is much more difficult, in that in Israel Jews must assume responsibility for all aspects of life — from military service to garbage collection. Perhaps the most difficult facet of living as a Jew in Israel is that we can no longer romanticize or idealize the Jewish past. One must confront negative realities as well as positive ones.

The recently deceased Professor Moshe Greenberg was an important Jewish scholar of Bible who was always concerned with the educational implications of his scholarship. Greenberg was especially concerned with problematic Jewish texts relating to the Other.[59] He has pointed out the

on Near East and South Asian Affairs, October 15, 2003; the entire text is available on www.foreign.senate.gov/testimony/2003/MelchiorTestimony031015.pdf.

59. See, for example, his "A Problematic Heritage: The Attitude towards the Gentile in the Jewish Tradition — An Israel Perspective," *Conservative Judaism* 48, no. 2 (Winter 1996): 23-35.

tremendous educational challenge we have today in dealing with these questions in our study of traditional Jewish culture. In Israel he was made aware "that the main stream of Jewish thought is permeated by notions of the genetic spiritual superiority of Jews over gentiles."[60] This is in the category of a closely guarded secret in most Jewish educational contexts throughout the diaspora. But in the religious — i.e., Orthodox or ultra-Orthodox — networks of schools in Israel, these views are often expressed and taught freely and in an uncritical manner. To this, Greenberg responded:

> I am more than ever convinced that the hold that Judaism will have on this and future generations will be gravely impaired unless these notions are neutralized by an internal reordering of traditional values — a reordering by which the cherished value of the universality and oneness of God is matched by an equally cherished value of the universality and oneness of humanity.[61]

Challenges in Israel

The Jewish assumption of responsibility in Israel involves assuming responsibility not merely for Jewish life and civilization. It also involves responsibility for all citizens of the democratic state, between one-fifth to one-fourth of whom are gentiles. "Israeli" is not synonymous with "Jewish."[62] There are nearly a million and a half Palestinian Arabs who are citizens of the State of Israel. Additionally, since the war in 1967, between one million and a half to three million Palestinians — depending on which point in time is being scrutinized, and what stage has been reached in the process of peace negotiations — have lived under Israeli rule. This situation has posed great practical, political, and moral challenges to the Zionist movement, the State of Israel, and to Jewish thought today.

Another great challenge to the State of Israel, related to the above, is the ongoing threat to its security and the need for vigilant self-defense. The threat comes from some surrounding Arab nation-states, from Iran, from terrorist groups like Hezbollah and Hamas, and from some Palestinian peo-

60. Greenberg, "A Problematic Heritage," p. 23.
61. Greenberg, "A Problematic Heritage," p. 23.
62. Similarly, many people don't realize that "Arab" isn't synonymous with "Muslim." Most Muslims are not Arabs, and some Arabs are Christian.

ple of the West Bank and Gaza. Although peace treaties were reached with two of its neighbors, Egypt and Jordan, Israel has not known a year in its history without either open warfare or terror.

One must draw a distinction between using power for self-defense and using it to inflict punishment as an act of revenge. As a friend of mine put it, "Zionism means that the Jews must get our hands dirty. But there's a difference between getting your hands dirty and wallowing in the mud."[63]

Given the direction that Rabbi Kook's theology developed in the thought of his son and his followers, it is surprising that Kook once said, "It is not fitting for Jacob [i.e., the Jewish people] to engage in political life at a time when statehood requires ruthlessness and demands a talent for evil."[64] In other words, Zionism should not necessitate even getting our hands dirty. That is, indeed, highly utopian. And, bearing in mind that he died in 1935, one must ask if Rabbi Kook might not have changed his mind had he lived long enough to see the horrors of the Holocaust.

Seasonal Pruning

I previously mentioned the important work of Moshe Greenberg in identifying and confronting some of the problematic texts within the Jewish tradition. In another essay, Greenberg has given us a useful approach to dealing with these texts: "Even the choicest vine needs seasonal pruning to ensure more fruitful growth."[65] One of the techniques of "pruning" would be to contextualize the problematic texts within Jewish history. Jews, who were a persecuted minority in most periods and in most places, sometimes treated violently by the surrounding societies, developed defensive, insulating postures. The victimhood of Jewish history and the feeling of abject powerlessness reached their tragic climax in the Holocaust in Europe 1933-1945. If many Jews today are mistrustful of the outside world, it is not without cause.

A well-known jest goes: "Just because you're paranoid, it doesn't mean they're not out to get you." Even paranoids can have real enemies. The phenomena of anti-Semitism and even neo-Nazism are still very much with

63. Private communication with Daniel Seidmann, education officer in the Israeli Defense Forces, August 1980.

64. Avineri, *The Making of Modern Zionism*, p. 197.

65. As quoted in Seymour Fox, Israel Scheffler, and Daniel Marom, eds., *Visions of Jewish Education* (Cambridge: Cambridge University Press, 2003), p. 145.

us. In the Middle East, both the Israelis and the Palestinians see themselves as the victims of the conflict. They seem to compete in a "suffering sweepstakes." One problem with victimhood is that it prevents the victim from assuming responsibility for his actions, including the victimization of others. In the Israeli-Palestinian conflict, I believe that both sides are victims and both sides are victimizers.

> It was the experience of exile that forged the Jews and the Palestinians both. We are who we are, in no small part, because of the hardships, longings and insecurities conferred by displacement from home. . . . For the Jews, the insecurity manifests itself as fear, fear of being annihilated, fear of being cast out by force. For the Palestinians, the insecurity finds expression in humiliation and profound loss of honor, that stretches over the decades that the State of Israel has existed. . . . We are, all of us, Jew and Palestinian, victims of our refugee mentality, the one we cannot shake, that makes us into villain and victim both.[66]

Victimhood gives one a sense of self-righteousness. It gives the victimized group a basis for solidarity, through suffering together. Yet it also blinds them to other aspects of their reality.

With regard to the Jewish people and the gentile world, important and far-reaching changes have taken place in the post-Holocaust era. The changes that seem most dramatic began in the Roman Catholic Church with Vatican II, but similar changes have been noted in other denominations as well.[67] In recognizing the sincere transformation that has been undertaken by many Christians in reforming their texts and theologies, Jews need to undertake our own process of going through classical Jewish sources and teachings regarding the Other. Some of these teachings may be contextualized historically or reinterpreted; others should be seen as part of an ongoing internal debate. The first document, I believe, that calls for parallel processes of historical, cathartic, liturgical soul-searching on the part of both Christians *and* Jews is the document published on July 5th, 2009, in Berlin by the International Council of Christians and Jews, titled "A Time for Recommitment: Building a New Relationship between Jews and Christians."[68]

66. Bradley Burston, *Haaretz,* April 26, 2006, distributed by Common Ground News Service, May 1, 2006.

67. See, for example, www.jcrelations.net for the relevant historical documentation.

68. For the full text of the Berlin Document, see www.iccj.org.

Deborah Weissman

Historical Time and Eschatology

I noted earlier that the weekly celebration of *Shabbat* lends credence to the deferred eschatological hope. We should strive to find ways in which we could apply similar reasoning to the pre- (or perhaps even, non-) messianic role of the State of Israel, recognizing that

> [Zionism] has brought about a national revival, but not religious redemption. . . . [T]he supporters of this stance would claim Jews have always distinguished themselves from Christians precisely in that they taught their sons and daughters to find positive religious meaning even in a pre-messianic world. . . . Historical time is not to be judged only from the perspective of eschatological time.[69]

Some Jews might say that the State is an opportunity for avenging the victims of the Holocaust. Clearly, its establishment, only three years after the end of the Second World War, was like shouting to the world, "We are still alive! We are still here!" But we would do well to reflect upon the suggestion of the seventeenth-century Welsh poet George Herbert that "living well is the best revenge."[70]

So the question now remains, of what importance is clinging to a messianic hope? Ultimately, the messianic belief can serve as a safeguard against two potentially destructive tendencies:

1. Human *hubris,* overweening pride in the ability of human beings to change our situation by ourselves. This recognition can help put things in perspective and give us a sense of our own limitations as human beings.
2. Deep existential despair, which emerges out of understanding how limited we mortals really are. Correct messianic belief gives us a sense that if we do our "bit," there will be some assistance coming from a transcendent source.

   > "I have experienced many difficulties and hardships in my life and yet despair is a state in which I rarely remain for long. This is largely because despair cannot share the same place as wonder. . . ."[71]

69. Ravitzky, *Messianism, Zionism, and Jewish Religious Radicalism,* p. 209.

70. http://www.quotationspage.com/quote/26999.html, accessed September 9, 2008.

71. Alice Walker, *We Are the Ones We Have Been Waiting For: Inner Light in a Time of Darkness* (New York: The New Press, 2006), p. 36.

282

The wonder we experience, for example, in celebrating the exodus from Egypt, can help us navigate between the Scylla of *hubris* and the Charybdis of despair. The *Mishnah* put it well, "It is not incumbent on you to finish the task; but neither are you entirely free to desist from it."[72] The establishment of the State of Israel, three years after the end of the Holocaust; its continued existence amidst a host of challenges; the many accomplishments it has achieved — all these can give us a sense of wonder, and can help us cope with despair, without necessarily equating them with the fulfillment — and certainly not the total fulfillment — of biblical prophecies.

> Without hope, we lose our faith in life. And without a belief that we can make things better, we become disempowered, rendered ineffective in the world. Without hope, we die, if not physically, then mentally and emotionally. Hope is an attitude of effectiveness and a source of energy. . . .
>
> There is always something constructive we can do, even if it is just by changing our attitude. And it is in our response — and that of others — that we find cause for hope. *To hope is our greatest responsibility.*[73]

72. *Aboth* 2:16.

73. Wayne Visser, "Corporate Sustainability & Responsibility," Csrinternational .blogspot.com/2008/10/faith-hope-and-responsibility.html — Accessed March 18, 2009 (emphasis added).

Afterword: Where Do We Go from Here?
Future Theological Challenges
for Christians and Jews

Robert W. Jenson

The whole arena of Jewish-Christian relations is obviously too big to touch on here in one short essay — especially when prophecy is mandated. I will limit myself to what I can at least claim to have some ideas about: Jewish-Christian theological conversation.

There are — or can be — two Jewish-Christian conversations, which are closely related and often in practice impossible to keep separate, but are nevertheless different: there is dialogue, which, when it occurs, is often shaped on the pattern of intra-Christian ecumenical dialogue; and there is joint work on shared problems, the sort of converse to which ITI groups are dedicated, but which can break out in various settings, as when David Novak and I used to feed ideas to each other in Richard Neuhaus's colloquia.

Thus, for example, the understanding of covenant, on which one of the two ITI working parties labored, is a central theological locus of both communities; and the Jewish and Christian members tried hard, and to some considerable extent succeeded, to think *together* about the Lord's covenant or covenants with his people. At the same time, the question of the church's claimed inclusion in the covenant with Israel has been and remains controversial between the two communities, and our group could not altogether ignore the divergence. Perhaps the covenant claimed by Christians is *different* from the Lord's covenant with the descendants of Abraham, but Christians *cannot agree that it is separate*. The divergence shows up in the essays.

It will be apparent that joint work on shared problems is the conversation I most want to see as our future — and I will come back to that. But both conversations must be vigorously pursued, and for like reasons. I will suggest two reasons, of different sorts.

Perhaps we may now admit: during the long centuries in which Jews and Christians pursued each their own agendas, each determined by opposition to the other, the thinking of both suffered from the separation. But in our time there is light at the end of at least this tunnel: the generally less hostile relation between many Jews and many Christians opens the possibility of mutually committed theological discourse. It is not for a Christian to probe deformations that Jewish thought may have suffered from closure to Christianity — though I have some guesses about that. Hence I will confine myself to *Christian* theological deformations resultant from closure to Judaism.

Let me start with observation of a remarkable *positive* phenomenon: the New Testament brings almost no theology in the narrow sense, that is, informative discourse directly about God. Why is that? As soon as you ask, the answer is plain: It is because the New Testament's tradents and authors didn't need to carry on about this; they simply presumed Judaism's daily discourse for and to God, as found in Scripture and in the communities in which they lived. The God to whom the witnesses of Jesus' resurrection attributed the event was antecedently present in their consciousness as the God who had called Abraham to be the father of his people, who had chosen Jacob and not Esau, who gave the Law at Sinai, who fought for Israel and sometimes against her, who sent prophets with messages of judgment and salvation, who could be angry — and could also be funny, given to pranks like ambushing Jacob in the guise of a river god, or making a donkey a prophet — etc. The tradents and authors of the New Testament did not need to make all that explicit.

Thus in the second century when Marcion wanted to sever Christianity altogether from Jewish faith, this required some heavy critical lifting. He of course simply rejected the Old Testament, but he had also to exclude from his canon most of the documents that would shortly come together as the New Testament, leaving only Luke's Gospel and the letters of Paul, and these too had to be severely edited.

But as the church became mostly gentile, the discourse of Judaism was no longer native to most of her members, though a few explicit scriptural doctrines, notably the creation, remained central in the church's life. It is another strange, and this time ominous, phenomenon: by around 170, the church lived by a *regula fidei,* an unwritten but nonetheless authoritative creed, whose narrative skipped straight from creation to Mary's pregnancy — as do the Apostles' and Nicene creeds to this day.

The result has been a lamentable narrative emptiness in Christian doctrine of God, a vacuum into which other air than that of Scripture quickly rushed. We may summarize the result: the replacement of living narrative by abstract predicates, like the *omni*'s. And since the substantiating predicates of any substance — notice the language I am sliding into — do not come or go unless the thing itself comes or goes, God's being comes to be understood as fixed, the eternity of his being comes to be construed as mere immunity to time, instead of as Israel's Scripture construes it, as his *faithfulness* in his history with his people. I can go on and on about this, and I will give myself the liberty of mentioning my suspicion that the problem has afflicted some sorts of Jewish theology as well.

Through much of the church's theological community there is now increasing awareness that Israel's Scripture must do much more than provide cultural background for the New Testament. It must tell us what God is like. And as we turn to that Scripture for instruction, we willy-nilly turn to the community with which we share that Scripture.

A second and quite different impetus to Jewish-Christian solidarity is external pressure. There is a sort of spiritual globalization afoot, which is very unlikely to be friendly to either Judaism or Christianity. Whether the secularization thesis belatedly works out on a global scale, or whether — as I suppose — Chesterton's Father Brown has the right of it, that those who refuse to believe in the Bible's God will believe instead in anything and everything, the more primitive the better, the one thing the homogenized world is very unlikely to admire is serious dedication to the God of Israel.

How the relation with Islam, the one great block of humanity that is not secularized, will work out over time, also remains to be seen. It is in any case plain that, despite once-flourishing and in many respects assimilated communities of Christians in Islamic territories, Islam generally regards Jews and Christians together as the "West."

So to matters for Jewish/Christian *dialogue:* a first and fundamental question: What exactly do we disagree about? Is it the Law? The doctrine of Trinity? The number and relation of covenants? It is perhaps the most significant fact of Jewish/Christian history, that in all these centuries of quarreling we have never gotten it quite clear what we are quarreling about.

For my own part, I have a proposal, which perhaps might be debated in some future dialogue. We are separated by just one question: Did the God of Israel in fact raise his servant Jesus from the dead or did he not? All the other clashes are, in my judgment, consequences of the one circumstance that when Jesus' Resurrection was proclaimed, some Jews who heard the preaching believed it and most did not. If Jesus was raised, then I think it can be argued that it simply follows that the God of Israel is triune, that God did become incarnate, that gentile converts to his worship are not to be circumcised, and so on. If he is in *Sheol* with the rest of the dead, then such doctrines are indeed heresies within or indeed apostasies from Judaism.

To be sure, the traditional matters of contention must be explored, whether or not they have a common root.

So — both communions loudly affirm the oneness of God: "Here, O Israel: the Lord your God is one God." "We believe in one God. . . ." And each distrusts the other's affirmation. The Christian teaching of Trinity is an obvious bone of this contention. But so is the abstract "monotheism" of much "Jewish thought."

From the Christian side, it often seems that what Judaism so vehemently rejects is some other doctrine of Trinity than the one that we actually teach.

Why is that? Is the doctrine itself unclear? Or have we done very badly in explaining it? Or do Jews just not want it to be explained? In any case, Christians do not take well to having our doctrine of the one God classified as idolatry, even of a sort that can be excused in gentiles. There is, I think, ample matter for renewed discussion by both faith communities.

Then there is the question of the church's claim to inclusion in the covenant with Israel. In our group on covenant, we discovered that there was no unanimity of opinion among either Jews or Christians, except that Christianity does in one way or another make that claim, and Judaism in one way or another rejects it. Question for dialogue: Is there any common ground between some forms of the church's claim and some forms of Judaism's rejection?

And finally, of course, the Law. Plainly, there can be no meeting of minds between the antinomianism of much current American Christianity, which excludes biblical law from the life of the church, and the view of my esteemed colleague Meir Soloveichik, according to whom "Torah study" is the one legitimate link between humanity and God. But is that the end of the matter?

Then to the kind of work to which ITI is primarily dedicated.

I may mention the two matters to which the new round of ITI groups will be dedicated: the theological significance of the Jewish return to Zion, and the relation of religion and violence. On neither topic is there consensus within either community, which is just the sort of question we are looking for.

Could converse with diverse Jewish thinkers help Christians make up their minds? And even vice versa?

An obvious chief candidate, as it seems to me, is resurrection itself. When both communities "look for the resurrection of the dead" — to use Christian liturgical language — what do they have in mind? Among Christians, it's a long stretch between Bultmann and those who line up for the rapture. And superficial observation suggests that Jewish eschatologies show a remarkably similar range of teaching.

And last on my list, or at least on the list I will inflict on you, is the relation between time and eternity, or between the finite and the infinite. It seems to me the way in which — again in either community — the two terms are regularly defined as contradictories, prevents the realms to which they point as having any relation at all. Despite the current calamities of my tradition of Christianity, Lutheranism, I continue to cherish a few of its maxims. One of these is *finitum capax infiniti* ("the finite is capable of the infinite"), originally formulated to contradict the maxim of another branch of the Reformation, *finitum non capax infiniti*. Maimonides would, I think, applaud the latter. Can I find some Jewish thinkers who might stand with me for the former?

How much effect either theological dialogue or doing theology together can or will have on the life of our communities is arguable. How much effect ideas can have on life has, after all, been disputed since the first time anybody had an idea. I can only say that I lean to Socrates' view — I had better, given my profession — and that I myself have been changed first by involvement in the Christian ecumenical movement and then by converse with Jewish thinkers in several settings, including the sessions of ITI.

In any case, both communities are too fragmented in themselves for there to be much likelihood of general theological or practical sharing. All that is likely is outbreaks of increased common understanding and purpose here and there — which is a lot.

And then — hope differs from anticipation of the likely. We do not — and indeed should not — hope for Judaism and the church to become one community in this age. But we can hope for converse of the type to which ITI is dedicated to become more a part of the life of both communities than seems likely.

When he was Prefect of the Congregation for the Faith, Joseph Ratzinger used to say that further progress toward unity of Christians would depend on an uncovenanted intervention of the Spirit. *Mutatis mutandis . . .*

Contributors

Robert W. Jenson is Co-Director with Eugene Korn of the Institute for Theological Inquiry. He has taught systematic theology and philosophy at Oxford, Notre Dame, and Princeton. He was the Senior Scholar for Research at the Center of Theological Inquiry in Princeton for eight years. Besides his two-volume work, *Systematic Theology,* he is the author or co-author of seventeen books. He was co-founder and long-time associate director of the Center for Catholic and Evangelical Theology, and co-founder and long-time editor or co-editor of the journals *Dialog* and *Pro Ecclesia*. Most recently, he has written commentaries on Song of Songs and Ezekiel. It is his conviction that Christianity needs a theological understanding of Judaism, and that Christian and Jewish thinkers must work together on shared theological questions.

Douglas Knight is editor of *The Theology of John Zizioulas* (Ashgate, 2007) and of John Zizioulas' *Lectures in Christian Dogmatics* (T. & T. Clark, 2009). He is the author of *The Eschatological Economy: Time and the Hospitality of God* (Eerdmans, 2006). His recent articles include "The Son and the Spirit in the Providence of God"; "Oliver O'Donovan on the Church and the Public Square"; "The Eucharist and the Whole Christ," presented at the Cheyneygates seminar, Westminster Abbey; "Sacrifice, Atonement and Christian Unity"; "Pope Benedict on Liturgy and Sacrifice"; and "John Zizioulas on Eschatology and the Eucharist." He resides in London.

Eugene B. Korn is Co-Director with Robert Jenson of the Institute for Theological Inquiry, and the American Director of the Center for Jewish-

Christian Understanding and Cooperation in Israel. He is the author of *The Jewish Connection to the Land of Israel — A Brief Introduction for Christians* (Jewish Lights, 2006) and *Land and Covenant: The Religious Significance of the State of Israel* (American Jewish Congress, 2004). In addition to this volume, he co-edited the third edition of *End of an Exile* by James Parkes (Micah Press, 2004); *Two Faiths, One Covenant?* (Rowman & Littlefield, 2005); and *Jewish Theology and World Religions* (Littman, 2012). He has penned over thirty scholarly essays on Jewish ethics and Jewish-Christian relations, most recently "Rethinking Christianity: Rabbinic Positions and Possibilities," in *Jewish Theology and World Religions;* "American Jewish Interfaith Relations," in *The Future of American Judaism* (Columbia University, 2011); "Orthodoxy, Contemporary Pluralism and the Christian Other," in *Mishpatei Shalom* (KTAV, 2010); and "Divine Commands, Genocide and Amalek: Moralization in Jewish Law," *The Edah Journal* (2006). He also edits *Meorot — A Forum for Modern Orthodox Discourse.*

Gerald McDermott is the Jordan-Trexler Professor of Religion at Roanoke College, in Roanoke, VA. One of the leading authorities on "America's theologian," Professor McDermott has authored four books on Jonathan Edwards: *Understanding Jonathan Edwards* (Oxford, 2008); *Jonathan Edwards Confronts the Gods* (Oxford, 2000); *One Holy and Happy Society: The Public Theology of Jonathan Edwards* (Penn State, 1992); and *Seeing God: Jonathan Edwards and Spiritual Discernment* (Regent College, 2000); as well as *Can Evangelicals Learn from World Religions?* (InterVarsity, 2000); *The Baker Pocket Guide to World Religions* (Baker, 2008); and *God's Rivals: Why Has God Allowed Different Religions?* (InterVarsity, 2007). Professor McDermott is now editing *The Oxford Handbook of Evangelical Theology* (Oxford) and co-editing *Handbook of World Religions* (Baker Academic). His most recent book is *The Great Theologians for Beginners* (InterVarsity, 2010).

Alan Mittleman is Professor of Modern Jewish Thought and head of the Department of Jewish Thought at the Jewish Theological Seminary, where he serves as Director of the Seminary's Louis Finkelstein Institute for Religious and Social Studies. Professor Mittleman is the author of four books, *Hope in a Democratic Age* (Oxford, 2009); *Between Kant and Kabbalah* (SUNY Press, 1990); *The Politics of Torah* (SUNY Press, 1996); and *The Scepter Shall Not Depart from Judah* (Rowman & Littlefield, 2000). He is also the editor of four books, *Uneasy Allies: Jewish and Evangelical Relations*

(Rowman & Littlefield, 2007); *Religion as a Public Good* (Rowman & Littlefield, 2003); *Jewish Polity and American Civil Society* (Rowman & Littlefield, 2002); and *Jews and the American Public Square* (Rowman & Littlefield, 2002).

David Novak holds the Shiff Chair of Jewish Studies as Professor of the Study of Religion and Professor of Philosophy at the University of Toronto since 1997, where he is also a member the Centre for Ethics of the Joint Centre for Bioethics. From 1997 to 2002 he also was Director of the Jewish Studies Program. He is secretary-treasurer of the Institute on Religion and Public Life in New York City, Fellow of the American Academy for Jewish Research and the Academy for Jewish Philosophy, and a member of the Board of Consulting Scholars of the James Madison Program in American Ideals and Institutions at Princeton University. He is the author of thirteen books, including *The Jewish Social Contract: An Essay in Political Theology* (Princeton, 2005); *Talking with Christians: Musings of a Jewish Theologian* (Eerdmans, 2005); and *Covenantal Rights: A Study in Jewish Political Theory* (Princeton, 2000). He has edited four books and is the author of over 200 articles in scholarly and intellectual journals.

Russell R. Reno is Professor of Theology at Creighton University and the general editor of the *Brazos Theological Interpretation of the Bible* series. His recent books include *Genesis* (Brazos, 2010); *"Sanctified Vision": An Introduction to Early Christian Interpretation of the Bible* (Johns Hopkins, 2005); *In the Ruins of the Church: Sustaining Faith in an Age of Diminished Christianity* (Brazos, 2002); and *Redemptive Change: Atonement and the Christian Cure of the Soul* (Trinity Press, 2002). His recent essays include "Theology and Biblical Interpretation," in *Sharper Than a Two-Edged Sword: Preaching, Teaching, and Living the Bible* (Eerdmans, 2008); "The End of the Road," *First Things* (October 2008); "Nietzsche's Deeper Truth, *First Things* (January 2008); "Reading the Bible with the Church," *Calvin Theological Journal* (2008); "Faith in the Flesh," *Commentary* (November 2007); "Rebuilding the Bridge Between Theology and Exegesis: Scripture, Doctrine, and Apostolic Legitimacy," *Letter and Spirit* (2007); "Origen and Spiritual Interpretation," *Pro Ecclesia* (2006); "Pride and Idolatry," *Interpretation* (2006); "Ethics and Redemption," in *The Oxford Handbook for Christian Ethics* (Oxford, 2005); and "God or Mammon?" in *The Ten Commandments for Jews, Christians, and Others* (Eerdmans, 2007).

Shlomo Riskin is Chancellor of the Center for Jewish-Christian Understanding and Cooperation in Israel, and Chief Rabbi of Efrat, Israel. An internationally renowned religious thinker, educator, and author, he is founder and Chancellor of Ohr Torah Stone Colleges and Graduate Programs. Rabbi Dr. Riskin has published scores of articles and monographs on Judaism and contemporary issues, and is the author of five books: *A Jewish Woman's Right to Divorce: A Halakhic History and a Solution for the Agunah* (Maggid, 2009); *Torah Lights — Genesis Confronts Life, Love and Family* (Urim, 2005); *Torah Lights — Exodus Defines the Birth of a Nation* (Maggid, 2009); *Torah Lights:* Vayikra, *Sacrifice, Sanctity and Silence* (Maggid, 2009); *The Rebellious Wife: Women and Jewish Divorce* (KTAV, 1989); and *The Passover Haggadah with a Traditional and Contemporary Commentary* (KTAV, 1984).

Naftali Rothenberg is a Senior Research Fellow at the Van Leer Jerusalem Institute (since 1994), where he holds the Chair in Jewish Culture and Identity. He also serves as the rabbi and spiritual leader of Har Adar, a Jerusalem suburb town, where he resides with his family. He has been a member of the International Committee of Religion, Science and the Environment (London, 1995-1997) and 2005 Martin Marty Center visiting Scholar at the Divinity School, University of Chicago. He has published numerous articles on philosophy, Jewish thought, and Jewish Law. His recent books include *Studies on Jewish People, Identity and Nationality* (2008); *Meditations on the Parasha — The Weekly Torah portion as inspiration for Jewish thought and creativity* (Hebrew, 2005); *Beloved Doe — Studies in the Wisdom of Love* (Hebrew, 2004); and *Jewish Identity in Modern Israel — Proceedings on Secular Judaism and Democracy* (Urim, 2002). His most recent book is *The Wisdom of Love — Man, Woman & God in Jewish Canonical Literature* (Academic Studies Press, 2008).

Richard Sklba recently retired as Vicar General/Auxiliary Bishop of Milwaukee, WI. He served as President of the Catholic Biblical Association of America in 1982, was Chairman of the United States Conference of Catholic Bishops' Committee on Ecumenical and Interreligious Affairs from 2005 to 2008, was Co-Chair of the National Evangelical Lutheran/Catholic Dialogue, and a member of the Orthodox/Catholic Bishops Dialogue. He has written a number of books, articles, and papers on Catholic theology, and in 1988 he was awarded the Catholic Theological Society of America John Courtney Murray medal for outstanding achievement in theology.

Miroslav Volf is Director of the Yale Center for Faith and Culture and Henry B. Wright Professor of Systematic Theology at Yale. His books include *Free of Charge: Giving and Forgiving in a Culture Stripped of Grace* (Zondervan, 2006); *After Our Likeness: The Church as the Image of the Trinity* (Eerdmans, 1998); *The Sun Is Not Afraid of the Darkness: Theological Meditations on the Poetry of Aleksa Santic* (Izvori, 1986); *Zukunft der Arbeit — Arbeit der Zukunft. Der Arbeitsbegriff bei Karl Marx und seine theologische Wertung* (Grunewald, 1988); *Work in the Spirit: Toward a Theology of Work* (Wipf & Stock, 1991); *Gerechtigkeit, Geist und Schöpfung: Die Oxford-Erklärung zur Frage von Glaube und Wirtschaft* (Brockhaus, 1992); *The Future of Theology: Essays in Honor of Jürgen Moltmann* (Eerdmans, 1996); *After Our Likeness: The Church as the Image of the Trinity* (Eerdmans, 1998); *A Spacious Heart: Essays on Identity and Belonging* (Trinity Press, 1997); *Exclusion and Embrace: A Theological Exploration of Identity, Otherness, and Reconciliation* (Abingdon, 1996). He was editor of *A Passion for God's Reign: Theology, Christian Learning, and the Christian Self* by Jürgen Moltmann, Ellen T. Charry, and Nicholas Wolterstorff (Eerdmans, 1998).

Darlene Fozard Weaver is Associate Professor of Theology at Villanova University and Director of the Theology Institute at Villanova. Her classes focus on fundamental moral theology, ethical theory, ethics and the family, sexual and reproductive ethics, and healthcare ethics. She is the author of *Self Love and Christian Ethics* (Cambridge, 2002) and the forthcoming *Involvements with God and Goods: Persons and Actions in Christian Ethics* (Georgetown). She is editor of and contributor to *The Ethics of Embryo Adoption and the Catholic Tradition* (Springer/Kluwer).

Deborah Weissman is a resident of Jerusalem, where she has devoted her life to Jewish education and interfaith relations. She is President of the International Council of Christians and Jews, and a member of the Academic Advisory Council of the Swedish Theological Institute in Jerusalem, the International Editorial Advisory Board of *Nashim: A Journal of Jewish Women's Studies & Gender Issues,* and the editorial board of *Studies in Christian-Jewish Relations.* Her latest publications include "Jewish Religious Education as Peace Education," in *Peace Education and Religious Plurality: International Perspectives* (Routledge, 2008); "Towards a Humanistic Hermeneutic of Jewish Texts," in *Hermeutical Explorations in Dialogue: Essays in Honor of Hans Ucko* (Indian Society for Promoting Christian

Knowledge, 2007); "What We Are and Who We Are: Educating for the Universal-Particular Dialectic in Jewish Life," in *Languages and Literatures in Jewish Education: Studies in Jewish Education in Honor of Michael Rosenak* (Hebrew University, 2006).

Michael Wyschogrod is Professor of Philosophy Emeritus, City University of New York. From 1994 to 2002 he served as Professor of Religious Studies at University of Houston. His books include *Kierkegaard and Heidegger: The Ontology of Existence* (Routledge & Kegan Paul, 1954); *Jews and "Jewish Christianity"* (Ktav, 1978); *The Body of Faith: Judaism as Corporeal Election* (Seabury-Winston, 1983), reprinted in paperback as *The Body of Faith: God in the People Israel* (Harper & Row, 1989) and second edition as *The Body of Faith: God and the People Israel* (Jason Aronson, 1996); *Understanding Scripture: Explorations of Jewish and Christian Traditions of Interpretation* (Paulist Press, 1987); *Parable and Story in Judaism and Christianity* (Paulist Press, 1989); and *Abraham's Promise: Judaism and Jewish-Christian Relations* (Eerdmans, 2004). He has published more than sixty scholarly articles and reviews in philosophy and Jewish thought, including "Breaking the Tablets: Jewish Theology after the Shoah, by David Weiss Halivni," *Modern Theology* 24, no. 3 (July 2008); "Responses to Friends," *Modern Theology* 22, no. 4 (October 2006); "On the Christian Critique of the Jewish Sabbath," in *Sabbath: Idea, History and Reality*, ed. G. Blidstein (Ben Gurion University, 2004).